✻ INSIGHT GUIDES

GUATEMALA BELIZE & THE YUCATÁN

DISCOVERY CHANNEL

APA PUBLICATIONS
Part of the Langenscheidt Publishing Group

INSIGHT GUIDE
Guatemala
Belize &
The Yucatan

Editorial
Editor
Huw Hennessy
Editorial Director
Brian Bell

Distribution

United States
Langenscheidt Publishers, Inc.
36–36 33rd Street 4th Floor
Long Island City, NY 11106
Fax: 1 (718) 784 0640

UK & Ireland
GeoCenter International Ltd
Meridian House, Churchill Way
West Basingstoke, Hants RG21 6YR
Fax: (44) 1256 817988

Australia
Universal Publishers
1 Waterloo Road
Macquarie Park, NSW 2113
Fax: (61) 2 9888 9074

New Zealand
Hema Maps New Zealand Ltd (HNZ)
Unit D, 24 Ra ORA Drive
East Tamaki, Auckland
Fax: (64) 9 273 6479

Worldwide
Apa Publications GmbH & Co.
Verlag KG (Singapore branch)
38 Joo Koon Road, Singapore 628990
Tel: (65) 6865 1600. Fax: (65) 6861 6438

Printing

Insight Print Services (Pte) Ltd
38 Joo Koon Road, Singapore 628990
Tel: (65) 6865 1600. Fax: (65) 6861 6438

©2006 Apa Publications GmbH & Co.
Verlag KG (Singapore branch)
All Rights Reserved
First Edition 2000
Updated 2006
Reprinted 2006

CONTACTING THE EDITORS
We would appreciate it if readers
would alert us to errors or out-
dated information by writing to:
**Insight Guides, P.O. Box 7910,
London SE1 1WE, England.**
Fax: (44) 20 7403 0290.
insight@apaguide.co.uk

www.insightguides.com
In North America:
www.insighttravelguides.com

ABOUT THIS BOOK

The first Insight Guide pioneered the use of creative full-colour photography in travel guides in 1970. Since then, we have expanded our range to cater for our readers' need not only for reliable information about their chosen destination but also for a real understanding of the culture and workings of that destination. Now, when the internet can supply inexhaustible (but not always reliable) facts, our books marry text and pictures to provide those much more elusive qualities: knowledge and discernment. To achieve this, they rely heavily on the authority of locally based writers and photographers.

How to use this book

This first edition of *Insight: Guatemala, Belize and the Yucatán* is carefully struc-tured to convey an understanding of this fascinating region, as well as to guide readers through its sights and activities:

◆ The **Features** section, indicated by a yellow bar at the top of each page, covers the history and culture of the destinations in a series of informative essays.

◆ The main **Places** section, indicated by a blue bar, is a complete guide to all the sights and areas worth visiting. Places of special interest are coordinated by number with the maps.

◆ The **Travel Tips** section, with an orange bar, is a point of reference for information on travel, hotels, restaurants, etc. Its index can be found on the back flap.

Map Legend

–––– - ––	International Boundary
– – – –	State/Province Boundary
⊖	Border Crossing
–•–•–	National Park/Reserve
– – – –	Ferry Route
✈ ✚	Airport: International/ Regional
🚌	Bus Station
❶	Tourist Information
✉	Post Office
⊞ † ⸸	Church/Ruins
†	Monastery
☾	Mosque
✡	Synagogue
⌂	Castle/Ruins
∴	Archeological Site
Ω	Cave
𝟏	Statue/Monument
★	Place of Interest

The main places of interest in the Places section are coordinated by number with a full-color map (e.g. ❶), and a symbol at the top of every right-hand page tells you where to find the map.

The contributors

Insight Guides managing editor **Huw Hennessy** assembled an impressive team of experts to write this book: HISTORY AND FEATURES: **Nick Caistor**, Latin America editor at the BBC World Service, wrote the history chapters for all three countries. **Krystyna Deuss**, of the Guatemalan Maya Centre in London, wrote Highland Life, and the picture feature about Guatemalan textiles. **Iain Stewart**, an expert travel writer on Central America, wrote the main introduction as well as features on the Maya World Today, Food and Drink, and Outdoor Adventure. **Peter Hutchison**, a specialist Latin America travel writer, wrote The Forces of Nature. **Phil Gunson**, Latin America correspondent for London's *Guardian*, wrote about Guatemalan Wildlife. **Ellen McRae**, a marine biologist

based on Caye Caulker, wrote about the Flora and Fauna of Belize and Belize's Barrier Reef. **Barbara Mac Kinnon**, of the Sian Ka'an Biosphere Reserve, in the Yucatán, wrote The Coast of the Yucatán and Mass Tourism. **Neil Rogers**, an expert Mayanist, wrote the Unearthing the Ruins and Ecotourism in Belize picture features. The feature on the Treasures of Tikal was written by **Simone Clifford-Jaeger**, who studied archeology whilst living in Tikal.

GUATEMALA: **Iain Stewart** wrote all the Places chapters and Travel Tips as well as features on Rigoberta Menchú, Antigua's churches, Lake Atitlán, and Maximón.

BELIZE: **Ian Peedle**, travel writer and former NGO worker in Belize, wrote all the Places chapters, as well as the Music and Dance feature. The Travel Tips were written by **Jo Clarkson**, a specialist Central America travel writer. Contributors to *Insight Guide: Belize* whose work has been adapted here include: **Tony Perrottet**, **Karla Heusner** and **Tony Rath**.

THE YUCATÁN: The Places chapters and Travel Tips were written by **John Wilcock**, a long-standing Insight Guide contributor. The feature on the architecture of the Yucatán was written by **Chloe Sayer**, an experienced writer on Mexican history and culture.

Special thanks go to **Peter Eltringham**, who checked and revised the original Guatemala and Belize chapters and to **Anna Vinegrad** for checking the Maya history chapters. **Karla Heusner** keeps the Belize section up to date. Thanks also to **Joanne Potts** and **Sylvia Suddes**.

The main photographers, contributing to a stunning gallery of images, were **Andreas Gross**, **Jamie Marshall** and **Mireille Vautier**.

CONTENTS

INSIGHT GUIDE
Guatemala
Belize &
The Yucatan

The majestic
temples of Tikal

Travel Tips

Full Travel Tips index is on page 339

Places

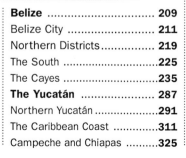

BIENVENIDO

The magnificent architecture and cultural brilliance of the

ancient Maya are attracting a growing tide of visitors

I f we had wished to give this book a subtitle, it would have been "The World of the Maya", for that is the evocative theme that brings together these two Central American countries and a thumb-shaped region of Mexico. The first Maya settled in the south of the region, along the Pacific coast between Mexico and El Salvador, and concentrated on farming and fishing. By 2000 BC there were villages sparsely scattered throughout the area and rudimentary pottery was being made. The first stone civic and religious buildings were erected around 750 BC in the heart of the region at Nakbé, close to the modern borders where Guatemala, Mexico and Belize meet today.

Gradually these settlements expanded and flourished, and formed a loosely-connected network of city states, centered around groups of awesome temple-pyramids, decorated with fine murals and carved stelae. The ruins at Chichén Itzá, Uxmal, Palenque, Copán, Tikal, Calakmul and El Mirador are some of the most impressive archeological remains in the Americas, produced by whom most experts consider to to be the most advanced people the continent has known.

Masters of time

The Maya studied the stars, and developed several interconnecting calendrical systems that rival even today's technology for their precision and complexity. They developed a hieroglyphic form of writing, producing paper codices, which related every last detail of their sacred rituals in meticulous mathematical order. They were highly skilled artists and craftsmen, producing a treasure-trove in ceramics, precious stone and metals, and breathtakingly beautiful weavings.

Above all, though, the Maya were the masters, or rather the worshipers of Time. Every day and every daily routine, from the birth of a child to the planting of a crop, had its sacred procedure laid down in the *Chilam Balam*, the Maya Bible. In fact, even royal marriages and wars would be planned around the calendar, each according to the propitious date and time, when the appropriate deity was in ascendance in the heavens.

And then suddenly, sometime around AD 900, the whole Maya civilization collapsed, almost a chain reaction that saw every major city deserted throughout the region. Magnificent temples and palaces were desecrated or were abandoned to the encroaching jungle. The priestly hierarchy fell from grace and the people dispersed. Theories explaining this tragic end are still being offered: drought, invasion, epidemic disease, even abduction by aliens. Recent studies indicate

PRECEDING PAGES: girls from Nebaj in Guatemala's western highlands; sugarcane workers from the Guatemalan Pacific coast; spectacular costumes from the Ixil Triangle, Guatemala; Lago de Atitlán, the most beautiful lake in the world.
LEFT: El Castillo, Chichén Itzá's most important temple-pyramid.

that over-exploitation of land created an environmental collapse, a theory that has been backed up by strong evidence at Copán in Honduras, one of the best-studied of all the Maya sites.

One fallacy should be exposed here and now, however. The Maya as a people did *not* disappear. More than 6 million still live in Guatemala alone. They are still spread over a similar territory as at the peak of their culture, and many still maintain the same beliefs and traditions as their ancestors. Others, however, have become assimilated into modern society. The Spanish Conquest and subsequent historical upheavals have decimated their numbers and hounded many more into cultural submission.

The terror returned in the late 1960s and '70s in Guatemala, with a vicious civil war between the state and guerrilla armies – one of the bloodiest periods of the region's history. Ostensibly aimed at stamping out the threat of communist insurrection, military-formed death squads soon turned the conflict into a virtual genocide, with many Maya hig hland villages completely wiped out and their inhabitants either slaughtered or driven into exile. Many thousands of Maya villagers died and human rights investigators are still working to establish the truth.

EL Mundo Maya

In recent years, however, a new optimism and pride in Maya culture has emerged, given expression in an ambitious initiative combining tourism and environmental conservation, El Mundo Maya. Devised in the late 1980s, the plan is to identify, protect and draw together the various regions and archeological sites belonging to the Maya region, and enable the Maya themselves to regain their sense of identity on a practical, economic level, by developing these sites as major tourist attractions. Going against the example set by Cancún on Mexico's Caribbean coastline, whose massive multinational resorts do their best to appear culturally anonymous, the Mundo Maya is set on reviving age-old Maya traditions, and protecting their land, to which their culture is intrinsically tied.

The project still has a way to go to realize its ambitious aims, particularly as the Maya communities are faced with the same economic and population pressures as their fellow citizens. Furthermore, concerns have been raised about Mundo Maya drawing a disproportionate share of the region's finances, which may lead to other, equally needy regions being left worse off.

Nevertheless, it's the astounding diversity of the landscape, flora and fauna that's the Mundo Maya's best-kept secret. The heart of the region, where the civilization first emerged, is covered in dense, subtropical forest, much of it protected in a cross-border network of national parks. A fearsome chain of volcanoes pierces the skies in the south of region. There's the world's second greatest coral reef, off the Caribbean coast. There are mighty non-volcanic mountain ranges such as the Sierra Madre and the Cuchumatanes and great lakes like Bacalar, Atitlán and Izabal; desert zones and impressive wetlands along the northern coast of the Yucatán that are ideal for birding.

Jaguar, ocelot, tapir, spider and howler monkeys can be found here in the rainforest reserves. The giant ceiba, which is sacred to the

RIGHT: market day in Chichicastenango, in Guatemala's western highlands.

Maya, is the greatest tree in the vast jungle areas that remain, but the biodiversity in the Maya area is almost overwhelming. You may even get a glimpse of the elusive manatee, the resplendent quetzal, or the monkey-eating harpy eagle (the world's largest) if you have time, patience and luck. Offshore, there are spectacular pelagic visitors to the region. Huge whale sharks, up to 15 meters (50 ft) long, migrate along the Caribbean coastline; green, leatherback and Pacific Ridley sea turtles come ashore to lay their eggs on Pacific beaches; there are dolphins and many species of bluewater sharks. On the outer Belizean cayes, divers and snorkelers regularly encounter eagle rays, manta rays and other forms of pelagic life.

People and cultures

Latino (*ladino*) culture dominates the Maya region, and competes with the USA for cultural hegemony. Whether it's Brazilian TV soap operas or Argentinian theater, influence from the rest of the Latin world is very evident, especially its musical influence. You'll be lambasted with rhythms from all over the continent in the buses, bars and clubs as merengue tunes from the Dominican Republic, salsa from Colombia, son from Cuba, latin house from Argentina and even Hispanic hip hop from California add lyrical joy, sorrow and social comment to everyday life.

The region's elite is largely of white, European origin and concentrated within a select group of families. Sometimes called criollos, this oligarchy retains ties with Spain, but also increasingly with Miami and the USA's Latino diaspora.

Indigenous Maya culture is much less flamboyant, and in traditional villages dancing is something which is reserved for fiestas. Ancient, unmistakably pre-Columbian, dances are performed by costumed performers reenacting themes like the flight of the Hero twins of the Popol Vuh during the spectacular Palo Volador. The musical soundtrack to a Maya fiesta above all is the hauntingly hypnotic melodies of the xylophone-like marimba.

The third important cultural leverage is from the Caribbean, and in most of the Central American coastal towns the offshore influence is very evident. In Belize thunderous reggae basslines direct from Jamaica shake the dancehall while the inimitably reflective wit and harmonies of Trinidadian calypso fills the airwaves. You may even see a game of cricket on the village green.

In Southern Belize and on the Caribbean coast of Guatemala, there are several Garífuna communities. The incredible story of the Garífuna, the Afrocaribs who trace their origins back to shipwrecked slave boats, intermarriage with Carib island Indians, wars with Britain and exile in Roatán and the journey to the Central American mainland, is told on page 233.

Finally, there are also several, quite small communities of Mennonites, whose fascinating culture originated in Holland in the 16th century and who subsequently formed settlements all over the continent (*see page 185*). The most significant Mennonite groups can be found in Belize where, in the past 40 years they have made a tremendous contribution to the agricultural sector. ❑

RIGHT: San Francisco El Alto, Guatemala.

Decisive Dates

THE PRE-HISPANIC ERA

c. 10,000 BC Earliest animal remains:mammoth bones found at Loltún in Yucatán.
c. 2000 BC First evidence of fixed Maya settlements: at Nakbé, Cuello, Loltún, and Mani.
1000 BC Remains found of villages on Pacific coast of Mexico, at Ocnos.
700 BC Evidence of large-scale settlement at Kaminaljuyú in Guatemala.
500 BC Period of first monumental buildings at sites such as Tikal. Influence of the Olmec culture.

300 BC Izapa-style pottery, and the first hieroglyphs. Nakbé thought to be at its height.
100 BC El Mirador established as the first Maya superpower.
AD 100 Early Classic period. Sites such as El Mirador and Cerros have already been abandoned.
300 Start of Classic period. Dominance of Tikal and Calakmul in central Maya region. First stelae found with exact dates, eg Stela 29 at Tikal, dated AD 292.
400 Life of the fourth king of Copán in Honduras, Cu Ix, accurately dated AD 455–95.
700–850 peak of Maya Classic period, all through the region: sites such as Uxmal and Kabah at their height in Yucatán, Palenque in Chiapas.

850–900 Decline of Classic Maya sites: the last recorded inscription at Palenque is from AD 799.
900 Dominance of Chichén Itzá in north Yucatán.
1000 Post-Classic period, with the emergence of fortified sites in Yucatán region, and several competing groups in Guatemala.
1250 The fall of Chichén Itzá and emergence of Mayapán as center of influence in Yucatán. In Guatemala, K'i che's, Kaqchikeles and Mames dominate region. Tulum, on eastern seaboard of Yucatán, emerges as important trading center.
1440 Decline of Mayapán, and break-up of Maya groups in Yucatán into small areas of influence.

THE SPANISH CONQUEST

1512 Shipwreck leaves first two Spaniards, Gonzalo Guerrero and Jeronimo de Aguilar among the Maya of Yucatán. The family Guerrero forms with his Maya wife is the beginning of the mixed race or *mestizaje* of Mexico.
1517 Arrival on coast of Yucatán in Mexico of Francisco Hernandez de Córdoba.
1519 Hernán Cortés arrives on island of Cozumel off Yucatán at the start of discovery and conquest of Mexico. First Mass held in Mexico.
1523 Spanish exploration and conquest of Guatemala under Pedro de Alvarado, who defeats the K'iche' and other Maya armies.

THE COLONIAL ERA

1527 First Spanish capital of Guatemala founded. Francisco de Montejo begins conquest of Yucatán.
1541 Pedro de Alvarado dies. Capital of Guatemala is moved to Antigua.
1542 Foundation of Mérida, which becomes Spanish capital of Yucatán.
1540s Franciscan friars set out to bring Christianity to Maya. In Yucatán, Bishop Diego de Landa publishes *Relación de las cosas de Yucatán*, an invaluable insight into Maya way of life. But he also persecutes the Maya, and in 1562 organizes huge burning of Maya manuscripts and sculptures.
1576 Report to Spanish crown on ruins of Copán by Diego Garcia de Palacio.
1600s First "Baymen" begin to settle near mouth of Belize River and to exploit forests of the region.
1697 Last Maya stronghold in Guatemala falls with conquest of the Itzá on a Lake Petén Itzá island.
1739 First of the Maya manuscripts rediscovered in Vienna and taken to the German city of Dresden, to become known as the Dresden codex.
1857 The *Popol Vuh*, the sacred book of the K'iche' Maya, is published in a French translation.

1746 Father Antonio de Solis is first European to discover the site of Palenque in Chiapas, Mexico.
1765 "Burnaby's Code" drawn up as first constitution for what became British Honduras (Belize).
1786 Spanish captain Antonio del Rio explores Palenque for Spanish king. When his report is published in English in 1822, with engravings by J-F de Waldeck, it creates immense interest. Waldeck and others are convinced that the Maya civilization must have come from Europe.

INDEPENDENCE MOVEMENTS

1798 The Battle of St George's Caye between British and Spanish naval forces. Defeat of Spanish fleet firmly establishes British rule of Belize region.
1821 Mexico and Central America win independence from Spain. Guatemala, Honduras, Nicaragua and El Salvador form Central American federation. Yucatán and Chiapas also join federation, but join Mexico in 1823. The United Provinces of Central America breaks up in 1839.
1841 *Incidents of Travel in Central America, Chiapas and Yucatán* by the explorer John Stephens, illustrated by Frederick Catherwood, begins the era of scientific investigation of the great Maya sites.
1847 Guatemala becomes independent republic.
1847 War of the Castes in Yucatán. Maya revolt that is to last more than 50 years.
1859 Convention between the UK and Guatemala recognises the boundaries of British Honduras, but has been disupted by Guatemala ever since.
1862 Belize becomes official British colony.

THE MODERN ERA

1880s Englishman Alfred Maudslay begins first modern scientific exploration of Maya sites.
1893 Mexico renounces its claim to territory of British Honduras.
1910 Mexican revolution against Porfirio Diaz.
1923 Yucatán governed by revolutionary socialists.
1924 Governor Felipe Carrillo Puerto assassinated.
1930 Dictator Jorge Ubico president in Guatemala: banana boom led by United Fruit Company.
1937 Mexican president Lázaro Cárdenas orders massive land redistribution in Yucatán.
1944–54 Progressive nationalist governments in Guatemala under presidents Arévalo and Jácobo

PRECEDING PAGES: replica of Maya fresco from Bonampak, Mexico.
LEFT: late-Classic Maya jadeite mask.
RIGHT: Rigoberta Menchú, from Guatemala, winning the Nobel Peace Prize in 1992.

Arbenz. Land reform and attempts to curb power of US-owned banana companies.
1954 A CIA-backed coup in Guatemala leads to overthrow of Arbenz, start of military rule and civil war.
1976 Earthquake in Guatemala leaves 23,000 dead.
1981 Belize gains independence from the UK.
1982 Guatemalan guerrillas form Guatemalan National Revolutionary Unity (URNG). Dictator Ríos Montt intensifies war in countryside: thousands of Maya are killed or forced into exile.
1986 Guatemala returns to civilian government with election of Christian Democrat Vinicio Cerezo.
1992 Rigoberta Menchú is awarded the Nobel Prize for peace.

1994 On January 1, Mexico joins North American Free Trade Agreement with the US and Canada. The same day, Lacandón Maya Indians and the Zapatista National Liberation Army rebel in Chiapas.
1996 Final peace accords signed in Guatemala, end more than 30 years of civil war in which about 200,000, mostly Maya, were killed or disappeared.
1998 Hurricane Mitch sweeps Central America, causing massive damage and many casualties.
2004 Military numbers and budget cut in Guatemala; CAFTA trade agreement approved.
2005 Hurricane Wilma hits Mexico's Yucatan Peninsula, several people are killed. The same year archeologists discover a mural, believed to be more than 2,000 years old, at the San Bartolo site. ❏

MAYA ROOTS

Human settlement of the Maya region dates back thousands of years, with their cultural origins linked to the mysterious civilization of the Olmecs

The Maya people settled what are today five different countries in Central America: the Yucatán Peninsula in Mexico, almost all of Guatemala and Belize, and parts of Honduras and El Salvador. In total, the Maya occupied territory of more than 300,000 sq. km (115,850 sq. miles), in very varied natural surroundings. These included the highlands of Guatemala, the dense jungles of the Petén and Belize and Chiapas, and the flat limestone peninsula of the Yucatán. The Maya groups adapted to survive in these varied environments, but shared common beliefs, social structures, languages and an architecture that clearly define them.

Archeological remains

The first remains of human settlement in these areas date from around 2000 BC. Archeologists have found traces of villages, and of clay figurines they think were used in fertility cults, but little more than this.

One of the earliest villages to have been explored is at Ocos on the Pacific coast of Guatemala. Thought to date from around 1500 BC, the inhabitants of Ocos seem to have lived primarily on shellfish, fish and iguanas. Another early village at Las Charcas in central Guatemala shows that by the 5th century BC the Maya villages were much larger. The people of Las Charcas were already skilled at making pottery with red on white decorations. This period, generally known as the Preclassic, continued until around AD 300, by which time some of the Maya villages had several thousand inhabitants. They used irrigation systems to supply water to their fields, and were already writing and erecting monuments.

As these agricultural settlements prospered, Maya society became more stratified. Most of the Maya still lived as farmers, cultivating

LEFT: artist's impression of Maya city Rio Azul at its peak, from Guatemala City's Museum of Archeology.
RIGHT: early Maya glyphic inscriptions on Stela 31, from Tikal, Guatemala.

maize and other vegetables. They lived in small family units in thatch-roofed huts as they had done for hundreds of years. The huts were raised on mounds of earth and stone to protect them from wet season flooding, and were usually sited near a source of fresh water. But the ordinary Maya were governed by an elite who

enjoyed religious and military power, and who passed the power on in dynasties. They increasingly celebrated that power in vast ceremonial buildings, and in inscriptions and *stelae* (carved stone monuments) which recalled their deeds as well as depicting their gods. By AD 250–300, what is known as the Classic period of Maya civilization began. This lasted until approximately AD 900, and is the period when most of the great Maya centers were built and amplified by successive generations.

One of the most important early centers was at Kaminaljuyú, close to the modern Guatemala City. (So close, indeed, that it has now been swallowed up within the city, much of it being destroyed as new houses and roads were built on the ancient site; *see page 113*.) Here, local obsidian was worked into tools and traded all over the Maya territory. More than 400 ceremonial mounds have been located at Kaminaljuyú. In one of them, a jade covered corpse of a leader was found, accompanied by the remains of sacrificed adults and children.

Palaces and pyramids

Other important early sites are El Mirador and Tikal, the latter deep in the jungle of the northern Petén in Guatemala. Tikal (*see page 162*) is one of the few Maya centers to have been fully excavated, giving a good idea of how a settlement might have looked some 1,200 years ago. Archeologists estimate that 12,000 people may have lived there, in dwellings and ceremonial buildings spread over an area of 6 sq. km (16 sq. miles). Most of the inhabitants lived in huts scattered throughout the area. The several dozen palaces and pyramids were not placed at the center, but took advantage of the terrain and were placed on high vantage points.

Tikal has several nuclei of important buildings, connected to each other by causeways. These buildings are typical of Maya sites: low palaces and stone platforms arranged around

THE MAYA CALENDAR

The observation of the heavens, and the calculation of time based on the movement of the stars, the sun, and the moon, was of the utmost importance to the Maya. Many great Maya sites, such as Chichén Itzá, had observatories from where the experts could calculate the calendar.

Over the centuries, the Maya elaborated two different but inter-related calendar systems. The first consisted of 20 named days, which interlocked like a cogwheel with the numbers one to 13, giving a total cycle of 260 days. No-one knows why this number of days was chosen, although it has been pointed out that it is close to the period of human gestation. In some of the more remote Maya villages in Guatemala, this calendar is still remembered, and some elders still tell the meaning and portents of each day.

Alongside this system was one more closely based on the sun's movement. In this calendar, there were 18 months – again, each one 20 days long. Then at the end of the year came five days to complete the solar cycle (the extra quarter day of the annual solar cycle was ignored). These five days were regarded with dread, and only the knowledge and skill of the priests could guarantee that the yearly round would continue as normal. These two calendar systems, one based on 260 days, the other on 365, came back to their starting point every 18,980 days, or 52 years.

courtyards, and several tall pyramidal constructions, built on a base of earth and rubble and covered with limestone blocks. At the summit of these pyramids are narrow rooms decorated with plaster and vividly painted with murals, probably reserved for sacred rituals. The whole construction is topped off with a further extension – a roof comb of stone that adds height and solemnity, and was usually covered in brightly painted stucco reliefs.

Stone stelae

In the courtyards in front of the palaces, the Maya placed stelae or free-standing stone

the strong hierarchy in their society, and their sense of history as reflected in the written inscriptions on the many stelae erected.

Rule by religious leaders

During this Classic period, there are thought to have been as many as five million Maya, although it is impossible to confirm this figure. It seems that Maya society involved rule by an extremely powerful individual who was also the religious leader of his community. In the tomb of one of these leaders, Pacal, in the Temple of the Inscriptions at Palenque in Mexico, he is carrying a jade sphere in one hand and a

columns on which the figure of the ruler who put up the building is shown, with elaborate dating and details of his dynastic position inscribed in hieroglyphic writing.

The other main ceremonial centers such as Palenque (*see page 332*), Piedras Negras, Bonampak, Copán, Uxmal and part of Chichén Itzá were also built during the Classic period. These sites show not only the complexity of the religious beliefs of their inhabitants, but also their fascination with astronomy and time,

LEFT: replica of the Rosalila Temple, from the Museum of Maya Sculpture at Copán.
ABOVE: detail of Stela 12 at Piedra Negras, Guatemala.

dart in the other, representing the powers of heaven and earth. On the lid of his sarcophagus is a sculpture of a dragon in the form of a cross. This is the dragon Itzamna, the most powerful god in the Maya pantheon.

Classic Maya architecture

The architecture of this Classic period is one of the greatest glories of the Maya. They used earlier ceremonial mounds to construct tall and graceful pyramids, topped off with rooms using the corbel arch. They built intricate observatories such as the one at Chichén Itzá to carry out their studies of the stars, the sun and moon and Venus, on which they based their calendar.

The Maya Codices

The Maya not only engraved monuments with hieroglyphs depicting their gods and their history. They also wrote and drew about their beliefs on long strips of tree bark or animal hides. These were then folded like a screen to form books or codices. When the Spaniards arrived in the 16th century, hundreds of these sacred books were in existence. Bishop Diego de Landa in Yucatán had an important collection of them, but in 1562 he decided they were all heretical, and so organized a huge burning of his collection of manuscripts.

Because of this and other accidents or deliberate acts of destruction, only four of the ancient Maya codices have survived to our day. Three of them are known after the cities where they can be found: Dresden, Madrid and Paris. The fourth, which came to light in the 1970s, is named the Grolier Codex after the association of bibliophiles who helped identify and authenticate it. The Grolier codex is the only one still in Mexico.

These books are thought to have been owned originally by Maya priests, who consulted them to make sure that the proper rituals were carried out on different days of the cycle. These sacred books told the priest which god was to be worshiped when, and what kind of sacrifice or offering was to be made. In this way, the Maya knew when to plant their maize, when it was propitious to go hunting, when to start out on a new venture. No single book contained all the necessary information, and these "scientific books" were zealously guarded in special libraries.

The Dresden Codex is thought to have arrived in Europe during the reign of Carlos V, that is, early on in the conquest of Mexico. It is a single piece of bark more than 3 meters (10 ft) long, covered in white plaster with black, red and yellow pictures and writing. These show a series of seated gods, but also human beings, animals and fish. The celebrated British Mayanist Eric Thompson argued that there were 13 chapters in the codex, showing different calendars, the movements of Venus, a torrent of rain, and other calculations.

The codex in the Museo de America in Madrid is almost twice as long as the one in Dresden. It has 56 pages, but the drawing and writing are less perfected. It too shows the rituals associated with different activities such as hunting, beekeeping, and trade. It also has a section on the rites to be observed during the key period of five days when one year was at its close, and the Maya feared the next might never start unless the gods were properly propitiated.

The Paris Codex is especially interesting for its astronomical data. It shows the gods who govern each *katun* or period of 20 years that was important to the Maya. In the glyphs around this central figure are the predictions for this period, and the ceremonies to be observed.

The Grolier Codex is kept in the National Library of Anthropology and History in Mexico City. It is not on public display because many experts question its authenticity as it only came to light in 1971. Like the Dresden Codex, it is concerned above all with the movements of the planet Venus, which was considered a dangerous influence.

The codices are remarkable works of art. They show a great ability to combine writing with the skilfully depicted figures of deities, animals, and other creatures of this world and the complicated pantheon of their deities. And looking at them, it is hard to suppress a strangely pleasing sense of satisfaction in the fact that these few remaining examples of a vast and complex library of signs can still resist almost all attempts to decipher them, centuries after they were conceived. ❑

LEFT: detail from the Madrid Codex, discovered in the 19th century and now kept in the Museo de America in Madrid.

They built stone platforms and temples for their religious ceremonies, lined up with the movements of the sun and moon. They constructed paved roads or *sacbeob* that linked one ceremonial center with another. And most of the ceremonial sites also had a court for the famous ball game, with stone hoops for the ball to pass through, and platforms for spectators that are as regular and harmonious as any Greek stadium. The ball game itself was a battle between cosmic opposites: sun and moon, night and day, the life-giving gods versus those of the underworld. It has often been said that the losing team was sacrificed after these games, but some archeologists dispute this.

PLANET OF VICTORY

The Maya carefully monitored the movements of Venus as it was linked with success in war. Many stelae record its appearance prompting the decision to attack.

Although for many years the idea prevailed that the Maya were a peaceful people, interested only in science and art, more recent theories suggest they were just as warlike as any of the other civilizations of Mesoamerica. Like many of them, the Maya also used human sacrifice as a guarantee of cosmic order, to help ensure that nature did not destroy mankind.

A culture in decline

By the 9th century of our era, there were signs that this great flowering of the Maya culture was in decline. Again, there have been many different attempts to explain this. Some experts believe it was due to over-population; others speak of a natural disaster while others still think there may have been disastrous civil wars between the different Maya dynasties.

Whatever the reason, the large centers in Guatemala and Chiapas seem to have been abandoned, with many of them disappearing for centuries into the jungle undergrowth. Other archeologists argue that there was no sudden collapse, but that the hub of Maya culture moved to the northern lowlands of the Yucatán, to the Puuc region, and above all to the great center of Chichén Itzá.

Over a lengthy period of time, an immense and elaborate ceremonial center was built on this site in the north of the Yucatán Peninsula. At its heart was the sacred *cenote* or pool,

which was a place of pilgrimage for people throughout the region. Thousands of votive offerings, as well as the remains of human sacrifice, have been found in the mud at the bottom of this pool.

Chichén Itzá itself is a hybrid of styles and influences, which suggests that the Maya came into contact with, or had been conquered by, groups from further north in Mexico. The Toltecs brought in the worship of Kukulcan, a feathered serpent worshiped in other Mexican cultures as Quetzalcoatl. The most important

building at Chichén Itzá, the so-called Castillo, is a temple built in his honor, which is clearly in the style of the Toltec Maya. At some point in the 13th century, however, the Toltec also seem to have abandoned Chichén Itzá, which soon became part of the kingdom of the Itzaes.

Defensive strongholds

The center of this kingdom was Mayapan, a walled city in the west of the Yucatán Peninsula. As many as 12,000 people are thought to have lived in this important trading city, which covered more than 5 sq. km (2 sq. miles) of land and where up to 2,000 dwellings have been discovered. Although the Itzá

RIGHT: terracotta figure of a Maya ruler from the Classic period, in the Museo Nacional de Antropología, Mexico City.

did build temples and various other ceremonial buildings, they had lost many of the skills of the Classic Maya. Mayapan appears to have been the defensive redoubt of a warlike group of people who exacted tribute from neighboring tribes.

Another center built during this last phase of the Classic Maya culture was the breathtaking site of Tulum, on the Atlantic coast of the Yucatán Peninsula (*see page 319*). This too was a defensive stronghold, surrounded by walls on three sides and the ocean on the fourth. Its buildings, paintings and inscriptions show it to have been a mixture of styles and influences. Its

isolated position means that it may have survived on into the Spanish era.

In 1441, Mayapan itself was apparently overrun by its enemies. Mayapan was the last of the major Maya centers; when the Spaniards arrived 150 years later they found the sites deserted, and the Maya of Mexico living in small, dispersed groups.

Warring local factions

The Maya in Guatemalan highlands underwent a similar fate. The Toltec-Maya arrived in the region from further north in the 13th century. They appear to have overcome the local indige-

THE MAYA LONG COUNT

In addition to their two intermeshing calendars, which completed their full cycle every 52 years, at some point the Maya also developed a system designed for calculating longer historical dates and distinguishing the 52-year cycles from one another. Confusingly, this seems to have been based on a year made up of 360 rather than 365 days, known as a *tun*. The system, called the Long Count, came into use during the Classic Maya period, and is based on the great cycle of 13 *baktuns* – a period of 1,872,000 days, or 5,125 years.

Many of the Maya monuments have the date of their construction written in this Long Count in hieroglyphs. Most

archeologists have followed the idea of the British Maya expert Sir Eric Thompson that these dates of the Long Count began from a fixed date far in the past when the Maya thought the world had begun. Thompson calculated that this must have been on August 11, 3114 BC, which in the Maya script was 4 Ahau 8 Cumku. The date written on Classic Maya monuments is meant to show how many days had elapsed between 4 Ahau 8 Cumku and the moment the stela or temple was built. And, according to some inscriptions, the world is supposed to come to an end when the entire great cycle of the Maya calendar is completed – which will be on December 23, 2012.

nous Maya, and formed several local empires. The most powerful of these were the K'i che', whose capital was Utatlan. Other groups included the Kaqchikel and the Mam, but these last two were conquered by the K'i che' in the 15th century. But when Quicab, the powerful leader of the K'i che', died in 1475, the other Guatemalan Maya tribes broke away from their rule. As in Mexico, when the Spaniards arrived they found the local tribes at war with each other, and were quick to exploit this enmity to their own advantage.

The Classic Maya held deep religious beliefs. They thought that the gods found their purpose were the four Bacab who occupied each corner. They were each identified with a color (white for north, yellow for south, red for east and black for west) and between them held up the heavens, where the other gods lived. Each of the Bacabs was worshiped in a quarter of the days of the 260-day calendar.

Heavenly hierarchy

There were 13 layers in the Maya heaven. In the topmost layer lived Itzamna, the "celestial dragon" or serpent, the male figure who was the god of creation, of agriculture, writing, and the all-important calendar. Itzamna was also

in the creation of mankind, who repaid them for their existence by showing fidelity to them and the rituals the gods demanded. They carved stylised representations of their gods on temples and stelae, and wrote about them in the codices (*see page 28*). They conceived of the world as flat and square (some paintings and codices suggest it was seen as the back of a huge crocodile floating in a pond full of waterlilies), and among their most important gods

---

LEFT: jaguar altar or throne, El Castillo, Chichén Itzá.
ABOVE: mural in the Museum of Archeology in Guatemala City, after an original in the Maya site of Uaxactún in Petén province, painted by Antonio Tevedaf.

identified with the sun, with maize and semen, and with blood. His companion was Ixchel (Rainbow Lady) who was also identified with the moon. All the other gods in the Maya pantheon were the offspring of these two.

Each of the 13 layers was identified with a particular god, among whom were the north star god, the maize god, and the young moon goddess. The benevolent rain gods, or Chacs, were also to be found at the four corners of the earth, together with the Bacabs.

The exact number and attributes of these gods is difficult to ascertain. It seems that each of them had four different aspects, corresponding to the colors of each corner of the world.

Then too, they all seem to have had a counterpart of the opposite sex, reflecting the dualism that underlies much of Maya thought. To complicate matters still further, it is thought that the Maya gods had a double in the layers of the dark underworld where, like the sun, all the gods had to pass in order to be reborn.

Rhythm and ritual

Each day had its appropriate ritual according to its place in the 260-day calendar. The most important rites seem to have taken place during the five-day period at the end of one year and the beginning of the next. For the Maya, the cosmos was in constant movement, and only by fulfilling the rituals could they be assured that not only would the land be fertile, but that the sun and moon would continue their course through the heavens.

Reading the Maya

The Maya ceremonial centers contained many examples of their writing. These beautifully chiselled small pictures or glyphs accompanied the sculptures on temple lintels, and were included in the decoration of the many stelae (stone columns) that were characteristically placed in rows in front of the main buildings.

The meaning of these glyphs was lost by the time the Spanish entered the Maya territory in the 16th century. Attempts to decipher them have been one of the most exciting adventures in Maya studies, and have only recently been truly successful.

The first to try to understand Maya writing was the redoubtable Bishop Diego de Landa, the Franciscan who was in charge of bringing Christianity to the Yucatán in the middle of the 16th century. While on the one hand he was the man responsible for burning most of the Maya manuscripts which he considered heretical, on the other he was genuinely interested in the culture and language of the Maya among whom he lived. He learned their language, and compiled the first dictionary of Mayan and Spanish. He also suggested that the writing in the ancient Maya manuscripts might be closely related to what the Maya around him were speaking.

Attempts to read ancient Mayan language after him were often hampered by racism and far-fetched notions of antiquity. In the 18th and 19th centuries, there were several attempts to demonstrate that the Mayan language must be derived from an Indo-European one, that had somehow been taken across the Atlantic. Just as there have been many fantastic theories to explain the extraordinary buildings of the Maya sites – including visits from outer space – so it was a long time before researchers into Maya writing were free of similarly distorted views that the ancient peoples of Mexico and Guatemala were not capable of producing such an elaborate system unaided.

Towards the end of the 19th century, though, attempts were made in earnest to decipher the Maya inscriptions. The rediscovery of Maya sites by John Lloyd Stephens and in particular

PEON POWER

Maya society was highly structured, with strict divisions between the classes. Most numerous were the *peones*, at the bottom of the scale, whose primary role was to work the land intensively to provide food for the community. In addition, they performed regular military service duties. But their most lasting contribution was to provide the labor needed to construct the temples found in the center of every Maya city. These great structures were achieved by human power alone, without the use of wagons or wheelbarrrows – the Maya did not have the wheel – and without the aid of any draught animals such as horses, mules or oxen.

the marvellous engravings of buildings and stelae by his companion Frederick Catherwood in the late 1840s paved the way. But it was a French priest, Charles André Brasseur de Bourbourg, who made the first important breakthrough in reading Maya scripts when he discovered a manuscript of Bishop Diego de Landa's work in a Madrid library.

Calendars and counting systems

This manuscript helped de Bourbourg to decipher some of the Maya calendar, and to work out Maya numerals, based on a dot for the numbers one to four, a bar for the number five, and an adapted conch shell for the all-important zero. However, he too was convinced that the Maya had not developed these ideas all alone – his pet theory was that their writing "proved" they were the lost civilization of Atlantis.

Another Englishman, Alfred P. Maudslay, made further forays into Maya territory at the end of the 19th century, and brought back plaster casts and accurate drawings of the hieroglyphs. These were studied by perhaps the most influential of all the Mayanists, Eric Thompson. His great contribution was in working out the extraordinarily complex calendar systems employed by the Classic Maya. But at the same time, he was dismissive of the idea that many of the hieroglyphs could be related to other things, and might be phonetic rather than just pictures – that they might represent the sounds of the Mayan language as it was spoken and not just be commonly recognized pictorial short-hand.

Symbols as sounds

The counter-argument – that the inscriptions on Maya buildings could be read and pronounced in a similar way to other early languages, was put forward in the late 1940s by an extraordinary Russian scholar, Yuri Knosorov. He reinterpreted Bishop de Landa's observations, and offered a method to understand the grammar and phonetic construction of the language.

It was Knosorov's approach which has proved more fruitful. In 1976, the North American researcher Dave Kelley published his book, *Deciphering the Maya*, based on a pho-

netic reading of the symbols. More researchers continued the work, and discovered that the inscriptions, rather than being wholly concerned with astronomy or religion, were a description of the history of the royal families who were commemorated in the buildings.

It is now plain that many of the glyphs found on Maya monuments represent phonetic syllables. One example is the word for *cacao* (chocolate), which was of great symbolic importance for the Maya. So it is that after being lost to the world for centuries, and after defying attempts to decipher them for several hundred years, Maya inscriptions are now

yielding their secrets – just as the ancient Egyptian or Cretan languages revealed the secrets of their societies.

The Spanish era

The first Spanish expedition to land in the Maya world was led by Francisco Hernandez de Córdoba in 1517. Hernan Cortés followed two years later. He landed on the island of Cozumel, where the first Christian Mass was said on the American continent. It was in the Yucatán too that he picked up a survivor from an earlier expedition, Gerónimo de Aguilar, who acted as a translator both among the Maya, and with the famous Doña Marina (Cortes'

LEFT: Francisco de Montejo, founder of Mérida.
RIGHT: Dominican missionaries baptize the Maya, as part of the Spaniards' campaign to win the indians' hearts as well as their lands.

translator and mistress) when Cortés moved further north into Mexico.

It was one of Cortés's lieutenants, Francisco de Montejo, who returned to the Yucatán in 1527 to extend Spanish rule to the Maya living there. At first he was unsuccessful, both on the Caribbean coast near Campeche, and on the Atlantic side, where one of his men, Alonso Davila, set up a short-lived colony at Villa Real, near today's Chetumal. By 1534, the Spaniards had to withdraw once again. It was Montejo's son and nephew who in 1540 began a second conquest of the Yucatán. This time, the Spaniards succeeded in establishing their rule. In

1542 they founded the city of Mérida, and as in Mexico City, built the new cathedral directly on top of the ruins of a Maya temple.

Systematic repression

From their base in newly-established towns, the Spaniards spread their control in several ways. They defeated and killed the leaders of the Maya. They took their lands, and forced the Maya to work for them. They imposed their own system of local government and set up their own authorities. They forbade the native religions, and brought in Franciscan friars to spread the Christian message throughout the peninsula. The Europeans also carried with

them diseases such as measles and smallpox to which the Maya had no resistance, leading to more deaths and greater demoralization. Even so, the Maya of Yucatán and Chiapas never accepted Spanish rule entirely, and rose against it on many occasions.

Legendary ferocity

The Spanish conquest of the Maya in Guatemala was entrusted to Pedro de Alvarado. He achieved it with a ferocity that became legendary. In 1523, he and some 800 men defeated the main army of the K'i che' and slew their leader Tecun Uman. Alvarado then advanced on the K'i che' capital Utatlan, and burned it down. He was equally ruthless with the Kaqchikel, and set about conquering the many mountain tribes. In 1527, Alvarado founded the first Spanish capital of Guatemala at Santiago de los Caballeros, close to the modern-day city of Antigua.

Resistance to Alvarado's rule continued through the 1530s, especially in the highlands of Verapaz, where in the end it was Christian missionaries led by Fray Bartolomé de las Casas who managed to get the Maya to accept Christianity and Spanish rule. By the time of Alvarado's death in 1541, almost the entire Maya population of Guatemala was under Spanish control. As in Mexico, however, this did not mean a complete end to resistance, and it was more than a century and a half later, in 1697, that the last descendants of the independent Maya kingdoms, who lived in Tayasal, an island on Lake Petén Itzá in northern Guatemala, were finally subdued.

Life under Spanish rule

By the mid-16th century, the original Spanish *conquistadores* had died, and Spanish rule was directed more impersonally from Spain and from the capital of the viceroyalty in Mexico City. The Yucatán and Guatemala (from where Honduras and Chiapas were governed) were far from these centers, and this distance on the one hand led to greater abuses, but on the other protected the Maya way of life, as it was never entirely dominated by the newcomers.

Among the first measures taken by the Spanish adminstration was the concentration of the native population in villages and towns, known as *reducciones*. Each of these was laid out in the Spanish style, with a central square where the Catholic church and the town hall or *ayuntamiento* were situated. The local population was brought into these new villages for several reasons. It was easier for the Spaniards to control them, and to make sure they paid their taxes. They were on hand for the communal work demanded of them, while at the same time it facilitated the missionaries' work of evangelization.

> **ON THEIR METTLE**
>
> The Maya had no metal tools – they were ignorant of iron and bronze – yet they produced a mass of finely-worked gold objects, jade carvings and pottery.

In this way, the Maya were forced to become part of Spanish colonial society – which, in a very racist way, always regarded them as the lowest element in that society. As the Spaniards developed agriculture and their estates or *haciendas* extended throughout the region, they also forced the Maya to work there – and in Guatemala for example, began the wholesale transfer of laborers from the highlands down to the plantations on the Pacific coast.

Skilful adaptation

Although some Maya were given posts of minor authority in the new Spanish villages, there was little chance of them wielding any real power. Instead, they continued their traditional practices and communal organization in parallel with the Spanish system.

Authority in the more remote villages continued to be held by the *principales* or village elders. Communal efforts were organized among Maya *cofradías* or brotherhoods, who used their role as keepers of the local saints to run self-help schemes, joint work on the *milpas* (maize fields) or even land transfers among villagers. Together with this, the colonial Maya were skilful at adapting the Christian religion to their own beliefs, continuing to worship the old gods in the guise of the Christian pantheon.

Bourbon influence

For more than two centuries after the Spanish conquest, these efforts and the isolation of much of the Maya world from the centers of Spanish interest helped to protect the Maya from the worst ravages found elsewhere in the empire. But the Maya's position worsened con-

---

LEFT: a 16th-century lithograph of the hated Pedro de Alvarado attacking the Kaqchikel in Guatemala.
RIGHT: Pedro de Alvarado (1485–1541), scourge of the Maya in Guatemala.

siderably during the second half of the 18th century, however, when the Bourbon monarchy in Spain attempted to regain effective control of its rebellious colonies. The provinces were subdivided and reorganized into *intendencias* and *partidos,* and indigenous officials were removed from office and replaced by Spaniards or *criollos.*

At the same time, an effort was made to redistribute land and to make the *haciendas* more productive. The profitable new crops of sisal, tobacco, sugar cane or cotton

demanded more land, which was seized from communal Maya holdings. And increasingly, the Maya were employed as laborers on these estates, often in conditions of near slavery.

When the struggle for independence began in Spanish America during the first decades of the 19th century, the Maya were still regarded as the lowest sector of society. Their customs and beliefs were largely ignored, if not actively despised. They themselves by this time had very little idea of their ancestors' glorious achievements, and yet many elements of their distinctive culture – language, dress, beliefs, social habits and structures – had managed to survive against the odds. ❑

UNCOVERING THE MYSTERIES OF THE PAST

The secrets of 5,000 years of Maya history are being painstakingly unravelled as archeologists explore the remains hidden by the tropical forests

Scientists are piecing together the spiritual and intellectual legacy left by a civilization that was ruled by living gods from more than 50 city-states, such as Tikal, Copán, Palenque, Calakmul, and Caracol. The classic Maya society (200 BC to AD 900) developed through trade, religion and statecraft, and left its imprint in hieroglyphical texts and superb monumental architecture. Fine artwork in jade, stone and clay pottery depicted scenes from mythology, the supernatural, politics, science, warfare and recorded events from everyday life. Etchings chronicled Maya kings' births, coronations, marriages, conquests and deaths.

ARCHEOLOGISTS VERSUS LOOTERS

Today the texts written on tombs' interior walls help unlock Maya secrets, yet these texts are all too often destroyed by looters foraging for artefacts for the lucrative, illegal pre-Columbian art trade. Regional governments and archeologists are racing against time to find and protect important undiscovered sites. Today, scientists are turning to airborne sensors operated from aircraft and satellites. The Landsat satellite provides data that delineates natural and large, man-made features. This data could help find as yet unknown ancient cities.

▷ **COPAN'S STELAE**
The magnificent carved stelae at Copán in Honduras are considered the finest in the Maya world.

▷ **TIKAL**
The towering temples of Tikal are now restored to their former glory, after a long renovation project.

△ **EARLY DISCOVERIES**
The natural blanket of the jungle helped to preserve the ruins of Tikal for the first explorers.

▷ **UNDERGROUND CAVE**
The huge network of potholes and caves in Belize and the Yucatán have revealed some rich finds of Maya ceramics.

◁ EDZNA
The Chenes-style ruins at Edzná in the Yucatán are crowned by an impressive five-story temple, adorned with huge stucco masks.

△ DETAILED MURAL
Colorful Maya murals on temple walls provided a mass of information about their everyday life, in particular, work and trade.

ARCHEOLOGICAL EXPEDITIONS

The birth of modern Maya archeology traces its popular origin to the epic expeditions, between 1839 and 1842, of adventurers John L. Stephens and Frederick Catherwood. Their discovery of immense ruined cities among the tropical jungles of Mesoamerica caught the imagination of the academic world.

Catherwood's beautiful lithographs of the ruins of Chichén Itzá, Uxmal, Palenque and Copán were widely published in Europe and North America. The explorers' tales of discovery were hailed as the greatest of the century.

Some 50 years later, archeologists such as Thompson, Morley, Tozzer, Joyce and Maler led expeditions to the jungles of Central America to try and unlock the mystery of the Maya civilization.

But it was only in the 1950s, with the help of modern technology, that archeologists began to decipher more than dates and numerals. Today's research is cracking the "Maya code" to reveal intricate details of Maya history.

△ CATHERWOOD'S ART
The 19th-century drawings of Maya ruins by Frederick Catherwood captured the world's imagination.

▷ JADE FIGURINE
A huge cache of finely worked jade pieces was found at Altún Há, a major Maya site in northern Belize.

THE MAYA WORLD TODAY

The Maya definitely didn't disappear; there are millions of them living today in Guatemala, Belize, Mexico, Honduras and El Salvador

The rapidity of the breakdown of the Classic Maya civilization, roughly between AD 800 and 900, has still not been convincingly explained. It seems it was not caused by cataclysmic natural forces: there was no earthquake, flood or volcanic eruption that devastated the region. There may have been a class-based uprising against the ruling elite. There may have been harvest failures and hunger due to man-made environmental over-exploitation. The failure of calendar-based prophesies could have triggered revolt. Whatever the reasons, all the cities in the heartland of the Maya world were all but deserted by AD 909. But the Maya did not disappear.

Maya and *ladinos*

There are around 9 million Maya spread across Guatemala, Mexico, Belize and Honduras today – about half of of the region's total population. These are the survivors; the descendants of the temple builders, astronomers, the mathematicians, the architects, artists and artisans, the farmers and soldiers.

As in ancient times, the modern Maya are a far from homogeneous race – they speak some 30 different languages, and worship at Catholic, Protestant and Evangelical churches. Yet many still also continue Maya religious practices forged over thousands of years, and blend pagan and western faiths: prayer keepers use the Tzolkin 260-day calendar while celebrating Christianity's holy days. After centuries of cultural attack, ridicule and humiliation at the hands of the state, this unique fusion of western and indigenous faiths prevails in most indigenous communities and permeates many more *mestizo* minds.

The other half of the population are *mestizo* (of mixed Maya and European blood), though

PRECEDING PAGES: bullfight in Tizimín, Yucatán state.
LEFT: members of the *Cofradía de San Gaspar*, from Chajul, in Guatemala's Ixil Triangle.
RIGHT: a Maya boy from Akumal, in the Yucatán Peninsula, where the Spanish influence is dominant.

mestizo is a term that you will rarely hear in Central America. In Guatemala and the other Central American states those of mixed blood are usually called *ladinos*. Complicating matters somewhat, a *ladino* is, strictly speaking, someone who is identifiably "western" in outlook, someone who speaks Spanish, someone

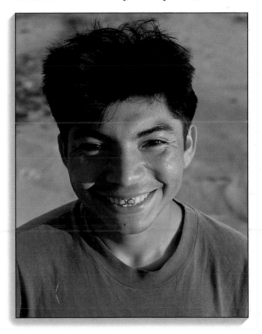

who sees themselves as Latin American rather than Native American. There are *ladinos* who are pure-blood Maya but no longer speak a Mayan language or dress in indigenous style. Generally, most *ladinos* have much more Maya than Spanish blood in their veins, though there are a few *ladinos* who are of pure European ancestry. The ruling elites of the majority of Latin American countries tend to be of European origin – for example, Alvaro Arzú, the president of Guatemala from 1996 to 2000, is fair-haired and and blue-eyed.

Maya and *ladinos* may account for 99 percent of the region's inhabitants, but there are myriad other ethnic groups, most obviously in polyglot Belize, a veritable Central American and Caribbean melting pot of peoples, cultures and tongues.

Belize: a complex ethnic mosaic

English-speaking Creoles (blacks and mixed black-white) form around a third of Belize's tiny 250,000 population, living mainly in Belize City and the towns. Culturally most Creoles feel much closer to Jamaica and the islands of the British West Indies than the rest of Latin America and listen to reggae, soca and calypso and other Caribbean rhythms. In recent years, African-American influence has also grown noticeably: musically, rap and R&B are becoming much more prevalent, and on the sports fields basketball is now more widely played than cricket.

The other black Belizeans are the Garífuna (*see page 233*), a people with an extremely rich history that they trace back to Africa, two shipwrecked slave boats, and the Caribbean islands of St Vincent and Roatán. The Garífuna are sometimes called Black Caribs – ethnically quite accurate as the Garífuna are also descendants of Africans and Carib indians – though the people themselves now prefer the name Garífuna. There are some 17,000 Belizean

(*see page 233*)

WAR REFUGEES

The population of Belize has been swollen in the past three decades by refugees fleeing from devastating civil wars in neighboring countries, particularly from El Salvador. Although El Salvador has only about 6 million inhabitants, this is some 20 times the number of Belize's population, and the task of absorbing numerous distressed refugees placed considerable pressure on Belize's infrastructure. El Salvador's tragic civil war, which lasted throughout the 1980s, resulted in thousands dead and tens of thousands exiled throughout Central America. Some 4,000 settled in Belize, many becoming squatters and small landowners around Belmopan and other towns.

Garífuna, mainly around Dangriga, though many more live in Honduras (and the United States). There are also a few Garífuna villages in Nicaragua and Guatemala.

Mestizos now form 45 percent of Belize's population, a figure that has increased markedly in the past few decades. Thousands of Central Americans have migrated to Belize from wars elsewhere in Central America and joined an established number of *mestizos*. Most are farmers, and live predominantly in the north of the country and Cayo district. Similarly, a few thousand Q' eqchi' Guatemalan Maya have fled from the civil wars of their homeland to settle in southern Belize close to an established

Mopán Maya population. In northern Belize, around Orange Tree Walk, there are a few thousand Yucatec Maya; and in Botes perhaps a few hundred remaining Icaiché Maya. In total, there are no more than 25,000 Maya in Belize. Completing the complex Belizean ethnic mosaic are small numbers of Mennonites (*see page 185*) who arrived there from Mexico in 1958, as well as more recently arrived North Americans, Europeans, Indians (from the subcontinent), Chinese and Middle Eastern immigrants.

A MAYA PRESIDENT?

According to the prophesies of a number of latter-day shamans, in the year 2012, a Maya citizen will be elected to serve as the president of Guatemala.

The Maya mainly live in the western highlands of Guatemala, between the Mexican border and the capital. In these highlands they form some 80 percent of the population, and it is here that Maya customs and traditions remain strongest and continue to defy mainstream Latin American and North American cultural influence. The K'i che' Maya are the most numerous (more than 1 million), the descendants of the warrior Tecún Umán, who was defeated in 1535 by Pedro de Alvarado the conquistador, close to

Guatemala's many Maya groups

Guatemala is far more homogeneous: it's 99.8 percent Maya and *ladino*. There are just 5,000 Garífuna, a tiny number of Creoles, a few thousand European and North American immigrants and maybe 1,000 Chinese (most of whom live in the eastern highlands). There are a few dozen indigenous (but non Maya) Americans called the Xinca. It is the sheer quantity of different Maya groups, however, that gives the country its special character: some 21 languages are spoken, as well as many more dialects.

LEFT: a distinguished Guatemalan *cofrade* elder.
ABOVE: Maya women from highland Guatemala.

the modern-day town of Quezaltenango. The K'i che' have adapted relatively well to life in modern Guatemala and have a reputation as skilful entrepreneurs and traders. Rigoberta Menchú, the 1992 Nobel Prize winner (*see page 83*), is from a K'i che' family.

West and north of Quezaltenango is Mam Maya country, encompassing some of the highest terrain in the country in the Sierra Madre and Cuchumatanes mountains. The main Mam town is Huehuetenango, and the ancient Mam capital of Zacaleu just outside. Todos Santos Cuchumatán, famous for its horse race and fiesta, is one of the best places to glimpse a traditional Mam village: it now attracts a steady stream of western travellers. The other most numerous Guatemalan Maya groups are the Kaqchikel, who live between Antigua and Lago de Atitán, and the Q' eqchi' who live outside the western highlands in a swathe of territory that includes the north coast of Lago de Izabal, much of Alta Verapaz and southern Petén.

The Maya in Mexico

Most of Mexico's Maya live in the southeastern state of Chiapas and in the Yucatán Peninsula. The Chiapas Maya are very traditional, with customs that are very similar to those of the highland Guatemalan Maya over the border. In

the Yucatán Peninsula there has been severe pressure placed upon the resident Maya to integrate into Mexican *mestizo* society, though at least they have been spared the massacres that have devastated the Guatemalan Maya.

Many anthropologists concur that the traditions and dress of the jungle-dwelling Lacandón Maya are probably closest to that of their ancestors, due to their relative isolation in the Lacandón rainforest of Mexico. Today much of the forest is gone, evangelical preachers eager for converts moved in, and ancient traditions have been lost in one generation.

Repression and discrimination

It is impossible to analyze the modern Maya world without a brief examination of the historical background of the region. In a nutshell, the arrival of the Spanish was a catastrophe for the Maya. Not only were they outgunned and outmaneuvered by Cortés, Alvarado and company, but the Spanish also brought a host of diseases to which the Maya had no resistance – around 90 percent of the original population was wiped out in a few decades. The other critical factor was that, at the time of the Spanish arrival, the Maya were divided into disparate, warring tribes; a situation which the Spanish cunningly exploited, forming a series of alliances in order to defeat hostile opponents.

When the governments of Spain and Central America sought to celebrate the 500-year anniversary of Columbus's "discovery" of the Americas, indigenous groups throughout the continent were quick to assert that they had nothing to celebrate and there were widespread protests. Quezaltenango hosted an alternative

THE COFRADIAS, OR RELIGIOUS BROTHERHOODS

If you visit Chichicastenango or Sololá on a Sunday morning, look out for a procession of serious, silver emblem-bearing men dressed in their finest *traje* heading for and from Mass. The men are *cofrades,* members of a *cofradía* (religious brotherhood), dedicated to a Christian saint. Most Maya towns have a number of *cofradías*. It is a great honor to be a *cofrade,* a social status given only to respected male members of the community. Membership involves considerable financial sacrifice, as *cofrades* are expected to contribute significantly towards the village celebrations and annual fiesta arrangements, including the provision of costumes and alcohol. The image of the saint

must also be maintained. Outwardly, the *cofradías* may seem integrated within the Catholic Church, but they also perform a crucial function in maintaining ancient Maya religious beliefs – keeping the Tzolkin calendar, venerating Maya "idol saints" and worshipping Tiox Mundo, the earth god. For centuries the Catholic hierarchy accepted these practices, but from the 1950s the Catholic Action movement and evangelical denominations began to forbid "pagan" worship and upset age-old community traditions. Today many young men choose not to enter *cofradías* because of their evangelical faith or for financial reasons. In Chiapas the word *cargo* is usually used instead of *cofradía*.

quincentenary conference dedicated to the world's indigenous people, which was attended by thousands from all over the globe. There were significant demonstrations in Guatemala City and Sololá. To many onlookers it looked like the beginning of a new Maya activism, encouraged by the success of Rigoberta Menchú after the very dark years of the Central American civil wars had all but stifled democratic opposition.

Grim statistics

The inequalities of life in the Maya region are brutally divided on race lines. The statistics make grim reading and are comparable to those of South Africa during the apartheid years. A Guatemalan Maya can expect to reach an age of just 48 (men) or 49 (women), *ladinos* to 66 (men) and 67 (women). These are some of the very lowest figures in the world, rivalling only those of AIDS-ravaged sub-Saharan Africa and Afghanistan. By the Guatemalan government's own estimates, 81 percent of Maya live in poverty and 75 percent are illiterate. In Mexican Chiapas and Yucatán the figures are a little better, but way below the national averages.

Land reform is another very significant issue. In both Mexico and Guatemala, much of the best agricultural land is controlled by a handful of wealthy families and more and more marginal plots are being farmed by desperate *campesinos,* with severe environmental repercussions. Thousands of Maya from remote communities (many barely able to speak Spanish) flee north to the USA in search of work. Even in sparsely-populated, land-rich Belize there have been angry conflicts between the government and Maya over state-backed logging schemes in the Toledo district.

Winning concessions

Against the odds, and despite continuing discrimination, there are a number of indigenous groups fighting hard and winning concessions for Maya people throughout the region. It is in Guatemala that this is most noticeable. The Indigenous Rights Accord was finally passed in 1995; hundreds of schools have been established so that Maya children can study in their

Belize has the greatest cultural mix in the Maya region, including Mennonites (**LEFT**) and Garífuna (**RIGHT**) of Afro-Caribbean origin.

own language and people again feel free to protest publicly without fear of intimidation. In Mexico, the Zapatista rebellion has brought the discrimination, racism and land conflicts present in the troubled state of Chiapas onto television screens and the front pages of newspapers all over the globe (*see page 268*).

Political apathy

One of the biggest problems in the region is political apathy and a lack of voter participation; most Maya still feel that voting is something that *ladinos* do, to elect a *ladino* government to run a *ladino* state. Despite the

commendable efforts of groups such as the Rigoberta Menchú Foundation to register the indigenous electorate, turnout remains woefully low in Maya areas. This lack of participation was one of the reasons why changes to the Guatemalan constitution that would have benefited the Maya were not passed in 1999.

The insular nature of Maya society is one of the main reasons for this lack of political appetite. For hundreds of years, traditions have been maintained in Maya communities by excluding outsiders from village affairs. The power structure in indigenous communities is controlled by the village elders, the *alcalde* (mayor), *cofradías* (religious brotherhoods) aj *q'ijab* (prayer keepers), shamans, teachers and healers. In larger settlements, the state may have more of an influence. In some towns with large mixed populations (such as Chichicastenango and Sololá) there are two separate municipal councils: one for *ladinos* and another for Maya.

Traditional justice

Maya cultural traditions have also been perpetuated through *costumbres,* customs that include a legal system which has survived in rural areas where the state's influence

> ## ROYAL BLOOD
>
> Blood-letting dates back to the days of the ancient Maya rulers: the king would draw blood from his penis, which was soaked up by paper and then ritually burned.

is minimal. In isolated communities, justice is often dispensed according to restitution (confession and compensation) rather than punishment for minor crimes. The inertia and endemic corruption of the state legal system in Mexico and Guatemala; the expense, time and travel involved and the fact that court business is conducted in Spanish further discourage the Maya from attempting to use conventional legal procedures. Unfortunately, this extreme lack of confidence in the courts is prevalent throughout the Maya world and has resulted in a series of public lynchings of suspected criminals in the late 1990s, in indigenous and *ladino* areas, and many innocent people have died.

On a more esoteric level, virtually all villages will have *costumbristas,* keepers of Maya customs, including shamans, day keepers and healers. Shamans are specialist practitioners who narrate between the physical and spiritual worlds utilizing crystals, sacrifices, incense and sometimes taking advantage of natural psychedelics including mushrooms, the white water-lily flower, herbs and alcohol to achieve a trance-like vision state. This vision quest has been a feature of Maya spirituality since ancient times, and the most famous images are depicted on the stone carvings of Yaxchilán that can now be found in the British Museum in London. On a Yaxchilán door lintel, Lady Xoc practices blood-letting by gruesomely pulling a thorny rope through her tongue, no doubt after consuming copious quantities of hallucinogens. This bloody ritual is guaranteed to stimulate trippy visions in abundance.

Day keepers

The role of the day keeper or calendar priest (*aj q'ijab*) is to ensure that the Tzolkin 260-day and 365-day solar calender (Haab) are observed correctly. As a *costumbrista* he may combine this with shamanic duties and some fortune-telling. All over the Maya world, especially in the Chiapas and Guatemala highlands, you see shrines on hilltops (such as Pascual Abaj, *see page 130*), the stone images blackened by candle smoke, the earth littered with incense wrappers, flowers, *aguardiente* bottles and perhaps feathers from a chicken sacrifice.

At all the main ruins throughout the highlands (including Iximché, K'umarcaah, El Baúl, Zaculeu) day keepers visit on important dates in the calendar to make an offering, pray to Tiox-Mundo and the day lords and perhaps chant the sacred text of the *Popol Vuh*. The most important town in the Maya region for the training of shamen, day keepers and Maya priests is Momostenango (*see page 135*) and every Guaxaquib Batz (Maya New Year) hundreds of *costumbristas* descend on Momostenango to celebrate, pray and burn offerings. ❑

LEFT: Westernised Maya from the Yucatán, where only the women still wear traditional Maya clothing today.
RIGHT: Antigua's famous Semana Santa pageant.

GASTRONOMIC GUIDELINES

Corn-based tortillas and tamales, rice 'n' beans, tropical fruits, nuclear-strength aguardiente and fresh seafood are the specialties of the region

In Maya mythology, the gods created man from maize, after earlier unsuccessful attempts with clay and wood. Even today, corn retains a semi-sacred status throughout the Maya region for many indigenous people, and is certainly regarded as more than just another staple crop. In the more traditional Maya areas, it is considered morally wrong to throw away uneaten corn, and children are taught to finish every last scrap on their plates.

The first foods

Some ten thousand years ago, hunter gatherers began successfully to domesticate corn – a seminal development that enabled the first Americans to settle and farm, and much later enabled the Maya civilization to flourish. The Preclassic and Classic Maya diet was very similar to their modern range of foodstuffs, with corn (*maíz*), beans (*frijoles*), squash (*calabaza*) and chilli eaten most mealtimes.

Corn or maize is most often eaten in the form of a *tortilla*, a thin, circular pancake made from corn dough, either shaped by hand (in Guatemala) or by a machine press (the usual method in Mexico) and then toasted on a metal tray (*comal*) over a fire. In rural Guatemala, the first noise of the day (along with the inevitable rooster) is the pat-pat sound of the making and shaping of *tortillas* by the village women, long before the sun has risen.

Tortillas are eaten as an accompaniment to virtually every meal in Guatemala. They are best served while still warm – often wrapped inside a cotton cloth. Fresh, warm *tortillas* are delicious, often combining a wonderful smoky flavor from the woodfire and a dense, but pliable texture. If you are served tough, dry *tortillas,* send them back, just as Guatemalans do.

In Mexico, the *tortilla* is also used as the basis of a number of delicious dishes that are now familiar all over the world. *Enchiladas* are *tortillas* stuffed with mince or cheese; *quesadillas* are *tortillas* covered with melted cheese; *tacos* are fried, filled *tortillas*, and *tostadas* are crispy, deep-fried *tortillas* served with salad. Other variants include *flautas*, *chimichangas* and *tlacoyos*.

Tortillas aside, the other way maize is consumed is in the form of a *tamal*: maize dough stuffed with a little meat or a sweet filling and steamed in a corn husk or a banana leaf. In Guatemala, a mini *tamal* (*chuchito*) is a popular street snack and considerably more traditional than other fast foods; it is known that *tamales* were prepared and cooked in an almost identical fashion by the ancient Maya.

In Belize, eating habits are more divided on ethnic lines, with *ladinos* eating tortillas, *tamales* and *tacos*, while Creoles prefer beans cooked with rice, seasoning and coconut oil – a dish they call "rice 'n' beans" – or served separately with meat, fish or seafood.

LEFT: Antojitos, meat-stuffed *tortillas*, from Retalhuleu, in Guatemala's Pacific coastal region.
RIGHT: the Mesón del Marqués Hotel, Valladolid, Yucatán.

In fact, after maize, beans (*frijoles*) are the second fundamental ingredient in the regional diet, and were also cultivated by the ancient Maya. They are the most important protein source for the vast majority of people, for whom meat is a luxury they can seldom afford. *Frijoles* are often grown in maize fields as companion plants; the bean plant winds itself around the corn stalk and is harvested a little later in the season.

Black beans are the most popular variety, but red pinto (literally "painted") beans are also eaten. Black beans are usually served whole (*volteados*) in a little brine, often with

some onion or garlic added. Pinto beans are prepared *refritos* (refried). The beans are boiled then mashed and fried in a pan; sometimes a little cream is added to the bean pulp, and occasionally a little chopped *chorizo* (spicy sausage) is mixed in for flavor. You'll find that wherever you are in the Maya world, and whatever time of day it is, mealtimes usually include a portion of *frijoles* – in some shape or form.

Vitamin providers

Historically, squash (*calabaza*) has always been one of the most frequently cultivated vegetables, and it remains very popular today as it grows well in the cornfield (*milpas*) after the maize and beans have been harvested. Chilli – which is super-rich in vitamin C, native to the region and has been domesticated for 7,000 years – is another dietary essential, and over 100 varieties are eaten.

Chilli is commonly served in the *salsa* sauce that you'll find at every dinner table. In Guatemala this *salsa* is often called just called "picante" (spice), but in Mexico the art of *salsa*-making is taken extremely seriously, and every establishment from restaurant to street stall will produce a bottle or two of homemade *salsa*. Reputations live or die by it. Belizean diners also invariably keep a bottle or two of hot, chilli-based sauce on standby.

A great variety of other vegetables is also grown: carrots, peppers, onions, and greens including cabbage, spinach, green beans and broccoli (which is mainly exported to North America). And the region's extensive micro-climates support the cultivation of almost every

EATING OUT WITHOUT MEAT

Traveling as a vegetarian (*vegetariano*) in the Maya region can be a frustrating experience, and dining out is rarely a real pleasure. But there are worse places in the world to eat a meat-free diet.

In the major towns geared towards tourism, places like Panajachel, San Cristóbal de las Casas and Antigua, plenty of itinerant veggies have trodden the trail before, and waiters and restaurateurs are fairly familiar with the concept. In these places you'll find plenty of choice on most menus. And as foreigners have also settled and opened their own restaurants, so you'll find good meat-free European, American, Asian and wholefood dishes offering a

change from the sometimes predictable vegetarian options in traditional Central American establishments.

Off the beaten track, the main problem is simply that few locals will understand the principle that some people choose not to eat meat, and no matter how many times you try to tell them, "I don't eat meat" ("*yo no como carne*"), it seems to find its way onto your plate somehow. Seasoned travelers find that explaining it as a religious issue (*es mi religión*), even if inaccurate, is the simplest and most effective way to get the point across. Luckily, there are always eggs, beans and *tortillas*, and plenty of fruit in the market.

conceivable variety of fruit. Bananas are everywhere, but avocados, tomatoes, blueberries, raspberries, apples, oranges, limes, papayas and mangoes also feature. There are in addition other, highly exotic fruits. The creamy pink flesh of the zapote fruit, for example, is amazing. Fruit is often consumed as part of a shake or *licuado* (*see page 52*).

Protein on the menu

Historically, turkey, wild pig and iguana were all eaten, but except in jungle areas, you'll find that these days chicken, pork and beef are the meats specified on most menus, either grilled,

The tourist's choice

You'll find the best and most varied cuisine in Mexico. In Belize, there's some superb and inexpensive seafood available on the coast and cayes, but away from the top hotels, inland menus usually only offer a limited choice. In Guatemala there is a two-tier structure in evidence, which effectively means that the more adventurous traveler must forego culinary pleasures (*see box below*).

Any establishment in the region that calls itself a "restaurant" has upmarket pretensions; it may sell wine and the menu is usually reasonably varied, and prices a bit higher than in

fried or in a stew. Except in the best restaurants, you may find that the meat is tough, but usually tasty. Eggs are very commonly eaten for protein and prepared in many different styles: *rancheros*; *a la mexicana* or *motuleños*.

You'll find plentiful fish and seafood served near the coast. Snapper, grouper, barracuda and shark are all popular, while lobster is on many up-market restaurant menus, as well as shrimp, crab and conch; *ceviche* (raw seafood marinaded in lime juice) is a favorite in many areas.

LEFT: local markets are the best source for a wide range of fruit and vegetables.
ABOVE: the elegant La Pigua restaurant, Campeche.

COSMOPOLITAN CUISINE

In Guatemalan towns off the tourist trail the food is usually very basic (often just eggs, beans and *tortillas*), but it's cheap (around US$2 a head) and filling. However, it is a completely different story anywhere in the country where groups of tourists gather. In popular tourist spots in Guatemala you'll find a wide choice of local and international cuisines at relatively high prices.

In Antigua and Panajachel the penchant for culinary variety is taken to extremes. In these towns you can order Asian, American, Middle Eastern, Italian and even Indian dishes in restaurants, but expect to pay around US$6–$10 a head for the privilege.

other places that will provide you with a meal. A *"comedor"*, by contrast, is the local equivalent of an American diner – a basic line-up of popular local dishes, nothing exotic, served up quickly and priced cheaply.

There are plenty of fascinating street snacks as well, but hygiene standards can be dubious so take care. In the larger towns and cities you'll find most of the big American fast food outlets, plus home-grown equivalents like Pollo Campero, which sells fried chicken. There are also Chinese restaurants in most towns, which usually serve up a fairly good selection of dishes, but don't expect anything very exciting

or authentic. (They do, however, offer plenty of vegetarian options.)

Liquid refreshment

Though the water is heavily chlorinated in the main towns, it's better to play it safe and stick to bottled water, which is cheap and widely available. Many locals drink *fresca* with their lunch or dinner, which is a iced water with a little lime or orange juice added. It's very refreshing, but will generally have been made with tap water. The usual international brands of soft drink are all readily available; confusingly however, all canned soft drinks are known as *"aguas"* in Guatemala.

A little more exciting is a *licuado*, which is a water- or milk-based fresh fruit shake. You'll see specialist vendors chopping and blending fruit for *licuados* at markets and bus stations all over the region, except in Belize. Fresh fruit juices (*jugos*) are less commonly available. Orange juice (*jugo de naranja*) is the one most likely to be on offer, often consumed by local people with a raw egg.

Bad brew

One of the biggest disappointments of travel in the Maya region is the coffee (*café*), which is usually awful. Though some of the world's finest, most aromatic beans are grown locally, the best quality is usually reserved for export.

As is the case with so many things, in the popular tourist towns you'll be able to find a good quality brew, but anywhere else you'll either be served instant coffee or a murky, watery and nearly always highly-sweetened, banal blend of inferior beans.

Tea (*té*) is quite popular in Belize, thanks to the British influence, but is rarely on offer elsewhere – except camomile tea (*té de manzanilla*), which is commonly served in Guatemala and Mexico. Cacao beans were used to make a sacred chocolate drink in ancient times, and were so highly prized that they were used as a unit of currency. Today you'll still find cocoa on the menu, though it's usually sweetened rather than in its bitter, original form.

Beer (*cerveza*) is best and cheapest in Mexico, where there are several excellent local and national brands. Lager-style brews include Sol, Bohémia and Dos Equis, and darker beers include Negra Modelo and Tres Equis. In Guatemala the bland Gallo brand has a near-monopoly, though there's also Cabro and the dark Moza. In Belize beer is quite pricey; the Beliken brand has a monopoly, but the company brews four different beers.

Rum (*ron*) is the most widely available liquor; in Mexico tequila is, of course, the national drink. Any rum or tequila labeled *"añejo"* (aged) is worth paying a little more for. And if you are feeling brave, try one of the local firewaters: Guatemala's *aguardiente*, or *mescal* (the one with the worm) in Mexico. ❑

LEFT: typical Creole cuisine – fish, seafood and rice.
RIGHT: an exotic platter at La Fonda de la Calle Real, one of Antigua's finest restaurants.

OUTDOOR ADVENTURE

Options include trekking in Belizean rainforest, climbing a volcano in Guatemala,
diving on the spectacular coral reef, or white-water rafting down the Río Usumacinta

With more than 30 volcanoes, 4,000-meter (13,000-ft) high mountains, Pacific and Caribbean coastlines, huge swathes of virtually untouched rainforest, subtropical moist forest, vast savannas, wetlands, intriguing limestone cave complexes, and the world's second largest barrier reef just offshore, the Maya region's wealth of exciting natural settings makes it a paradise for hikers, scuba divers, cavers or anyone with a sense of adventure.

In many ways the governments and tourism boards of Mexico and Guatemala are only just beginning to realize this potential, and to market the region in Europe and North America accordingly. The Belizeans have been quicker off the blocks – Belize is viewed internationally as second only to Costa Rica in the embryonic Central American ecotourism league. On the ground, there are a number of excellent, established specialist companies catering for divers, hikers, bikers and rafters, with the number growing on a daily basis.

Highland hiking

The Maya region offers some of the finest walking – jungle, mountain and coastal hikes – in the world. In Guatemala the spectacular highland scenery is the main attraction: it is a spellbinding landscape of lofty peaks, verdant river valleys, thick pine forests, traditional adobe villages and huge whitewashed colonial churches. Villages are linked by a web of well-maintained trails, paths and dirt tracks that the locals use to get to the market or to distant cornfields, making hiking a real pleasure. There are simple accommodations in *hospedajes,* and *comedores* in most of the larger villages serve cheap local food.

Some of the best highland hiking in Guatemala is in the mountains north of Huehuetenango, around Todos Santos Cuchumatán, one of the most picturesque and traditional

Maya villages in the country (*see page 137*). There are many superb trails through epic Cuchumatán mountain scenery, but one of the most popular routes is the six-hour hike from Todos Santos Cuchumatán to the equally traditional Mam Maya village of San Juan Atitán.

The countryside around the Ixil Triangle vil-

lages of Nebaj, Chajul and Cotzal is equally rewarding to hike across, with breathtaking, craggy mountaintops, vast, grassy valleys interspersed with humble farmhouses, cornfields and fast-flowing streams. If you trek to the village of Acul from Nebaj, you can return via an Italian-Guatemalan *finca*, where you can buy some of the finest cheese in the country.

Lake Atitlán, a mandatory destination for every visitor to Guatemala, is also world-class trekking country (*see page 125*). There is an idyllic network of trails that snake around the steep banks and volcanic slopes of the lake, connecting all the 13 shoreside settlements, past patchwork cornfields, vegetable gardens, and

---

LEFT: snorkeling in Laguna Chankanab National Park.
RIGHT: windsurfing is one of the many watersports on offer around Cancún.

avocado and fig trees. It is possible to walk around the entire lake in three days, but if you only want to walk one section then the five-hour trail between Santa Cruz la Laguna and San Pedro La Laguna is especially picturesque.

Wildlife and ruins

Moving up from Guatemala, the **Maya Mountains** of Belize offer more spectacular walking country. Here the altitude is lower, and the subtropical vegetation much denser, with thick forests of mahogany and ceiba trees, epiphytes and giant ferns all protected in a series of protected reserves. These mountain forests offer

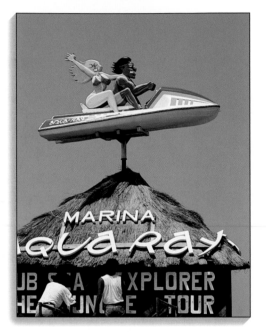

superb opportunities to see some of the area's magnificent wildlife, including birds of prey, tapirs and perhaps even a jaguar. The village of Maya Centre is a good place to head for to explore the **Cockscomb Basin Wildlife Sanctuary** (*see page 232*). Here there are some short trails, or it's a two-day trek to the summit of Victoria Peak, and excellent guides are on hand.

Another fine hiking destination in Belize is the **Mountain Pine Ridge** and Macal River area, where there are the Río On pools, the Thousand Foot waterfalls and, in the rainforest south of Mountain Pine Ridge, the large Maya ruins of Caracol. A number of agencies offer tours to the area from San Ignacio, or there are several accommodation possibilities, including some luxurious lodges.

Still closer to sea level, the huge forest that straddles the Guatemalan-Mexican border was the cradle where the Maya civilization first flourished. Dozens of ruined cities lie buried in the **Maya Biosphere Reserve** and bordering forests. This is the best place to arrange an expedition into the jungle. The town of Flores in Guatemala now has trekking companies that will provide the expertise, guides and supplies to explore this frontier zone. There are dozens of ruins in the jungle north of Flores, but one of the most popular excusions is to the ruins of El Zotz, a two- to three-day trip. The ruins of Nakbé and El Mirador are best approached from the village of Carmelita, and Río Azul from Uaxactún. To get to the amazing ruins of Piedras Negras, high above the Usumacinta River, you'll need a specialist rafting company.

Over the Mexican border, the huge **Calakmul Reserve** is the place to experience the jun-

---

MOUNTAIN BIKING

Off-road trails in the Guatemalan highlands and the western districts of Belize are perfect for mountain biking. Antigua is an excellent base – biking specialists there organize trips and rent bikes. Maya Mountain Bike Tours and Old Town Outfitters will both take you on an escorted tour of the countryside around Antigua or Lago de Atitlán; the latter firm also offers volcano tours and rock climbing.

Many of the dramatic trails around Antigua and Lago de Atitlán skirt volcanoes and run through coffee plantations and cornfields, past hot springs. You can rent bikes in Panajachel in order to explore the hillsides around the beautiful Lake Atitlán (*see page 128*) and, further west,

Quezaltenango is another good starting point, with its rugged setting among high mountains and volcanoes. You can hire bikes here from the Xela Sin Limites travel agency.

In Belize, head for the Mountain Pine Ridge/Macal River area of the Maya Mountains, where there is a vast network of isolated forest trails (*see page 227*). The main town of San Ignacio makes a good base for budget travelers, but if you want more comfort, try a jungle lodge deep inside the reserve. Waterfalls, jagged peaks and dramatic rivers are also ideal for canoeing and tubing, and a wide range of such activities is available in the area. Mountain bikes can be hired from tour operators in San Ignacio.

gle and perhaps catch a glimpse of some endemic wildlife. The ancient city of Calakmul, in the midst of the jungle, is also one of the largest ruins found to date; it supported a population of up to 100,000 in the Classic era. Above all, jungle trekking in the Maya world presents a wonderful opportunity to see the magnificent ruins that lie deep within the forest.

Volcano climbing

There are more than 30 volcanoes in the Maya region, concentrated in Guatemala, where a spectacular chain of peaks rises above the Pacific coast and forms a barrier between the highlands and the coast. You won't need any special equipment to climb Guatemala's volcanoes, just hiking boots and warm layers if you plan to camp out on the summit.

Altitude sickness can occur at heights of more than 3,300 meters (10,800 ft), so it's a good idea to postpone any attempt on Tajumulco or Tacaná, which are both above 4,000 meters (13,000 ft), until you're sure that you have acclimatized. If you experience symptoms such as headaches, descend immediately.

Volcán de Agua, at 3,763 meters (12,346 ft), is the most popular of all the big peaks to climb. It's a fairly straightforward five-hour trek to the summit from the village of Santa María de Jesús, close to Antigua (*see page 122*). Of the three volcanoes that surround Lake Atitlán, Volcán San Pedro (3,020 meters/9,900 ft) is by far the easiest to climb. Hire a guide in the village of San Pedro la Laguna; it takes about six hours to reach the summit. The Atitlán and Tolimán volcanoes (respectively 3,537 meters/11,604 ft and 3,158 meters/10,360 ft) present a much stiffer challenge. Pick up a guide in either Santiago Atitlán or San Lucas Tolimán.

From Quezaltenango there are numerous more peaks to conquer, the almost perfect cone of Santa María being the most obvious choice. In addition to this, there's the stunningly beautiful crater lake atop the 2,900-meter (9,500-ft) high Chicabal. Expeditions to Volcán Tajumulco which, at 4,220 meters (13,846 ft), is the highest peak in Central America, also begin in Guatemala's second city.

Of the dozen extinct volcanoes in the eastern highlands, Volcán de Ipala (1,650 meters/ 5,413 ft) is the one to climb. It's an easy two-hour hike from the village of Aguas Blancas and, as with Chicabal, there's a glorious crater lake at the summit that is ringed by rainforest and is perfect for a refreshing dip.

Diving on the reef

Tracking the entire Caribbean coast of the Maya region, from Puerto Morelos in Mexico south through Belizean waters to the Bay Islands of Honduras, is the world's second longest barrier reef, an aquatic paradise for scuba divers. Like the Australian Great Barrier Reef, it's not just one continuous barrier or

LEFT: jet skiing is one way of burning up your energy.
RIGHT: game fishing, Hemingway-style, is energetic too.

ACTIVE VOLCANOES

The most spectacular volcano in Guatemala is Volcán Pacaya *(see pages 64–65)*, which has been in a constant state of eruption since 1965, spewing a stream of lava, gases and rocks into the sky above Guatemala City. Every year many thousands of people climb the 2,550-meter (8,370-ft) peak to witness its colorful pyrogenics. Guided tours of Pacaya are run from Guatemala City or Antigua.

There are several volcanoes near Antigua, which also make popular hikes *(see page 122)*. Volcán de Fuego, at 3,763 meters (12,346 ft), is highly active, and last erupted in 1999. It is a tough climb of at least seven hours, and is recommended only for experienced hikers.

coral wall, though in many places the reef crest stretches for miles just below the surface. Additionally there are hundreds of large and small coral-fringed islands or cayes, underwater seamounts and ridges, and four coral atolls. The magnificent but fragile barrier reef is spread across the waters of Mexico, Belize, Guatemala and Honduras.

Starting in the north, there's some excellent diving around Isla Mujeres and Cancún, and there are several well-established dive schools on both islands. The famous Gar-

THE REEF'S TOP STATUS

Belize's barrier-reef reserves were given UNESCO World Heritage Site status in 1996, confirming the global importance of the Caribbean reefs and their wildlife.

of dive schools in Cozumel. There's also some decent diving and snorkeling to be found off Playa del Carmen and, again, plenty of dive schools exploit this.

Following the coastal path south to Tulum, there are a number of small, less developed beaches, and dive schools at Puerto Adventuras and Akumal. There is some amazing diving and snorkeling in these parts, not just in the sea offshore but also inland in *cenotes* (freshwater pools). If you're a diver, a *cenote* dive is an unforgettable experience.

rafón Reef off the southern tip of Isla Mujeres, however, is now in poor condition after many years of abuse by snorkelers, boat skippers, divers and day-trippers, which have severely degraded the reef. As a result of the sheer numbers of tourists (and dive schools) in the Cancún area, you might find that many of the local sites are overcrowded with divers and snorkelers, especially during the high season.

Cozumel is the next important location, with some world-class diving. Palancar Reef, which was first popularized by the French underwater explorer and marine biologist Jacques Cousteau, is justly famous throughout the diving world for its incredible coral wall. There are plenty

It's a skilled activity, however, and unless you have the necessary cave-diving qualification, you need to be accompanied by a dive master. Specialist courses are organized by dive centers in Puerto Adventuras, Tulum and Akumal. At Tulum, snorkeling trips can be arranged, but there is no dive school here.

Continuing south, the spectacular Sian Ka'an Biosphere Reserve incorporates the offshore reef within its boundaries, and, although there aren't any dive schools in this region, snorkeling trips can be organized in nearby Punta Allen, to the north of the reserve. The final underwater Mexican jewel is Banco Chinchorro, a remarkably pristine coral atoll about

20 km (12½ miles) off the coast at the southernmost tip of the country, which has now become a National Park *(see page 322)*.

Best in Belize

Belize offers arguably the best diving in the western hemisphere. The sheer number and variety of dive sites is astonishing, the marine environment is well protected and there are some excellent dive schools. The reef off San Pedro and Caye Caulker is fine, but if you yearn for some really dramatic diving consider heading out to one of

TAKE THE PLUNGE

For details of recommended dive schools and other watersports operators in the Yucatán and Belize, *see Travel Tips, page 344.*

In southern Belizean waters there is good diving around most of the cayes – Tobacco Reef, Columbus Reef and South Water Caye particularly – but Glover's Reef, further offshore, is the place that people rave about *(see page 241)*. Glover's Reef, designated as a marine reserve, is a large atoll with some epic wall diving and beautiful snorkeling gardens. The real thrills for most visitors, however, are the close encounters with pelagic sea life, including the enormous, migrating whale sharks in October.

the coral atolls further offshore, which are best visited by dive boats with sleeping berths.

Lighthouse Reef, one of the atolls, is where you'll find the much-touted Blue Hole, which looks as if it was created by a bomb blast but is actually the result of a collapsed cavern. There are several shipwrecks that have formed artificial reefs, which you can explore in the area, and there's the Half Moon Caye Natural Monument, which in 1982 became the first marine location in Belize to be made into a reserve.

LEFT: one of the well-marked trails inside Belize's Cockscomb Basin Wildlife Sanctuary.
ABOVE: hang-gliding over Lake Atitlán.

High-altitude diving

Guatemala has a few tiny patches of reef on its Caribbean coast, but most divers head to the southern Belizean reefs (Hunting and Sapodilla cayes) on trips that can be organized in Río Dulce or Lívingston. There's also an excellent dive school based on Lago de Atitlán, if you fancy some freshwater, high-altitude diving. It's an amazing experience to surface after an Atitlán dive and see volcanoes. One Guatemala City dive school occasionally runs dive trips in the Pacific Ocean, which are recommended for experienced divers only.

Finally, the Honduran Bay islands of Roatán, Utila and Guanaja, at the southern edge of the

Maya region but easily accessible from Guatemala or Belize by air, sea or land, are all first-class dive destinations. Utila is one of the cheapest places in the world to learn to dive (a 10-dive package is around US$120), there are over a dozen dive schools and the walls on the north coast of the island are awesome. Roatán has both exclusive dive resorts and independent dive schools in the island's West End, where prices are a little higher than Utila but still very competitive. Most diving on Roatán is wall diving, and the coral is generally in superb condition. Guanaja, the third island, was hit very badly by Hurricane Mitch in 1998 and,

though the reefs survived with limited damage, the island's infrastructure took a hammering.

Rafting, canoeing and tubing

The Maya region offers phenomenal white-water rafting all year round. There are at least a dozen exceptional rivers to raft down throughout Guatemala and Belize, with all grades represented from one (easy) to five (very challenging). There are no rivers in the Yucatán.

Typically, a day trip on Guatemala's Río Naranjo costs from US$65 per person; a three-day expedition down the Río Cahabón around US$220. Perhaps the most remarkable rafting trip in the region is along the Río Usumacinta

that divides Mexico and Guatemala, passing the ruins of Yaxchilán and Bonampak and finishing at Piedras Negras. Contact Maya Expeditions in Guatemala City.

In Belize there is more outstanding rafting, canoeing and tubing, especially in the Cayo district, and there are plenty of specialist white-water companies. The Macal River valley is a favorite place for these sports, and more and more people are kayaking, canoeing and tubing the Sibul and Mopan rivers. In the south there's more fun to be had on South Stann Creek, Placencia Lagoon and Big Falls.

Caving

To the ancient Maya, caves were entrances to the underworld – *Xibalba* – the Place of Fright. Recent research indicates that every major Maya settlement was built near a cave, usually a natural one, though in some cases an artificial chamber was hollowed out of the rock. Caves were essential elements in the Maya belief system and, although the ancient Maya never made permanent settlements in caves, every cave so far explored in the region exhibits evidence of a Maya presence long ago. From cave entrances to deep underground, records of ceremonial visits remain in the form of pottery, petroglyphs, carvings, fire-hearths and occasionally even complete skeletons. Flowstone grips, rounded pots and glittering crystals adorn ancient bones. Viewing these artefacts, abandoned for over 1,000 years, is an unforgettable experience.

"Show caves" apart, the best caves remain inaccessible to the visitor. In Belize, however, visitors can take an amazing journey into the realm of *Xibalba*. Caves Branch Jungle Lodge, on the Hummingbird Highway, 21 km (13 miles) south of Belmopan, has the best guided caving trips in the Maya world. The Lodge, on the bank of the Caves Branch River, midway between the huge St Herman's Cave and the Blue Hole National Park, has a range of accommodations, from dorm rooms to secluded cabaña suites. Yucatán's impressive caves are at Loltén, Balankanché and Dzitnup. ❑

● *See the Travel Tips section, page 344, for details of recommended companies specializing in the activities described in this chapter.*

LEFT: ferry across the Belize River to Xunantunich.
RIGHT: tranquil landing at tiny Queen Cayes, in the far south, near Sapodilla Cayes.

Weathering the storms

Periodically wracked by volcanic eruptions, earthquakes and hurricanes, the land of the Maya has been as prone to natural disasters as it is to man-made cataclysms. Indeed, there is a certain symmetry between the history and the geology of the region, its strategic location where the opposing forces of north and south meet appearing at times to generate this political and environmental upheaval. The forces of nature have

often helped to shape the region's history, compelling the relocation of capital cities and ravaging entire populations and economies. Yet the power and fury of these natural cataclysms have also produced the spectacular landscapes for which Guatemala, Belize and the Yucatán are so famous, while the active Pacaya volcano continues to attract sightseers from around the world.

Hurricanes and tropical storms

The path of destruction left in the wake of Hurricane Wilma in 2005 and Mitch in October 1998 follow a long series of natural disasters, which have left their mark on the history of this region. One of the earliest recorded hurricanes was the Great Hurricane of 1780, which struck the eastern Caribbean, killing approximately 20,000 people.

Devastating tropical storms build in the Gulf of Mexico before winging their way through the Central American isthmus. Positioned to the west of the hurricane's usual path, Belize has managed to avoid a good many of the Caribbean hurricanes of the past 40 years, but those that have scored a direct hit have been disastrous.

In 1961 Hurricane Hattie leveled Belize City, prompting the building of the modern, planned capital of Belmopan and the relocation of all government offices. Six years earlier, Hurricane Janet completely destroyed the northern town of Sarteneja and in 1931 another powerful hurricane killed around 15 percent of the population. While Honduras and Nicaragua bore the brunt of the havoc wreaked by Hurricane Mitch, in Guatemala the weakening storm brought heavy rains causing landslides and flooding. Some 260 Guatemalans died in the storm and another 27,000 were left homeless. The long-term economic effects of the catastrophe are impossible to calculate, but damage included the destruction of over 95 percent of Guatemala's banana crop and more than half of the season's corn and bean plantings, staple foods for the Maya and *mestizos* of the region.

Tectonic activity in Guatemala

Beneath the Earth's crust, minute movements of continental tectonic plates cause seismic convulsions and volcanic eruptions in a region plagued by the most powerful natural forces that planet earth can muster. Historically, Guatemala has been on the receiving end of much of the region's seismic activity, located as it is between the Pacific and Caribbean coasts, and with a chain of volcanoes spanning the southwest of the country. The Mesoamerican Pacific coast belongs to the continent's active tectonic field, where the small Cocos Plate is pushed and shoved by the forces of the larger Caribbean Plate to the east.

Just two days after Pedro de Alvarado's widow had been installed as governor of the newly-established colonial capital at Ciudad Vieja in 1541, the Agua volcano buried the city under a torrent of mud and water – an event recorded somewhat gleefully in the Maya Annals of the Kaqchikeles. The Spaniards then moved the capital 8 km (5 miles) to the north to Antigua, until an earthquake in 1773 forced another move to the Guatemala City site.

The present capital was virtually flattened by quakes in 1917 and 1918 and again most recently in 1976 when at least 25,000 people were killed and a million left homeless. With its epicenter in Chimaltenango and measuring 7.5 on the Richter Scale, the tremendous reach of this disaster exposed and exacerbated governmental corruption alongside the progressive suffering of the poor.

Under the volcanoes

The Sierra Madre in the southern Mexican state of Chiapas marks the beginning of a long volcanic chain which stretches down along the Pacific Coast and into the western highlands of Guatemala. Forming the backbone of the Central American isthmus, this rugged range of mountains and volcanic

Great balls of fire

Starkly beautiful and at the same time darkly threatening in appearance, many of the thirty-three volcanoes towering over Guatemala's highlands are either dead or long dormant. Several remain active, however, in particular Volcán Pacaya, which has been in an almost constant state of eruption since 1965. This activity ranges from minor gaseous emissions and gentle steam eruptions, to explosions so powerful as to hurl "bombs" up to 12 km (7½ miles) into the air. Although such serious outbursts are rare, Pacaya, which looms over the village of San Vicente Pacaya to the south of Guatemala City, does emit lava flows on a daily

peaks cuts a swathe through the land of the Maya, dividing it into highlands and tropical lowlands. This central range and the proximity of two coasts which lie to either side of it contribute to the wide variety of micro-climates which occur, each with their own ecological characteristics. The rich volcanic soils, fed by ash spewed out millions of years ago, also proved perfect for growing coffee, the crop which more than any other has shaped Guatemalan history and society since the late 19th century.

LEFT: satellite image of the swirling path of Hurricane Mitch, which devastated Central America in 1998.
ABOVE: the active San Pedro volcano, one of the dramatic peaks overlooking Lake Atitlán.

basis, and an ashy pall often hangs over the immediate area. Occasionally local villages need to be evacuated, as in 1996, when an unusually powerful eruption spewed out a lava flow which stretched for over 1.5 km (1 mile) and caused ash to settle over the town of Escuintla, more than 10 km (6 miles) to the east of Pacaya.

The spectacle of erupting Pacaya is most impressive at night when its brilliant orange plume lights up the sky. Equally breathtaking, if less dramatic, are the views that can be had from the peaks of the country's many other dormant volcanoes, which can also be climbed. If you want to climb Pacaya and other Guatemalan volcanoes, see the Travel Tips section, page 349, for details of tour agencies. ❑

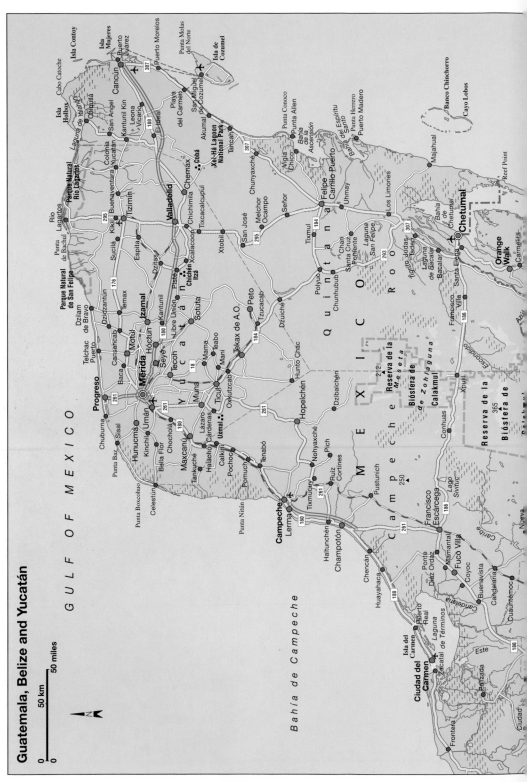

Guatemala, Belize and Yucatán

G U L F   O F   M E X I C O

Bahía de Campeche

M E X I C O

Y u c a t á n

C a m p e c h e

Q u i n t a n a   R o o

Isla Contoy
Cabo Catoche
Isla Mujeres
Puerto Juárez
Puerto Morelos
Punta Molas del Norte
Isla de Cozumel
Cancún
Isla Holbox
Chiquilá
San Angel
Kantunil Kin
Leona Vicario
Colonia Yucatán
Playa del Carmen
San Miguel de Cozumel
Akumal
Xel-Há Lagoon National Park
Cobá
Tancah
Punta Allen
Punta Conoco
Punta Chico
Bahía de Ascensión
Bahía del Espíritu Santo
Puerto Madero
Puerto Herrero
Banco Chinchorro
Cayo Lobos
Reef Point
Majahual
Vigía Chico
Chunyaxche
Felipe Carrillo Puerto
Uhmay
Los Limones
Punta de Bachul
Río Lagartos
Parque Natural Río Lagartos
Buenaventura
Tizimín
Valladolid
Chemax
Chichimila
Tixcacalcupul
Xcalacoop
Chichén Itzá
Piste
San José
Melchor Ocampo
Señor
Tixmul
Polyuc
Chunhubub
Chan Santa Cruz Poniente
Laguna San Felipe
Tihosuco
Judas
Badeb
Laguna de Bacalar
Bahía de Chetumal
Chetumal
Santa Elena
Orange Walk
Carmelita
Kiki
Sucilá
Espita
Dzitas
Xtobil
San José
Melchor Ocampo
Dziuché
Peto
Tzucacab
Tzucacab
Francisco Villa
Xpujil
Reserva de la Biósfera de Calakmul
Reserva de la Biósfera de
Reserva de la Meseta de Zohlaguna
Conhuas
Lago Silvituc
250
365
212
Punta Baz
Punta Boxcohuo
Celestún
Sisal
Chuburna
Chubuna
Hunucmá
Kinchil
Umán
Chocholá
Bella Flor
Maxcanú
Tankuche
Halacho
Lázaro Cárdenas
Calkiní
Pochoc
Pomuch
Tenabó
Nohyaxché
Pich
Ruiz Cortines
Hopelchén
Dzibalchén
Pustunich
Progreso
Telchac Puerto
Dzilam de Bravo
Dzilam
Dzidzantún
Temax
Dzidzantún
Canansanchac
Baca
Motúl
Seyé
Cansahcab
Mérida
Hóctun
Kantunil
Libre Unión
Izamal
Tecoh
Tekax de A.O.
Acanceh
Sotuta
Mama
Teabo
Maní
Ticul
Muna
Uxmal
Oxkutzcab
Hunto Chac
18
Parque Natural de San Felipe
Dzilam Puerto
Punta Nitún
Champotón
Haltunchén
Chencán
Huayahaca
Isla del Carmen
Ciudad del Carmen
Puerto Real
Zacatal
Laguna de Términos
Frontera
Ciudad
Palizada
Candelaria
Cuauhtémoc
Buenavista
Coyoc
Mamantal
Fuco Villa
Ponté Díaz Ordaz
Candelaria
Nueva
Este
Campeche
Lerma
Tixmúcuy
Francisco Escárcega
Bahía del Espíritu Santo
Laguna de Términos

Roads
307
180
295
176
261
180
184
295
293
184
261
262
186
365
186
180
261
18
250

0 ─ 50 miles
0 ─ 50 km

N

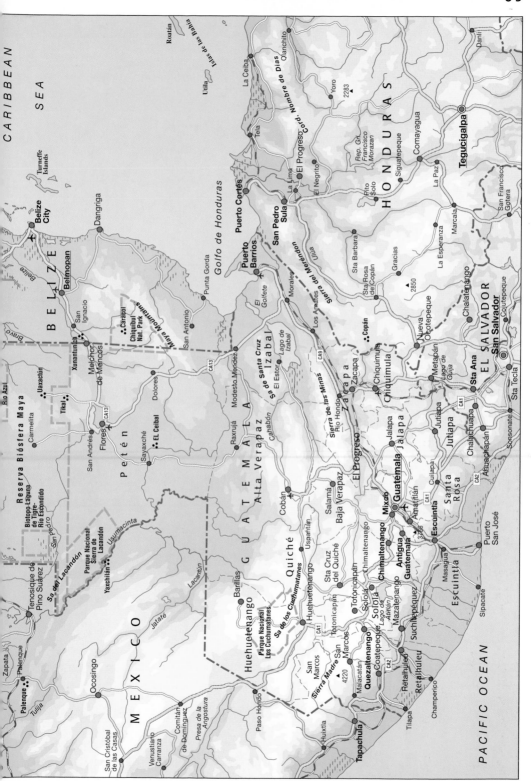

GUATEMALA

With its awesome cultural heritage and breathtaking scenery,

Guatemala is the supreme wonder of Central America

An incredibly diverse, beautiful and complex nation, Guatemala is both the ancient and modern heart of the Maya world. Around 7 million Maya live in Guatemala, forming some 60 percent of the country's population, and it is their dynamic, unique cultural tradition that is the nation's most distinctive feature. With the possible exception of Bolivia, Guatemala is the least latin of all Latin American countries, a land where sophisticated pre-conquest traditions, language, religion, culture and dress still endure over 500 years after the Spanish first arrived in the continent.

For such a small country, Guatemala combines a multiplicity of landscapes. Vast tropical forests cover the Petén, in the northern third of the country, a sparsely-populated region rich in wildlife and studded with the ruins of dozens of ancient Maya cities. The east of the country has an extreme juxtaposition of geophysical systems: cloud forests; the gorge systems of the Río Dulce; a humid Caribbean coastline and even a small desert region near Chiquimula.

The southern swathe of the nation, where most of the population live, is extremely mountainous, and crowned by volcanoes. Most Guatemaltecos live in this southern belt between the capital, Guatemala City, and the second city of Quezaltenango, where the fertile land is dusted by ash from sporadic volcanic eruptions. Below these highlands are the black sand Pacific beaches and vast agribusiness cotton and sugar plantations.

In the beautiful highlands, the rural population is mostly indigenous, and life revolves around the unique community traditions that have evolved since the conquest. Though most Maya are nominally either Catholic or belong to evangelical churches, ancient Maya spiritual beliefs are integrated into highland worship and fiesta celebrations. Beans and vegetables are farmed, but above all it is maize which remains the important crop – it also retains a sacred status, in Maya mythology man was created from corn.

Political and economic power is concentrated in the hands of the largely *mestizo* population, however, called ladinos. Differences between the two halves of Guatemalan society are sharp. Ladino culture is heavily influenced by the rest of Latin America and the the USA: consuming tropical musical rhythms from Cuba and Hollywood movies with equal relish. Ladino Guatemalans also control the military, which remains a powerful force in Guatemala, with civilian rule only re-established in 1986. A 36-year guerrilla conflict waged by a number of small rebel groups is over, and since the 1996 peace accords *(see page 82)* political violence has largely

PRECEDING PAGES: Lake Atitlán, the "most beautiful lake in the world"; market day at Chichicastenango, a feast for the senses.
LEFT: the dazzling colors of the church of San Andrés Xecul, near Quezaltenango.

disappeared, though rising crime rates threaten social stability. Nevertheless, the outlook is positive, as Guatemala looks forward to a period of building prosperity.

Guatemala has been the center of power in Central America since Preclassic Maya times when the great trading cities of the region, El Mirador and Kaminaljuyú first emerged. Tikal later dominated the Classic period. When the Spanish conquistadors arrived from Mexico in 1523 they established their first capital in Guatemala before moving down through the rest of the isthmus. The colonial capital of Antigua was one of the glorious cities of the Americas, ranking alongside Mexico City and Lima as one of the greatest in the continent. Today, Guatemala is the most populous of the seven Central American nations, with a population of around 14 million, and Guatemala City is the region's largest and most important industrial and commercial center.

Climate

The Inguat (tourist board) hyperbole is that Guatemala is the "Land of Eternal Spring," a country in perpetual bloom, where the days are warm and the evenings mild. There is actually a lot of truth in this, as much of the country is blessed with an extremely agreeable, almost benign climate – but there are significant exceptions.

The most important climatic consideration in Guatemala at any time of year is the altitude. Broadly, in most of the highlands, including Guatemala City, Antigua, Lago de Atitlán, Chichicastenango and Huehuetenango, the altitude is between 1,300 and 2,100 meters (4,260–6,890 ft) and the daytime climate is usually delightful – between 18 and 28°C (64–82°F) – fine for wearing T-shirts and shorts in the day and jeans at night. Humidity is never a problem. Above 2,100 meters (6,890 ft) it can get quite chilly at night, so pack a few layers if you plan to do some volcano climbing.

By the coasts, and in the Petén jungle lowlands, the heat and humidity can be exhausting, with temperatures regularly above 30°C (86°F) at all times of the year. If you're visiting Tikal in Petén, be prepared for these steamy, humid conditions.

There are two seasons in Guatemala. *Invierno* (winter) is between May and October and is the rainy season. Though the skies may be a mix of sunshine and cloud, often the rain is a short, tropical downpour in the late afternoon and the evenings are frequently clear. The dry season, *verano* (summer) is between November and April. Paradoxically, though this is the Guatemalan summer and skies are usually clear, the coolest nighttime temperatures occur in December and January, with the occasional snowfall and frosts not unheard of at high altitudes. For most of the country, however, this is the best time of year to visit Guatemala, though by March temperatures are climbing rapidly – April and early May is the hottest time of year.   ❑

RIGHT: mother and daughter at Joyabaj, in the western highlands.

MODERN HISTORY OF GUATEMALA

Dictatorships and bloodshed have plagued Guatemala since independence.
But peace and stability seem finally to be taking hold

Guatemala formally declared itself independent from Spain on September 15, 1821. Almost immediately, however, its territory was taken over by Mexico, which had been the center of the Spanish viceroyalty and was now ruled by an emperor, Agustín Iturbide.

By 1823, the Central American provinces of Guatemala, Honduras, El Salvador and Nicaragua had broken away from Mexico and formed a united federation based in Guatemala City. The Guatemalan Manuel José Arce became the federation's first president. This arrangement lasted only six years before, in 1829, rebel troops, calling themselves "the allied army for the protection of the law" under General Francisco Morazán from Honduras took Guatemala City.

Despotic legacy

Morazán was the first in a long line of dictatorial rulers in Guatemala, setting the precedent by declaring himself the head of the federation in 1830. Over the next eight years, Morazán set about reforming Guatemala single-handedly. He abolished the privileges of the Catholic church, reformed land ownership, and encouraged new settlement.

In 1833, Morazán transferred the capital of the Central American Federation to San Salvador in El Salvador. Guatemala itself was governed by Mariano Galvez, then by Rafael Carrera. Morazán struggled with increasing difficulty to maintain the federation, and in 1838 it was dissolved.

From 1839 to 1871, Guatemala was governed by the Conservatives: until 1865 under the *mestizo* Rafael Carrera, and then by Vicente Cerna. These years of Conservative government were little different from the colonial period. Political power was firmly in the hands

of a small *mestizo* elite. The majority Maya indians were excluded almost entirely from the political process, and their lands were taken over by large estates.

Throughout the 19th century, Guatemala was essentially an agricultural country, exporting first of all cochineal and indigo for dyes. These

were replaced by plantations of cacao and coffee and, around the turn of the century, by the first large-scale banana plantations run by the United Fruit Company of Boston.

Guatemala in the 20th century

A series of weak presidents and military coups characterized the first decades of the 20th century in Guatemala. Then, in 1931, General Jorge Ubico was elected as president; he was to rule until 1944. During his 13 years in power, Ubico managed to improve Guatemala's economic situation and bring about political stability. But individual freedoms were restricted, and he manipulated the constitution,

---

PRECEDING PAGES: window of opportunity; a family in Retalhuleu wait for the carnival procession to pass.
LEFT: an 1885 engraving of a coffee plantation.
RIGHT: General Justo Rufino Barrios, whose dictatorship from 1873 to 1885 was marked by tyrannical reform.

legislative and legal powers for his own ends. He is said to have surrounded himself with busts of Napoleon, and to have imposed military discipline throughout Guatemala to such a degree that even the national symphony orchestra played in military uniforms.

Ubico was finally overthrown in 1944, and the reformist Juan José Arévalo was elected president under a new constitution in 1945. Arévalo set in train important changes in education, land ownership, and labor laws.

THE OCTOPUS

The United Fruit Company grew so big in the 1950s, taking over the railway, radio, telegraph and electricity companies, it was nicknamed *El Pulpo* – "The Octopus".

from Honduras led by Castillo, Arbenz was forced to resign on June 27, 1954, paving the way for Castillo Armas to take over.

For the next 30 years, Guatemala was governed by a succession of military rulers. US-supported Colonel Castillo Armas was assassinated in the National Palace in 1957, and from then on the country was rocked by increasing violence, as trade unions, left-wing guerrillas and other groups fought against brutal military rule. The church too was subjected to violence by the

These measures brought resistance from the more conservative sectors of Guatemalan society, and there were several attempts to depose him. Despite these plots, Arévalo succeeded in completing his six years in office, and in 1950 handed over to another reform-minded president, Jácobo Arbenz Guzmán. His attempts to break up the huge rural estates through land reform programmes and to control the power of the United Fruit Company soon led to protests.

The United States branded Arbenz a communist, and in 1954 they backed a coup by Colonel Carlos Castillo Armas and the National Liberation Movement. Faced with an invasion

armed forces, who resented the clergy for their support of Maya villagers. Between 1978 and 1983, 13 Catholic priests were killed and more than 100 fled the country.

Repressive regime

In 1982 a military junta toppled the government of Lucas García and, in 1983, General Ríos Montt took control. It was during his period in power that the repression in the countryside reached a peak. Counter insurgency techniques ruthlessly implemented by the Guatemalan army led to the murder, torture and displacement of many thousands of peasants in these years, among Guatemala's darkest.

In 1984, the military ruler of the time, General Óscar Mejía Víctores, called a Constituent Assembly to draw up a new Constitution. This led to free elections in December 1985, at which Guatemala's first civilian president in more than 30 years was chosen. Vinicio Cerezo Arévalo, a Christian Democrat, moved only cautiously during his four years in office to try to curb the power of the armed forces and to bring the continuing civil war to an end.

Cerezo's successor in 1990 was President Jorge Serrano, who fared even worse. Although talks between the armed forces and the Guatemalan National Revolutionary Unity

opposed by politicians and the armed forces, and was forced to resign on June 1, 1993.

Peace at last

Following a caretaker government, elections were organized for the end of 1995. These gave victory to a new party, the National Progressive Party or Partido de Avanzada Nacional (PAN), which represented modernizing business interests.

The PAN leader, Álvaro Arzú, became president at the beginning of 1996. In March 1996, the guerrilla organization URNG agreed to a ceasefire. This was followed by rapid progress

(URNG) guerrillas began in Mexico City in 1991, very little progress was actually made toward peace.

The deteriorating situation within Guatemala ultimately led Serrano to attempt to take dictatorial powers in 1993. He dissolved Congress and the Supreme Court, and announced that he would rule by decree. These actions brought swift condemnation from the international community, and internally Serrano was

LEFT: Panzós, a typical thatch-roofed Maya village in the eastern lowlands, during the late 19th century.
ABOVE: early 20th-century church group in Santiago Atitlán, one of the highland's most traditional villages.

in other areas of the peace negotiations, and on December 29, 1996, an agreement for a firm and lasting peace was signed by the government and the rebels in Guatemala City.

Since then, the government has gradually sought to apply the accords. The rebels handed in their arms and were re-integrated into civil society, forming their own political party. Some reforms of the armed forces were carried out, and controversial units such as the Mobile Military Police were disbanded. A new Constitution was framed which, among other things, promised an inclusive role for the many indigenous groups. In February 1997, a Commission for Historical Clarification (akin to a Truth

The Evangelists

Although officially a Roman Catholic country, in the 1970s and 1980s Protestant and Evangelical sects won many converts among the Maya population in Guatemala. The Catholic church was often seen as distant from their needs and disinterested in their language and traditions.

Catholicism had been imposed by the Spaniards and their successors in the "white" centers of power for almost five centuries. In that time, the Church hierarchy had made little effort to reach out to the Maya – there were few attempts to

translate the Bible into the indigenous languages, and the liturgy was remote and often inexplicable to the local population. In the turbulent years from the 1950s onwards, the Catholic church hierarchy largely sided with the armed forces and with repression, and consequently was viewed with increasing suspicion as violence in Guatemalan society increased.

In spite of this growing tension, many rural Catholic priests had made efforts to win over local Maya communities, supporting development projects and campesinos' unions. Unfortunately these activities provoked the suspicions of the military authorities, who labelled the priests communists and troublemakers. Para-military death squads

hunted down and brutally murdered many of these campaigning Catholic priests, to such an extent that by the early 1980s the Catholic church withdrew altogether from some of the guerrilla-based areas of the highlands, by way of protest and for its own self-preservation. The vacuum thus created by the Catholic church left many highland Maya wary and fearful of being associated with the guerrilla movement.

The Baptist and other missionaries from the United States adopted a very different approach. They lived in the indigenous communities, and from the start learned the languages and translated the Bible into the local tongues. They also taught converts a way of life that was strict but appealing. They forbade alcohol and openly condemned social behaviour they saw as sinful, whereas the Catholic church had remained aloof on these matters. Significantly, the evangelists openly voiced their support for the army over the guerrillas, a policy which gained acceptance from those keen to survive further military oppression.

They also attracted many converts because of their promise that by leading a proper Christian life, the faithful would advance in their lives on this earth as well as in the next world. This Evangelical message was extremely seductive for many among the Maya who felt they had been excluded at all levels of society. As a result, by the beginning of the 1980s, the Evangelical churches had become a powerful force in Guatemala. Their position was further reinforced when one of these new converts, General Efrain Rios Montt, came to power.

Ríos Montt, who had become a born-again Christian in the 1970s when he became a member of the El Verbo Evangelical sect, was the first Protestant president of Guatemala. Although condemned internationally for the vicious counter-insurgency war that he fought in the Guatemalan countryside, his stern, uncompromising message of bringing law and order to a godless society won him a substantial political following.

This support continued in the 1990s. Ríos Montt was the most popular candidate prior to the 1995 presidential elections, before he was disqualified because he had taken power illegally in the 1980s. However, his Republican Front of Guatemala (FRG) party won the 1999 elections, while the number of Guatemalan evangelists continues to grow, currently around 40 percent of the population. ❑

LEFT: Efraín Ríos Montt, whose1982 presidency brought evangelism to the political forefront.

Commission) was established to investigate the human rights crimes that had been committed during the three decades of civil war.

Civil war

The civil war that rocked Guatemala for more than three decades is widely regarded to have started with the 1954 coup that overthrew Jácobo Arbenz. The Castillo government had built up a "blacklist" of more than 40,000 politicians, trade unionists, grass roots leaders and intellectuals whom it regarded as a threat.

Army of the Poor and ORPA (Organización Revolucionaria del Pueblo en Armas) or Revolutionary Organization of the People in Arms. In February 1982 these and several other insurgent groups got together to form the URNG (Unidad Revolucionaria Nacional Guatemalteca), or Guatemalan National Revolutionary Unity, in order to co-ordinate their struggle.

It was during the late 1970s and early 1980s that the war reached its climax. The guerrillas initially scored a number of military victories,

> ### WAR VERSUS PEACE
>
> Rios Montt was ousted in 1982 by his defense minister, Mejía Víctores, who observed that, "Guatemala doesn't need more prayers, it needs more executions."

Many were imprisoned, or forced into exile.

The left-wing groups responded by forming a variety of organizations. Among these, by the beginning of the 1960s, were several groups who believed that the only way to change Guatemalan society was by fighting a guerrilla war.

The Cuban revolution, which had successfully toppled Batista in 1959, provided the model as well as direct support. The main guerrilla groups were the ERP (Ejército Revolucionario de los Pobres) or Revolutionary

ABOVE: memorial in Nebaj to victims of the civil war that raged for three decades from the 1950s.

but the army hit back using scorched-earth tactics and a murderously successful terror campaign in the highlands.

Several thousand people were killed each year at this time, the vast majority Maya indigenous peasants who had nothing to do with the struggle.

The long road to peace

With the return of civilian government in 1986, the attempts to achieve a negotiated peace began in earnest. The guerrilla organizations had come to realize that they could not overthrow the Guatemalan state by violence. One of the chief problems for these negotiations was the fact that the army considered it had eliminated what it called "subversion", and therefore there was nothing to negotiate.

Gradually, however, the military was persuaded to participate in talks which continued for several years. The guerrillas wanted peace accords that would guarantee substantial change in Guatemala, including the promotion of the rights of the indigenous Maya peoples.

The armed forces were anxious not to be held responsible for the 200,000 deaths that had

> **LAW OF THE GUN**
>
> "In Guatemala there are two presidents, and one of them has a machine gun with which he is always threatening the other."
> Juan José Arévalo (1945–50)

occurred during the violence. They also wished to avoid any sweeping reforms to the army or the police.

Peace accords

The peace accords were finally signed in 1996. The principal parts of the agreement were to carry out an investigation of the human-rights abuses committed during the civil war, a commitment to demilitarize society, and to introduce constitutional changes to safeguard indigenous rights in Guatemala.

Initially, the outlook was positive as the guerrillas handed in their weapons and formed a political party while MINUGUA (the United Nations Mission to Guatemala) arrived to oversee the implementation of the accords.

Progress proved very slow however, as the Guatemalan military stalled on key commitments and proved reluctant to relinquish their powerbase.

Army personnel were later implicated in the assassination of Bishop Juan Geradi in 1998, two days after his offices had published a report that blamed the military and civil-defense patrols for 93 percent of civil war deaths. Meanwhile, a referendum rejected a constitutional amendment to legitimize Maya rights.

Guatemala today

Rising crime rates and the influence of criminal cartels were two of the most pressing issues facing Guatemala in the early years of the new millennium. Mafia-style networks, many with ties to the military, established Guatemala as a key country for cocaine smuggling and acted with near impunity against a chronically weak judiciary and corruption-riddled police force.

The cult of gang membership in the cities also threatened social stability. Former military dictator Efraín Ríos Montt dominated the political scene for many of these years, with his FRG party winning the 1999 election with its candidate Alfonso Portillo, carried by promises to restore law and order to the nation.

But Portillo's term proved to be disastrous, as he and leading members of his cabinet and team were caught up in a string of corruption scandals, while the security situation deteriorated further. Unsurprisingly, the FRG (with Ríos Montt as its presidential candidate) lost the 2003 elections as Óscar Berger of the pro-business GANA coalition swept to power. He quickly announced a crackdown on criminal gangs and corruption, arresting several former members of Portillo's administration.

By 2005, there were indications that security in Guatemala was at last beginning to show signs of improvement, although Berger's decision to sign up to CAFTA (Central American Free Trade Agreement) proved controversial and divided the nation. ❑

LEFT: former president, Alvaro Arzú, who signed the peace accord with the guerrillas in 1996.

Rigoberta Menchú

Globally, the best-known Guatemalan isn't the president, a drug baron or even a sporting figure, but the K'i che' Maya peasant-turned-human rights activist Rigoberta Menchú, who won the 1992 Nobel Peace Prize for her work on behalf of Guatemala's and the world's indigenous people. Menchú is a controversial figure in Guatemala, idolized by most Maya and the political left, but also provoking vitriolic polemic from her ideological opponents who consider her a subversive, ill-educated ex-guerrilla.

Rigoberta Menchú was born in 1959 near the isolated highland town of Uspantán in Quiché. In the first volume of her autobiography, *I, Rigoberta Menchú*, published in 1983, she describes how the horrific brutality of the Guatemalan civil war affected her family, how her mother, father and brothers were branded guerrilla-sympathizers and killed by the military in their fight to protect the family's farmland. In powerful, unambiguous language Menchú castigates the inequalities of that ruptured Guatemalan society: the cultural chasm between *ladino* and Maya, the gross disparity of wealth, health education and opportunity between the country's rich and poor. She also details that she had no formal schooling, how her family had to work in the plantations of the Pacific coast to survive, and her flight to exile in Mexico in 1980.

I, Rigoberta Menchú sold strongly all over the globe, catapulting the author into the international limelight. Menchú became a familiar face at the United Nations in Geneva, tirelessly campaigning for the rights of the Guatemalan Maya and forging connections with other oppressed minorities. This period of her life is recounted in *Crossing Borders*, the second volume of her autobiography, a less harrowing read. It tackles the controversy over her Nobel Peace Prize award, which split the country on familiar lines as ecstatic supporters celebrated in San Marcos while the president failed to turn up to a rally in the capital, complaining of an ear-ache. The Nobel laureate returned to Guatemala in 1994 as an iconic if contentious figure, but internationally she remained beyond reproach until the publication of David Stoll's biography *Rigoberta Menchú and the story of all poor Guatemalans*, in 1998. Stoll's book shook this enshrined reputation, con-

tending that important parts of *I, Rigoberta Menchú* were false: that Menchú had been educated at a convent school and had never had to work in the Pacific coast plantations; that her family's land dispute was an internecine family quarrel rather than a racially charged indigenous-*ladino* clash; he alleges a guerrilla past and questions the accuracy of her story about the death of one of her brothers from malnutrition.

Menchú has since admitted that she received some education at the convent, but remained silent about other allegations. It's fair to say (and Stoll still considers that the Nobel prize was rightfully awarded) that despite doubts over certain details

of Menchú's story, her reputation remains largely intact among her supporters. It is not in dispute that her mother, father and another of her brothers died at the hands of the military.

Menchu's success bringing global attention to the suffering of the Guatemalan Maya is unquestionable. Her work on behalf of the world's indigenous peoples for the UN has been tireless and she continues to campaign in Guatemala for political and social justice through her foundation and as a goodwill ambassador for the peace accords in the Berger administration. But Stoll's research has added further controversy to the Menchú legend, to a woman touted by many as a future presidential candidate. ❑

RIGHT: Rigoberta Menchú, whose story exposed the inequalities that are still rife in Guatemalan society.

HIGHLAND LIFE

All-important village ties and a rich melange of cultural influences are revealed in the western highlands' Maya communities on market day and at fiestas

The majority of Guatemala's 7 million Maya live in small towns and villages in the western highlands (a vast area comprising part of the volcanic Sierra Madre mountain range, which rises in Mexico and stretches south-eastwards to the doorstep of Guatemala City). In this heartland, the Maya have – to some extent – remained at arm's length from the events of the past century.

As it is traditional for extended families to stay together, married sons are given rooms within the family compound. Young men lead relatively restricted lives under their father's authority, and only those who become traders or make money working in the United States have the option of independence. Few children attend school for the full duration; older girls help their mothers at home and look after younger siblings, whilst the boys accompany their fathers to the fields or markets.

Village economy is based largely on subsistence agriculture. Most Maya men own a plot of land on which they try to grow enough corn and beans to feed their families. If space allows, cash crops such as carrots, avocados, onions, and squash are also grown and sold at market. However, since many villages were forced to give up their best land to coffee growers in the late 19th century, and as it is customary for fathers to divide their land among their sons, the plots become smaller with each generation and it is increasingly difficult even to remain self-sufficient – making annual migrations to pick cotton or coffee a necessity.

Sacred corn

Corn has a mystical significance, for besides being the Maya's main subsistence crop, in the *Popol Vuh*, the sacred book of the K'iché Maya, it is written that the first men were made of corn paste. Black and red corn, as well as the more common yellow and white strains, are indige-

nous to Guatemala, and the historian Sylvanus Morley has suggested that these four colors were sacred to the ancient Maya because of their association with corn.

Religion is fundamental to the life of the Maya. The majority claim to be Catholics, although many of them practice a unique type

of "folk Catholicism" which incorporates traditional beliefs. It was easy for the Maya to adapt to Catholic doctrines taught to them by the Spanish: elaborate ceremonies accompanied by incense had always been a part of religious life, as had the veneration of the cross, an important Maya symbol. Pagan gods simply assumed the identity of Catholic saints and their worship continued as before.

The *"cofradía"* system *(see page 88)* was introduced by the Spaniards to promote Catholicism, but soon it also acquired its own syncretic identity. However, although traditional villages like Nebaj, Chichicastenango, and Santiago Atitlán still have up to 10 working

---

PRECEDING PAGES: carving out a living on a *milpa*.
LEFT: colorful pageant in Chichicastenango.
RIGHT: tilling the fields is still a manual task.

cofradías, their influence has been in steady decline since the influx of foreign Catholic priests in the 1950s.

The shaman

Besides worshipping in church, traditionalists also pray at Maya shrines in the mountains. These older rites are the province of the shaman, who acts as an intermediary. He is also called upon to give advice, invoke or revoke curses, foretell the future, cure illness and officiate at ceremonies asking for rain. He is conversant with the 260-day Maya calendar and chooses propitious days for his ceremonies.

Shamans are particularly numerous amongst the K'iche' Maya of Quezaltenango and Totonicapán, where they hold court in the *cofradías* that contain the figure of Maximón, also known as San Simón. This figure is a seated effigy dressed in European clothes who is rated as having special powers, not only for good, but also evil *(see page 123)*.

Maya rituals are also well preserved amongst the Q'anjob'al Maya of Huehuetenango, where priests use both the 260-day ritual calendar and the 365-day calendar. The priest's function is to pray for the good of the community and the success of the harvest. Turkeys are sacrificed at relevant times during the year and blood-stained incense and candles are burned at the sacred places. If the rains fail to come, or the crops are ruined by frost, then the Maya priest is blamed; in the past he would have been jailed for not doing his job properly.

The 1990s saw a Maya religion revival movement amongst young Maya intellectuals, who now openly claim to be either followers of the religion or even Maya priests. This is a good example of the growing awareness and pride the younger generation is taking in its cultural heritage.

Distinct costumes

The Maya today identify with their villages rather than with their ancestral tribes, although the languages they speak still conform to the pattern of ancient tribal boundaries. Marriages between members of different communities are relatively rare, and village identity is consolidated further by the distinctive clothes worn by the women and some men.

DECLINE OF THE COFRADÍA

Each *cofradía* group within a village serves a single Catholic saint, organizing all the required rites and processions. The saint's image is enshrined in the house of the chief *cofrade*, which assumes the status of a chapel. Members are elected annually from the respected men and women of the community. A strict hierarchy is observed and young men can progress to the position of chief *cofrade* of the patron saint of the village (its foremost saint) by first serving in the minor *cofradías*. The head of the top *cofradía* may also be a practising shaman.

However, in recent years church committees have usurped many traditional *cofradía* functions, such as caring for the church, providing flowers, and officiating at burial ceremonies. Indeed, in many villages there is now considerable friction between the *cofrades* and the parish priest with his modern Catholic Action groups, not least because some *cofradía* ceremonies are accompanied by shamanistic rituals and very heavy drinking.

The decline in *cofradía* membership is also due to the high costs involved in organizing a saint's *fiesta*. Whereas in the old days the whole community would contribute to *cofradía* expenses, a typical village today is split between an ever increasing number of Evangelical groups, modern Catholics, and a diminishing number of traditionalists.

Costumes fall into three categories: everyday dress; more elaborate wear for special occasions, and the ceremonial garments worn by the *cofradías*. Although colors, designs and the way of wearing particular garments differ from village to village, all women's apparel consists of the same basic articles: a *huipil* (a loose rectangular blouse), a skirt, sash, hair-ribbon and *tzut* (multi-purpose carrying cloth) or shawl. Each item is hand-woven, either on a simple hip-strap loom or a foot-loom.

Modern trends

Twenty years ago, it was easy to identify a woman's village by the clothes she was wearing, as not only her *huipil*, but also her belt, *tzut* and skirt conformed to the colors and designs of her community. Today this is no longer so, as many women are switching from making (or commissioning) village dress to buying the cheaper Totonicapán trade pieces. *Huipiles* woven on foot-looms, or made of commercial cloth with machine embroidery round the neck, are far less expensive than those woven on hip-strap looms with village designs. Brightly striped belts and colorful acrylic shawls also make cheap and cheerful substitutes for traditional sashes and *tzutes*, though the wrap-around skirt is still the style used most, and only in Quezaltenango and Alta Verapaz have European-style gathered skirts been adopted.

The change from village specific to generic dress styles began during the civil war in the early 1980s, when thousands fled their villages for the relative safety of large towns. In addition to the cost factor, the anonymity of the Totonicapán textiles gave protection from being identified as possible guerrilla supporters. Now, because more and more young girls leave home to work or study in the large towns, it has become socially acceptable to wear not only trade items of dress, but also the *huipiles* of other communities. These developments are most evident around Guatemala City, Quezaltenango and Totonicapán.

Despite such changes, traditional costumes are the norm in many villages around Lake Atitlán, in Nebaj and Chajul, and among the Mam-speaking Maya of Huehuetenango, where even skirts are still woven on hip-strap looms and very young girls wear full village dress too.

Adaptive men

Men's traditional costumes have been preserved in only a few villages, most notably in those around Lake Atitlán, and in the mountains of Huehuetenango. Men have always been more open to change than women as they leave their communities for longer periods of time to trade in the larger towns, try their fortunes in the USA, or serve in the army. Because of continuing discrimination, it is always more advantageous to be taken for a mixed-race

LEFT: boys from Santiago Atitlán, dressed in a cultural mixture of traditional and modern styles.
RIGHT: *cofrade* from Chajul in the Ixil Triangle.

NO CHANGE IN DRESS STYLE

Women's clothing today differs little in style from that worn in pre-conquest times. Although only small fragments of cloth have been found at archeological sites, the carvings, figurines and pottery that have survived have left us clear pictures of pre-Columbian Maya dress.

Women are depicted wearing elaborate headdresses and knee-length *huipiles* which hang over wrap-around skirts – the type of costume still worn by *cofradía* women today, for example in Santiago Atitlán, Nebaj and Sololá. In a number of communities, such as Palín, Cobán, Joyabaj and San Mateo Ixtatán, *huipiles* are worn loose at all times.

ladino than an "indian". Men's clothing these days has more in common with Western dress than with ancient Maya loincloths and cloaks.

You can recognize Maya men from Lake Atitlán by their striped trousers decorated with village motifs and held up by sashes; sometimes a length of woolen fabric is wrapped around the hips too. Black split overtrousers are used in Todos Santos and by Sololá officials, whilst the men of San Juan Atitán wear woolen *capixays* that resemble the cassocks used by the Spanish friars. In Santiago Atitlán men embroider their own trousers, copying pictures of birds or Maya hieroglyphs.

cialties include woolen blankets from Momostenango, rope from agave fibers in San Pablo La Laguna and San Juan Cotzal, and *metate* (grinding stone) mats made from the reeds growing around Santiago Atitlán. Totonicapán is the center for glazed terracotta bowls and cooking pots, whilst in Chinautla plant containers and ornaments are produced for the Guatemala City market, as well as beautiful clay nativity tableaux.

Although a large number of craft co-operatives were established by foreign aid workers in the 1970s and 1980s, very few of them have continued to function successfully, as the Maya

Although modern Western clothes may be worn on a day-to-day basis, in some villages older dress styles are retained for *cofradía* use. Examples of this are the elaborate costumes worn by *cofrades* in San Juan Sacatepéquez and Chichicastenango. Items such as split over-trousers, knee breeches, capes and cloaks stem from 18th- and 19th-century Spanish fashions.

Crafts and markets

Crafts make an important contribution to village economy. Some communities specialize in the manufacture of particular items which are traded throughout the highlands. Regional spe-

SKIRTS ON THE ROAD

Artisans in the communities of Salcajá and Totonicapán specialize in weaving skirts and shawls with attractive tie-dyed (jaspé) patterns, which they sell in the markets.

Tie-dyeing is a process in which a given number of yarns are bound at specific intervals so that when they are immersed in the dye solution the tied areas retain their original color. The resulting patterns range from simple checks to more complex tree and doll designs.

In Salcajá much of the work takes place in the streets, as the warp yarns for a series of skirts are often 50 meters (160 ft) long and need to be stretched out and aligned before they are put on the loom.

are on the whole too individualistic to share profits with anyone outside the immediate family. A notable exception is the the Zunil Santa Ana Co-operative, established in 1970 by the German parish priest's assistant after whom it is named, and now run by a committee of women.

The main outlet for the sale of craft items is the town or village market. Market day is an important social as well as commercial occasion. Although large towns support daily markets, most villages have one

> ## FIESTA GLITZ
>
> Masks and opulent costumes, decorated with metallic threads, mirrors and ostrich feathers, are hired for the festival dances from costume houses in San Cristóbal Totonicapán or Chichicastenango.

Saturday market day in Almolonga is dedicated mainly to the sale of vegetables (baskets piled high with radishes and carrots make an impressive sight). The Chichicastenango market has developed primarily into a handicraft market for tourists, where very attractive souvenirs and gifts can be bought directly from the people who make them.

Queens and music

Every town and village has a patron saint, whose feast day is celebrated annually with a

main market per week which takes place around the central square and surrounding streets; relatively few villages have covered market halls.

Traders may journey for many hours to participate in important regional markets such as Tecpán, Sololá, San Francisco El Alto and Totonicapán. Whereas women carry heavy items on their heads, men carry goods on their backs, hanging from a leather strap wrapped around their foreheads.

LEFT: livestock market, San Francisco El Alto.
ABOVE: costumed performers at the Dance of the Conquest, in Chichicastenango's May festival.

three- to five-day *fiesta.* Traders from all over the country flock to the *fiesta* locations with their goods, packing the streets round the central square with colorful stalls and fairground rides for the children.

"Festival queens" are elected at the start of the festivities and are driven around town on floats. In mixed-race communities, one of the "queens" is a *ladina* (part indigenous, part Spanish descent), the other a Maya girl. The municipality lays on a band and dancing in the town hall, whilst various trade organizations sponsor bands to play in the square. It is not unusual to find three bands playing different tunes within 20 meters (66 ft) of each other!

No *fiesta* can claim to have been a total success unless at least one wealthy individual has sponsored the presentation of one of the masked dances. These fall into two categories: simple fancy dress dances (usually presented by *ladinos*), where the participants dress up as various comic characters; and the older traditional dances which tell the story of the conquest (La Conquista) and the battles between the Christians and the infidels (Los Moros). The deer dance (Baile de los Venados) is of pre-conquest origins and is now

performed regularly only in Santa Eulalia, as it requires a large cast and months of training to learn the text. The traditional dances are accompanied by music played on the *marimba* (a type of xylophone) and the native flute and drum.

The culmination of every *fiesta* is the patron saint's procession, in which an image of this saint is accompanied by all the lesser saints, musicians, the masked dancers, and the event is trumpeted by fireworks.

Fire crackers and bullocks

Fireworks are always an important and integral part of the annual *fiesta* throughout the highlands. They range from the fire crackers, bombs

ANNUAL FESTIVAL

For a list of Guatemala's public holidays and its most important festivals around the country, see Travel Tips, page 347.

and rockets that accompany the saints' processions, to the more sophisticated (and highly dangerous) cane structures in the shape of bullocks, which fit over each dancer and shoot rockets out in all directions.

Recommended are the particularly colorful festivals that take place in Patzún for Corpus Christi (late May or early June), in Chichicastenango around December 21, and in Sololá and Nebaj on August 15. The exceptionally strong *cofradía* involvement gives these *fiestas* an added dimension.

On November 1 and 2 each year, all Maya communities remember their dead with a traditional celebration. A *marimba* band usually plays in the cemetery and families picnic by the graves of their relatives. In Santiago Sacatépequez, giant kites are brought to the cemetery. Their launch can be a memorable sight if there's enough wind. The village of Todos Santos Cuchumatán also holds its annual patron saint's festival at this time, which is renown for its zany horse race *(see page 135)*.

Easter is celebrated with large-scale Holy Thursday and Good Friday processions everywhere. In Antigua Guatemala, beautiful carpets of colored sawdust are created for the chief participants in the processions to walk over, and the youths accompanying the processions dress up as Romans, Jews and Penitents. Stuffed dummies representing Judas are hung from lampposts and burned on Good Friday. In many Maya communities there are also colorful enactments of the Last Supper inside the village church complex, and Passion Plays take place on Good Friday, which culminate in Jesus and the Thieves being crucified.

So, important dates in the Catholic and Maya calendars are marked in carefully orchestrated, visually arresting and varied ways, often with centuries' old symbolism that may have syncretized the Maya and Christian religions. In fact, it could be said that some of the same characteristics are echoed year-round in the striking handmade costumes worn by Maya men and women, particularly those of the *cofradía*, which not only reflect the individual identity of each village, but also the wearer's status in the community. ❑

LEFT: the colorful Sumpango Kite Festival, in August.

Men of Maize

Together with beans and squashes, maize or Indian corn has always been a staple of the Maya diet. Since they first settled in Central America, the Maya have grown maize in much the same way. Towards the end of the dry season, they clear the ground – burning off trees and shrubbery in the jungle areas – and make a field known as the *milpa*. Then they dig a row of simple holes with a stick, and place in them the seeds kept from the previous year's crop. If the rains did not fail, in a few months they can hope to have a fresh yield of maize. Often the planting and harvesting was done by several families in the same village, so making the cultivation of maize another element that bound the community together.

After being picked, the ripe kernels are either boiled with water and a small amount of white lime, making a paste that is the basis for a dough that can later be steamed and made into *tamales* or shaped into flat cakes which are toasted or grilled to make *tortillas*. Archeological digs have found mortars (*metates*) and pestles (*manos*) for grinding the maize kernels similar to those still used in Guatemalan villages today. Another preparation was the broth known as *atole* that was often drunk with chilli peppers in it as the first meal of the day, or fermented to make an alcoholic drink.

But beyond the use of maize as a food, it also occupies an important symbolic role for the Maya. The *Popol Vuh*, the great epic poem of the Guatemalan Maya, describes how the world was created. At first, the gods made mankind from mud, but this was washed away. Next, they made them of wood, but found that this creation was without life and imagination. The third attempt, in which men were made from flesh, ended when these creatures of flesh and blood turned to evil ways, and were finally wiped out in great rains.

Finally, the gods decided that to make proper men, they must fashion them from maize meal; "the making, the modelling of our first mother-father, with yellow corn, white corn alone for the flesh, food alone for the human legs and arms, for our first fathers..."

Not only was mankind made from maize, but several of the classic Maya gods represented maize. The figure known to archeologists as God K

from the hieroglyphic codices is thought to represent the dragon who is one of the main gods in the Maya pantheon. This god is associated with semen and seeds in general and is seen as a life-giving principle.

This sacred aspect of maize has survived into the present day. Ceremonies for the fertility of the earth and a successful harvest are still common throughout the Guatemalan highlands in Maya villages. And the religious and ritual importance of the crop has also been brilliantly captured in modern Spanish literature by the Guatemalan writer Miguel Ángel Asturias in his novel, *Hombres de Maíz* (Men of Maize). Asturias, who in 1971

became the first Latin American novelist to win the Nobel Prize for literature, was always concerned with the social conditions of the poor, largely Maya in his native country. In *Men of Maize* he draws on sources such as the Popol Vuh or the Book of Chilam-Balam to paint a complex picture of Maya life, their struggle to fit into the modern world, and their continuing dependency on the bounty of nature: "Yes, the earth was a huge nipple, one enormous breast to which every peasant was fastened, hungry for harvest, for milk with the real taste of woman's milk, the way the maize stalks taste when you chew them young and tender. A miraculous crop, the way they all shot up with the first downpours." ❏

RIGHT: the first man, made from maize, from a mural in Mérida, by Fernando Castro Pacheco.

GUATEMALAN WILDLIFE

*The country's diversity of landscape – from cloud forest to mangrove swamp –
provides a habitat for an equally varied range of flora and fauna*

The wide variety of climate and habitat in Guatemala, along with its privileged position on the "bridge" between North and South America, has resulted in a remarkable degree of biodiversity for such a relatively small nation. Sadly, large areas of formerly rich habitat have been seriously degraded – in some cases effectively destroyed – by human activities. But efforts have been increasing since the 1950s to preserve the most significant ecosystems, with the result that more than 40 protected areas have so far been established and several dozen more are under consideration.

The country can be roughly divided into three regions: a narrow Pacific coastal slope, around 50 km (30 miles) wide; the highlands, comprising two principal mountain chains and the high plateaux of central Guatemala; and the huge lowland area in the northeast known as the Petén. There is also a much smaller lowland region stretching inland from the short Caribbean coastline, along the Polochic/Dulce and Motagua river valleys.

Along with the rest of the Central American isthmus, Guatemala is seismically very vulnerable, forming as it does part of the Pacific "ring of fire". Parallel to the Pacific coast runs a chain of 33 volcanoes, many of them active, which includes the region's highest peak, the Volcán Tajumulco 4,220 meters (13,700 ft). Rainfall varies from 500mm to 5,000mm (20–200 inches) a year. Combined with altitude and other factors, this results in more than a dozen different "life zones", which range from semi-desert and savanna to cloud forests, where precipitation is almost constant.

Among the trees

The name "Guatemala" is said to be derived from a Nahuatl word meaning "among the trees," and, despite deforestation, over a third of

LEFT: water lilies on the wildlife-rich Río Dulce, in the tropical eastern lowlands.
RIGHT: the spider monkey's innate sense of curiosity makes it a common sight in the wild.

the country still fits this description. The jungles of the Petén form part of the largest remaining block of moist tropical forest in Central America. Such forests comprise the world's richest ecosystem in terms of diversity of flora and fauna. Those of Guatemala, however, which are close to the northernmost limit

of tropical jungles, are less densely populated with species than the equatorial forests of South America. The plant life varies from rubber trees and tall (up to 30-meter/100-ft high) tropical hardwoods, such as mahogany, to the country's 500 species of orchid.

Around the mangroves

Mangrove swamps, occurring on both coasts, are highly specialized habitats in which the vegetation tolerates alternating fresh and salt water. Dominated by the red mangrove (rhizophora), they provide a vital breeding ground for fish and crustaceans and are often home to nesting colonies of birds such as egrets, herons, storks, ducks and kingfishers. The endangered, elusive West Indian manatee – once prized for its meat but now a protected species – as well as crocodiles, iguanas and otters, are among the creatures that can be seen in mangrove swamps such as in the **Biotopo Chocón Machacas**, on the north bank of the Río Dulce *(see page 154)*.

Also on the Caribbean coast is the **Biotopo Punta de Manabique**, on the peninsula which separates the Bay of Amatique from the Gulf of Honduras. Among its attractions are a swamp featuring a rare type of palm, known as confra, and beaches on which sea turtles lay their eggs. Turtle eggs are considered by some Central Americans to be an aphrodisiac and so they are often stolen, adding to the problems facing this endangered species.

Giant reserve

In 1989, a government decree set aside the entire area north of 17° 10'N as the **Maya Biosphere Reserve**. This huge tract of the department of Petén, totalling around 1 million hectares (2½ million acres) – or nearly 2 million hectares (5 million acres) if you include its severely degraded outer "buffer zone" – includes seven other protected areas in its boundaries. It covers 15 percent of the national

TIPS FOR BIRDWATCHERS

Visitors from temperate zones are often overwhelmed by the sheer variety of birds in a tropical woodland. For the novice, here are some tips worth following:

☛ The best time of day for observing most species is the early morning.

☛ At times it may seem as if nothing is moving, then the arrival of a mixed feeding flock of small birds suddenly places huge demands on your identification skills. At such times, take notes rather than looking up details of each bird, which may cause you to miss several others.

☛ Bear in mind that fruiting trees and columns of ants often attract many birds; stay close to one or the other for a while; this may be more productive than moving around.

☛ Wear long trousers and long-sleeved shirts to deter insects, and use plenty of insect-repellent cream.

☛ Boots with ankle support, or rubber Wellingtons, are advisable – and always watch where you step.

☛ If you come across a snake, it will usually slither away, unless you inadvertently corner it or step on it.

territory and borders on two other significant reserves, in Belize and Mexico. It is controlled by CONAP (National Council for Protected Areas), which is the controlling body for all of Guatemala's national parks and *biotopos* (scientific conservation areas).

Biosphere wildlife

The Maya Biosphere Reserve is home to some of Guatemala's most spectacular animal species, including flamboyant parrots, parakeets and toucans, as well as the region's largest mammal, Baird's tapir. This

A REAL HOWLER

The long-tailed "howler" monkey is so called due to the deep roar emitted by the male, which has enlarged vocal cords.

cat in the Americas – are also encountered, but the noisy spider and howler monkeys (the latter known locally as *zaraguates*) are more easily seen by the casual visitor than these denizens of the dense forest cover. For the best sightings, it is recommended you tour with an informative local guide.

There are more than 300 species of bird in the Tikal national park alone, and this covers less than 6 percent of the total area of the biosphere reserve. They range from various tiny hummingbirds to the raucous and spectacular scar-

900–1,300-kg (400– 600-lb) relative of the rhinoceros has a snout that looks like a small trunk. Usually found near water, the tapir is shy and hard to spot without a guide. If approached, this stocky creature is very likely to bolt away from you.

A variety of wild boar called a peccary rummages for scraps on the forest floor, while other animals commonly found here include porcupines, opossums and armadillos.

White-tailed deer and jaguars – the biggest

LEFT: the coati, frequently seen around Tikal.
ABOVE: the spectacularly colorful, ocellated turkey, which lives on the forest floor in the tropical lowlands.

let macaw. One rare but well known bird found only in this region is the brightly-plumaged ocellated turkey.

A less appealing discovery is the fearsome fer-de-lance, one of Latin America's most poisonous snakes, which inhabits the forest floor. You are unlikely to encounter many snakes in Guatemala, and the vast majority are not even venomous, but it's always best to give these potentially deadly creatures a wide berth.

Freshwater wetlands

In the rainy season (May–November), the flooded Río Escondido forms the largest area of freshwater wetlands in Central America, a type of ecosystem which has almost vanished from the region as a result of drainage and land reclamation for farming.

In the northern part of the biosphere lies the **Biotopo El Zotz**, which takes its name from the Maya word for a bat. The fruit bats that live here provide a wonderful spectacle each evening as they emerge in their thousands from cliffside caves in the central part of this heavily wooded area.

South of the Petén near San Agustín, and close to the border with Honduras, lies a highly

> ### BUTTERFLIES
>
> Guatemala is home to many beautiful, colourful butterflies, including the stunning blue morpho. Look out for the butterflies' huge caterpillars.

here, the latter often a victim of the former. Other cats, such as pumas, may also be seen.

With peaks more than 3,000 meters (9,000 ft) above sea level, the biosphere reserve contains within its boundaries the largest remaining area of cloud forest in the country. This is a highly localized type of habitat, dependent on plentiful moisture throughout the year. Typically, cloud-forest trees are laden with moss and epiphytes and interspersed with tree ferns.

Ecotourism

Conservation International, which has been very active in Guatemalan ecotourism, has established the Alianza Verde (Green Alliance), an initiative which promotes responsible tourism in the Maya Biosphere Reserve. Participants are required to meet agreed environmental, operational and service standards in order to market their products under the Alianza Verde seal. Conservation International's emphasis is on community-based ecotourism, such as the newly-created system of Caminos Mayas (Maya Trails). The trails allow visitors to observe wildlife, to take part in the harvesting of forest products, or to visit Maya ruins. By providing an alternative source of income for the local community, the programme aims to help curb the destruction of the forest by subsistence farmers. For more information about voluntary work, contact Arcas (www.arcasguatemala.com) or Fundary (www.guate.net/fundarymanabique).

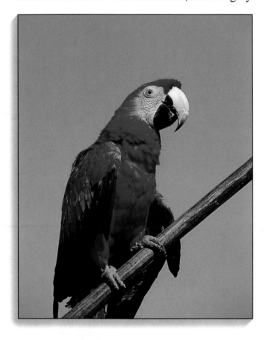

specialized biosphere reserve and national park: the mountain chain known as the **Sierra de las Minas**. Noted for its high degree of endemism (the existence of flora and fauna unknown elsewhere), it is also thought to host species as yet unknown to science.

Last refuge

The sierra is a known refuge for many threatened birds including the endangered Guatemalan national bird, the quetzal *(see facing page)*, and is the only place in Guatemala where the harpy eagle *(harpia harpyja*, one of the world's largest birds of prey) has been seen in recent years. Jaguar and deer are also found

A taste of the wildlife

For those unable to make the trip to the Petén, or to the mountains and valleys of eastern Guatemala, a visit to the **San Buenaventura de Atitlán** reserve near Panajachel may be a good way to get a sense of the variety of flora and fauna in the country.

The reserve contains a butterfly farm, where 25 different species can be seen, along with 50 kinds of orchid. Native plants, including fruit trees, have been planted to attract birds, which can be observed from a series of walkways, rope bridges and elevated platforms. ❏

LEFT: the distinctive scarlet macaw, an endangered species sometimes still seen in forested foothills.

A Resplendent Bird

Spectacularly beautiful but rarely seen, the subject of ancient legends, the appropriately named resplendent quetzal (*pharomachrus mocinno*) is a strong contender for the title of most magnificent tropical American bird.

A member of the colorful trogon family, the resplendent quetzal is Guatemala's national bird. It has even lent its name to the country's currency, which bears a striking portrait of a male quetzal in flight, its tail streaming behind.

This rare creature is found only in undisturbed cloud forest at around 1,500–3,000 meters (5,000–10,000 ft). It can be found virtually anywhere in Central America, from southern Mexico to western Panama, but habitat destruction and humans' quest for plumes have placed it high on the list of endangered species.

The adult male quetzal is bright, iridescent green with red underparts and an extraordinary tail, which can reach more than half a meter (2 ft) in length. Its striking feathers were highly prized by the pre-Columbian peoples of Mesoamerica, who used them in the headdresses of their priests and rulers, and even in warfare. The Mexica (Aztecs) called the bird a *quetzaltototl* and towards the end of a battle would sometimes name a *quetzal-owl* warrior, a practice which (until the arrival of the Spanish) was believed to guarantee victory. The birds' feathers were woven onto a frame and they completely concealed the warrior inside.

This warlike aspect also featured in the mythology of the Maya. The *nahual*, or spirit guide, of the great Maya *cacique* Tecun Uman was a quetzal which fought on after his death at the hands of the Spaniards. According to the Maya, the red belly-plumage of the bird was the result of its having been dipped in the blood of slain warriors after the battle of Xela (Quezaltenango).

The steep reduction in the quetzals' numbers today is a reflection of the specialized nature of their dietary and habitat requirements. Although they will eat various kinds of fruit and insects – and even lizards – their movements are closely tied to the presence of the wild avocado, whose fruit is a major part of their diet. They nest in tree-trunk hollows, but – unlike woodpeckers and parrots for example – their bills are too weak to carve out

RIGHT: the resplendent quetzal, whose favored delicacy is the wild avocado.

holes, unless the tree is thoroughly rotten. They therefore often depend on nesting holes already carved by other birds.

Their breeding period is March–June, with a peak in April–May, which is the best time to look for them. Under normal circumstances quetzals spend most of their time in the upper branches of trees and are thus easily missed. Their plaintive, cooing call is unlikely to be noticed, except by the trained ear. In the breeding season, however, they are obliged to move around in lower branches because of the location of their nest sites, some 3–5 meters (10–16 ft) above ground. Sometimes it is possible to detect their presence by the sight of tail

plumes emerging from a hole in a tree trunk. The best time of day to look for them, as with most tropical birds, is in the early hours of the morning, when they are at their most active. However, they are also reported to feed in the early evening.

One of the key sites in Guatemala for quetzals is the Biotopo Mario Dary Rivera in Purulhá municipality, in Baja Verapaz. Located on the road to Cobán, this 1,000-hectare (2,500-acre) reserve reaches an altitude of 2,300 meters (7,500 ft) and was established specifically to conserve quetzals and their cloud-forest habitat. It consists of two sections, of which the upper one is accessible only with permission, and is one of the best preserved areas of cloud forest in the country. ❑

PLACES

A detailed guide to the entire country, with principal sites clearly cross-referenced by number to the maps

With a multitude of ancient Maya sites to explore, an extravagant colonial architectural legacy to enjoy and spectacular natural sights, Guatemala is unsurprisingly many people's favorite country in Latin America.

For such a small country there are an astounding number of wonders. The western highlands are breathtakingly beautiful – an inspirational landscape of steep hillsides, sleepy adobe-walled villages and whitewashed churches. The vast forest reserves of the northern lowlands once contained dozens of thriving Maya city-states. The grace and colonial splendor of the former capital, Antigua, make it the country's most beautiful and most comfortable city.

We begin in the capital, Guatemala City, the largest city in Central America. "Guate" as it is known throughout the country, is in many ways a typical Latin American capital, with the nation's most affluent suburbs and, conversely, the worst poverty and pollution. It's not an especially attractive city, though there are three excellent museums and some interesting modern and historic buildings – it's probably best to make your base in Antigua, less than an hour away.

Antigua, the former capital, is everything that Guate is not: compact, relaxed and visually stunning. It's a supremely rewarding place to spend a few days; exploring the great ruined baroque churches and convents, wandering the cobbled streets and enjoying some of the fantastic courtyard cafés and restaurants. Antigua is also a great base for a number of excellent excursions into the surrounding countryside. There are four volcanoes to climb, including Volcán Pacaya, one of the most active in Central America – if it's safe to do so when you visit; the shrine of the wicked saint Maximón at San Andrés Itzapa, coffee plantations and textile markets.

Antigua sits on the cusp of the western highlands, an intoxicatingly beautiful world where most of Guatemala's Maya live, and which is many people's favorite part of the entire country. The volcanic scenery is magnificent, crowned by the awesome beauty of Lago de Atitlán, with its lakeside resort, Panajachel, and 15 other Maya villages to visit. The color and sheer spectacle of Chichicastenango's twice-weekly market is another amazing sight – this is one of the best places to purchase traditional Guatemalan textiles and crafts. There are more fascinating villages around the second city of Quezaltenango to the west. The nearby market towns are especially interesting, and include Zunil, where there is another shrine to Maximón and the heavenly hot springs of Fuentes Georginas above the village. San Francisco El Alto hosts possibly the

PRECEDING PAGES: waiting for the last boat home, on Lake Atitlán.
LEFT: the perfect peak of Volcán de Agua, overlooking Antigua.

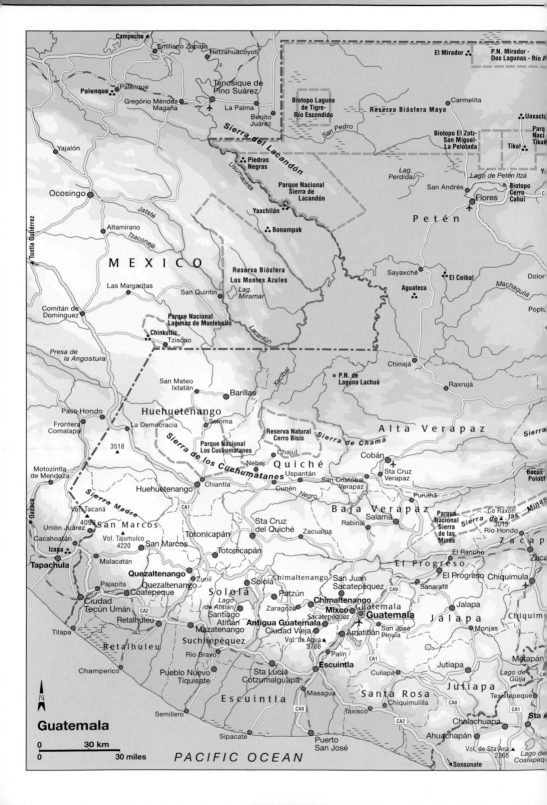

Guatemala

N

0	30 km
0	30 miles

PACIFIC OCEAN

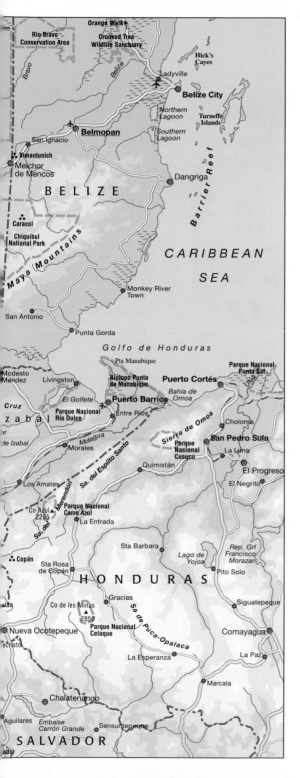

largest market in Central America every Friday; it's an essential experience if you are anywhere near Quezaltenango.

Below the highlands, the Pacific beaches are not Guatemala's best attraction, but the small resorts of Monterrico, Iztapa and Champerico are worth a visit. The coast's climate is always hot and humid, however, the hotels are not great value and the beaches are all black sand.

Heading east of the capital, there are hot springs, waterfalls and a Spanish-built fortress to see around peaceful Lago de Izabal and the momentous Río Dulce gorge. Right on the Caribbean coast, the Garífuna village of Lívingston is home to Guatemala's only black population, and the cuisine and music (reggae and punta rock) make a fascinating cultural diversion from the rest of the country. There's the alpine scenery and cave systems of the Verapaces around Cobán, a town that's fast establishing itself as Guatemala's top ecotourism destination. Not far from Cobán are the exquisite pools of Semuc Champey and the Quetzal Reserve, where there are significant numbers of this beautiful national bird. Also covered in this chapter are the first-class Maya ruins of Copán, just over the border in Honduras.

In the far north of Guatemala are the magnificent jungles and savannas of Petén, which comprises nearly one-third of the national landmass. This region was once the very heart of the Classic Maya civilization, led by the city states of El Mirador, Tikal and Piedras Negras. The delicate ecosystem is home to a plethora of exotic animals, including jaguar, tapir, toucans, and monkeys.

At the magnificent ruins of Tikal you have every chance of seeing the wildlife as well as its superb monumental architecture and carved stelae. There are hotels at the ruins or alternatively stay at the pleasant island town of Flores or El Remate, another village on the great lake of Lago de Petén Itzá. Dozens more Maya cities lie in the Petén's jungles, including the huge site of Yaxhá. An organized trip is the best way to see the more remote ruins of El Mirador, Nakbé, Piedras Negras and Aguateca. ❑

GUATEMALA CITY

Maps:
City 108
Area 112

*The capital city is mostly an ugly urban sprawl, but for all that
it offers an undeniable taste of local life in the raw,
as well as several excellent museums*

Guatemala

Though it is the political and administrative hub of the country, sights are few and there is little to attract most visitors. The city stands on the 2,000-year-old remains of Kaminaljuyú, one of the dominant Maya city states of Mesoamerica, but little of historic interest remains outside the museum rooms.

An urban vortex of humanity and traffic, Guatemala City, colloquially known as "Guate", is in most respects everything that the rest of the country is not. Plagued by pollution, the crumbling streets of the central zone are an intimidating sight for visitors. The downtown area is nearly empty after dark. In the richer suburbs in the south of the city, the atmosphere is more relaxed, but even here the bougainvillea flowers draped over middle-class homes are intertwined with razor wire, put up to deter intruders.

Nevertheless, if you want to get a real flavor of the the complexities (and inequalities) of the country, then a day or two in "Guate" is essential. Mingle with the Guatemalan élite in the Zona Viva, visit one of the many markets full of *indígenas* and *ladinos* from every corner of the country. There are three excellent museums, a cosmopolitan plethora of restaurants, bars and clubs. The climate – as the city is at 1,500 meters (4,900ft) – never gets oppressively hot.

LEFT: adding a splash of color to the Parque Central, Guatemala City.
BELOW: corn on the cob, part of the national diet.

Origins

Guatemala City ❶ is actually the country's fourth capital city, only established after a series of catastrophic earthquakes all but destroyed nearby Antigua in 1773. Yet the new capital was built close to the ruins of Kaminaljuyú, which 2,000 years ago was the most important highland Maya city, and later was allied with mighty Teotihuacán, the Mesoamerican superpower.

Today, the plazas and temples of **Kaminaljuyú** have been all but swallowed by Guatemala City's suburbs and the architectural remains in Zona 7, 3 km (2 miles) from the center of town, give no impression of the Maya city's size (around 50,000 inhabitants) and its position as a pivotal trade centre for the transportation of obsidian and quetzal feathers.

Aside from a tiny Spanish settlement, the plunging highland bowl where Guatemala City stands was unoccupied until 1773. The new capital did not develop quickly at first, but following the 1902 earthquake that decimated the rival city of Quezaltenango, Guatemala City grew rapidly and uncontrollably as waves of migrants arrived in the capital. Many are landless *campesinos* (landworkers), who have been forced to settle in totally inappropriate *barrio* shantytowns, situated tight against railway tracks and highways and on the fringes of the ravines that surround the north of the city.

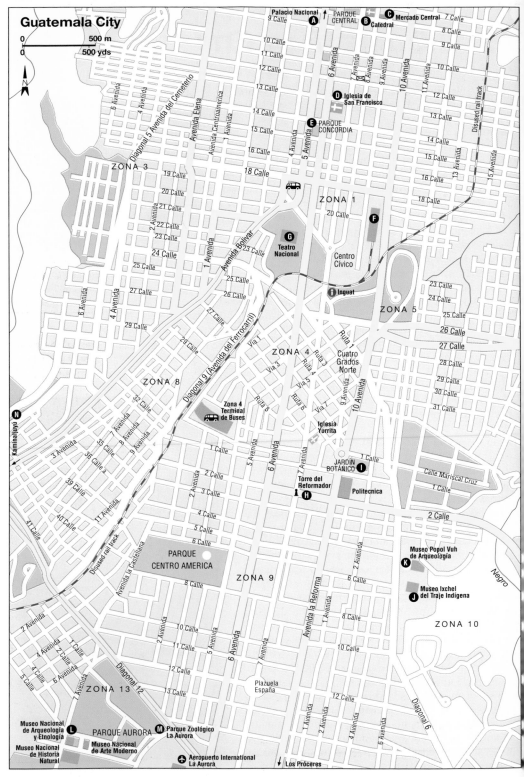

Guatemala City

0 ────── 500 m
0 ────── 500 yds

N

Palacio Nacional **Ⓐ**
9 Calle
PARQUE CENTRAL
Catedral **Ⓑ**
Mercado Central **Ⓒ** 7 Calle
8 Calle
9 Calle
10 Calle
11 Calle
12 Calle
13 Calle

6 Avenida
4 Avenida
Diagonal 5 Avenida del Cementerio
Avenida Elena
Avenida Centroamérica
1 Avenida

ZONA 3

10 Calle
11 Calle
12 Calle
13 Calle
14 Calle
15 Calle
16 Calle
18 Calle
19 Calle
20 Calle
21 Calle
22 Calle
23 Calle
24 Calle
25 Calle
27 Calle
29 Calle

6 Avenida
4 Avenida
2 Avenida

Iglesia de San Francisco **Ⓓ**
PARQUE CONCORDIA **Ⓔ**

4 Avenida
5 Avenida

14 Calle
15 Calle
16 Calle
18 Calle

13 Avenida
5 Avenida

Disused rail track

ZONA 1

20 Calle **Ⓕ**

Teatro Nacional **Ⓖ**
Centro Cívico

ZONA 8

Diagonal 9 (Avenida del Ferrocarril)
Avenida Bolívar
1 Avenida

25 Calle
26 Calle
27 Calle

Inguat **ⓘ**

ZONA 5

23 Calle
24 Calle
25 Calle
26 Calle
27 Calle
28 Calle
29 Calle
30 Calle
31 Calle

ZONA 4

Ruta 1
Ruta 2
Ruta 3
Ruta 4
Ruta 5
Ruta 6
Ruta 7
Ruta 8

Vía 1
Vía 2
Vía 3
Vía 4
Vía 5
Vía 6
Vía 7
Vía 8

Cuatro Grados Norte

9 Avenida
10 Avenida

Zona 4 Terminal de Buses

Iglesia Yurrita

32 Calle
35 Calle
36 Calle a
39 Calle
40 Calle
41 Calle

7 Avenida
8 Avenida
9 Avenida
3 Avenida
11 Avenida

Ⓝ Kaminaljuyú

JARDIN BOTANICO **ⓘ**
1 Calle

1 Calle
2 Calle
3 Calle
4 Calle
5 Calle
6 Calle

Torre del Reformador **Ⓗ**

Politécnica

Calle Mariscal Cruz
1 Calle
2 Calle

5 Avenida
6 Avenida
7 Avenida
4 Avenida

Avenida la Castellana
Disused rail track

PARQUE CENTRO AMERICA

8 Calle

ZONA 9

Museo Popol Vuh de Arqueología **Ⓚ**

Museo Ixchel del Traje Indígena **Ⓙ**

ZONA 10

Negro

2 Avenida
1 Calle
2 Calle
3 Avenida
5 Calle
6 Avenida

Diagonal 12

10 Calle
11 Calle
12 Calle
13 Calle

2 Avenida
5 Avenida
6 Avenida
7 Avenida

Avenida la Reforma

8 Calle
10 Calle
12 Calle

1 Avenida
2 Avenida
4 Avenida

Diagonal 6

ZONA 13

Plazuela España

Museo Nacional de Arqueología y Etnología **Ⓛ**
PARQUE AURORA
Parque Zoológico La Aurora **Ⓜ**

Museo Nacional de Historia Natural
Museo Nacional de Arte Moderno

Aeropuerto International La Aurora

Los Próceres

Guatemala City, in common with most capitals in the developing world, faces tremendous problems in the third millennium. The concept of civic pride has been neglected for years. The rich have long decamped to the green outer suburbs, and the central zones remain stagnant from a lack of investment and political inaction, breeding crime and decay. Despite this neglect, there are pockets of interest, but much work needs to be done before Guate becomes a rewarding place to visit.

Map on page 108

Getting your bearings

Fortunately, almost everything of interest is in five zones: Zona 1 in the north of the city; Zona 4 in the center and Zonas 9, 10 and 13 in the south. In common with most Latin American capitals, Guatemala City is organized according to the Spanish grid system: all calles run east to west and all avenidas north to south. The Parque Central in the heart of Zona 1 is the most important landmark. Other landmarks include the Centro Cívico bureaucratic buildings and the Torre del Reformador, a Guatemalan copy of the Eiffel tower in Zona 9.

To find an address, first find the zona, followed by the street and then the number. If you're given the address "10 C, 12–15, Zona 9", first look for Zona 9, then the street (10 Calle) then the number (12–15); 12 means the street is between 12 and 13 avenidas, and 15 is the number of the house.

The military has always played a dominant role in Guatemala's history.

Zona 1

Though it's now towards the north of Guatemala City, the Parque Central is considered both the heart of the city and the nation, indeed all distances are measured from here. The Parque is surrounded by some of the most historic and prestigious edifices in the country but, strangely, it's usually devoid of the energy and metropolitan bustle that define other capital-city squares except on Sundays, when it's occupied by a huge indigenous textiles market, and public holidays.

BELOW: lofty interior of the Iglesia de San Francisco.

The Parque's stone-flagged expanses are largely bare and featureless, and it's only the colossal Guatemalan flag, a giant fountain and the small eternal peace flame that relieve the monotony.

Presiding over the Parque, on the northern side, is the monumental bulk of the **Palacio Nacional Ⓐ**, built by the architect Rafael Pérez de León during the Ubico dictatorship between 1939 and 1943. The Palacio contained the presidential offices until 1998, if you visit you can take a free guided tour (in English and Spanish). The sober grey-green stone exterior belies an eclectically decorative interior of Moorish and neo-classical influences. Giant stairwell murals by Alfredo Gálvez Suárez depict an idealized history of Guatemala, and in the reception hall on the first floor a massive chandelier groans under the weight of crystal and four bronze quetzals. Don't miss the two attractive Mudéjar (Moorish) inner courtyards planted with palm trees on the ground floor. The Palacio is open daily 9am–4.45pm.

Dominating the east side of the Parque Central is the city **Catedral Ⓑ**, constructed in a mixture of baroque and neo-classical styles between 1782 and

Colorful cashews are among the many exotic fruits, vegetables and flowers sold at the Mercado Central.

1809, though its blue-tiled dome and towers were added later in 1868. It doesn't rank amongst Guatemala's most impressive churches, but its sturdy construction has at least survived two earthquakes. The somewhat austere interior contains three naves and 16 altars, some painted in gold leaf (open daily, 8am–1pm, 3–7pm; free).

Around the corner from the Catedral on 8 Calle is the **Mercado Central ©**, in an inauspicious triple-deck sunken concrete block. Though it doesn't look especially inviting, this is quite a good place to shop for textiles, leather goods, basketry and other handicrafts. If you're feeling adventurous there's a huge number of foodstalls on the middle floor serving up a range of *caldos* (stews) and snacks.

Heading south from the Mercado, the **Correo** (post office), on 12 Calle and 7 Avenida, is the next place of interest. Its great arch spans 12 Calle and the whole building is painted salmon pink.

Situated one block to the west, up on 6 Avenida, is the **Iglesia de San Francisco ©**, close to the castle-like Police Headquarters, and in the commercial heart of the city where the streets are thick with traders, food stalls and neon-lit signs. Built in 1780 in an Italianate neo-Classical style, the mortar used to construct the church consisted of milk, cane syrup and egg white. Many of the paintings and relics inside were brought from the original church in Antigua. There is a terrific collection of paintings of martyrs, and the relics include the sacred heart of Trujillo and the cork figure of Ecce Homo. A small but worthwhile museum inside the church houses the belongings of Fray Francisco Vásquez, a Franciscan friar (open daily, 9am–noon & 3–6pm).

Heading south down 6 Avenida you pass the **Parque Concordia ©**, a small

BELOW: a neon jungle dominates much of Guatemala City's skyline.

Map on page 108

green oasis with a good percentage of Zona 1's very few trees. It's popular with evangelical preachers, *limpiabotas* (shoe-shine boys), street performers, quack medicine sellers and amateur philosophers. The only other landmark in Zona 1 is the Estación, the old train station, opposite a plaza at 18 Calle and 9 Avenida. The station no longer functions, but it has been converted into the excellent **Museo del Ferrocarril** ⓕ, devoted to the history of Guatemalan railways. There are several superb old steam engines plus a small collection of classic cars.

The Centro Cívico – Zona 4

Bridging the divide between the old quarter of Zona 1 and the richer, leafy environs of Zonas 9 and 10 is the cluster of concrete buildings known as the Centro Cívico. Here you'll find **Inguat**, the tourist board HQ, housed in a large block on 7 Avenida, near the railroad tracks. Zona 4 is best known for **Cuatro Grados Norte**, the city's dynamic artistic quarter. Centered around the pedestrianized street of Vía 5, this hip area has an ever-expanding array of bars, boutiques and restaurants.

The **Teatro Nacional** ⓖ, part of the Centro Cultural Miguel Ángel Asturias, is also in this zone, set superbly above the traffic on the remains of the old Spanish fortress of San José – the ancient ramparts are still evident. The views over the city and of the surrounding mountains, including Volcán de Pacaya, are excellent. The Teatro Nacional was completed in 1978 to a radical design that has a distinctly nautical flavor; painted blue and white, with port-hole windows, reminiscent of a great ocean liner. A Greek-style outdoor theater, a small chamber-music auditorium and a small armament museum complete the complex (open Mon–Fri; grounds open to guided tours only).

TIP

Guatemala City has a certain, edgy appeal, but always take basic precautions to minimize the risk of being robbed: keep your valuables out of sight and take taxis after dark.

BELOW: the Teatro Nacional, the city's main architectural highlight.

The city museums have a vast range of superb archeological artefacts.

In the south of Zona 4, the neo-gothic **Iglesia Yurrita** on Ruta 6 is a startling sight (note the leaning spire, damaged in the 1976 earthquake).

Zonas 9 and 10

These two wealthy zonas are bisected by Avenida la Reforma, an attractive tree-lined boulevard. Zona 9, to the west, is the less exclusive of the two, with a mixed combination of businesses, mid-range restaurants and hotels. The one landmark in this part of the city is the **Torre del Reformador ⓗ**, a small-scale imitation of the Eiffel Tower in Paris, erected in honor of President Rufino Barrios (1873–85). At the southern end of the boulevard is the Parque El Obelisco, containing the obelisk commemorating Guatemalan independence.

On the opposite side of Avenida la Reforma, in Zona 10, there is much more of interest. This is the natural abode of Guatemala's wealthy elite, with a good proportion of all the city's luxurious hotels, restaurants and nightlife. At the **Jardín Botánico ⓘ** (Botanical Garden), just off the Avenida la Reforma on Calle Mariscal Cruz, there's a diverse range of nearly 1,000 species of Guatemalan plantlife, and a small museum with some stuffed birds, including a quetzal (open Mon–Fri, 8am–3pm, Sat 9am–noon; entry fee).

Top museums

Perhaps the two biggest attractions in the city are twin museums inside the verdant grounds of the Universidad Francisco Marroquín, down 0 Calle in the valley of the Río Negro. **Museo Ixchel del Traje Indígena ⓙ**, superbly set in a dramatic Maya-esque structure, is dedicated to Maya culture, especially textiles. All the exhibits are clearly presented and explained in English as well

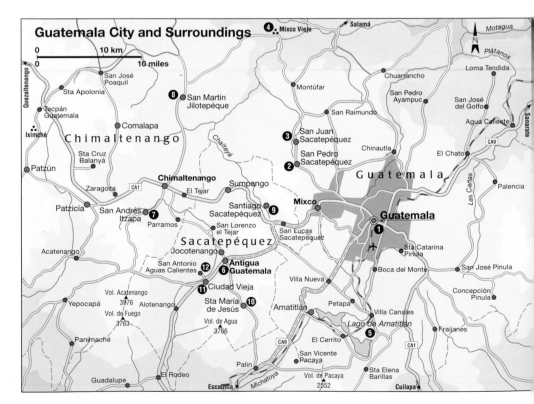

Guatemala City and Surroundings

as Spanish; it also has a good gift shop selling some unusual textiles (open Mon–Fri 9am–5pm, Sat 9am–12.50pm; entrance fee).

The **Museo Popol Vuh de Arqueología** , adjacent to the Ixchel, is another private museum with a small range of top-quality archeological artefacts arranged into pre-Classic, Maya Classic, post-Classic and Colonial rooms. Highlights include a replica of the Dresden Codex and some stunning funerery urns (open Mon–Fri, 9am–5pm; Sat, 9am–1pm; entry fee).

There are also a couple of museums worth a visit in Zona 13, just to the south (all open Tues–Fri, 9am–4pm, Sat–Sun, 9am–noon, 1.30–4pm). By far the most impressive is the **Museo Nacional de Arqueología y Etnología** (entry fee), in the Parque Aurora, which has some spectacular Maya art, costumes, masks and jade artefacts. Spend an hour or two at the **Parque Zoológico La Aurora** ⓜ, close by, where you'll find plenty of endemic wildlife, and even elephants, tigers and lions, all looking quite healthy (open Tue–Sun, 9am–5pm; entry fee).

Around Guatemala City

Heading northwest of the capital, along Calle de San Juan Sacatepéquez, you pass close to the ruins of **Kaminaljuyú** ⓝ, once one of the most important cities of the Maya World, and believed to be one of the very first centers where writing developed. It's now reduced to an inauspicious collection of grassy mounds, and the best of Kaminaljuyú's fine pottery and stone carvings can be seen in the capital's museums (open daily 9am–4pm).

Continuing further out of the city, you pass through the Maya villages of **San Pedro Sacatepéquez** ❷ and **San Juan Sacatepéquez** ❸, both sharing a prestigious weaving tradition and the same market day – Friday, when they come alive, particularly the larger San Juan, where the women wear striking *huipiles*.

Some 28 km (17½miles) from San Juan Sacatepéquez are the ruins of **Mixco Viejo** ❹, the former capital of the Pokoman Maya. The site, comprising nine temples and two ball courts, has been well restored, forming a dramatic setting on flat-topped ridges surrounded by steep ravines (open daily 8am–5pm; entry fee).

About 30 km (18½ miles) to the south of Guatemala City, following the Carretera del Pacífico, is one of the most beautiful lakes in Guatemala, **Lago de Amatitlán** ❺. Unfortunately, its waters have been polluted for years and are not safe for swimming, though hundreds of city-dwellers still flock here at weekends to splash about. For a less threatening dip, take a boat trip to one of the numerous thermal pools scattered close to the shore.

High above the lake is **Volcán de Pacaya**, one of the most active volcanoes in Central America, which has been in a state of almost constant eruption since 1965. Pacaya is an astonishing sight, especially at night when the finest sound and light show in Guatemala can paint the sky orange with great plumes of lava and gas. Go to a reputable tour agency in Antigua or Guatemala City to arrange transport and a guide to see the spectacle (going alone is not advised as robberies and assaults have been reported; see the Travel Tips section, page 349, for contact details). ❑

Maps:
City 108
Area 112

TIP

The Museo Ixchel has a superb collection of *huipiles* complete with explanations about the weaving process and the importance of Maya symbolism in the colorful patterns and designs.

BELOW: kite festival in Santiago Saquetepéquez, near "Guate".

ANTIGUA

The colonial charm of this tranquil city and its setting amid forest-clad volcanic peaks make it one of the most popular tourist destinations in Guatemala

Maps:
Area 112
City 117

Serene, civilized **Antigua ❻**, the former capital, is the most beautiful city in the entire Maya region. The attractions are outstanding. Primarily, there is the vast legacy of stunning colonial architecture. The city's compact size (population around 35,000) is another factor – walking the almost traffic-free cobbled streets is a pleasure and the pace of life is easy-going. The city's inhabitants, Antigüeños, are an outward-looking and cultured bunch, well-used to playing host to visitors from overseas. Enhancing the cosmopolitan atmosphere, hundreds of people from all over the world have been seduced by Antigua's charm and the temperate climate and settled in the city to run European and North American-style restaurants, cafés and bars.

The setting is also spectacular, in a beautiful, broad highland valley where the hills are thick with pine trees and even cloud forest on the upper slopes, interspersed with coffee plantations and small *milpas* (cornfields). Even higher, above the tree line and enveloping the city, are three giant cones: Volcán de Agua, which destroyed the first Guatemalan capital; Volcán de Fuego, active and smoking plumes of gas; and slumbering Volcán Acatenango, the largest but least threatening of the trio.

LEFT: looking over Antigua, toward Volcán de Agua.
BELOW: the Arco de Santa Catalina.

Disaster and destruction

Few cities anywhere in the world can claim such a cataclysmic history, founded on disaster and punctuated by periods of glory and seismic destruction. Antigua was actually the third capital of Guatemala. The Spanish first settled close to the modern town of Tecpán, near the ruins of their allies, the Kaqchikel Maya, at Iximché, but quickly moved to set up a permanent capital near the town of Ciudad Vieja in 1527. Disaster soon struck here, though, and after torrential rain, a massive mudslide from nearby Volcán de Agua destroyed the settlement and killed the widow of Alvarado the conquistador. The site chosen for the third capital, in the Panchoy valley just 5 km (3 miles) away, is where Antigua stands today.

The city we know today as Antigua, originally called Santiago de los Caballeros de Guatemala, grew steadily after it was founded in 1543 to become the most important city in the Americas between Mexico City and Lima. Prestigious political and municipal buildings were constructed and a wave of religious orders moved in and added churches, monasteries, convents and schools. Bishops and wealthy merchants commissioned imposing palaces. A printing press, only the third in the Americas, was installed in 1660. A university was established in 1681. Yet the entire colony was underpinned by a complex apartheid system that divided the population into rigid social

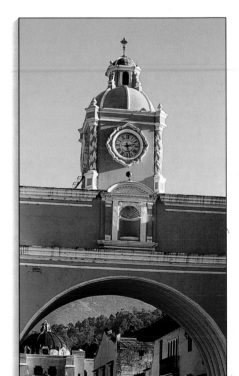

Antigua's Churches

A ntigua's numerous churches are, to many visitors, the most dazzling jewels in this colonial city's crown. They are characterized by a unique, "squat-baroque" architectural style, with immensely-thick walls, supported by colossal foundations and giant buttresses, which were developed in a futile effort to resist the perpetual tremors that have plagued the city since it was founded in 1543.

The fledgling capital city was all but destroyed by a series of earthquakes between 1585 and 1586. More tremors shook the city in 1607, 1651, 1681, 1684, 1689, 1702, 1717, 1751, 1765 before the final ruinous quake of 1773 precipitated the evacuation of Antigua and the establishment of the new capital, Guatemala City. Immediately before the 1773 earthquake, Antigua had been a thriving city of some 75,000 inhabitants.

Ironically, the destruction of 1773 saved the city: the subsequent abandonment prevented the ruined city from the ravages of industrialization, shoddy construction and the inevitable population boom, which have tainted all other Latin American capitals.

Structurally, 21st-century Antigua is almost entirely an 18th-century city. A few earlier details have survived, but the dominant style is Iberian-American Baroque, a supremely pictorial, decorative and flamboyant style that's expressed on virtually all Antigua's church façades. It's also called Churrigueresque, and not to everyone's taste. The Maudslays, who wrote *A Glimpse at Guatemala*, based on visits in the late 1890s, the height of the Victorian Gothic revival, considered it vulgar, garish and ostentatious. But at its best, as witnessed at the recently-restored La Merced, or at Santa Cruz, the depth, fluidity and theatrical nature of Antiguan Baroque is astounding – undeniably grandiose, with dreamy façades embellished with astonishing detail.

These remarkable façades were created by applying layers of plaster over the exterior masonry, a technique called *ataurique*. The masonry itself was a humble mix of tamped-earth and brick, which was always given a lime-based plaster finish. Little stone has ever been used in Antigua – the local basalt rock is extremely hard to quarry and shape.

The sheer number of ecclesiastical buildings in Antigua is amazing, there are over 30 within a few blocks of the Parque Central. By the mid-17th century, all the main denominations and many more minor ones were established in the city. The religious orders were possibly the greatest power in Central America: free from taxation, granted huge swathes of the most productive land where sugar, tobacco, wheat and, most lucratively, cochineal and indigo were farmed.

The orders were also allocated vast numbers of Maya labourers to work in the fields and construct the grand edifices of the capital. These laborers managed to implant indigenous imagery onto some of the great church façades: corn cobs (sacred to the Maya) at La Merced and the white waterlily (a vision-quest hallucinogenic) at San Francisco. ❑

LEFT: the spectacular façade of La Merced, the most ornate church in Antigua.

classes: Spanish-born whites, Guatemalan-born whites, *mestizos*, mulattos, African-born slaves and Mayans at the bottom of the heap.

Santiago expanded further following the 1717 earthquake, which demolished many weaker buildings and necessitated the strengthening of those remaining. Many of Antigua's colonial structures date from this period, built in an uniquely "squat baroque" style with colossal walls in an attempt to resist future seismatics. The city prospered again until 1773, its population growing to around 75,000, when a six-month long series of tremors all but crippled the capital. Damage and disease epidemics forced the government out of the city and the king of Spain ordered the city to be evacuated in favor of a new capital (Guatemala City) some 45 km (28 miles) away in the valley of Ermita.

Antigua was never completely abandoned however, as the fertile hillsides around the old capital proved perfect for the production of cochineal dye and later in the 19th century, coffee. Wealthy enthusiasts renovated colonial mansions, such as Casa Popenoe *(see page 120)* and middle-class Guatemalans again repopulated the city. Today, Antigua is one of the most international cities in the Americas and the most prosperous place in Guatemala. It's estimated that at least 80 percent of its economy is dependent on the booming tourist trade and language school industry.

Map on page 117

Antigua is a thriving center for Spanish language schools.

The Parque Central

The heart of Antigua is the Parque Central, the delightful main square, popular night and day with locals and visitors who come to snack, chat and soak up the atmosphere. The parque is bounded on all four sides by imposing, graceful colonial buildings that represented the epicentre of the Spanish empire in Central

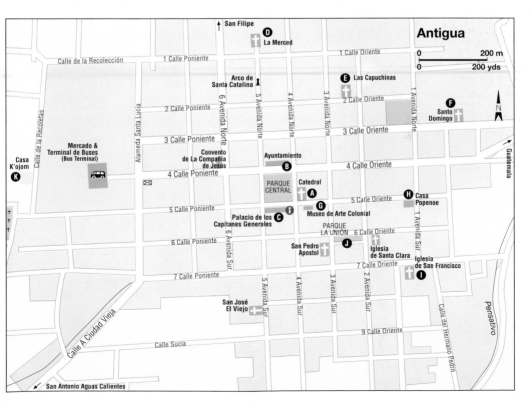

Bust of Fray Bartolome de Las Casas, outside the church of La Merced.

America for more than 200 years, now occupied by local government offices and museums. Note the risque fountain in the centre of the square.

The **Catedral Ⓐ**, on the east of the square, dates from 1669, though it was built above the ruins of an earlier building that dated back to 1543. The Catedral survived the 1717 earthquake, but was all but reduced to rubble after the 1773 tremors. What's left today is only about half of the original building, which had a 21-meter (69-ft) dome, twin belltowers, three naves, eight domed bays and measured almost 100 meters (328 ft) in length. Inside the Catedral sparkled in a riot of tortoiseshell, marble and bronze. Now the building is much more perfunctory, with half of the original in ruins to the rear and the interior relatively bare. Below the Catedral are several crypts and the remains of the Royal Chapel, and supposedly the remains of many historic figures, including Pedro de Alvarado, Francisco Marroquín and Bernard Díaz de Castillo.

Situated on the north side of the square is the **Ayuntamiento Ⓑ**, the city's municipal offices, with its twin-deck façade of solid-stone arches built in a Tuscan style. This has changed little in appearance since it was built in 1740, surviving both the 1773 and 1976 earthquakes.

The Ayuntamiento houses two museums, the **Museo de Santiago** (also known as the Museo de Armas), where there is a collection of colonial art and artefacts, as well as some weapons dating back to the days of the conquest, including Alvarado's sword and Maya clubs. Next door is the small **Museo del Libro Colonial**, dedicated to publishing, where there is a replica of the first printing press in Central America, and a collection of colonial books. Both of the Ayuntamiento museums are open Tues–Sun 9am–4pm, and both charge entry fees.

Facing the Ayuntamiento on the other side of the parque is the **Palacio de los**

BELOW:
public washing area outside the Iglesia Santa Clara.

Capitanes Generales , occupying the whole of its southern side, again built over an earlier civic construction. The two-story colonnade building dates from 1761 and originally extended back to cover the whole block behind. The building survived the 1773 quake, but was cannibalized to provide building material for the new capital in Guatemala City. The site was the nucleus of power in Central America for over two centuries, the home of the colonial rulers and also the Courts of Justice, the Mint, a prison and barracks. Now the Palacio holds the tourist office (Inguat) and the headquarters of the local police force.

The west side of the square has much less historical interest, its polyglot occupants currently include several stores, Café Condesa, an evangelical church, numerous cookshacks and two good bookshops.

North of the plaza

From the plaza, heading up 5Avenida Norte, you'll immediately notice the Arco de Santa Catalina – one of the great Antiguan landmarks. The arch was built in 1693 to connect the convent of Santa Catalina to orchards and gardens on the other side of the street so that the nuns could cross the street without fear of contamination by the outside world. The arch was later restored in the nineteenth century. Continuing up 5 Av, you'll soon reach a small plaza at the junction with 1 Calle Poniente, and the church of **La Merced** , whose "wedding cake" façade is the finest in all Antigua, recently restored and painted a fantastic shade of yellow with white detail. Inside at the end of the south nave is the figure of Jesus Nazarene, sculpted by Alonso de la Paz in 1650, and in the ruins of the adjacent cloisters a fountain that's said to be the largest in Central America.

Perhaps the most evocative of all Antigua's ruins, **Las Capuchinas** , also

Map on page 117

TIP

You can get an excellent bird's eye view of the city from the neaby Cerro de la Cruz hill (*picture on page 114*). Robberies have been reported up here however; tell the tourist police, office on Av Norte, just off the main square, and they will accompany you.

BELOW: the Romanesque Good Friday procession.

BELOW: colorful carpet, with offerings of food, inside La Merced during Holy Week.

lie in the north of the city at 2 Avenida Norte and 2 Calle Oriente, set in beautiful gardens (open Tues–Sun 9am–5pm; entry fee). The Capuchin order was an extremely severe splinter group of the Franciscans: nuns were permitted no contact at all with the outside world. The unique (and intriguing) feature at Las Capuchinas is the Torre de Retiro (Tower of Retreat), a circular courtyard of 18 tiny cells – it's not certain what its function was exactly, but possible uses include a retreat cloister or an isolation sick bay.

One block to the south and two to the east on 3 Calle Oriente is **Santo Domingo ⑪**, once a monastery, now a luxury hotel and cultural center. The site given to the Dominicans in 1541 was the largest occupied by any religious body, and the monastery grew to become the wealthiest order in the city, also starting up a college for the study of theology, philosophy, art, Latin and – Mayan language, which in 1676 was established as the University of San Carlos. The monastery was reduced to rubble in 1773, but a superb restoration has transformed much of the site, though the outer buildings remain in ruins.

South and east of the plaza

Just off the parque, on 5 Calle Oriente is the **Museo de Arte Colonial ⑫** (open Tues–Sun; entry fee) sited in the old premises of the University of San Carlos, which has now moved to Guatemala City. The university only occupied this site for ten years between 1763 and 1773, but the building did survive the earthquake of that year, leaving its Moorish-style patio intact. The museum is arguably less interesting than the building, but there are paintings of the life of St Francis of Assisi by Villalpando and Christ Passion by Tomás de Merlo.

Two blocks further down 5 Calle Oriente, at the junction with 1 Avenida Sur, is the **Casa Popenoe ⑬**, an exquisite and immaculately restored colonial mansion that dates from 1634. It's the attention to detail of the restoration that's most impressive here, a project that Dr Popenoe of the United Fruit Company and his wife Dorothy Popenoe commenced from ruin and rubble, and which involved scouring Antigua for the correct period paintings (which include one of Pedro de Alvarado himself), fabrics and furnishings (open Mon–Sat, 2–4pm; entry fee).

The **Iglesia de San Francisco ⑭**, situated around the corner on 1 Avenida Sur, is another mighty church. It is most noticeable for the tomb and shrine of Hermano Pedro de Betancourt, a teacher-friar who tirelessly cared for the sick, street children and the poor and established hospitals and convalescent homes. Pope John Paul II made the friar Central America's first saint in 2002.

Today hundreds of Guatemalans visit his shrine to ask for his help and he is credited with many miracles, as the plaques on the wall testify. Don't miss the extensive ruins (open daily; entry fee) behind the church.

To get back to the parque from here, return by the **Parque la Unión ⑮**, a small plaza where indigenous women from all over the highlands gather to sell and weave textiles. At the east end of the plaza there's a large *pila* (wash house) still in use, and Santa Clara, the site of a church and a convent which was founded in 1699 by nuns from Puebla, in Mexico, becoming popular with ladies who desired a little extra comfort after taking their vows. Facing Santa Clara across the plaza is San Pedro Apostol which was built as a hospital and church.

Maps:
Area 112
City 117

To the west of the plaza

Leaving the Parque Central down 4 Calle Poniente, you pass the remains of the Convento de La Compañía de Jesús on the corner of 6 Avenida Norte, which currently houses a cultural center. At the end of the road is the busiest, most "Guatemalan" part of town where you'll find the main *mercado* (daily), the terminal de buses, and a row of stores. This is the noisiest part of town, the air thick with diesel fumes, the streets packed with villagers from the surrounding region.

Around Antigua

There are some fascinating sights in the stunning countryside of pine trees, coffee bushes and volcanoes around Antigua, and many interesting villages; both indigenous and ladino. It's best to explore the area as a series of day and half-day trips, using Antigua as your base.

Aguardiente *liquor is often given as an offering to Maximón.*

To the north of Antigua, on the road to Chimaltenango, you pass through the village of Jocotenango, almost a suburb of Antigua, where you will find the impressive Centro La Azotea (open Mon–Fri 9am–4.30pm, Sat 9am–2pm; entry fee). One half of this center contains a museum, the **Casa K'ojom** (House of Music), which has an incredible wealth of musical recordings, instruments and information about Maya musical traditions. Next door is an organic coffee *finca*, which has guided tours of the plantation. Regular minibuses leave Antigua's 4 Calle Oriente for the Centro La Azotea.

BELOW:
a marimba band.

Heading north from Jocotenango, the next place of interest down a dirt road before you reach the Interamericana, is **San Andrés Itzapa** ❼, where there is a Tuesday market, but also a shrine to the pagan saint of Maximón *(see page 123)*. This Maximón (or San Simón) is particularly interesting because he attracts a primarily ladino clientele, especially prostitutes. It's customary to light a candle or two in Maximón's chapel, to ask for good fortune, but if you want to take things further, pay one of the cigar-smoking women attendants for a *limpía* (soul cleansing) which involves you both drinking *aguardiente* liquor and getting thrashed by a bundle of herbs. Maximón's abode is open daily, 6am–6pm.

North of the Interamericana there are three more villages worth a visit. **San Martín Jilotepéque** ❽ is a pleasant place with an excellent Sunday market, with beautiful local *huipiles* and good value weavings for sale. It's 19 km (12 miles) north of the regional capital, Chimaltenango, from where there are local buses to the market, but which is of little interest itself. At Comalapa to the west, there is a long-established tradition of *primitiva* (folk art) painting, with plenty of artwork on sale locally and also the spectacular crumbling baroque façade of the village

Map on page 112

church. Market day is on Tuesday in Comalapa. Heading in the other direction towards Guatemala City along the Interamericana highway, the village of **Santiago Sacatepéquez ❾** is famous throughout Guatemala for its giant kites, constructed by the villagers every year to be flown on the Day of the Dead (November 1). The kites, which can be up to 7 meters (23 ft) in diameter, are flown in a symbolic act to release the souls of the dead. At other times of the year there's much less going on, but there is a market (Tuesdays and Sundays) and a small museum full of pottery and figurines.

To the south of Antigua there are three main villages of interest. Set on the northern shoulder of the Volcán de Agua, **Santa María de Jesús ❿** is the most traditional Maya village in the vicinity. It's a scruffy place, but the base camp for hikers should you want to climb Agua. The trail is easily followed and takes around five hours to the summit. On the northwest flank of the Agua volcano is the village of **Ciudad Vieja ⓫**, site of the second Guatemalan capital, which was devastated by a vast mudflow in 1541, killing Alvarado's widow, Doña Beatriz de la Cueva, who had been made ruler of Central America for all of two days. There's little to see in the village now except a fine church that dates from the 19th century and nothing left of the former capital, whose center was actually 2 km (1 mile) to the west.

Textile enthusiasts may want to head for **San Antonio Aguas Calientes ⓬**, just 2 km (1 mile) from Cuidad Vieja, which is the premier weaving center in the Antigua area. The sprawling village is mainly Maya, and is the base for a number of different collectives and stores selling textiles from all over the country, some of which also give weaving lessons. The local *huipil* design combines floral and geometric patterns on a predominantly red background. ❑

BELOW: Volcán de Agua, towering over Antigua, is the easiest to climb of the nearby volcanoes.

CLIMBING THE VOLCANOES

The three spectacular volcanic peaks near to Antigua, Volcán de Agua, Volcán de Fuego and Volcán Acatenango, can all be climbed, offering unrivalled views of the surrounding landscape.

The easiest of the three is Volcán de Agua (3,763 meters/ 12,346 ft). You start from Santa María de Jesús, heading uphill from the plaza, past the cemetery and out of the village, up a well-marked path that crosses a road, which goes most of the way to the top. At the summit there is a shelter (often full overnight) and a small chapel, but it gets bitterly cold at night. In total, the walk takes most people 4–6 hours up, and 2–4 hours down.

The adjacent Fuego (3,763 meters/12,346 ft) and Acatenango (3,976 meters/13,045 ft) volcanoes are a much more serious challenge altogether and Fuego should only be attempted if you are an experienced hiker and conditions are favorable. The climb for both starts from the village of Soledad, southwest of Ciudad Vieja; it takes a full day to ascend Acatenango, and Fuego is at least a 12-hour hike.

For all three walks, you need to wear warm clothing and proper climbing boots are recommended. Ask at the Antigua tourist office about organized trips with climbing clubs and agencies (*and see Travel Tips, page 344*).

The Maximón cult

The pagan-Maya cult of Maximón or San Simón is the most enigmatic in Guatemala. Its origins are obscure, but it's generally accepted that he is a mischievous, evil saint, a powerful figure who can impregnate women, confront Christ, cure illnesses and bring all sorts of misfortune to his enemies. He's said to be a combination of Judas Iscariot, the conquistador Pedro de Alvarado and various Maya deities.

Though the cult of Maximón is widespread through the highlands of Guatemala, his physical appearance is remarkably consistent. At first sight he's a comical figure, a stunted statue with a wooden face that's unmistakably *ladino* in appearance, with stumpy legs and arms, a hat, a cigar in his mouth and draped in scarfs and a towel or two to soak up alcohol spillage. He's surrounded by a bevy of attendants who ensure his appetite for *aguardiente* liquor is satisfied and his cigars are regularly lit. Maximón's house is truly a den of iniquity: a smoky abode where the air is thick with candle and tobacco smoke and the floor littered with empty bottles and spittle.

The three best known Maximón chapels are at Zunil, San Andrés Itzapa and Santiago Atitlán, though many other highland villages share the cult – every village around Lago de Atitlán has its own figure. At Zunil (*see page 135*), near Quezaltenango, Maximón can often be seen wearing sunglasses and sporting a bandana, buccaneer-style. The San Andrés Itzapa Maximón entices hundreds of devotees daily, largely *ladinos,* who come to seek cures from maladies and protection from their enemies. The walls are covered with plaques from all over Guatemala, and even Mexico and El Salvador, acknowledging his help. Uniquely, the San Andrés Maximón is especially popular with prostitutes.

In Santiago Atitlán, the Maximón cult involves a highly charged, symbolic confrontation with an image of Christ every Good Friday. To the sound of drums and a mournful brass band, Christ emerges from the colonial Catholic church, carried by the faithful, with hundreds crowding the plaza. The tension reaches fever pitch until Maximón appears, supported by his *telinel* (bearer), from a neighboring chapel and faces Christ across the plaza, a challenge that mirrors the conflict between the Maya *costumbristas* (traditionalists) and Catholic Action (mid-20th century orthodox priests) for Santiago's hearts and minds.

It's essential to respect local etiquette when visiting Maximón – be careful not to offend local sensibilities. Maximón actually moves from house to house every year or so (except at San Andrés Itzapa), so you'll need a guide to take you to his current residence – plenty of children will offer to escort you there for a quetzal or two. Buy a small bottle of Venado or Quezalteca liquor to give to quench Maximón's thirst and a cigar or two for him to puff on. Before you enter Maximón's chapel greet his keepers and pay them a dollar or two to enter, and, crucially, ask their permission to take a photograph (which may be refused). ❑

RIGHT: the San Simón/Maximón shrine in Santiago Atitlán.

THE WESTERN HIGHLANDS

*This is the heartland of the Guatemalan Maya,
a place of living traditions amid the most beautiful
landscape in the whole country*

Map
on page
126

The rugged mountain scenery and the absorbing Maya culture alive in the western highlands are the apex of most visitors' experience in Guatemala. The natural setting really is awesome, epitomized by the chain of volcanoes that strides through the heart of the land. There is Lago de Atitlán, one of the most beautiful lakes in the world, the Cuchumatanes mountain range to the north, the hot springs and market villages around Quezaltenango.

This landscape would entice tourists anyway, but these highlands are also the heartland of Guatemala's Maya. The strength of indigenous culture is all-apparent in the peoples' costume, fiestas, religious practice and language – a dozen different tongues (plus Spanish) are spoken in these mountains. If you can, get to a fiesta *(see box, page 135)* to see one of the many often somber, sometimes joyous, and always acutely symbolic Maya dances. Visit all the markets you can: the spectacle of Chichicastenango, the tranquility and hushed tones of Chajul, the frenetic hustle and commerce of San Francisco El Alto.

Lago de Atitlán

Of all Guatemala's natural attractions, perhaps the most beautiful is the volcanic *caldera* of **Lago de Atitlán ❶**, and its unforgettable highland setting that has seduced travellers for centuries. Its various bays and inlets give the lake an irregular shape, but it measures about 19 km (12 miles) long by 12 km (7½ miles) at its widest point. Atitlán is transcended by three towering volcanoes, its shores are dotted with Maya villages, and its 305-meter (1,000-ft) deep waters conjure up a spectrum of shifting color changes. Even Aldous Huxley was overwhelmed, describing the lake as the most beautiful in the world.

Of all the 13 lakeside villages, Panajachel is the place that most people head for first, though in the last few years a number of excellent hotels and lodges have mushroomed all around the shores of the lake. While Panajachel has a superb selection of restaurants and hotels, each of the 13 lakeside villages has its own character and appeal. Santa Cruz is supremely peaceful and relaxing, San Pedro is a backpacker haven, there's traditional Santiago Atitlán and the "new age" center of San Marcos. Santa Catarina and San Antonio Palopó are different again, both villages specializing in textile weaving.

Gringotenango

Panajachel ❷, on the lake's northern shore, is where most people stay. Dubbed *Gringotenango* by the locals because of the heavy influx of tourists and the high density of Westerner-owned bars and cafés, "Pana" has become something of a boomtown in

LEFT: Volcán San Pedro, framed by foliage.
BELOW: glorious sunset on Lake Atitlán, seen from Panajachel.

Pana attracts an intriguing mix of "new agers" and traditional artisans.

recent years. It is the only lakeside village where tourism really dominates the economy. Yet, despite the vast lakeside kasbah of *típica* textile shops and stalls and the dozens of hotels, restaurants and cafés, Panajachel remains a pleasant place to relax and a good base to explore the rest of the lake. There are no sights in the town itself to see; Pana's appeal is all about its position overlooking the lake and volcanoes and its inimitable laid-back atmosphere. Transport connections are also superb, with regular buses and shuttles running up to the Interamericana and a flotilla of boats linking Pana with the other lakeside villages.

Back in the 1960s, Panajachel was Guatemala's hippie mecca, and Atitlán a legendary place where ley lines were said to meet and the lake was a "vortex energy field". This hippie consciousness has never quite left Panajachel, surviving dark days of the civil war, and today the town remains a magnet for a greying tribe of new agers clad in tie-dyes and *típica*s (Westernised traditional clothing) who run many of the cafés and export businesses in town. Westerners apart, Panajachel is a Kaqchikel Maya and ladino town.

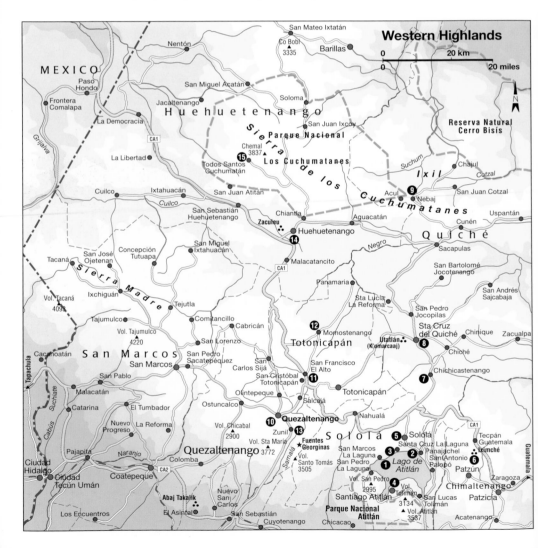

The north shore of the lake is sparsely populated, road-free and the perfect place to head for some real relaxation. The first place the boat heading west to San Pedro stops at is **Santa Cruz La Laguna ❸**, the main village high above the water, while its shoreside hotels, popular with independent travellers, make this an excellent base for hiking and scuba diving. More lodge-style hotels have been constructed in Jaibalito and Tzununá, the next two tiny, very traditional settlements – ideal if you seek some isolation.

At **San Marcos La Laguna**, a larger village, the dense foliage has been left in an aromatic tangle of jocote, banana, mango and avocado trees and there's a meditation-yoga center, and some excellent budget and mid-range hotels. There's not much to see or do in San Pablo, the next village, but you may want to drop into the weaving co-op run by the village women of San Juan la Laguna, close by – it's signposted from the dock. **San Pedro La Laguna**, a short distance beyond San Juan, attracts the second greatest number of tourists after Panajachel, almost all young backpackers, creating perhaps the most distinctively bohemian atmosphere anywhere in the Maya region. Suitably, the hotels and restaurants here are some of the cheapest in the country, and if you plan to climb **Volcán San Pedro** this is the ideal base for an early-morning start.

A road runs around the east side of the lake, connecting Pana with two more interesting villages. **Santa Catarina Palopó**, the first place, 4 km (2½ miles) from Pana, is famous for its weavings. You'll see the turquoise and purple *huipiles* at markets all over the highlands. There's not much to see in the village itself, though as ever the volcano views are magnificent. **San Antonio Palopó**, another 5 km (3 miles) from Santa Catarina, shares a fine weaving tradition; here many men also wear *traje* (traditional dress) – interestingly both the men's and women's shirts are nearly identical. There are many workshops in the village, though the villagers can be a little pushy in an effort to sell their weavings as you walk up to the fine colonial church.

Sacred Shrine of Maximón

Continuing around the lake, on the south side is San Lucas Tolimán, the least interesting of the villages, but the best place from which to climb either of the nearby Atitlán or Tolimán volcanoes. Ask at your hotel or the town hall about hiring a guide, which is recommended as some paths are difficult to follow. Much more interesting is Santiago Atitlán ❹, a Tz' utujil Maya village on one of the lake's inlets around the western flank of Volcan Tolimán, 30 minutes from Pana by fast lancha boats. A shrine is kept here to Maximón (see box, page 123), part evil saint, part pagan idol, said to be a combination of San Simón, Judas Iscariot and Pedro de Alvarado, the conquistador. Any young Atiteco will guide you to his abode for a quetzal, it's customary to make a donation for his upkeep. The two other points of interest are a small weaving museum to the left of the dock, and the Catholic church. Inside this imposing colonial structure there's a giant altar and a memorial to Father Stanley Rother, an American priest who served in the village between 1968 and 1981, and who was murdered here in 1981 by a paramilitary death squad.

Map on page 126

TIP

If you're in Santiago Atitlán at Easter, on Good Friday there is always a symbolic confrontation in the plaza between Jesus Christ and Maximón.

BELOW: farmer from Santiago Atitlán, overlooking the lake.

The History of Lake Atitlán

The region around Lago de Atitlán has probably been volcanic in character for at least 12 million years, when a colossal cauldera, much larger than the present lake, extended several kilometers, further to the north. More eruptions around nine million years ago then formed another slightly smaller bowl-shaped cauldera, the walls of which can still be seen to the west of Panajachel around San Jorge la Laguna.

Lago de Atitlán's present outline is the result of a third volcanic explosion 85,000 years ago. This eruption blocked all access to the sea, so that the three rivers that tumble into the newly-formed crater formed today's vast, high-altitude lake, some 1,562 meters (5,125 ft) above sea level.

Further volcanic energy then threw up the three huge cones, – Atitlán,Tolimán and San Pedro, which ring today's lake's waters. The

final addition to the scene is the small cone called Cerro de Oro, which sits on the south side of the lake between the villages of San Lucas Tolimán and Santiago Atitlán on the slope of the much larger Tolimán volcano.

The Maya probably first visited Atitlán around 2000 BC, as they formed small farming and fishing communities just to the south along the Pacific littoral.

There's little evidence that Lago de Atitlán was an important center in Preclassic or Classic times, but by the times the first Europeans arrived in 1523 the lake was inhabited by Tz'utujil' and Kaqchikel Maya. Today there is nothing left of the old Tz'utujil capital Chuitinamit, which was on the lower slopes of the San Pedro volcano, but legend has it that the city's gold and silver were buried in the small cone of Cerro de Oro or "Hill of Gold".

During the colonial period, Santiago Atitlán was the most important village on the lake, as its fine church from that era testifies, because of its position on the edge of the highlands and access to the Pacific.

In the last hundred years, the environment, economy and character of the lake has radically changed. Firstly a new road from Sololá was completed in the 1930s. By the late 1960s the road had turned the previously sleepy lakeside village of Panajachel into a legendary hippie tourist retreat. Then in the 1970s, the lake environs became a battleground, as guerrillas and the Guatemalan army fought a protracted war on the volcanic slopes. Terrible atrocities were committed by the military, especially in Santiago Atitlán, where there was a large base.

The great challenge for the new millennium is to safeguard the lake's environment, which has been ravaged in recent years by population pressure (over 100,000 people now live around its shores), over-exploitation of land, and the effects of tourism. Fields are being planted higher and higher up the hillsides, the waters are increasingly tainted with pesticide and sewage, and hundreds of new holiday homes have been built. The Atitlán grebe, a flightless bird once endemic to the lake, is now extinct, its chicks all eaten by the black bass, a predatory fish that was introduced in the 1950s for sportfishing. ❑

LEFT: the calm waters of Lake Atitlán.

The market at Sololá

Close to Lago de Atitlán are a number of other fascinating places, the nearest is Sololá ❺, just to the north of the lake. Unusually, Sololá has parallel Maya and *ladino* governments and is one of the largest indigenous towns in Guatemala. Despite its proximity to Atitlán, Sololá is bypassed by most travelers, leaving the huge Friday market almost wholly a local affair. The town itself is pretty unremarkable, but on market day the whole place erupts in a frenzy of activity as traders and villagers besiege the plaza and surrounding streets. You can't help but gawk at the iridescent local costume, worn by both sexes, though the men's outrageous "space cowboy" shirts are especially eye-catching.

Some 28 km (17 miles) east of Sololá are the ruins of **Iximché** ❻, former capital of the Kaqchikel Maya, who were allies of the Spanish. The ruins (in common with the remains of all the highland Maya cities) are not large in scale, consisting of a few pyramids, plazas and ball courts. But the setting is beautiful, surrounded by stunning highland countryside, and the ruins are still used as a place of Maya worship. Iximché is open daily 8am–5pm; entry fee.

Just 3 km (2 miles) away, the town of Tecpán was the first ever Guatemalan capital (1524–26), but there's nothing here today to hint at this illustrious past.

Quiché: the Maya heartland

North of Sololá is the mountainous department of Quiché, stretching from Chichicastenango northward as far as the Mexican border. As the name suggests, this is the heartland of the two million or so K'i che' Maya, the most numerous Maya group in Guatemala. Quiché has had a long history of bloodshed; from the days of the conquest when, in 1524, Alvarado's men massacred Maya warriors

Women and girls in Santiago Atitlán wear a headdress, called a tocoyal, *made of a long strip of cloth wound around the head.*

BELOW:
market day crowds, Chichicastenango.

after a final battle at K'umarcaaj, near Santa Cruz del Quiché, to the horrors of the "scorched earth" policy of the 1980s, when thousands of Maya civilians were massacred in a series of paramilitary operations. The department is crossed by several mountain ranges and travel to the Ixil Triangle in the north is a long slog, taking up to three hours from Santa Cruz del Quiché on poor roads.

Chichicastenango

Turning off the Carretera Interamericana at the Los Encuentros junction, you enter Quiché department along a winding road, plunging down into river valleys, through pine forests, then zig-zagging upwards to dizzying passes. After some 20 km (12½ miles), you'll reach **Chichicastenango ❼**, a quiet highland town with an intriguing past that has become one of the chief tourist destinations of the highlands. Twice a week, the normally calm "Chichi" hosts the most famous market in the entire Maya region, coming to life in a maelstrom of furious commerce. From the dead of night every Thursday and Sunday, traders arrive to set up their stalls by candlelight and by daylight the roads into town are crammed with trailers, trucks and *camionetas* (buses). The market is probably the best place in the country to buy *típica* textiles and handicrafts – short of venturing to their place of origin – if you have your haggling skills well-honed.

Sitting pretty in the main plaza, the whitewashed **Iglesia de Santo Tomás** is an overwhelming sight, the air around the crecsent-shaped stone steps thick with the sweet, smoky aroma of smoldering pine-based incense called copal. The church, dating back to 1540, is one of the most fascinating in all Guatemala, a place where Maya religious traditions have long been tolerated and fused with Catholicism. Enter by the side door (the front door is reserved for priests and *cofrades* – religious officials). The atmosphere inside is magical on Sundays, the aisles and the altar packed with Maya families and groups softly praying. Candles, *aguardiente* liquor and flowers are offered at different platforms spread around the church, each dedicated to the souls of the deceased. Photography is not allowed inside the church.

As you leave (again though the side door) the neighboring building holds the former monastery where, in about 1702, a Spanish priest, Francisco Ximénez, first discovered the *Popol Vuh*, the K'i che' bible, containing their story of creation involving the hero twins – it's considered one of the great literary masterpieces of the pre-Columbian Americas. On the south side of the main plaza is the **Museo Rossbach**, with an interesting collection of pre-Columbian ceramics and jade (open daily except Tues, 8am–noon, 2–4pm; entry fee).

The smaller church opposite Santo Tomás is El Calvario, another hallowed place where incense is burned and prayers offered.

There's another sacred site on a hill just outside Chichi: **Pascual Abaj**, where sacrifices and flowers are regularly offered to the *Idolo*, a blackened pre-Columbian sculpture. It's a 20-minute walk from the plaza: go up 9 Calle, and across a stream. Then follow the signs through the yard of a workshop making wooden masks and continue up into the pine forest.

"There is the original book and ancient writing, but he who reads and ponders it hides his face."

– FOREWORD FROM THE POPOL VUH

BELOW: maize ready for storage in Nebaj, Ixil Triangle.

Santa Cruz del Quiché

Heading north some 15 km (9 miles) from Chichicastenango, the next stop is **Santa Cruz del Quiché ❽**, the departmental capital. The town of Quiché is not especially interesting and there's little in the way of cosmopolitan distraction except for a pizza parlor or two and a row of unappetising cake shops on the west side of the plaza. Best to head straight out of town to **K'umarcaaj** (also called Utatlán), the former capital of the K'i che' Maya, 4 km (2½miles) southwest of the plaza. Like all the highland Maya capitals, K'umarcaaj is set superbly in a defensive position, surrounded by pine trees and ravines, and the ruins are low-rise and lack initial impact. Yet this is the fortified capital where Pedro de Alvarado and the conquistadors burned alive two K'i che' kings in 1524 and sealed their control of the highlands.

Today K'umarcaaj remains an active site for Maya religious ceremonies and prayers, especially beneath the grassy plaza, where a long tunnel leads to an underground chamber. Maya priests frequently come here to pray, burn incense and candles and offer liquor. As you approach the tunnel, if you hear prayers it's best to keep some distance; and be careful if you decide to explore inside, some of the side tunnels end abruptly and plunge into oblivion. Take a flashlight or ask to borrow one from the site caretaker.

East of Santa Cruz del Quiché, a good road passes through a string of small villages in the foothills of the Sierra de Chuacús for some 54 km (34 miles) to the market town of **Joyabaj**. There is an excellent Sunday market here and one of the best *fiestas* in the country in the second week of August. Dances performed include the Palo Volador, a kind of Maya bungy jump, where men jump off a maypole and spin to the ground with a rope attached to their feet.

Map on page 126

The Ixil Triangle costumes are some of the most beautiful you'll see in all Guatemala.

BELOW: cornfields in a highland valley.

The Ixil Triangle

One of the most compelling regions of the highlands, the Ixil Triangle is an extremely traditional and beautiful area that also saw some of the bloodiest conflicts of the civil war during much of the 1970s and 1980s *(see page 81)*. Now the war is over, the Ixil Triangle (Ixil is the language spoken in these parts, triangle refers to the three main towns of Nebaj, Chajul and Cotzal) is again welcoming a steady trickle of visitors, especially hikers.

Getting to the Ixil involves a bone-jarring three hour journey from Santa Cruz del Quiché, via the interesting town of **Sacapulas**, an ancient salt-producing center on the banks of the Río Negro, where there is a fine colonial church and the reasonable Restaurante Río Negro. From Sacapulas, a lofty dirt road snakes eastwards towards Uspantán, and then on to Cobán in Alta Verapaz. There is little of interest in Uspantán, but the Maya Nobel Peace Prize laureate Rigoberta Menchú grew up in the mountains north of the town and many chapters in her two-volume autobiography *(see page 83)* are set here.

Nebaj ➒ is the largest of the Ixil towns, set dramatically in a broad green valley that's encircled by steep-sided ridges. The first thing you'll notice is the startling costume worn by the Ixil women, arguably the finest in the entire Maya region: incredibly tightly-woven white, green and red *huipiles* and waist sashes, scarlet *cortes* (skirts) and Medusa-like headdresses of fabric and colorful woolen pom-poms. By contrast, most men are dressed in bland second-hand *ropa americana* (US clothing sold in the market), but on festival days colonial-style scarlet jackets are worn. Check out the market for its colorful bustle, but you'll find better prices for textiles at the cooperatives in the main plaza or from the women who regularly visit the town's *hospedajes* to sell their wares.

There's an imposing colonial church in the plaza, but otherwise there is little else of architectural interest to see in Nebaj itself. The hill-walking is tremendous, however. One hike takes you to the "model village" of **Acul**, a strategic hamlet two-hours' walk from Nebaj, where villagers were resettled under pressure from the military during the civil war. Continuing through the village, just the other side you'll come to the Finca San Antonio, a beautiful Italian-Guatemalan farm where some of the best cheese in the country is made, and for sale. The two tour operators in Nebaj can organise many more terrific treks, including trips to the area around Cocop, and Salquil Grande *(see Travel Tips, page 349)*.

The other two Ixil towns are an hour or so away by bus or pickup from Nebaj. If you decide to go, try and travel on a market day when there is more to see and more traffic. Chajul's market days are Tuesdays and Fridays, Cotzal's are on Wednesdays and Saturdays. **Chajul** is the more interesting – and traditional – of the two villages, a scruffy but beautiful place dominated by the massive white basilica in the main plaza. The Chajul women also wear an elaborate costume of scarlet skirts, *huipiles* woven with images of animals and birds, pom-pom accessories, and earrings threaded with old coins.

Cotzal (officially San Juan Cotzal), the third town, is the least traditional of the trio, with a higher number

The Spanish attacked Nebaj and burnt it to the ground in 1530; captive "rebels" were branded and sold into slavery.

BELOW: colonial façade in downtown Quezaltenango.

of *ladinos* and more Spanish spoken. It's also set in a lovely valley, beneath the Cuchumatán mountains, and again it's a sleepy place best visited on market days. It has one simple pensión, and the pharmacy sometimes rents out a room.

Maps:
City 133
Area 126

Quezaltenango and around

Southwest of Quiché, beyond the small department of Totonicapán, is the department of Quezaltenango, with its chief city of the same name, located high (over 2,300 meters/7,500 ft) in a mountain range. Also Guatemala's second city, **Quezaltenango ⑩** (population 135,000) for centuries rivaled the capital as the country's most important business, banking and cultural city, even declaring itself the capital of an independent state in 1820. By the 20th century, Quezaltenango (also known as Xela – pronounced Shella – from its Maya name Xelajú) was an impressive city, its wealth boosted by its pivotal position as a center for the coffee trade and a direct railtrack to the Pacific port of Champerico. But the stately architecture and theaters were all but destroyed by a colossal earthquake in 1902, and ever since Quezaltenango has been relegated to second division provincial status as a capital of the highlands, devoid of metropolitan swagger, but retaining a friendlier, less frenetic character.

Evenings and early mornings can be chilly in this high-altitude city, especially around Christmas. Looming above the buildings is the majestic Volcán Santa María, the most perfectly proportioned cone in Guatemala.

The heart of the city, the **Parque Centroamérica ④**, holds an an impressive assortment of buildings, including some fine-looking banks, the Municipalidad (city hall), the cathedral and in the center of the square a strange visual cocktail of neo-Grecian columns and stone benches. The **Catedral ③** is a mod-

TIP

San Andrés Xecul, about 8 km (5 miles) to the northeast of Quezaltenango, has a stunningly colorful church that is claimed to be the oldest in Central America.

BELOW: dazzling details of the church of San Andrés Xecul.

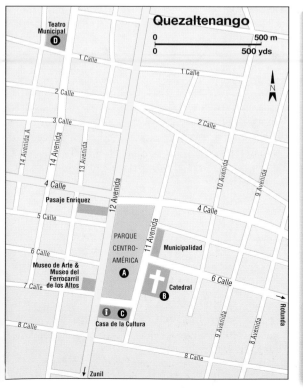

Baskets of red-hot chilli peppers are a common sight in many of Guatemala's highland markets.

BELOW: the misty lower slopes of the Cuchumatanes mountain range.

ern concrete building, with only the façade remaining of the original. The Bishop of the Highlands, an important post, is stationed here. Inside the cathedral is an image of El Padre Eterno (The Eternal Father) housed in a silver case. The **Casa de la Cultura ⒞**, on the south of the square, harbors the Tourist Office, exhibits about the city's history and the **Museo de Historia Natural**, where there's an assortment of stuffed creatures, as well as some impressive pre-Colombian artefacts (open Mon–Fri, 8am–noon, 2–6pm; Sat, 9am–1pm; entry fee). Almost next door is the **Museo de Arte** (same hours) with a moderate collection of modern material. Take a look at the fine shopping arcade, the Pasaje Enríquez, in the northwest corner of the square as well – for years it was very run down, but is now looking a little healthier thanks to the popular Salon Tecún bar. Away from the Parque Centroamérica, there is little to see in the center of town, though the **Teatro Municipal ⒟**, at the end of Avenida 14, on the corner of 1 Calle, is another stolid neo-colonial edifice. The theater faces a plaza, which contains various busts of local artists, including Guatemala's first Poet Laureate, Osmundo Arriola (1886–1958).

Unlike the city itself, there is much of interest in the countryside around Xela. Going north of Xela for 17 km (10½ miles) up a steep hill, you come to the village of **San Francisco El Alto ⑪**, which hosts the biggest market in the entire Maya region (and probably Central America). The Friday morning market is a wonderful spectacle, and a real assault on the senses, as thousands of traders descend on the small village to buy and trade everything from honking hogs to fine fabrics. Textiles are bought here to be sold around the country, and some good bargains can be found, also in the town's many textile shops. Most of the market is given over to fruit and vegetables;

however, for a bird's-eye view of the action, pay the main church's caretaker one quetzal to climb up to the roof.

A further 19 km (12 miles) from San Francisco is another famous market town, **Momostenango** ⓬, this time specializing in *chamarras* (woolen blankets) and carpets. Some good quality textiles can be bought here, especially at its Sunday market. Momostenango is also a center for Maya religious study, with many shamans working here, attracting students from all over Guatemala.

Ten kilometers (6 miles) southeast of Xela is **Zunil** ⓭, another traditional K'i che' Maya village, where there is a shrine to Maximón, a Monday market and a good weaving cooperative close to the plaza. The village economy is based on the cultivation of vegetables, which thrive in the rich volcanic soil. From Zunil a steep road leads to **Fuentes Georginas**, a beautiful natural hot spring spa. Perched on the lush slopes of the Volcán Santo Tomás, it is smothered by dense foliage of ferns, moss and plants. There are seven rustic cabins and a simple restaurant.

The Cuchumatanes

In the far west of the country, the highland scenery becomes even more dramatic, dominated by the blunted peaks of the Cuchumatanes mountains. Above Huehuetenango there's a huge high-altitude plateau known as the *altiplano*, a dauntingly inhospitable environment where trees are stunted by the cold and little else will grow. In the valleys, the warmer climate permits a limited amount of corn, vegetables and some fruit to be grown, but only enough to sustain a small population and many villagers are forced to leave and look for work elsewhere in the country or, increasingly, in the United States.

The Cuchumatanes have always been an isolated region – the Spanish had

Maps:
City 133
Area 126

Momostenango means "Citadel of the Altars," after the many altars found around the town, and reflecting the long-standing religious devotion of many of the townspeople.

BELOW: a merry band on their way to the fiesta at Todos Santos Cuchumatán.

TODOS SANTOS' FIESTA

At the end of every October, *Todosanteros* (men from Todos Santos Cuchumatán) return to the village from all over Guatemala – and even from the United States – to celebrate the festival of All Saints (Todos Santos), which is probably the most famous in the country.

The festivities start the week before the horse race, which takes place on November 1 (All Saints' Day). Music and dancing is held on 31 October, in the costume of the next day's race. Riders, most of whom have been drinking hard liquor all night, must circumnavigate a course around the town, stopping to take another swig of *aguardiente* after each lap. The "race" in reality becomes a comical stampede, with the drunken jockeys urging their long-suffering steeds like demons possessed. The winner is the one who survives, still on his mount; all the riders gain considerable kudos, however, just for taking part.

On the next day, appropriately "the day of the dead", everyone moves to the cemetery for a day of eating, more drinking, and commemorating the lives of their dearly departed. Marimba bands play in the town center for days, and in the cemetery itself on November 2. Many traditional dances are performed, including the dance of the conquistadors. Absolute bedlam!

Traditional head-dresses are obviously not used just for decorative purposes.

little interest in the area, and the inhospitable terrain has helped shield the over-whelmingly Maya inhabitants from changes that have affected villages closer to the Interamericana. In many villages, the Maya Haab and Tzolkin calendars are still observed by prayer keepers. Travel in the mountains is tough, hotels and restaurants are simple, but the spellbinding scenery is apt compensation.

Gateway to the mountains

The first port of call for visitors to the Cuchumatanes is **Huehuetenango** ⓮, a pleasant town that's both a transport hub and a departmental capital. The main sight, however, is **Zaculeu**, Maya ruins 5 km (3 miles) from the center of "Huehue." Zaculeu was the capital of the Mam nation, one of the main tribes that confronted the Spanish. The former capital, like the other highland Maya centers, was well-fortified and the Mam held out for six weeks before they sur-rendered. Unfortunately, Zaculeu was insensitively rebuilt in 1947, the temples covered in an unsightly stucco finish. Despite this, it is still worth a visit – the ruins are surrounded by ravines, providing tremendous views, and there's also a small museum on site (open daily, 8am–noon, 1pm–6pm; entry fee).

North of Huehue a single road clings to the massive southern flank of the Cuchumatanes, passing a lookout point after 12 km (7½ miles) where, if it's clear, you can pick out the chain of volcanoes that rises over the epic Guatemalan highland landscape. About an hour and a half from Huehue the terrain tempers a little and the flat, chilly *altiplano* lands beckon. Continuing down this road you pass through the villages of San Juan Ixcoy and Soloma (where there are *hospedajes*) and then to San Mateo Ixtatán, possibly the most interesting place on this isolated road. The circular design of the women's

BELOW: the pick of the tomato crop at San Francisco El Alto's market.

huipiles worn here is one of the most striking in Guatemala: a multi-colored star-like emblem woven upon a white background (*see Textiles feature on page 138*). Visit the village on its market days (Thursday or Sunday), when you can buy textiles much more cheaply than in Huehue.

Todos Santos Cuchumatán

The one village in the Cuchumatanes that draws a trickle of tourists is **Todos Santos Cuchumatán** ⑮, some 50 km (31 miles) north of Huehue, a magical place that has a few basic hotels and a language school, but which is most famous for its three-day *fiesta* (*see box, page 135*). Apart from this, the twin attractions are the sublime setting in a canyon-like valley beneath the 3,837-meter (12,589-ft) peak of Chemal and the purity of Mam Maya culture here – it's extremely rare to see any Todosanteros not wearing traditional costume. The women wear beautiful purple and navy *huipiles* that are some of the most tightly woven in the country, but it's the men who are the real peacocks – they wear an almost outrageous outfit of candy-striped trousers and thick cotton shirts with huge, flapping pink collars. Both sexes wear similar straw hats.

The countryside around Todos Santos is perfect for some challenging hikes, including one route which takes you out of town, south past the minor ruins of Tojcunanchén, up on to the spine of the Cuchumatanes and on to the equally traditional Mam village of San Juan Atitán, six hours' walk away. The men in San Juan wear a strikingly distinct costume: red cotton shirts with elaborately embroidered collars and cuffs, "short-long" white pants and leather sandals almost identical to those worn by the ancient Maya. From San Juan Atitlán, pickups return regularly to the relative civilization of Huehuetenango. ❑

Map on page 126

TIP

There are two language schools in Todos Santos Cuchumatán. Nuevo Amanacer teaches the local Mam language as well as Spanish. Summer residential courses are offered, for US$100–125.

BELOW: the men outdress the women in Todos Santos Cuchumatán.

RAINBOW COLORS OF GUATEMALAN COSTUME

Visit the markets and villages of the Guatemalan highlands and you will be dazzled by the glowing colors of the costumes worn by the Maya

The most beautiful textiles in Guatemala are the traditional clothes Maya women make for themselves and their families.

The most intricate weavings are made on simple hip-strap looms identical to those used by the ancient Maya, which consist of nothing more than a series of sticks. The vertical foundation threads (the warp) are suspended between the two end-rods, one of which is tied to a post and the other to the strap which passes round the weaver's hips to control the tension. The remaining sticks are used to separate the layers of warp yarns, to interlace the horizontal (weft) threads with the warp to form the ground weave, and to beat the woven threads together.

MATERIALS

Cotton is still the most commonly used fiber, although it is now in the process of being replaced by brightly colored, shrink-resistant acrylic yarns, which started taking over from wool in the 1960s. Very little cotton thread is hand-spun today. Metallic threads and artificial silks are very popular as they give the weavings a luxurious look.

▷ MIXED MOTIFS
Maya weavers and embroiderers draw from a wide range of designs, using sacred and secular images, both ancient and modern.

△ CHANGING FASHIONS
Highlanders express themselves through dress as they wear the latest fashions to church and on special occasions.

▽ MULTIPURPOSE *TZUT*
Women wear the square-shaped *tzut* on the head as a sunshade, slung across the shoulder, or as a wrap during festivals.

▽ SPINNING YARNS
The age-old practice of hand-spinning cotton has, for the most part, given way today to a vast array of commercially produced threads and yarns.

▽ COTTON COLORS
Brown and white varieties of cotton are grown in Guatemala – the scarcer brown is normally used for ceremonial garments.

◁ WARP AND WEFT
Through the continued use of the hip-strap loom, Maya women preserve the tradition of hand-weaving their own costumes.

△ TOURIST TRADE
Tourist items, such as the friendship bracelets being made here, represent an important supplement to the family income.

◁ FEAST OF COLOR
A dazzling row of hand-woven and embroidered belts on display at a market stall in the village of Chuarrancho.

△ SATIN STITCH
A few communities embroider their clothing with eye-catching designs, such as this one from San Mateo Ixtatán.

DESIGNS AND MOTIFS

Highland costumes are decorated with a wide range of bird, animal, and plant motifs as well as geometric forms, some are recalled from memory, without the use of patterns. Some motifs, such as the horse, peacock and chicken, are obviously post-Conquest as these animals arrived in the Americas with the Spaniards. Other animals such as deer, coyotes and double-headed birds figure in Maya mythology. The largest variety of such designs are found in the beautiful *tzuts* (multi-purpose cloths) of Santa María de Jesús, near Antigua. Today's artisans widen their range of designs by drawing from picture books and life around them. However, older designs are often preserved in ceremonial textiles. Tree, doll and lyre motifs decorate many skirts. These patterns are traditionally produced by a dye-resistant method known locally as *jaspe*.

THE PACIFIC COAST

Guatemala's longest coastline does not have the beaches to compete with the Yucatán, but it does have some interesting nature reserves and a few unusual archeological sites

Map on pages 142–43

Guatemala

G lance at a map of Guatemala, and the 300-km (190-mile) long Pacific coastline might appear to be the perfect place to chill out, swim and relax. But if you're dreaming of palm-fringed beach resorts, gourmet seafood and tropical cocktails, try the Caribbean. Guatemala's Pacific coast is the engine room of its agricultural economy, a humid strip of land that's almost entirely dominated by vast *fincas* devoted to sugar cane, cattle ranching, cotton and bananas, with coffee the main crop in the higher altitudes.

Attractions are few and far between. The beaches are all black sand, the climate is fiercely hot and humid, the few hotels and restaurants tend to be disappointing and the sea is plagued by a dangerous undertow that makes swimming treacherous. Most of the towns in the region are featureless, and there is little to detain you in comparison to other parts of Guatemala and the Maya region.

Yet between the vast cattle ranches and sugar plantations, there are important archeological remains of the Pipil culture at Takalik Abaj and in numerous sites around the town of Santa Lucía Cotzumalguapa. There are the colossal stone heads in La Democracia. The scale of these sites can't compete with the temples and pyramids of the Petén and Yucatán but some of the stelae and sculpture is fascinating. Parts of the original rich coastal ecosystem of mangroves and forest has survived, especially around Monterrico, one of the nicer places on this coast, and also a good place to see nesting sea turtles and abundant bird life.

Running parallel to the coast is Guatemala's fastest highway, the Carretera del Pacífico, and it's simple to get around this route by bus. To really explore the region, however, you'll need your own transport as many of the Pipil sites, and all the beaches, are a considerable distance off the highway.

From El Salvador to La Democracia

The border town of Ciudad Pedro de Alvarado is a quiet crossing, with most of the traffic between the two countries using the quicker San Cristóbal Frontera route to the north. Tourist attractions are limited in this remote corner of the country, but close to the tiny settlement of Las Lisas is the superb Isleta de Gaia hotel. Pressing on down the Carretera del Pacífico, there's a spectacular section of the road with the volcanoes Moyuta and Cruz Quemada defining the highlands to the north.

The Carretera del Pacífico bypasses the town of **Chiquimulilla ❶**, 48 km (30 miles) from the Salvadorean frontier, but if you need a break the town is quite interesting as it's an important center for the cattle ranch industry with a number of specialist stores selling superb leather goods. Taxisco is the next town, a nondescript place, but it's here where a branch road

LEFT: vast sugar cane fields still fill the landscape on the Pacific coast.
BELOW: colorful doorway in Retalhuleu.

Several species of sea turtle lay their eggs on the beaches in protected reserves along the coast near Monterrico.

leads to **Monterrico ❷**, probably the nicest place on the entire coast to spend a day or two. To get to Monterrico you'll have to cross the Chiquimulilla canal, which inconveniently separates the beach from the hinterland along much of the coast. Regular ferries (which can take cars) make the connection from the village of La Avellana.

Monterrico Nature Reserve

Much of the wetlands around Monterrico are protected as part of a national nature reserve, the **Biotopo Monterrico-Hawaii**, which forms an important habitat for herons, egrets and migratory birds, iguana, alligators, opossums, raccoons and anteaters. It's the three species of sea turtle that nest on these shores that makes Monterrico really special, however. The East Pacific Black turtle (up to 1 meter/3 ft in length) and Olive Ridley (reaching over 1 meter/3 ft) nest here between July and November, and the Leatherback (reaching over 2.5 meter/8 ft) between mid-October and February. All the turtles crawl ashore at night to lay their clutch of 80–100 eggs, a laborious effort that sends the turtles into a trancelike, exhausted state.

Despite the protected status of the reserve, egg collectors comb the beaches at night, seeking out nesting turtles and stealing the eggs, which are considered an aphrodisiac in Central America and which fetch a good price. Conservationists have set up two hatcheries on this section of the beach, however, and have had some success in persuading the egg collectors to donate a proportion of their cache. The collected eggs are protected until they hatch, when the baby turtles are released into the ocean. Some 10,000 baby turtles are released annually, though it's estimated only a few dozen of these will reach maturity and return to nest at

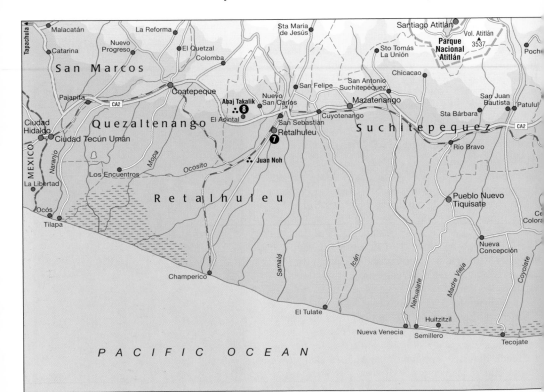

Monterrico. There are a number of hotels in Monterrico for all budgets, though the restaurant selection is mediocre. As is the case all along this coast, take care if you want a dip as the ocean is savage and prone to a strong undertow.

Chapín Safari Park

Back on the Carretera del Pacífico, heading west toward Mexico, the **Parque Auto Safari Chapín ❸** is a popular attraction at Km 87.5, with a diverse range of wildlife, both endemic (jaguar and tapir) and foreign (hippos and giraffes). There's a swimming pool here (open Tues–Sun, 9am–5pm; entrance fee). Escuintla (population 95,000) is the next town on the highway, an ugly, sprawling place that's an important center for agri-commerce, with plenty of cheap hotels and restaurants, but with no esthetic or cultural merit.

Evangelical bumperplate ("God is my driver").

From Escuintla a fast road runs south 38 km (23½ miles) to the formerly bustling **Puerto San José ❹**, the most popular "resort" on the entire coast, though this is entirely due to its proximity to the capital – the place itself is somewhat rundown. Around Puerto San José there are several other places that are more inviting. Just to the east, past the container port, Puerto Quetzal, the upmarket enclave of Likín is a sanititized private beach-dom for the Guatemalan oligarchy, while further east (12 km/7½ miles from Puerto San José), Iztapa has plenty of character, a more easy-going atmosphere but a limited choice of hotels.

To continue onwards to Monterrico, you'll have to cross the Canal de Chiquimulilla (there are regular ferries) from Iztapa – it's 25 km (15½ miles) down a paved road. To the west of Puerto San José, Chulamar is another resort geared to the capital's richer inhabitants, with a fine stretch of black sand beach and a hotel or two.

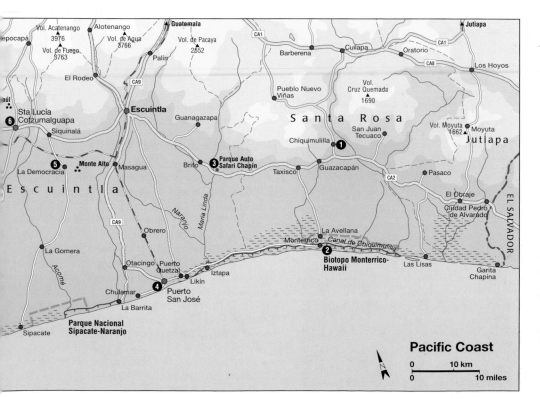

Pacific Coast

Map
on pages
142–43

TIP

If you feel in need of a cooling dip, spend a few hours in the sleepy resort of Champerico, south of Retalhuleu – but watch out for the dangerous undertow.

BELOW: inscrutable features of a stone head at La Democracia.
RIGHT: trucker's siesta time.

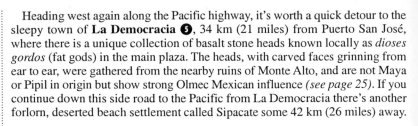

Heading west again along the Pacific highway, it's worth a quick detour to the sleepy town of **La Democracia ❺**, 34 km (21 miles) from Puerto San José, where there is a unique collection of basalt stone heads known locally as *dioses gordos* (fat gods) in the main plaza. The heads, with carved faces grinning from ear to ear, were gathered from the nearby ruins of Monte Alto, and are not Maya or Pipil in origin but show strong Olmec Mexican influence *(see page 25)*. If you continue down this side road to the Pacific from La Democracia there's another forlorn, deserted beach settlement called Sipacate some 42 km (26 miles) away.

Santa Lucía Cotzumalguapa to Mexico

There are more interesting Pipil archeological remains grouped around the town of **Santa Lucía Cotzumalguapa ❻**, some 17 km (10½ miles) west of La Democracia. Here the sights are spread out in the sugar cane fields that surround the town, and to explore them all you'll need your own transport, or hire a taxi in the main plaza. The Pipil weren't great temple builders, but astonishingly adept sculptors, carving from basalt (volcanic) stone. The nearest sculptures, the Bilbao stones (known locally as *las piedras*), are just to the north of the town; dozens more have been removed over the centuries and smuggled out to museums in Germany and elsewhere.

Just to the north of Santa Lucía Cotzumalguapa is **El Baúl**, a ceremonial center atop a small hill that's still used actively by Maya shamans – incense and candles are burned and occasionally a chicken sacrificed. There are two sculptures at El Baúl: one stela of a human figure crowned with a dramatic headdress and inscribed with the date "8 deer" (equivalent to AD 36); the second a giant stone head bearing a huge grin, its face blackened by centuries of candle wax and copal (pine resin incense). At the third site, nearby at the Finca El Baúl, there's a good collection of more carvings, and more stone heads inside a small museum that's open in daylight hours (open daily, free entry). Finally, take a look at the small museum attached to the Finca Las Illusiones, 2 km (1 mile) from the town center, just off the Carretera del Pacífico, where there are more stelae, Olmec-style carvings and some pottery.

Retalhuleu and Abaj Takalik

Back on the highway, heading west to Mexico another 94 km (58½ miles), the road passes through a collection of dull lowland towns before the turnoff for **Retalhuleu ❼**, usually shortened to "Reu" (pronounced "RAY-oo"). Reu is a civilized place as far as the Pacific coast goes, with an attractive, shady plaza, a relaxed air, and a good Museo de Arqueología y Etnología (open Tues–Sat 8am–5.30pm; entry fee), which is full of historical photographs and anthropomorphic figurines.

West of Reu, near the small village of El Asintal, is **Takalik Abaj ❽** (open daily 7am–5pm; entry fee), probably the most important ruins on the entire coast – though the Maya and Olmec-style temples have not survived well and lack visual impact. The stelae and altars are much more interesting and there is also a small but worthwhile museum. ❑

THE EAST

The main attractions of this varied region are the superb carved stelae of Quiriguá and Copán, a quetzal reserve, and the fascinating Caribbean coastal culture

Map on page 148

Eastern Guatemala only attracts a slim slice of the country's burgeoning tourist industry, a region that most visitors hurry through on their way to the ruins of Petén or Copán, just over the Honduran border. Yet there is plenty of interest here, most obviously the extreme juxtaposition of landscapes: desert, wetlands, both arid and humid mountain ranges, lowland jungle, tropical coastline and even (this being Guatemala) a volcano or two. Creditably, a network of protected reserves has been established to safeguard these remarkable ecosystems, and the unique habitat of species like the manatee and the quetzal, the national bird – but this reserve status is all too often poorly enforced.

This chapter covers a vast swathe of land, divided into three distinct regions: the twin departments of Alta and Baja Verapaz, to the northeast of Guatemala City; the huge department of Izabal, which encompasses the Caribbean coast and Lago de Izabal; and finally the dry mountainous departments of Chiquimula, Zacapa, El Progreso and Jalapa, known locally as "El Oriente."

Its population is as diverse as its landscape: most people are *ladinos*, but there are a number of Maya speakers (mainly Q'eqchi') and also a few Garífuna people on the coast. This is a sparsely-populated area, overwhelmingly agricultural, and devoid of a single city. Cattle ranching, bananas and tobacco dominate the lowland economy; coffee and cardamom are the most important highland crops.

Historically, the Motagua River that flows through the heart of the region to the Caribbean Sea was a crucial trade route. Close to the banks of the Motagua were the largest jade deposits in the entire Maya area, contested and controlled by the Maya settlements of Quiriguá and Copán (*see page 156*). Today the ruins of both sites are essential visits for their astonishing sculptural remains.

Leaving the capital down the busy Carretera al Atlántico, the only major route to the region (and to Petén and Belize), the scenery is an uninspiring deforested landscape of scrub bush that gradually gives way to succulents and cereus cacti. There's no reason to stop until the El Rancho junction, from where a good sealed road climbs into the Verapaz highlands and towards the town of Cobán.

The Verapaces

The twin departments of Baja and Alta Verapaz (*vera paz* = "true peace") were the last part of Guatemala to fall under Spanish control (apart from Flores) such was the ferocity of opposition from the indigenous Achi tribes, and dominance was only established in 1538 after a successful "softly-softly" approach pioneered by a group of Dominican priests led by Fray Bartolomé de Las Casas.

LEFT: the Maya cities of Quiriguá and Copán contain some of their finest carved stelae.
BELOW: the Castillo de San Felipe, Río Dulce.

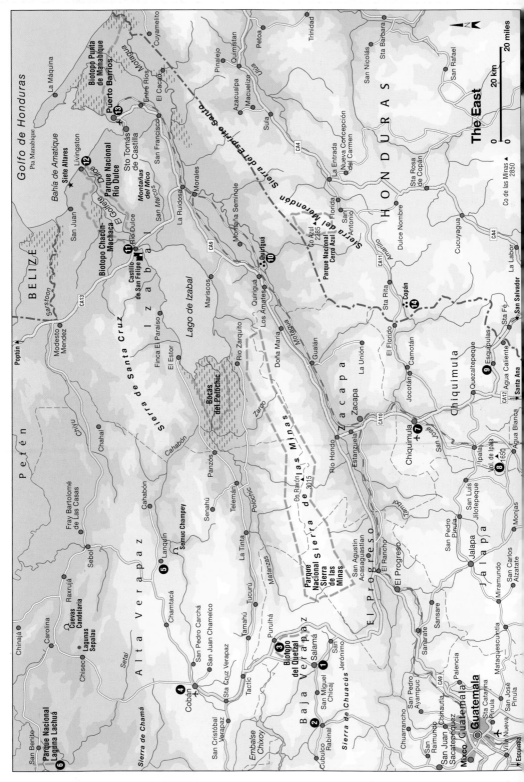

The East

Golfo de Honduras
Pta Manabique

BELIZE

HONDURAS

Petén

Alta Verapaz

Baja Verapaz

Izabal

Zacapa

El Progreso

Chiquimula

Jalapa

Sierra de Santa Cruz

Sierra de Chamá

Sierra de las Minas

Parque Nacional Sierra de las Minas

Sierra del Merendón

Sierra del Espíritu Santo

Lago de Izabal

Bahía de Amatique

Guatemala
Mixco

San Salvador

Santa Ana

20 km
20 miles

The Verapaces contain some of the most beautiful scenery in the country, at places almost Swiss alpine in appearance; a large spread of cloudforest home to the elusive quetzal; some of the world's best coffee-growing country and the fascinating market towns of Cobán, Salamá, Rabinal and Cubulco.

Map on page 148

Historic Salamá and Rabinal

Salamá ❶, the first of the towns in Baja Verapaz and also the capital of the department, lies some 60 km (37 miles) northeast of Guatemala City. The scenery around the town (altitude 940 meters/3,084 ft) is a delightful mix of productive pastoral land (everything from oranges to olives are grown) and extensive pine forests. It is an historic place set in a wide river valley with an excellent Sunday market. The 17th-century colonial church in the plaza is an absolute gem, with no less than fourteen gilded altars, and there's a rather dilapidated old colonial bridge on the edge of town, now only used by pedestrians. There are a few, good-value places to stay here, as well some reasonable restaurants.

Situated a further 19 km (12 miles) west is **Rabinal** ❷, the town where the leader of the Achi tribe accepted Bartolomé de Las Casas and his Christian priests. It also has a fine colonial church, and another superb Sunday market that's a good place to buy *artesanías* (handicrafts), especially ceramics. About a kilometer (half a mile) north of Rabinal are the unreconstructed Achi ruins of Cahrup – there's not too much to see but it makes a pleasant place for a picnic. The final town out this way is Cubulco, famous for its July 25 fiesta, where the Palo Volador, a Maya-style bungee jump, is performed.

Statue of Manuel Tot, revolutionary Maya leader, from Cobán.

BELOW: shrine near the church of El Calvario, Cobán.

Quetzal reserve

Baja Verapaz's other attraction is situated just to the south of Purulhá, off the Cobán highway, where an area of dense cloudforest has been declared a quetzal reserve, the **Biotopo del Quetzal** ❸ (open daily, 6am–4pm; entry fee). The quetzal, once the spiritual talisman of the Maya lords, now Guatemala's national bird, is a beautiful but notoriously elusive creature that is now very rare throughout Central America (*see page 99*).

The reserve (also called the Biotopo Mario Dary, after its founder, a conservationist who was murdered in 1981 whilst fighting to protect the area from loggers) is a permanently humid patch of forest thick with ferns, epiphytes, moss and lichen. Dawn is the best time to spot a quetzal, which feasts on the fruit of the aguacatillo (wild avocado) tree, but if you're lucky there are at least another 87 species of birds to look out for. A map available on site details the two trails that meander through the ever-dripping foliage. The season for spotting the quetzal is March–June.

Cobán

The commercial center of the Verapaces is **Cobán** ❹, which though founded by Las Casas in 1538, remained a slumbering backwater until the late 19th century when large numbers of German immigrants arrived. The Germans were granted authority to plant

coffee bushes, which thrived in the mild, moist Verapaz climate, and business prospered until World War II, when many of the coffee barons were expelled at the USA's insistence because of their open support for Adolf Hitler.

Tranquil Cobán has a few attractions and makes an excellent base to explore the beautiful Verapaz scenery. Though the town maintains a sleepy demeanour, there are some good-value cafés and hotels, so visitors should enjoy their stay here. It's worth a stroll up to the Templo el Calvario, a fine old church dating from 1599, which is popular with Q'eqchi' and Poqomchi' Maya worshipers. Don't miss the exquisite carvings and artifacts inside the small **Museo El Príncipe Maya**, or take a guided tour of the **Finca Santa Margarita**, a coffee plantation 300 metres (328 yds) south-east of the plaza.

Just out of town, situated 2 km (1 mile) to the west, is the Vívero Verapaz, a specialist nursery where thousands of plants, including more than 600 species of orchid are grown.

TIP

You can climb the 131 steps of the Calvario church tower in Cobán for a fine view of the town and surrounding countryside.

Underground caves and turquoise pools

Far more dramatic though are the stunning natural wonders near the village of **Lanquín ❺**, situated 45 km (28 miles) to the northeast. The gargantuan Lanquín caves are a speleologist's delight, stretching for several kilometers underground, and to the south of the village, on the banks of the Río Cahabón, is **Semuc Champey**, one of the most beautiful places in Guatemala.

The Río Cahabón eventually flows into Lago de Izabal, but at Semuc Champey most of the water plunges underground, leaving a great limestone bridge at the surface. A little riverwater spills over this natural shelf, creating a series of idyllic turquoise pools perfect for swimming, and a magical place to relax and enjoy the magnificent setting. Tour companies in Cobán also run regular trips here (*see Travel Tips, pages 348–9*).

BELOW: the gorgeous greenery of Semuc Champey.

Caves and lagoons

North of Lanquín, a poor dirt road winds through some spectacular Verapaz countryside, the first stretch almost alpine in appearance, then punctured by dramatic limestone hills as the route heads towards the Cruce del Pato junction. Near the isolated village of Raxrujá, the Candelaria caves are some of Guatemala's most impressive and include a 200-meter (650-ft) chamber known as Tzul Tacca. There is a small entry fee.

Heading north of Cobán toward Petén, it's 60 km (35 miles) along a smooth highway to the small town of **Chisec**, which has two natural attractions close by. Just 2 km (1 mile) north of town, **Bombil Pek** (painted cave) is a huge limestone sinkhole, which has a tiny cave adorned with faint images of monkeys that date from ancient Maya times. Some 8 km (5 miles) east of Chisec are the **Lagunas de Sepalau**, two stunning turquoise lakes surrounded by dense rainforest.

Continuing northwest from Chisec, it's 43 km (27 miles) to the **Parque Nacional Laguna Lachuá ❻**, a spectacular lake created by a stray meteorite. Ringed by dense rainforest, Lachuá is idyllic, if extremely remote, and a variety of wildlife, including otters and many birds, can be seen here. There's camping or you can rent a hammock, but no food is available at the lake.

Map
on page
148

El Oriente

Situated south of the Carretera al Atlántico is another highland region, known as El Oriente. This is the hottest part of Guatemala, a relentlessly uncompromising land where the thermometer regularly nudges 100°F (38°C). El Oriente is *ladino* country par excellence, the arid, dusty terrain is the natural home to *campesinos*, cattle ranchers and tobacco farmers. Probing the horizon are a scattering of ancient, extinct volcanoes – though much smaller in scale and more weathered in appearance than the chain across the western highlands. You'll have to cross through these eastern highlands if you plan to visit the ruins of Copán.

The main route into El Oriente branches off from the Carretera al Atlántico at the Río Hondo junction, where there is a gas station and a good selection of hotels. The first major town, **Chiquimula** ❼ is archetypal of the region – hot, dusty and featureless – but as this is the main route to Copán in Honduras, you may need to break your journey here. Because of its location, it is well served by buses, and has a reasonable choice of places to stay and eat. The only building of architectural interest is an old colonial church on the edge of town, badly damaged by the earthquake in 1765 and now reduced to ruins.

To the south of Chiquimula, down near-empty roads, is **Volcán de Ipala** ❽, a 1,650-meter (5,410-ft) eroded volcano with an exquisite crater lake at its rounded summit. It's a fairly easy two-hour hike to the top from the closest village of Agua Blanca. If you have your own transport, the most direct route is up

BELOW: pilgrims' bus, en route to the Esquipulas basilica.

Radiant devotion of a pilgrim at the basilica of Esquipulas.

a trail that begins at Km26.5 on the Ipala–Agua Blanca road, near to a drinks stall in the tiny settlement of Sauce. Once here, you can walk all around the forest-fringed summit of the lake in a couple of hours.

Esquipulas

Some 33 km (20 miles) south of Chiquimula, close to the border with El Salvador, **Esquipulas ❾** is famous as the site of the biggest pilgrimage in Central America. The object of veneration is an image of El Cristo Negro, the Black Christ, which is housed in a colossal white basilica. Inside the church, the atmosphere is heady with incense and smoky from burning candles, while a continuous procession of pilgrims lines up to receive a blessing, many on their knees and reciting prayers. The image itself, created from balsam wood, was carved by the fabled sculptor Quirio Cataño in the late 16th century, while the origins of the pilgrimage are thought to predate the conquest. The main pilgrimage date is January 15, and there is a smaller event on March 9, but Esquipulas is busy throughout the whole year with pilgrims and devotees paying homage and seeking cures to ailments.

The town itself is rampantly commercial, geared to extract as much as possible from its short-term visitors – you'll find hotel prices double on Saturdays and an unholy heap of tacky souvenirs in market stalls outside the basilica.

Izabal

BELOW: the basilica at Esquipulas.

Fringed by the Caribbean Sea, with Belize just to the north and the Honduran coastline to the south, the low-lying department of Izabal feels totally unlike the rest of the country. The population is a polyglot assortment of *ladinos*, Garífuna, Caribs and Q'eqchi' Maya. The scenery is also different: the landscape is lush and the heat and humidity are punishing at any time of year, creating a decidedly languid, tropical ambience.

Izabal is bounded by mountains: the Sierra del Merendón defining the Honduran border, the Sierra del las Minas to the southwest, and the Sierra de Santa Cruz to the north. In the very center of the department is **Lago de Izabal**, the biggest lake in the country, which drains into the Caribbean through the beautiful Río Dulce gorge. The economy has been geared around bananas for over a century, exported via the port towns of Puerto Barrios and Santo Tomás de Castilla to North America and Europe, though tourism centered upon the town of Río Dulce is also becoming more important, particularly for cruises on Lago de Izabal and El Golfete (*see below*).

Quiriguá ruins

The Carretera al Atlántico follows the Motagua River through much of the department, following the ancient trade route from the highlands to the Caribbean. The early Classic ruins of **Quiriguá ❿**, set in a beautiful clearing just off the highway, are well worth investigating for their remarkable stone carvings of sandstone stelae and giant flat boulders. Quiriguá had always been a minor site, possibly first settled in the Early Classic period by an elite group from the northern

Map
on page
148

Maya lowlands. It was subsequently dominated by nearby Copán, but in AD 737, the leader Cauac Sky (or Two-legged Sky) captured and sacrificed Copán's ruler Eighteen Rabbit, turning centuries of Maya power politics upside down.

To celebrate this success, Cauac Sky started rebuilding Quiriguá, commissioning the carving of the largest stelae anywhere in the Maya world, which were grouped around an enormous monumental plaza, enclosed on three sides by an acropolis.

The site's largest stela is 8-meter (25-ft) tall Stela E, which depicts Cauac Sky, crowned with an elaborate headdress. There are ten other stelae in the plaza, a small acropolis to the south, and a ball court. Don't miss the six fantastic carved boulders just below the acropolis, which are decorated with images of frogs, turtles and snakes, and a serene, buddha-like figure on Zoomorph P.

Lake Izabal

North of Quiriguá is Lago de Izabal, a huge freshwater expanse which is steadily being opened up to tourism. The western environs of the lake are protected as part of the Bocas del Polochic reserve, where there are alligators, iguanas and a riot of colorful birdlife. Most people stay at the eastern edge of the lake however, near the massive concrete bridge, at the town of **Río Dulce ⑪**. The town, scattered on both sides of the bridge, is no beauty, functioning mainly as a transport hub, but unexpectedly close by there are some delightful hotels, well-placed for exploring the lake.

Back in the 16th and 17th centuries, British pirates caused mayhem around Izabal, raiding Spanish merchant caravans, and the Castillo de San Felipe (open daily 8am–5pm; entry fee), just 3 km (2 miles) from Río Dulce town, was built

TIP

Boat cruises around El Golfete often stop at the hot springs that empty into the lagoon, so you can take a dip in the warm water.

BELOW:
Castillo de San Felipe, Río Dulce.

to combat these marauding buccaneers. There's a lot more to see around the lake, including an incredible hot spring waterfall near Finca El Paraíso, and the Boquerón canyon near the town of El Estor, originally called "the store", another reminder of English influence.

Manatee reserve

Heading towards the Caribbean from Río Dulce town, the lakeside scenery opens up again into a lagoon called El Golfete, where there's a manatee habitat reserve, **Biotopo Chacón Machaca** (open daily 7am–5pm; entry fee) though you'll be extremely fortunate to see one of the huge, timid mammals. The birdlife is usually much more in evidence, so keep your eyes peeled for pelicans, egrets, kingfishers, ospreys and herons. The banks then close in as you enter the spectacular Río Dulce gorge, its soaring 100-meter (328-ft) high walls covered in impenetrable rainforest, passing a bubbling underwater hot spring.

Lívingston

At the point where the Río Dulce meets the Bahía de Amatique is the Garífuna town of **Lívingston** ⓬, sometimes known locally as La Buga (The Mouth). Lívingston is one of the most interesting villages in Guatemala, its atmosphere seemingly much more in tune with Jamaica or the Honduran Bay Islands than the Central American mainland. Connections with the rest of Guatemala are somewhat tentative, and not just culturally, as Lívingston can only be reached by boat from Puerto Barrios, Belize or Honduras. With the melodic rhythms of reggae and Garífuna punta filling the village streets, it's easy to assume Lívingston is a some lost laid-back Caribbean paradise. Not so – unemployment

BELOW: the ferry leaving Lívingston, *en route* to Puerto Barrios

is very high forcing many to emigrate and it's said that more Lívingston-born men live in New York than in the village itself.

There is also some tension between the Garífuna and the town's *ladinos* and Asians, who own most of the businesses. Good excursions from Lívingston include the waterfalls called Siete Altares (best in rainy season); the best beach in Guatemala, Playa Blanca; and even snorkeling trips to the edge of the Belizean reef system.

Map on page 148

Puerto Barrios

Puerto Barrios ⑬, situated in the southeastern corner of Bahía de Amatique, is today little more than a transit point for tourists picking up boats for Punta Gorda in Belize or en route for Lívingston. For many years though, the town was the country's most important port. Now it has been eclipsed by the modern facilities available at Santo Tomás de Castilla, just 11 km (7 miles) to the west around the bay.

Puerto Barrios was established by president Rufino Barrios in the late 19th century, but developed by the United Fruit Company in the 1900s as the company's exclusive port for the export of its bananas. The UFC modelled the town on urban North American lines, and it retains this legacy today, with broad streets and sprawling city blocks.

Stunning stonework of Stela E, Quiriguá.

Most of the old wooden Caribbean buildings are crumbling and dilapidated now, unfortunately, replaced by faceless concrete constructions. The odd reminder of more prosperous times remains, however, and the town's one real sight is the Hotel del Norte, right on the waterfront, an immaculately preserved – and charming – living monument. ❑

BELOW: keeping the man from Del Monte happy, at the Quiriguá banana packing plant.

THE UNITED FRUIT COMPANY

For more than half a century, all Guatemala's political and economic decisions were effectively supervised by the United Fruit Company, Central America's biggest employer, and dubbed "*el pulpo*" (the octopus) because of its huge influence in the region. The UFC first began banana business in Guatemala in 1901, and quickly struck a deal to complete the Guatemala City–Puerto Barrios railway line in exchange for almost complete tax exemption and land concessions. By 1930 the company was worth $215 million, and its yellow tentacles controled the country's railways, the main port Puerto Barrios, and consequently, control over all the country's other exports.

This hegemony was largely unchecked until 1952, when president Arbenz drafted new reform laws, which redistributed land to peasants. US interests were deemed to be under threat and a plot was hatched by the CIA (whose director Allen Dulles was also on the the the UFO board) to support an invading force of Guatemalan exiles from Honduras, which overthrew Arbenz in 1954. The new CIA-backed strongman, Carlos Castillo Armas, returned all the confiscated land to the UFC, who merged with United Brands in the 1960s and finally quit Guatemala in 1972, selling its remaining land to Del Monte.

Copán Ruins

One of the most impressive ancient sites in Mesoamerica is **Copán** ⑭, a city on the banks of the Río Copán, only 12 km (8 miles) into Honduras from the Guatemalan border town of El Florido.

The explorers John L. Stephens and Frederick Catherwood visited the site in 1839, at which time the magnificent stonework was smothered in jungle vegetation. Today, however, after more than 20 years' dramatic excavation work and study, the site has been spectacularly restored. An increasing number of visitors to Guatemala make a special detour to these superb ruins, whose carved stelae are widely considered the finest yet found in the Maya world.

History

At its peak in the 8th century AD, Copán was a powerful city-state which dominated the Motagua Valley through its control of the important trade in jade, obsidian, cacao and

quetzal feathers. By this time the city was home to an estimated population of some 20,000 inhabitants.

There is evidence of human settlement in the Copán Valley as early as 1300 BC, but it was not until AD 426 that a nobleman from Teotihuacan in central Mexico, Yax K'uk Mo', took control of the area and established a new royal dynasty which would rule Copán for almost the next 400 years.

The dynasty of Yax K'uk Mo' held political sway throughout the southeastern Maya region, including Quiriguá, another city-state in the southeast of present-day Guatemala (*see page 152*). Eventually, however, the warriors of Quiriguá rose up under their new king Cauac Sky and rebelled against Copán in a bid for independence, crushing the once invincible city. Following the capture and ritual sacrifice in AD 737 of its 13th ruler, 18 Rabbit, Copán's supremacy began to wane. The quality of its ceremonial architecture and carved stonework also began to deteriorate from this time on. The glorious dynasty founded by Yax K'uk Mo' struggled on under three more rulers before the city finally collapsed.

Copán's slow decline coincided with that of the rest of the lowland Maya world at the end of the Classic period circa AD 800 . The city of Copán was abandoned in the early 9th century, although a small population remained in the valley for some time afterward.

Archeological work at Copán has been in continuous progress since 1975, and there were several earlier expeditions that mapped and excavated the site. To date, a large portion of the city center has been excavated and restored, with many monuments re-erected in their original positions. Over 1,000 structures have been found in this urban core alone, covering an area of 1.3 sq. km (½ sq. mile), which represents only the nucleus of the majestic city of Copán.

The visual impact of the city lies above all in the artistic achievements of its craftsmen and the site boasts some of the most ornate carving "in the round" to be found in Mesoamerica. Copán's masons developed an extremely fine and detailed form of high relief

LEFT: the artistic brilliance of Copán was in its superb carving, as shown here by Stela H.

sculpture using the local stone: a greenish andesite that was very soft and thus the ideal material for the intricately formed figures of humans, animals and birds.

The sculptures also contain a myriad of symbolic texts and images demonstrating what Aldous Huxley described as the Maya's "extraordinary preoccupation with time". Scribes were revered by the Maya, and the knowledge and use of hieroglyphics was vital to Copán's rulers for the affirmation of elite legitimacy and to ensure the continuation of the dominant ideology in future generations.

The site today

Copán is a well-kept site, which you could visit on a long day-trip from Guatemala City, but it is better to take your time and spend at least one night in the nearby town of Copán Ruinas. As you enter the site from the **Visitors' Center**, a main pathway takes you into the **Great Plaza**, a vast open space which, at one time, would have been paved. The Great Plaza houses some of the site's most beautiful sculpted stelae, many of which

depict King 18 Rabbit, including stelae A, B, C, D, F, H and 4. Stela A is particularly impressive, with deep carving and 52 glyphs decorating its sides. It is a reproduction of the original which is kept, together with most of the other original stelae, in the on-site **Museum of Maya Sculpture**. Stela C has faces carved on both sides, and an altar in the shape of a turtle at its base.

To the south of the Great Plaza lies the **Acropolis**, a colossal man-made mound upon which several successive pyramids, temples, terraces and plazas were built over the centuries. Altar Q, at the base of Pyramid 16, is one of Copán's most famous sculptures, its sides decorated with 16 seated figures, carved in exquisite relief. Together with the Great Plaza, the Acropolis constitutes what would have been the main hub of activity in the ancient city.

Just to the north of the Acropolis, is perhaps the most exceptional structure in Copán, which is known as the **Hieroglyphic Stairway**. Built by the city's 15th ruler, Smoke Shell in AD 756, the stairway was dedicated to the honor of his dynastic predecessors. Smoke Shell also hoped the achievement would serve to regain the support of his people and reaffirm the status of his dynasty after the earlier, humiliating defeat of 18 Rabbit.

With 62 carved steps leading up a pyramid, and adorned with six richly decorated figures representing the city's rulers, the Hieroglyphic Stairway contains the longest inscription known in ancient Mesoamerica, the meaning of which is still challenging epigraphers. The partial collapse of the structure at some point before its excavation left a "jigsaw in stone" of some 20,000 individual hieroglyphic inscriptions. At the base of the stairway is Stela M, depicting a royal figure in a feathered cloak, while at the front a plumed serpent swallows a human head.

The ruins of Copán are open daily (8am–4pm; entry fee). The **Museum of Maya Sculpture**, next to the Visitors' Center, is well worth a visit (entry fee US$5) – best before you see the ruins themselves – containing many of the original stelae, and a full-size reproduction of the startlingly colorful **Rosalilia Temple**, recently discovered intact beneath Temple 16. ❑

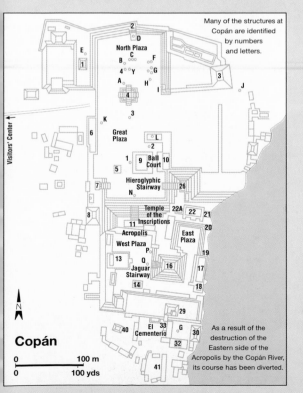

Many of the structures at Copán are identified by numbers and letters.

As a result of the destruction of the Eastern side of the Acropolis by the Copán River, its course has been diverted.

Copán

0   100 m
0   100 yds

PETEN

Hidden in this vast northern jungle department are some of the most spectacular Maya cities, including the indisputable, dazzling jewel in their crown: Tikal

Map
on page
160

Guatemala

Between 750 BC and around AD 900, arguably the greatest of all pre-Columbian cultures, the Maya civilization, evolved, excelled and ultimately collapsed in the lowland subtropical forests of what is now northern Guatemala. It was in the jungles and savannas of the department of Petén, which covers a third of the country, that the Maya city states succeeded in creating some of the greatest human advances in the continent: a precise calendrical system, pioneering astronomy, a complex writing system, breathtaking artistry and towering architectural triumphs.

There's compelling evidence that a combination of environmental and social factors (including overpopulation, warfare and revolt) prompted the disaster of the Maya collapse, but the exact reasons are still subject to animated academic debate. Whatever the truth, the jungle reclaimed the temples, plazas and palaces, so that by the time the 19th-century explorers arrived, buildings were choked with 1,000 years of forest growth.

Penetrating the Petén

The Spanish all but ignored the area until, in 1697, they finally bothered to defeat the tiny isolated Itzá Maya tribe that lived on the shores of Lago de Petén Itzá. Most of the entire department of Petén was all but inaccessible up until the 1960s, when the hellish trails that sneaked through the trees between the capital and Flores were upgraded to dirt roads. At this time, most of Petén was still covered in pristine forest, with only a few thousand human inhabitants. Government schemes opened up the forests to land-hungry settlers, loggers and oil prospectors and the population spiralled (now estimated to be over 500,000). As much as 50 percent of the forest may have already been cut, with destructive "slash and burn" farming and logging, at first clearing the trees, then moving on and leaving the degraded land to cattle ranchers.

Yet despite the population boom and environmental damage, vast areas of the Petén forest remain intact, and this is still one of the best places in Central America to see the region's spectacular wildlife. A number of national parks and reserves have been established (and combined as the Maya Biosphere Reserve) in a belated attempt to protect the subtropical habitat of over 4,000 plant species and animals that include jaguars, crocodiles, tapirs, ocelots, collared peccaries, blue morpho butterflies and 450 resident and migratory birds. Even if you only make it to Tikal, you should hear the deafening roar of the howler monkey, glimpse toucans and parrots squabbling in the forest canopy and perhaps spot an ocellated turkey or a gray fox in the undergrowth (*see page 168*).

LEFT: the majestic roof combs of Tikal, swathed in their jungle blanket.
BELOW: the calm waters of Lake Petén Itzá.

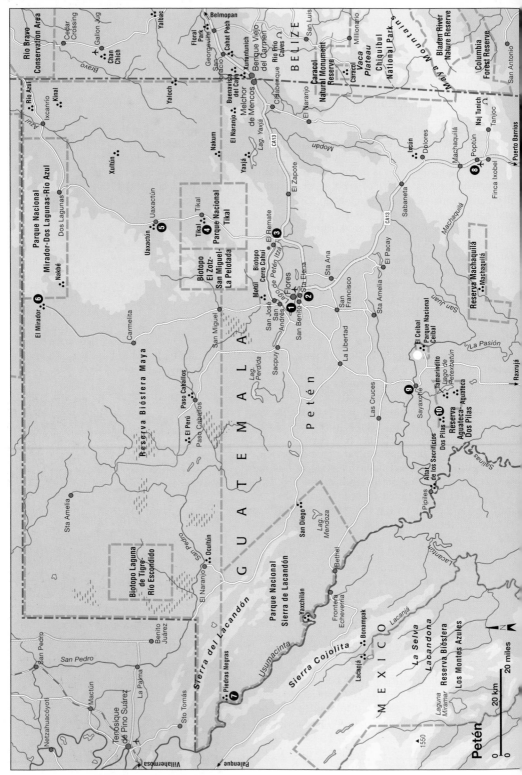

Petén

The Petén is still Guatemala's wild frontier province, and transport, communications, hotels and restaurants are pretty basic away from the main town of Flores. To get to Maya sites like El Mirador takes time, planning and local expertise – you'll need a guide and supplies – fortunately there are a number of excellent local organizations who operate expeditions to the remote ruins (*see Travel Tips, page 349*). The Petén climate is perennially hot and humid. The rainy season can extend until December, and can disrupt overland travel to isolated areas. Tikal and Flores are always accessible nevertheless.

Map on page 160

The horse is still the preferred means of transport in many jungle back routes.

Flores

Set on a natural island in Lago de Petén Itzá, connected via a small causeway to shore, **Flores ❶** (population 5,000), is a peaceful, civilized place that's now largely dependent on tourism. It is a small, tranquil and historic town that's by far the most pleasant urban center in the department. Today's town stands on the remains of the old Itzá Maya capital, Tayasal, which was first visited by Hernán Cortés in 1525, left alone, and only conquered in 1697. The Spanish had no appetite for jungle life and the town was made a penal colony, retaining closer contact with Belize and Mexico until the road links to the rest of Guatemala improved in the late 20th century.

The best way to explore Flores is to stroll around the lane that circumscribes the shoreline – it'll take you about fifteen minutes to walk around the whole town. Some of its architecture is delightful: the older houses are brightly-painted wooden and adobe constructions, many of the hotels have been painted in harmonious pastel shades, and there's a fine plaza in the center of town that boasts a twin-domed cathedral.

BELOW:
the town of Flores, on Lake Petén Itzá.

Just across the causeway, the ugly urban sprawl of **Santa Elena ❷** and San Benito (combined population 55,000) could not present more of a contrast. These are rough and ready frontier towns, typical of a region where laws can be ignored and the authorities bribed if necessary. Development is ramshackle, the streets are thick with dust and dirt. There's no reason to be here except to visit a bank (there are a couple in Flores anyway) or catch a bus out of town.

Around Flores

On the banks of Lago de Petén Itzá, around Flores, there's a number of things to see, most of which are best visited by boat – you'll find boatmen by the Hotel Santana and on the Santa Elena side of the causeway. The **Petencito zoo** (entry fee) and a lookout point on a small island, are the most popular destinations, but if you want to to see a traditional Petén village, head for San Andrés on the north shore. The neighboring village of San José, 2 km (1 mile) away, is another friendly place, where efforts are being made to preserve the Itza Maya language. Some 4 km (2½ miles) beyond San José are the minor ruins of Motúl where there are some small pyramids and a stela to see.

Some 2 km (1 mile) south of Santa Elena, the caves of Aktun Kan have some bizarre formations that vaguely resemble animals, plus plenty of stalactites, stalagmites and the odd bat.

The scarlet macaw, whose piercing screech is an intrinsic part of the jungle experience.

BELOW: luxurious comforts at the Hotel Camino Real Tikal, by Lake Petén Itzá.

The small but spread-out village of **El Remate ❸** is another good base for exploring Tikal. It is 30 km (18½ miles) from Santa Elena/Flores and particularly convenient if you're approaching the ruins from Belize, with a burgeoning number of hotels scattered around El Remate.

About 3 km (2 miles) from the center of the village is a small nature reserve, the **Biotopo Cerro Cahuí**. The reserve is home to a remarkable diversity of plantlife (mahogany, ceiba and sapodilla trees, orchids and epiphytes), animals (spider and howler monkeys, armadillos and ocelots) and particularly an exceptional quantity of birds, with an estimated 450 species recorded.

Tikal

Entombed in dense jungle, where the inanimate air is periodically shattered by the roars of howler monkeys, the phenomenal, towering ruins of **Tikal ❹** are one of the wonders of the Americas. Five temple-pyramids soar above the forest canopy, finely-carved stelae and altars in the plaza eulogize the city's glorious history, giant stucco masks adorn monuments and stone-flagged causeways lead toward other ruined cities lying even deeper in the jungle.

Tikal's scale is awesome. In the Classic period its population grew to almost 100,000. Trade routes connected the city with Teotihuacán (near modern-day Mexico City), the Caribbean and Pacific coasts. Temple IV was built to a height of almost 70 meters (230 ft), complete with its enormous roof comb. Exquisite jade masks, ceramics, jewellery and sculptures were created. There were ball courts, sweat baths, colorfully painted royal palaces, and another 4,000 buildings to house the artisans, astrologers, farmers and warriors of the greatest city of the Maya civilization.

Most travelers concur that Tikal is the most visually sensational of all the Maya sites. To really get the most out of your visit, try to stay overnight at one of the three hotels close to the ruins, to witness the electric atmosphere at dawn and dusk when the calls of toucans, frogs, monkeys and mammals echo around the surrounding jungle. The temperatures and humidity are punishing at any time of year, so take plenty of water, and also insect repellent.

History

Tikal is one of the oldest Maya sites, the latest evidence indicates only Nakbé and Cuello (in Belize) predate it. It's located in the central lowland Maya zone, the cradle of Maya civilization, in a dense subtropical forest environment. The earliest evidence of human habitation at Tikal is around 700 BC, in the pre-Classic period. By 500 BC the first simple structures were constructed, but Tikal would have been little more than a small village at this time and Nakbé, some 55 km (34 miles) to the north was the dominant power in the region.

By the time Tikal's first substantial ceremonial structures were built (the North Acropolis and the Great Pyramid) about 200 BC, powerful new cities had emerged, above all the enormous El Mirador, 64 km (40 miles) to the north and connected by a *sacbé* raised causeway. By the start of the Classic period in AD 250, El Mirador and Nakbé had faded and Tikal had grown to be one of the most important Maya cities, along with Uaxactún and Calakmul. The great Tikal leader Great Jaguar Paw and his general Smoking Frog defeated Uaxactún in AD 376, and Calakmul and Tikal were to contest dominance of the pivotal center of the Maya region for another two centuries. Huge advances were made in the study of astronomy, calendrics and

Map on page 160

After the death of a Maya ruler, the stelae describing his life were often broken up and placed in his tomb, as they were considered personal records rather than public monuments.

LEFT: Temples I and II, facing the Great Plaza at Tikal.
BELOW: the best way to get your bearings in Tikal is to climb one of the temples.

arithmetics under Stormy Sky (AD 426–457). But disaster struck in 562 when upstart Caracol (in Belize) defeated Double Bird of Tikal and forged a crucial alliance with Calakmul that was to humble Tikal for 120 years – no stelae at all were carved in this time.

Tikal's renaissance was sparked by Ah Cacau or Lord Chocolate (682–734) and continued by his son Caan Chac, who ordered the construction of most of the temples that bestride the ruins today, which are taller and grander than earlier buildings. Caan Chac also reassumed control of the core Maya area, eclipsing bitter rival Calakmul. Tikal continued to control the region, enjoying unsurpassed stability and prosperity into the 9th century; but it faded quickly by AD 900, along with all the other lowland sites.

The site

Before (or after) you enter the site, it's worth having a look in the **Visitors' Center Ⓐ**, where the **Museo Lítico** has an excellent collection of stelae and carvings, and opposite is the **Museo Morley**, where the exhibits include ceramics, jade, the burial ornaments of Lord Chocolate and Stela 29, the oldest found at Tikal (both museums are open daily, entry fee).

The **Great Plaza Ⓑ** is the first place to head for, the nerve center of the city for 1,500 years. The grassy plaza is framed by the perfectly proportioned Temples I and II to the east and west, the North Acropolis, and the Central Acropolis to the south. In Classic Maya days, these monumental limestone buildings would have been painted vivid colors, predominately red, with clouds of incense smoke smoldering from the upper platforms. Civic and religious ceremonies, frequently including human sacrifice, would have been directed by priests and kings from the top of the temples.

Temple I Ⓒ (also known as the Temple of the Giant Jaguar), was built to honor Lord Chocolate, who was buried in a tomb beneath the 44-meter (144-ft) high structure with a stately collection of goods (now exhibited in the Morley Museum). Three small rooms on top of the temple were probably the preserve of priests and kings, adorned with beautifully carved zapote wood beams and lintels. Facing Temple I across the plaza is **Temple II Ⓓ** (also known as the Temple of the Masks), slightly smaller at 38 meters (125ft) tall, and a little less visually impressive too because part of its massive roof comb is missing. Both temples were constructed around AD 740.

Between the two mighty edifices, on the north side of the plaza are a twin row of stelae and altars, about 60 in all. Many date form Classic Maya times, but were moved here from other parts of the site by post-Classic people in a revivalist effort – Stela 5 has some particularly fine glyphs. Behind the stelae is the untidy bulk of the **North Acropolis Ⓔ**, a jungle of disparate masonry composed of some 16 temples and an estimated 100 buildings buried underneath, parts of which are some of the oldest constructions at Tikal, dating back to 250 BC. Most of the temple structures are late Classic, and missing elaborate roof combs, but all are built over much earlier foundations. Among the remains are two colossal stucco masks.

TIP

Your entry ticket into the ruins at Tikal is officially only valid for one day, but if you enter the site after dusk, your ticket will automatically be stamped for the following day.

BELOW: fine Maya ceramic urn.

On the south side of the plaza is the **Central Acropolis ❺**, a maze of buildings, thought to function as the rulers' palace, grouped around six small courtyards. In front of the Central Acropolis is a small ball court, and behind it to the south is the palace reservoir and the restored 58-meter (190-ft) Temple V. A very steep staircase ascends this temple (which may be closed following heavy rain), and from its summit there's an astonishing view of the entire site.

The Lost World

Reached by a trail from Temple V, El Mundo Perdido (The Lost World) is a beautiful, atmospheric complex of buildings, dominated by the mighty **Great Pyramid ❻**, a 32-meter (105-ft) high pre-Classic monument that's Tikal's oldest-known structure. It's also an ideal base from which to watch sunrise or sunset. **Temple III ❼**, north from here, peaks at 55 meters (180 ft) and remains cloaked in jungle, while **Temple IV ❶** has been half-cleared of vegetation. Temple IV is the tallest of all Tikal's monuments, at around 64 meters (210 ft) or 70 meters (230 ft) if you include its platform, making it the (joint) highest pre-Columbian structure ever built – the El Tigre temple at El Mirador is of equal height. Getting to the top involves a tricky climb using giant roots and a ladder for support but the view from the summit really is astounding – mile after mile of rainforest, only broken by the roof combs of the other temples.

There are thousands of other structures to explore, some considerable like Temple VI, the **Temple of Inscriptions ❶**, down the Méndez causeway leading from Temple I, with its 12-meter (39-ft) high roof comb and intricate glyphs, most much more modest – the homes of the workers and farmers. Take a good map and great care if you go for a walk in the forest; people get lost every year.

Parts of Tikal, such as Temple IV, are still fighting an ongoing battle against the encroaching jungle.

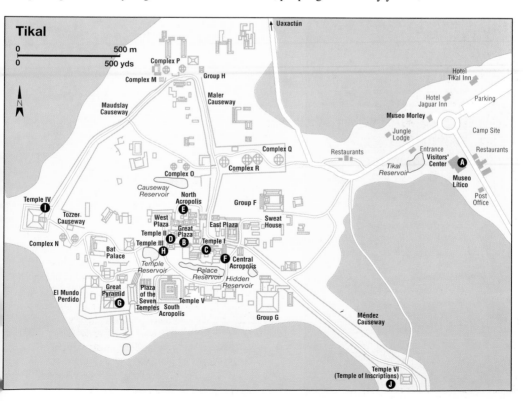

*One of the buildings
at Uaxactún, the
unimaginatively
named E-VII in
Group E functioned
as an observatory
in pre-Classic
Maya times.*

The northern ruins

In the thick jungle of the Maya Biosphere Reserve in the extreme north of Guatemala, there are dozens more Maya ruins, most almost completely unexcavated. The easiest to get to is **Uaxactún** ❺, 24 km (15 miles) away, and connected to Tikal by a dirt road, served by one daily bus form Flores/Santa Elena. If you can, visit Uaxactún before Tikal, because the ruins are much smaller. Uaxactún rivalled Tikal for many years in the early Classic era, but was finally defeated in a battle on 16 January AD 378. Today there is an interesting observatory (Group E), numerous fine stelae, simple accommodation and, of course, the jungle to explore and admire.

Just a couple of kilometers from the Mexican border, the pre-Classic metropolis of **El Mirador** ❻ matches Tikal in scale and may yet be found to exceed it. It is only accessible by foot, however, a tough three-day hike through the jungle from Carmelita, the nearest settlement (also served by a daily bus from Santa Elena). El Mirador's colossal temple in the El Tigre Complex touches 70 meters (230 ft), but the vast ruins have been barely excavated.

Nakbé is another pre-Classic ruin, some 10 km (6 miles) south, where there are more big temples and a mask measuring 5 meters by 8 meters (16 ft by 26 ft) has been uncovered. Right on the tripartite border where Belize, Mexico and Guatemala meet, **Río Azul** is a large site, also dating from the pre-Classic era, where grave robbers have plundered most of the tombs.

Finally, way over on the other side of the Maya Biosphere Reserve on the Río Usumacinta, is the extremely isolated **Piedras Negras** ❼. The site, which towers over the Guatemalan bank of the river, can only be accessed by boat, with trips organized in Guatemala City (*see Travel Tips, page 349*) or Palenque

BELOW AND RIGHT:
domestic chores in
the Petén have
changed little for
thousands of years.

Map on page 160

in Mexico. Some of the finest stelae in the Maya world were carved at Piedras Negras, and there is a megalithic stairway and substantial ruins to admire, including a sweat bath and an impressive acropolis, with extensive rooms and courtyards.

South and east of Flores

Two roads creep through the jungle south of Flores, the busiest of which, now paved, heads past **Poptún ❽**, a dusty featureless town 113 km (70 miles) away where a fine ranch makes an idyllic place to stay. At the American-owned Finca Ixobel, a short distance out of town, there are many opportunities to explore the region's cave and river systems and great company, while the home-cooked food gets most peoples' vote as the best in Guatemala.

Taking the other route south, 62 km (38 miles) from Flores is the town of **Sayaxché ❾**, a frontier settlement by the Río de la Pasión. It's an ideal base to visit the ruins of **El Ceibal**, set in a patch of rainforest 17 km (10½ miles) away, which was a large city dating from pre-Classic times. Much remains unreconstructed, but there's a fine plaza and stelae, an astronomy platform and many noisy howler monkeys. South of Sayaxché is the lovely, forest-fringed Lago de Petexbatún, with three interesting ruins close by. **Aguateca** is the most accessible, positioned high above the lake, the partly restored ruins are scattered between a natural chasm. **Dos Pilas ❿** is a bigger site with some fine altars, a ball court and four short hieroglyphic stairways. Finally, 73 km (45 miles) east of Flores are the substantial ruins of **Yaxhá**, which are steadily being restored, and were the location for *Survivor*, a US TV program aired in 2005. Structure 216, which tops 300 meters (980 ft), is Yaxha's most impressive construction. ❏

Stela I from Piedras Negras, in the Archeology Museum of Guatemala City.

BELOW: sunset over Lake Petexbatún.

TIKAL – JEWEL IN THE MAYA CROWN

Possibly the greatest of all the Maya cities, Tikal stands majestically in the Petén jungle, occupied now only by monkeys, toucans and other exotica

As the first sunlight filtered through the early morning mist, the high priest, Iahca Na, emerged from the inner sanctum of Temple 1. Yik'in Chan K'awiil, his son and successor, clad in jaguar pelt and jade jewels, nervously awaited approval from the shaman who had consulted the gods for their blessing. A discreet nod from the wise priest confirmed Caan's accession and the expectant multitude gathered in the plaza below erupted in celebration. Drums sounded and dancing began, heralding a new era for the city of Tikal.

COSMOPOLITAN CITY

As you walk through the ruins of Tikal today, it is easy to forget that it was previously a thriving metropolis with a population of around 100,000. The Maya city was once home to a multi-layered society; as well as the nobility there was a large middle class, comprising merchants, craftsmen and bureaucrats; and a workers' class, which included farmers, builders and servants.

Tikal represents over 1,000 years of continuous construction. In fact, wherever you stand, beneath your feet lie many layers of previous eras. More than 100 structures lie beneath the North Acropolis as we see it today.

△ **COMBING THE JUNGLE**
As seen from the top of Temple IV, the massive temple roof combs rise out of the dense tree canopy.

△ **STONE BOOKS**
Carved stelae depicted major events in Tikal's history and tales of Maya mythology.

BURIAL MASK ▷
This jadeite mask of Maya ruler Ah Cacau was found amongst a rich burial cache, entombed in Temple I.

▷ **SACRED ROOM**
Closer to heaven, the small room at the top of the temples was used for sacred rituals and ceremonies.

▽ SACRED TREE
The Ceiba is a symbol of national pride in modern Guatemala. In ancient times, the sacred tree was seen as a link to heaven.

▽ TIKAL AS IT WAS
This model of Tikal's city center at its height, c.600–700AD, shows the broad ceremonial highways, linking the main buildings.

△ TEMPLE III
Some temples in Tikal are still being recovered from the jungle, exposing them to the new threats from people and pollution.

▷ ALTAR FIVE
This carving depicts two figures standing over a human skull and bones, maybe a sacrificial victim.

▷ SACRIFICIAL CLUB
This carved stone axehead, which may have been used in ceremonial sacrifices, is now kept in the Tikal museum, at the site.

TIKAL'S NATURAL WONDERS

In addition to its awesome archeological heritage, the Tikal National Park offers visitors one of the richest rainforest environments in Central America. The protected territory saves trees, hundreds of years old, from logging, and rare animals from both the black market and the dining table.

Tikal has an incredible variety of animal life and as you wander around the site, you can tell that they have made it their home. Racoon-like coati-mundis scurry up to eat from your hand and troupes of spider monkeys playfully pelt you with berries from the treetops. The park is also home to over 200 species of birds, such as the keel-billed toucan, the ocellated turkey, parrots and eagles. Most thrilling of all are four of the world's rarest wildcats that live in the area; you might even be lucky enough to catch sight of a jaguar, puma, ocelot or margay.

BELIZE

This tiny Central American country, although only about the size of Massachusetts or Wales, is an ecotourism paradise

With so few people and so much space, Belize's main attraction for the visitor is its incredible, largely untouched natural environment. The steamy rainforest and spectacular coral reef, along with a chain of tiny paradise islands, are within touching distance of the USA, with Miami only a two-hour flight away.

Above all, Belize's greatest natural attraction is its superb coral reef, which shadows its entire coastline, the longest in the Western Hemisphere. The reef's dazzling underwater landscape hosts an astonishing array of sea-life, acts as a barrier, calming the inshore waters and creating excellent conditions for watersports. There are more than 200 small offshore islands and three coral atolls.

Belize has an astonishing quantity of plant and animal species. There are hundreds of birds, rare wild cats, and all manner of reptiles and insects. The forests are also home to thousands of flowering plants, including 70 varieties of orchids and 700 varieties of native trees.

The climate

Belize has a subtropical climate, with two distinct wet and dry seasons. It is most often hot and humid, particularly during the rainy season from May to December. The dry season is a cooler and more bearable time. The rainy season includes the hurricane season from September to November. Belize had suffered a direct hit from a hurricane on average once every 40 years, but that has changed – though the country does have an excellent warning system in place.

The government and the economy

In the political and economic arena, Belize usually gets lumped in with the other English-speaking Caribbean nations because of its British colonial heritage and contemporary status as part of the dwindling membership of the British Commonwealth. The present government, the marginally left-leaning PUP (Peoples' United Party), won a landslide victory in the 1998 general election, and was re-elected in 2003, a historical first in Belizean electoral politics.

The economy is still largely based on export cash crops – sugar, citrus and bananas being respectively the biggest foreign exchange earners. As all rely on preferential treatment – from either the US or European Union – it makes Belize vulnerable to external political pressures. Newer industries such as tourism and shrimp farming are beginning to make significant contributions without the need for artificial external protection, but the stability of the economy still remains largely at the mercy of the outside world.

PRECEDING PAGES: Queen's Caye; Cockscomb Basin Wildlife Reserve.
LEFT: Fort Street restaurant, Belize City, which is gradually renovating its colonial architecture, despite the ravages of seasonal hurricanes.

The land and the people

One of the main factors why the Belizean environment and wildlife has been able to survive and thrive is because of the country's tiny population – just 280,000. Its fellow Central American republic of El Salvador is smaller but has a population of more than 6 million.

Belize has an area of 8,867 sq. miles (22,962 sq. km), only about one-fifth the size of neighboring Guatemala. The Río Hondo marks the northern border with Mexico, while 175 miles (282 km) to the south the Sarstoon River forms the border with Guatemala.

Belizeans are a polyglot, culturally diverse people. The main groups are Creoles and latinos, with smaller numbers of Maya, Garífuna, East Asians and whites. Many thousands of refugees, mainly from El Salvador and Guatemala, settled in Belize in the early 1980s fleeing civil war and altering the racial balance of the country – there are now slightly more Spanish than English speakers. Most of the refugees settled to farm or work in citrus and banana plantations, many live around Belmopan and in the west of Belize.

The northern towns of Belize are also mainly Spanish-speaking with a population of *mestizos* (of mixed Spanish and Maya descent) and Yucatec and Maya who fled into Belize from Mexico after the Caste Wars in the mid-19th century. Most farm sugar cane. In the far south of the country are a few thousand Q'eqchi' and Mopán Maya who live mainly in isolated hill villages and practice subsistence farming. An innovative new ecotourism project based in a group of villages in the Toledo District is gaining popularity, helping to boost the Maya farmers' economy *(see page 229.)*

Creoles today form around one-third of Belize's population. They still dominate the country's largest town: Belize City. Belizean Creoles are descended from black African slaves and British buccaneers. The first European settlers or "Baymen" (because they were mostly based around the Bay of Honduras) arrived in the 17th century and set up mahogany logging camps along the main rivers. Villages and towns grew up around the camps, but the end of the logging industry in the 1960s left many of these communities in a state of poverty. Some have struggled on as subsistence farming communities, others have moved to Belize City or turned to tourism for economic survival.

Most of Belize's southern coastal towns – Dangriga, Hopkins, Seine Beight and Punta Gorda – are home to the Garífuna people *(see page 233)*, deported by the British from St Vincent to Roatán (off Honduras) in the 18th century. Displaying remarkable resilience, they retained their mixed Carib and African culture and identity, and quickly established communities along the coast of Central America.

Belize is also home to a sizable Mennonite community, who migrated from Mexico in the 1950s, drawn by promises of plentiful land and an official drive to develop agricultural production. The industrious Mennonites have helped Belize become self-sufficient in chicken, dairy products and corn, the country's main foods. ❑

RIGHT: the distinctive tin roofs of Belize City.

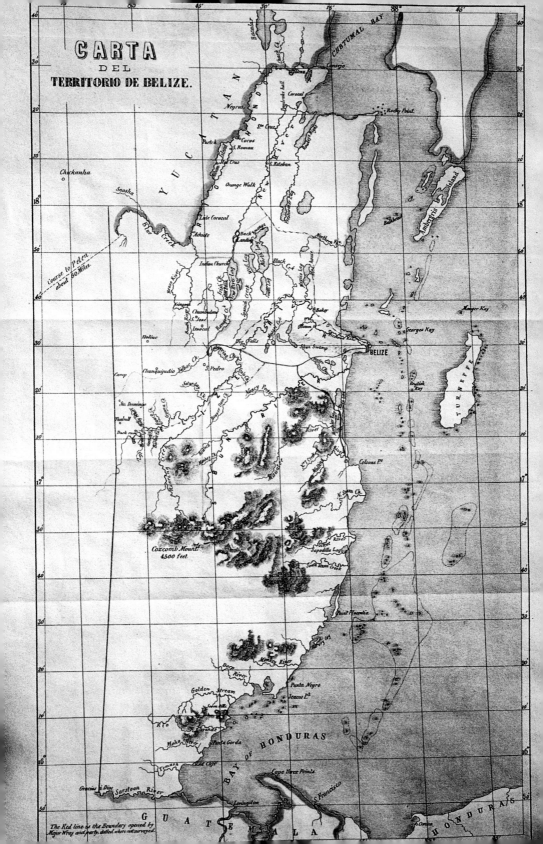

CARTA
DEL
TERRITORIO DE BELIZE.

MODERN HISTORY OF BELIZE

It took Belize many years to win its independence. Even then, it was a good few years before the country achieved true political freedom

After the decline of the Maya settlements in Belize, it was British settlers – known as "Baymen" – and their slaves from the Caribbean who began to occupy the territory in the 17th century. These new inhabitants were interested above all in the rich timber to be found in Belize's forests, especially logwood, then much in demand in Europe as the basis for fabric dyes, and mahogany. These loggers founded the first settlement on St George's Caye, a small island off the southern coast. Some time later, a larger colony was set up at the mouth of the Belize River, where the main city now stands.

In 1765, Admiral Sir William Burnaby, the commander of the British navy in Jamaica, wrote a first constitution for the territory. This became known as "Burnaby's Code" and was the basis of the laws and government in Belize for many years. In 1787, the first British-appointed administrator arrived in what was now officially called British Honduras.

Two further waves of immigration at the end of the 18th century changed the make-up of the population considerably. First, 2,000 people from the Mosquito Coast in Honduras and Nicaragua were brought in. Then, in 1797, the Garífuna, or people of mixed Amerindian and African blood, arrived in Belize after being deported from the island of St Vincent; since then they have formed a strong and distinct group in the south of the country.

Colonial conflicts

Relations with the Spanish rulers of neighboring Guatemala were frequently tense throughout the 17th and 18th centuries, as British pirate ships used Belize's sheltered waters as harbors from which to attack Spanish ships. On 10 September 1798, a decisive sea battle was fought at St George's Caye, in which the

PRECEDING PAGES: drawing of Belize City waterfront by the artist Barclay, after a 19th-century photograph.
LEFT: map of Belize dated 1869.
RIGHT: Captain Morgan, one of the most infamous pirates of the Caribbean.

Spanish force was soundly defeated. Following this victory, the local inhabitants considered themselves part of the British empire, although officially British Honduras still did not exist. In 1802, Spain was obliged to acknowledge British sovereignty over the area in the Treaty of Amiens. When Guatemala and Mexico won

their independence from Spain in 1821, both laid claim to the territory of Belize.

Fear of invasion

By the middle of the 19th century, the Guatemalan authorities were more concerned with a possible invasion by the United States. They were therefore willing in 1859 to accept a Convention with Great Britain which recognised the boundaries of Belize. Another article in the Convention called for Britain to help build a road from Guatemala City to the Atlantic seaboard in Belize, a promise which was never fulfilled. Three years later, Britain finally declared Belize a colony, and in 1871, it became a Crown

Colony, ruled by a governor appointed by Britain and a legislative council. A treaty signed with Mexico in 1893 saw the end of its claim to the territory, but successive Guatemalan governments upheld their right to sovereignty over the land. This claim lasted even after Belize was granted independence from the United Kingdom in 1981. It was not until the return of civilian government to Guatemala in 1986 that the position changed. In 1991 the Guatemalan government recognized the right of the Belizean people to "self-determination" while, in response, Belize limited its claim to territorial waters in the south to three miles, so ensuring Guatemala

access to the Caribbean. In 1992 the Guatemalan Congress officially ratified the decision to recognize Belize. This led to a final pull-out of the British garrison in 1993.

The fight for independence

The struggle within Belize to gain independence from Britain began in earnest after World War II. The People's United Party, under leader George Price, was founded in 1950. After universal adult suffrage was introduced in 1954, the PUP won huge majorities in the assemblies elected in 1954 and 1957, and in 1961 George Price became the colony's First Minister. Price also became the

THE CHICLEROS OR THE CHEWING-GUM MEN

There have been many extraordinary figures in the rediscovery of the Maya civilization. Perhaps the oddest were the *chicleros,* the men who went into the jungles of Belize, the Petén region of Guatemala, and the Yucatán Peninsula to gather *chicle* gum. As the habit of chewing gum became widespread in the US early in the 20th century, demand grew for the gum from the sapodilla tree and the *chicle macho* that was used in its manufacture. This *chicle,* obtained by slashing the trunks of the trees, was collected in the rainy season by a band of men many of whom were Maya or Waika indigenous people who had come to Belize from the Mosquito coast. They also had

intimate knowledge of the trails through the dense jungle where the Maya sites had been hidden for centuries. It was thanks to the *chicle*-hunters that the Austrian explorer Teobert Maler was able to find and photograph such important sites as Tikal, Yaxchilan, Piedras Negras and Naranjo.

At the end of their expeditions, the *chicleros* would bring back 10-kilo blocks of boiled gum for export to the US. The gum industry was badly hit in the 1950s, when an artificial substitute was created. But, with the recent renewed demand for *chicle* gum, Mayans and others are again being employed in this strange trade, and stumbling on yet more ancient sites not seen for hundreds of years.

first Belizean prime minister after self-government was granted in 1964, and he and the PUP began to press for complete independence.

The hurricane hits

On October 31, 1961, Belize was devastated by Hurricane Hattie. This particularly affected Belize City, the town on the coast which had been the capital since the 18th century. The hurricane killed hundreds of people and destroyed property to the value of millions of dollars. The authorities decided it was time to build a new capital, away from the coast and therefore less threatened by the hurricanes. The name Belmopan was chosen

Maya temples for the first time, so the gray concrete National Assembly building is flanked by the government offices in a long green court reminiscent of classical Maya sites, and its entrance is at the top of a flight of low, wide steps.

Belmopan soon became a symbol of the new, independent Belize, although admittedly it has struggled over the years to evolve from an administrative centre to a thriving city where ordinary Belizeans want to live.

Independence and beyond

The long-sought independence from Britain was eventually won in 1981, and once again George

for the new city, in honor of the Mopa, the Maya tribe who had resisted the Spanish conquistadors, and "Bel" for Belize.

By 1970, a new National Assembly building, government buildings and offices, and a national police headquarters had been constructed. The English firm who carried out the majority of the work declared that their intention was to create a similar experience to seeing one of the country's

LEFT: the volunteer guard boosted Belize's defenses when Guatemalan invasion was feared in the 1980s.
RIGHT: George Price, Belizean prime minister from 1964–84, meeting Britain's Foreign Secretary, Dr David Owen, in 1978.

Price was elected as the first prime minister of the newly independent country, now officially known as Belize. It was not until 1984 that the PUP dominance in Belizean politics was broken. In that year, the United Democratic Party (UDP), a more conservative political grouping led by Manuel Esquivel, won the legislative elections, and Esquivel was appointed prime minister.

But Esquivel and the UDP were unable to fulfil their promise of improving Belize's economic situation, and in 1989 the PUP was returned to power with a small majority. This situation was reversed in 1993, when the UDP once more secured a majority in the 29-seat House of Representatives.

Landslide victory

Once again, Belizeans soon became discontented with what they saw as the UDP's inability to deliver on its promises. In the next elections in 1998, the PUP accused the government of introducing "killa taxes", including a 15 percent value-added tax which they said was stifling business initiative. This time the voters returned massively to the PUP, giving its representatives 26 of the 29 seats. This overwhelming victory brought Said Musa to power as Belize's third prime minister.

Musa is a product of the strong Palestinian-Arab grouping in Belize's business sector. He

talks between the two sides have continued in an attempt to settle the dispute once and for all.

A further controversial issue in recent years has been the granting of "economic citizenship" to people from Hong Kong, Taiwan and other countries outside the region. This has allowed citizens from these countries to hold dual nationality and to buy land in Belize in return for paying a large US dollar application fee. Public pressure forced the PUP government to end the economic citizenship program soon after the party returned to power in 2003.

However, early into their second term, seven cabinet ministers threatened to resign if the

had returned to Belize in 1968 after studying at university abroad, and brought fresh and radical ideas with him. Having founded the People's Action Committee in 1969, he joined the PUP soon afterwards. On becoming Belize's fourth prime minister, Musa vowed to reduce unemployment and cut taxes. Since then, he has sought to present the PUP party as a modernizing force in Belize, and has looked for ways to diversify its economy and its political allegiances.

Following the withdrawal of British troops, the sovereignty dispute with Guatemala flared up again. In 1994, Guatemala formally restated its claim to the territory. Since then, however,

prime minister did not replace his finance minister and enact fiscal reforms. The internal crisis was averted, but a year later the government faced public protests over proposed tax increases and non-payment of pay rises for public officers.

The PUP's failed attempt at growth economics, which critics claim turned into "crony capitalism," left the administration facing widespread public skepticism and shattered confidence. Unfortunate, since they rode into power on a wave of unrivaled populist support in 1998. ❏

ABOVE: prime minister Said Musa, addressing the United Nations General Assembly in 1998.

The Mennonites

They stand out in any Belizean crowd: blond, blue-eyed men in denim overalls and cowboy hats; modestly dressed women whose home-made outfits – ankle-length, long-sleeved frocks and wide-brimmed hats tied down with black scarves – defy the tropical heat. Polite and reserved, they talk quietly among themselves, not in Spanish, English or Creole, but in guttural German.

These are part of Belize's Mennonite community, a resilient religious sect which traces its roots to the 16th-century Netherlands. Taking their name from a Dutch priest, Menno Simons, Mennonites live in isolated farming communities, calling themselves die Stillen im Lande, The Unobtrusive Ones. They reject state interference in their affairs and are committed pacifists.

Belize is the latest stop in a three-century odyssey – their beliefs have often led to persecution, driving them from the Netherlands to Prussia in the 1600s, to southern Russia and, when the Russian government suggested military conscription in the 1870s, they headed for Canada.

After World War I, the Canadian government demanded that only English be taught in Mennonite schools and, spurred on by anti-German feeling, reconsidered conscription. Again, many of the Mennonites moved on, this time to Mexico – only for the Mexican government to then try and include them in a new social security program.

Running out of obscure frontiers to settle, they discovered Belize (then British Honduras) encouraged by a colonial government desperate for farming skills. The colony had virtually no agriculture, and locals held farming in contempt, with even eggs imported from abroad. A Mennonite delegation toured Belize and was delighted to receive the British authorities' enthusiastic reception and promises of vast areas of virgin land.

In 1958, the first of 3,500 Mennonites arrived, to begin hacking roads through the forest, clearing a vast wilderness of land to create their farmsteads in the jungle. But, after centuries of traumatic upheaval, though the Mennonite religion's core had survived intact, deep cultural divisions had opened up. Conservative groups spoke German and used only farming implements available in the early 1900s (when an edict was passed

RIGHT: Belize's empty tracts of land are ideal for the hard-working Mennonites.

against the engine and science) while progressive Mennonites had learned English in Canada, and were happy to use tractors and fertilizer.

Settlements spread throughout Belize reflecting this cultural diversity: the progressive "Kleine Gemeinde" settled around Spanish Walk near San Ignacio; the conservative "Altkolonier" opted for the wilderness at Blue Creek on the corner of Mexico and Guatemala. Another contingent settled near Orange Walk Town at Shipyard and Richmond Hill.

The Mennonites are today the most successful farmers in Belize. They supply much of the country's food, including chicken, milk and eggs, and make most of the country's furniture. The modern

Mennonite town at Spanish Lookout would not look out of place in the USA.

Typical of more conservative Mennonites is William Freisen, an elder at Barton Creek – a breakaway group from Spanish Lookout's progressive ways. Freisen lives with his wife, 10 sons and three daughters in a wooden house without electricity and telephone in a remote community of a dozen families, linked to the highway by a rough dirt road.

Despite the isolation, Freisen and others are happy to meet interested visitors ("We want to show what Christian people do," he explains.) There is one caveat: strict Mennonites object to having their photographs taken, believing no memory should be left of a person after they die. ❏

FLORA AND FAUNA OF BELIZE

Belying its tiny size, Belize has an impressive range of abundant ecosystems, supporting great bird diversity and animals from jaguars to tree frogs

For centuries, Belize's small population, limited agricultural land and lack of industry caused it to be left behind in the race for development. This has worked to its advantage in many ways; Belize boasts the most accessible tropical wilderness in the Western hemisphere, and wildlife that lures travelers from around the world. Though not as biologically rich as the Amazon or Costa Rica, Belize is, for its size, unique in the number of different habitats and species within its borders.

The reasons for this diversity can be traced to its climate and geological history. Set in northern Central America, Belize is part of a landmass bridging two great continents. But North and South America were separated until roughly 2 million years ago, when giant continental plates began to rotate, grinding against each other and thrusting upwards to form mountains. As water became caught in the Poles' colossal ice sheets, the seas receded, exposing new land. Central America became a bridge between the two continents, opening an avenue of migration. The resultant mixture of endemic and immigrant creatures spawned one of the most varied faunas on earth.

Small but diverse

As a result of its complex geological history, Belize's landscape mixes mountains, savannas, and coastal lagoons in an area smaller than New Hampshire in the United States, while the tropical climate provides wet and dry seasons, hurricanes and heat. The resulting environmental mix creates an astonishing variety of animal and vegetable habitats: Belize has more than 4,000 species of flowering plants, including 250 orchids and more than 750 species of trees. In contrast, the whole of the US and Canada put together supports only 730 tree species, giving Belize on average a 1,000 times greater diversity of trees per square mile.

LEFT: the jaguar, largest wildcat in the Americas,
PRECEDING PAGE: the rugged Mountain Pine Ridge.
RIGHT: little blue heron, a mangrove-dweller.

Scientists have catalogued over 70 kinds of forest in Belize, grouping them into three basic types: 16–17 percent are open forests of pine and savanna; less than 5 percent are mangroves and other coastal habitats; while by far the largest type, 68 percent, is broadleaf forests. Vegetation, which is largely determined by soil,

in turn determines to a large extent which animals will thrive, and where they will do so.

Into the rainforest

The broadleaf forests (or, in Belize, all rainforests) support by far the greatest diversity of wildlife. They are the result of optimal conditions for life on land in this area – abundant sunlight, warmth and moisture. The essential core of a rainforest is its dense canopy, formed by the interlaced crowns of trees. One to three layers of trees and, in the understory, shrubs, twined together by twisting vines, create virtually a separate climate within, saving moisture and cooling temperatures.

Leaves, fallen branches and fungi litter the forest floor, where they are quickly broken down into minerals by soil decomposers. The secret of the rainforest is that most of the nutrients are stored not in the soil, but in its living biomass – the roots, trunks, leaves, flowers and fruits, as well as the animals. The nutrients are cycled and recycled throughout the system's plant and animal components.

Despite this, visitors to the tropics may be disappointed with the apparent lack of wildlife.

NOT CATS' EYES...

Spiders are some of the most conspicuous creatures encountered at night, the glinting reflections from their multiple eyes visible up to 15 meters (50 ft) away.

On the ground, it's easiest to spot leafcutter ("wee wee") ants, each carrying a leaf along the wide, clean highways they have cleared on the forest floor. The ants place the pieces of leaves in underground chambers, where they are chewed and processed to grow fungus. The fungus in turn feeds the ants. This relationship is so finely evolved that the fungus can no longer reproduce without the ants.

If you're lucky, you might spot snakes on the forest floor. The luck lies in the fact that 45 of

Although the animals are definitely there, most creatures of the rainforests sense human intruders long before they themselves are noticed, and they take advantage of the innumerable hiding places in the towering walls of green. But if you are patient, perceptive and well-informed, much of the biological wealth of the forest – birds in particular – will eventually reveal itself in all its spendour.

For birders and all wildlife watchers, the best time to visit such a forest is at sunrise, when the air is cool and filled with the sounds of birds feeding and declaring their territories. The broadleaf forest yields tremendous bird biodiversity – more than any other habitat on Earth.

Belize's 54 species are harmless, and even the most poisonous ones would rather slither away than fight. The surest way to steer clear of snakes lurking in the undergrowth is to stay on the trails; unless you are sure of identification, it is best not to interfere with them.

Rainforest nights

After sunset, rainforests come alive with a new, nocturnal shift of creeping, crawling, flying and jumping creatures, making the night a perfect time to scrutinize vegetation on well-marked trails. Tree frogs, gaudily colored lizards, and a multitude of insects and spiders awake and roam the dark jungle in search of sustenance.

The night is also a good time to view mammals. Bats and nighthawks dart above trails, gathering insects while startling hikers. Opossums, armadillos, kinkajous and anteaters are all nocturnal creatures that forage the forest's stream banks and fallen logs. Most nocturnal animals have big eyes that enable them to see in moonlight; point a flashlight at a rustling in the leaves and you might see a bright pair of eyes.

The paca, known as the gibnut in Belize, is a nocturnal rodent the size of a large rabbit. It can sometimes be heard chewing on cohune nuts and thrashing around the litter of the forest floor at night. Gibnut has traditionally been a

wildcats share the territory: jaguarundi, margay, ocelot and puma. All are endangered throughout their ranges, but Belize supports healthy populations. That five species of cat, so similar in their ecological needs, can coexist and thrive within the same rainforest is a tribute to the health of the Belizean habitat.

One of the smaller wildcats (and the most abundant), the jaguarundi moves like a fleeting shadow. Its long, lanky body, slender tail and short legs make the jaguarundi unmistakable. No bigger than a domestic cat, this animal feeds mainly during daylight hours on small rodents, birds and insects.

popular dish in local restaurants, but the eating of wild species is now discouraged – and is also hunted by the five species of Belizean wildcats.

Famous felines

As Central America's largest spotted cat, the jaguar is probably the most celebrated creature of the rainforest – Belize created the world's first wildlife sanctuary specifically to protect it. Roaming beneath the rainforest canopy and along the banks of mountain streams, four other

LEFT: park wardens at leisure in Cockscomb Basin Wildlife Sanctuary.
ABOVE: the shy tapir, Belize's national animal.

FOREST GIANTS

Belize's national animal, Baird's tapir, known locally as the "mountain cow", is the largest in the forest. Although weighing up to 300 kilos (650 pounds), tapirs can dissolve silently into the forest at the first sign of danger. A distinctive feature of these tapirs is their long prehensile lip, used to forage for leaves.

Tapirs prefer rainforest pools and swamps, although they may be seen in other habitats. Despite their adaptiveness, the tapir is endangered throughout its range (Mexico to Ecuador) by hunting and deforestation. Belize is one of the last remaining strongholds of this magnificent creature.

The shy, nocturnal margay has very large eyes, the extremely bright shine of which attests to its highly developed night vision. Superlative balance and great leaping ability make the margay ideally adapted for life in the forest canopy. Margays prefer primary or old-growth forests, but are rarely seen in the wild.

The ocelot's name comes from the Aztecan word *tlalocelotl*, meaning "field tiger", although it prefers second-growth or recently cut forests. Known locally as the tiger cat, the beautiful spotted ocelot – which was hunted nearly to extinction for its fur – is about the size of a medium dog. It keeps to the forest

floor, feeding occasionally on prey such as anteaters and brocket deer.

Of the larger cats, the jaguar inhabits lowland forests near streams and swamps, whereas the puma (known as the cougar or mountain lion in the United States) prefers the highlands and drier ridge areas of the forest. As a result, the two rarely encounter each other.

The call of the wild

Another celebrated inhabitant of the Belizean rainforest is the black howler monkey, whose aggressive and alarming roar is frequently mistaken for that of a jaguar. Baboons, as they are known in Belize, live in troops of between four and eight, and carve out a territory of favorite food trees. They defend their territories from intruding rival troops with their remarkable voices, which advise other black howlers of their presence. Howlers often begin and end their days with a roar – a noise that can carry for several kilometers.

The black howler monkey's range is limited to southern Mexico, northern Guatemala and Belize, and throughout this area, the populations are rapidly declining due to deforestation. Belize supports one of the last strongholds of baboons in the region: at the Community Baboon Sanctuary – the product of a grassroots project for which landowners have agreed to manage their properties in ways that will not be detrimental to the baboons – there are an estimated 1,200 monkeys *(see page 219)*. It is hoped that some of them will be transferred from the sanctuary back to their former homes, including the Cockscomb Basin Wildlife Sanctuary *(see page 232)*.

RISKS AND RULES

Though a naturalist's heaven, Belize can become purgatory for those ill-informed about the dangers of tropical wildernesses, so stay safe by following a few simple rules:
● Don't go alone. All forests begin to look alike once you're off the trail, and if you chase a bird or a red-eyed tree frog into the forest, it can be very easy to lose your orientation. It's best to hire a licensed guide.

● Stay on the trails. You are not only less likely to get lost, but also much less likely to stumble over nasties such as the deadly fer-de-lance and coral snakes that live among the litter of the forest floor. (Don't panic: most snakes are non-poisonous, and all will avoid you if they can.)

● Watch where you place you hands and feet. Some palm trees have needle-like thorns sticking out horizontally from their trunks, which will cause a nasty wound. Avoid unexpected meetings with snakes (see 2) by looking to see what's on the other side before stepping over fallen logs. And check for ants before sitting down.

● Carry sunscreen. You need only leave the protection of the broadleaf canopy for a short time to get burned.

The multitude of insects in Belizean forests is generally more of a nuisance than a serious hazard; but see Travel Tips: Health, *page 340*, for the relevant information on how to avoid the more disagreeable species.

In the savanna forests

Savannas are grasslands with trees, ranging from a few clumps to dense stands, embedded in them. With the exception of the high Mountain Pine Ridge in the Cayo District, most savannas are along the level lowlands of the north and on a strip east of the Maya Mountains, behind the coast. Islands of limestone, surrounded by oceans of wind-blown grasses and knurled trees, attest to the harshness of the habitat.

GRASSLAND ROUTE

The Manatee Road, running between Belize City and Dangriga, meanders through some of the most beautiful savannas in Belize.

Savanna flora in Belize evolved to subsist in extremes of climate and soil. Plants must deal alternately with water-logging during the rainy season and severe drought during the dry season. Savanna soils are poorly drained, acidic and nutrient-poor, allowing only hardy plants such as pines, oaks, craboo and palmettos to flourish. (The craboo is a small tree that produces a yellow, cherry-sized fruit that Belizeans use in jams, ice cream and wine.)

Caribbean pine is a prominent feature of the coastal savanna. Driving along stretches of the Northern Highway, the new coastal road and much of the Southern Highway, formations of this pine align themselves like silent sentries awaiting review. Many have scorched trunks, blackened by fire – usually from lightning strikes in the spring and early summer. Fires start at the tops of pines or in the tinder-like grass, and may burn or smoulder for days.

Many larger pines are protected by their thick bark, while the seeds of many shrubs and other trees actually need to be scorched in order to germinate. For this reason savanna plants are often referred to as pyrophytes. Not all fires in the savanna are started by natural causes. Though the practice is discouraged, hunters will often light fires to flush out deer and other game, or to clear land for other use. Savanna land is increasing in area in Belize.

Despite the inhospitable appearance of savannas, many mammal species forage there. The gray fox, one of the most common mammals in Belize, is about the size of a house cat, with a large bushy tail. It is an excellent climber, spending the hottest part of the day in the upper branches of the forest. The white-tailed deer is found in savanna areas as it emerges during the early morning to search for tender new shoots.

Unmissable birds

Though some luck is required to spot mammals in savanna lands, the wide open spaces are ideal for birding, and more than 100 species can be seen. The striking vermilion flycatcher, a sparrow-sized bright red bird, is often seen making repeated sorties to nab flying insects. The fork-tailed flycatcher, whose aerial

acrobatics make it an unmistakable inhabitant of the savanna, sports 10-inch (25-cm) long tail feathers, which make up half to two-thirds of this small bird's total length.

The most spectacular bird of the wet savanna is the jabirú, the largest stork in the Americas. Standing nearly 5 ft (1.5 meters) tall, the jabirú is white with a black head and a red band around the neck. It constructs a distinctive 8-ft (2.4-meter) diameter nest atop a pine, which is visible from a considerable distance away. In pre-protection days, this exposed nest made the endangered stork easy prey for hunters. Now fully protected, the jabirú is the symbol of the Central Bank of Belize. ❑

LEFT: park warden interacting with a howler monkey.
RIGHT: coral snake, one variety of which is deadly poisonous, and should be treated with great caution.

BELIZE – A MODEL FOR ECOTOURISM?

Belize offers some of the most pristine habitats in Central America. But how do you exploit such a bountiful legacy without ruining it in the process?

Belize's barrier reef, atolls, rivers, mountains and tropical forest along with its imposing Maya ruins and vibrant contemporary culture make it ideal for the development of ecotourism. This small Central American state of only 280,000 people has a low population density that has allowed a combination of state and private reserves to protect more than 40 percent of Belize's territory.

TOURISM WITHOUT TEARS

In the mid-1980s, the government recognized that small-scale, low-impact tourism was the way to provide stable economic growth while still safeguarding the environment. Rather than follow the mass-tourism path of Cancún 400 km (250 miles) to the north, Belize decided to follow one that would allow as many Belizeans as possible to participate in the tourism industry as stakeholders.

The development of a small number of up-scale lodges in the spectacular interior of Belize has provided a model of sustainable tourism that has both set standards and inspired many Belizeans to develop a network of accommodation and services to support the burgeoning industry.

Tourism is now Belize's number one foreign revenue earner. The government has begun to embrace cruise tourism and cruise ship passengers easily outnumber other travelers at many popular sites. Stakeholders must balance the economic benefits of mass tourism with its potential damage to the environment and sites of cultural value.

△ **PROUD HERITAGE**
Belize's numerous reserves and parks make it an ecotourism paradise – and a fine role model.

△ **RARE BIRDS**
Habitat loss and poaching has meant only isolated pockets of the magnificent scarlet macaw survive.

◁ **BIG CATS**
The *Panthera Onca*, or jaguar, largest of the New World cats. Rare in Central America, Belize supports healthy numbers.

▷ **TOLEDO GUESTHOUSE**
In the southern Toledo district, enterprising initiatives enable visitors to stay in small villages and visit local attractions.

BELIZE ZOO
The Belize Zoo mixes fun and education to promote the conservation of endangered species and critical habitats.

ON THE TRAIL
With the help of a guide, trail systems can be explored throughout Belize on horseback, by mountain bike or on foot.

WORLD-FAMOUS COCKSCOMB BASIN

Established in 1984 as a small forest reserve, the Cockscomb Basin Wildlife Sanctuary soon evolved into a reserve of over 98,800 acres hectares (40,000). Made famous by the Wildlife Conservation Society's Alan Rabinowitz's study of jaguars, this world-reknown sanctuary is a haven for many rare and endangered species such as puma, ocelot, margay, tapir, otter and scarlet macaw. Lodging facilities are available at the park administration center and well-maintained trails are constantly being expanded. Raleigh International built a trail that leads through the tropical forest for several days to the jagged granite summit of Victoria Peak. Many of the park rangers are from nearby Maya Center where there is a community guest house project, medicinal plant trail and crafts shop, while villagers act as nature guides and porters for expedition trips.

CORAL KINGDOM
Belize is home to the longest barrier reef system in the western hemisphere.

WELCOME TO BELIZE
You can be sure of a warm welcome and wonderful hospitality from the friendly, easygoing people of Belize.

BELIZE'S BARRIER REEF

Immerse yourself in a spectacular underwater world of colorful
corals, tropical fish, huge rays, barracudas, sharks and turtles

The seaward rim of Belize's barrier reef, referred to as the fore-reef, is a popular destination for scuba divers and snorkelers. It's not hard to understand why: imagine floating along an underwater mountain ridge; to the east stretches an abyss of indigo, below lies a 60-degree slope covered by a quilt of colorful coral plates and swaying fronds. A formation of eagle rays cruises past, their meter-long wings lazily flapping, grace in slow motion; groupers lurk in the shadow of coral heads, their skins darkening to blend into the surroundings; tiny damsel fish defend their territories against intruders (including divers); and parrotfish, the grazers of the sea, browse among the algae attached to dead corals while fluorescent blue chromis float above coral gardens.

Understanding the barrier reef

If coral reefs are visual poems that fill a diver's sense of sight with form, color and patterns, then Belize is a master poet, and the Belize barrier reef a colossal epic. At 300 km (185 miles) in length, and dotted with around 1,200 cayes, the Belize barrier reef is the second-largest in the world after Australia's Great Barrier Reef. The variety of reef types and marine life within its borders is unequaled in the northern hemisphere. Belizean waters are perfect for coral growth. Corals are finicky and they require warm, salty, clear water, steady sunlight and a shallow, firm foundation on which to grow.

The barrier reef and its offshore atolls lie perched atop underwater geological formations that appeared towards the end of the Cretaceous era about 65 million years ago. Coral has formed a crust on the shallow portions of three of these fault escarpments, separated by deep cuts. Windward of the best-developed scarp – off southern Belize – the sea floor lies more than 1,000 meters (3,300 ft) beneath the surface. Relatively recent reef growth commenced

5,000–8,000 years ago as seawater was gradually released from Ice Age glaciers.

Relics can still be seen, as scientists discovered when they drilled deep into the reefs. Closer to the surface, along the northern shore of Ambergris Caye, lies further evidence of these ancient reefs. Sharp, skeletal remains of

staghorn, elkhorn and brain corals lie exposed onshore, cemented together in a matrix of coral, sand and shells. These eroded fossils conjure up images of prehistoric landscapes; but you don't have to go far to see them come to life.

Hard and soft coral

South of these formations, hard coral begins to form a true barrier reef as it snakes toward the Bay of Honduras. Its structural framework is composed of limestone, on which billions of individual coral polyps form colonies connected by living tissue. Each polyp consists of a set of tentacles, a mouth, and a gut perched atop a limestone skeleton. The polyps have

---

LEFT: exploring the crystal waters off Queen's Caye.
RIGHT: Lighthouse Reef's Blue Hole, a sinkhole, one of Belize's most popular dive sites.

cells on the outside of their bodies that secrete calcium carbonate. As the colony grows, the polyps build their skeletons from underneath, pushing themselves up or out into a myriad of sizes and shapes. Growth rates vary with different species and conditions, but coral reefs in warm, tropical waters tend to grow upward by only about 10 mm (half an inch) every year.

A coral reef, then, is actually a thin layer of life on top of ever-accumulating pieces of limestone. When an inattentive swimmer or errant boat hits or brushes against a piece of coral, the damage may not be immediately apparent; but, much like a small wound on a human which

Diving on the reef

The Belize barrier reef is split into segments separated by relatively deep channels. Oxygen and plankton (free-floating microscopic plants and animals) carried by tides flush the Belize coastal zone twice daily through these channels, thereby feeding billions of hungry coral polyps and other reef creatures. As a result, the reef attracts large numbers of fish and is consequently excellent for diving and snorkeling.

Hundreds of species of fish are visible to snorkelers and divers over the coral reefs. Most ignore humans, unless the area has been heavily spear-fished. But there are exceptions. Bar-

can become infected if not properly treated, a coral wound may allow disease or infection to develop. Since the entire colony is connected by living tissue, a small, seemingly inconsequential injury may eventually wipe out a whole coral colony, one that took hundreds of years to develop.

Soft corals, close relatives, also secrete calcium carbonate, but they contain tiny pieces of limestone, protected by a leathery coat, inside their bodies. Soft corals, which can be distinguished by the branches that wave gracefully in the water currents, come in a range of hues – including yellows, reds and purples – and form colorful underwater forests.

racudas have an unnerving habit of approaching and even following swimmers. This is pure curiosity – they normally move away when approached. Moray eels have a nasty reputation; alarmingly, they open and close their mouths as if about to bite, when they are merely pumping water through their gills. Be careful nevertheless: morays can inflict a nasty bite if annoyed. Sharks will sense you long before you see them, and usually move away. However, all sharks should be treated with caution. Even the nurse shark can become aggressive if molested.

Fire coral lives in shallow water. Characterized by a smooth surface and a uniform mustard color, it grows in two distinct forms:

plate-like and encrusting. If touched, both cause intense stinging and welting. Some sponges also cause irritation, as do bristle worms and hydroids. The golden rule when exploring the coral reef is: don't ever touch anything. In fact it's a good idea to stay at least a yard/meter away from everything.

Coral atolls

Lying as close as 16 km (10 miles) off the barrier reef are three of the very finest coral atolls in the Caribbean: Turneffe Island, Glover's Reef and Lighthouse Reef. With almost 225 km (140 miles) of lush coral growth, the reef sys-

The mangrove coastline

Coral reefs do not exist in isolation. Mangroves line much of the Belizean coastline, the cayes and lower reaches of the rivers. Seagrass beds, their blades swaying in the current like the long grass of spring meadows, blanket the sea floor between reef and shore. These mangrove and seagrass beds may not look as spectacular as coral reefs but, as giant marine nurseries, they form the foundation of the continuing long-term health of the country's coastal zone. The quiet water protected by the reef – a self-repairing breakwater – supports mangrove roots and grass blades, which provide plentiful food and

tems surrounding these atolls rival Belize's barrier reef in length. Within the coral barrier surrounding the atolls lie thousands of patch reefs; in the case of Turneffe, the largest of the atolls with an area of more than 520 sq. km (200 sq. miles), there are some 175 small mangrove-covered islands. These three atolls provide some of the finest wall diving in the world. (For further details on all the diving and snorkelling possibilities in the outer reef, see Outdoor Adventure, page 59.)

LEFT: a close encounter of the shark kind, in Hol Chan Marine Reserve, Ambergris Caye.
ABOVE: a hawksbill turtle in Lighthouse Reef.

RESEARCH ON THE REEF

The basic structure of the barrier reef is consistent all along its 300-km (185-mile) length. At Carrie Bow Caye, a marine lab perched atop the edge of the barrier reef, scientists from the Smithsonian Institution have divided the reef up into basic zones or habitats. These are distinguished by conditions such as current, slope and type of bottom. Support communities of plant and animal life have adapted to these variable conditions.

Four major and 12 minor zones have been established along an east–west line north of Carrie Bow Caye. These zones include grass beds, reef flats and spur and groove formations, each with their own specialized lifeforms.

shelter for countless juvenile marine organisms. Most of the seafood caught off Belize depends on mangroves or seagrass.

As well as stabilizing the coastline against erosion and presenting a natural buffer against destructive hurricane winds, mangroves link rich nutrients on land with the billions of hungry mouths at sea. Every year Belizean rivers transport tons of sediment and debris to the sea from deep within the interior. The nutrients in these loads, deposited along the coast, may be in forms unavailable to marine life. Mangroves, which thrive on these frequent deposits, produce new foliage while protecting delicate

polyps from sediment and pollution.

When a mangrove leaf drops into the waters below, the process of decomposition begins. Millions of voracious micro-organisms attack the leaf, slowly releasing the nutrients within for coming generations. Small invertebrates such as worms, shrimp and crabs feed on these nutrients and microbes; these are in turn eaten by larger creatures, until the nutrients within are passed on through the food chain.

Many of these smaller fish become prey to the flocks of wading birds that comb the surf line for food. Roseate spoonbills, ibises, herons, and cormorants nest on the small mangrove islands in Chetumal Bay, leeward of Amber-

gris, while magnificent frigatebirds, boobies and terns have established nesting colonies on cayes to the south. Man-O-War Caye, 16 km (10 miles) east of Dangriga, has one of the largest colonies of frigatebirds in the Caribbean. Ospreys build nests, or rather loose piles of sticks, in the highest trees on the cayes.

Jewels of evolution

The entire coastal zone of Belize is awash with life. Jewels of evolution are continually being found. For example, Smithsonian scientists recently stumbled upon a tiny bay that may be unique in the Caribbean. A quirk of nature allows mangroves to grow on the edge of a series of deep sinkholes. Healthy colonies of lettuce coral carpet the steep slopes of the depressions. As the slopes rise into shallow water, the multicolored scene explodes into activity; crinoid arms perform silent ballets between tall loggerhead sponges; star and brain corals flourish among seagrasses and mangrove roots. Sponges, anemones and tunicates (diminutive barrel-shaped creatures better known as sea squirts) cling to the prop roots as they compete for limited space.

Researchers have identified an incredible 43 different tunicates in this one location, that is, more than was previously discovered throughout the entire Caribbean. The fish are so abundant that they form layers, with the smaller ones near the surface, the larger specimens a level down, and the fat-bodied herrings blanketing the carpet of lettuce coral.

The location of this bay will stay a closely guarded secret until scientists, the government and conservation groups can agree on proper management of the area. The risks cannot be overestimated. These organisms evolved over millions of years in a stable or gradually changing environment. Any sudden stress – from pollution, overfishing or injuries inflicted by a careless diver – can be devastating. A visitor might not even be conscious of kicking a piece of coral; for the coral it is a matter of life and death, and for Belizeans it is slow destruction of a priceless resource. The bay is a gauge of the local marine system's health. Areas such as this expose Belize as a raw wilderness, below the waves no less than in the rainforest. ❑

LEFT: delicate sea stars cling to mangrove roots.
RIGHT: the feather-like feeding antennae of tubeworms.

Music and Dance

Belize's music faces a similar plight to its food. Although the country has some wonderful raw musical talent and an array of local styles, much of what people listen to is imported – reggae and dancehall from Jamaica, soca and calypso from the eastern Caribbean, and salsa, merengue and boleros from Latin neighbors.

Belize's musical equivalent to rice 'n' beans is cooked up during the annual September celebrations when favorite imported dance songs are played night after night. Some of the country's

most talented musicians end up in show-bands, rehashing spotless cover versions of contemporary dance hits or serving up refried Caribbean reggae with a just a dash of Latin salsa.

The exception to the gloomy state of affairs facing local music is punta rock. Based on the traditional Garífuna drum beats of the country's south, punta evolved during the 1980s to become the Belizean sound and is now enjoying enormous popularity. The celebrated punta old guard – Andy Palacio, Bredda David, Chico Ramos and Titiman Flores – have been joined by new arrivals Sound Boys International, Griga Boyz and Punta Rebels, the hottest punta band.

Punta has been exported to North America and Europe with considerable success. Locally, it has won the hearts of virtually every ethnic group in the country and is the one native sound that manages to kick the imports off the radio and dance floors. The *punta*, an erotic mating ritual full of passion and spirit, has returned steamy romance to the dance floor and become the national dance.

The other exceptional modern Belizean band is the Christian group D-Revelation. Its music sounds good, and the band does good, using the success of its music to support a range of child-welfare and environmental causes. A "Stay in School Jam" gig, aimed at combatting Belize's truancy problem, attracted thousands of schoolchildren. D-Revelation is probably the country's single biggest musical draw in the field of pop. The band has toured extensively abroad on the strength of the albums *Virtually Live!* and *Payday*.

The Sound of Brukdown

The local music scene was a lot more vibrant during the logging days of the 19th century. Then the country's community let its hair down by "bramming" – groups of revelers would travel from house to house, push the furniture against the walls and use any available household object as a musical instrument on which to play "brukdown" music. In addition to drums, banjos, guitars, accordions and cow bells, purveyors of brukdown would utilize broom handles, wash basins metal graters and even an ass's jawbone. The Creole lyrics, spontaneously thought up on the spot, tended to be about famous people or local happenings.

After several years in the wilderness, brukdown is making something of a comeback with the release of albums by the uncrowned king of brukdown, Mr Peters and his Boom and Chime band. Mr Peters and his Belizean Creole sound is gaining an international reputation as he tours abroad.

In place of an ass's jawbone, Belize's festive partygoers are these days more likely to bring out the late-20th-century equivalent, the karaoke machine. Nearly every bar in every street in every town in Belize has karaoke and a night out isn't complete without at least one singalong session. These are fronted by a growing number of semi-professional karaoke singers, backed by aspiring vocalists plucked from the crowd.

The karaoke singers' inspiration most probably comes from local radio stations. Love FM and KREM play a wide range of music, while specialist stations such as Estereo Amor (the station for Latin lovers) cater specifically for certain ethnic groups.

Many Belizeans also watch MTV and Black Entertainment Television on cable, which explains why Creole youngsters have become so enamored with the latest American rap stars.

Annual Festivals

Party-time in Belize peaks during the annual September festivities, when the two most significant events in the country's history are celebrated: the Battle of St George's Caye Day on September 10 commemorates the 1798 sea battle which finally saw off Spanish claims to Belize; Independence Day on September 21 marks the day that British rule came to an end in 1981.

Music plays a vital role in the celebrations and every year an assortment of favorite old Tenth Songs – mainly patriotic march tunes and sentimental ballads – hits the airwaves. The party fire is usually stoked by Byron Lee, a veteran Jamaican soca artist who plays a selection of catchy dance songs.

A more cerebral musical offering during recent September revelries has been Francis Reneau's *Celebration* album, first released in 1996. Reneau, probably Belize's most talented musician and composer, wrote his first major work *Mass in Blues* when he was just 17. In 1994, he was commissioned to write an album drawing together all the country's musical threads; the resulting *Celebration* features Maya harp and marimba, Creole laments and humor, Garífuna singing and drumming, and Latin boleros and salsa, all performed by five generations of Belize's top musicians.

Throughout the country people enjoy discos and parties on the eve of the September public holidays. The following morning, they crawl out of bed to watch the parades weave through town. Trucks bearing huge speakers are followed by dancing crowds. While the flag-raising at the courthouse on Independence Eve and the official ceremonies the next morning are very solemn events, a party atmosphere prevails later in the day as people swarm the parks or main streets for the "jump up," or street fair, with lots of food and music.

Keeping the party going, Garífuna Settlement Day, on November 19, commemorates the 1832 arrival of the largest group of Garífuna to Belize's southern shores, and is a non-stop cultural fête. The best place to enjoy this is in Dangriga, where the celebratory music and dancing starts on the evening before Settlement Day. At dawn the following morning there is a re-enactment of the arrival of the early settlers in their *dories*. As they enter town from the mouth of the river, the travelers are greeted by women singing, drums beating and the waving of cassava sticks and the distinctive yellow, black and white Garífuna flags.

Both Garífuna Settlement Day and Christmas are greeted in Garífuna towns with Joncunu (John Canoe) dancers. Outfitted in pink wire masks, white tunics with flowing ribbons, elaborate crowns with tall feathers, and hundreds of tiny shells attached to their knees, the dancers go from door to door dancing the *wanaragua*, with arms outstretched

and legs together. Some say the dance is meant to imitate the behavior of white slave-holders, which might explain why it has traditionally been popular at Christmas, when master-slave relations would, for a short time, be more relaxed.

The *mestizo* and Maya communities have their own religious and other events, particularly at Easter time – costume parades begin the weekend before Lent. In Orange Walk, Las Mascaradas wear scary disguises and drag chains through the streets, while others perform skits or *comparsas* door to door. Most *mestizo* and Maya villages have an annual fiesta in honor of their patron saint, the largest of which is held in July in Benque Viejo del Carmen, near the Guatemalan border. ❑

LEFT: Mr Peters – on jawbone.
RIGHT: Garífuna group from Hopkins, near Dangriga.

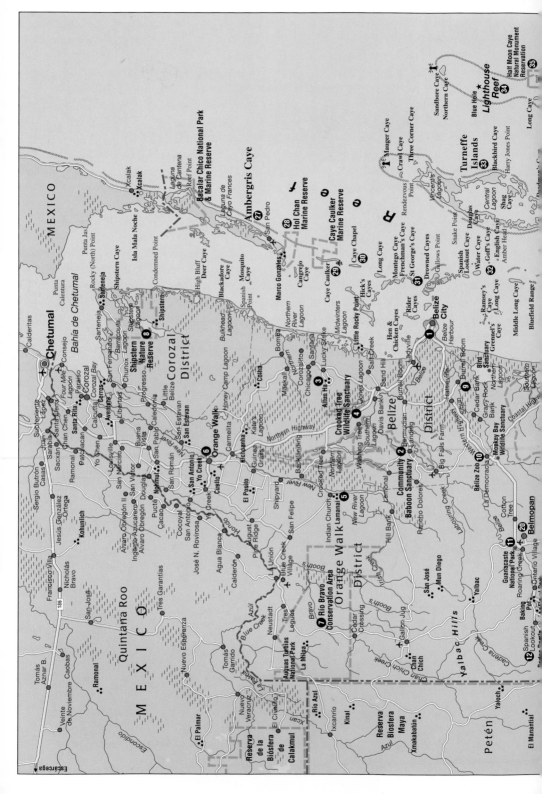

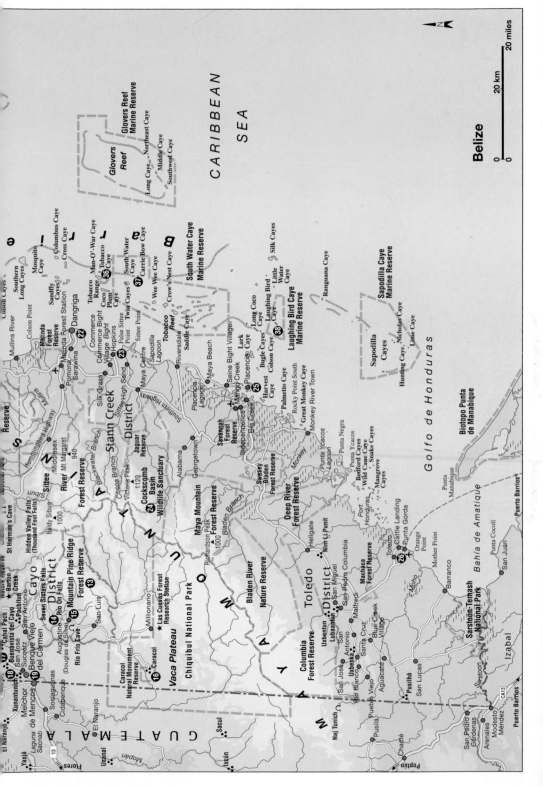

Belize

0   20 km
0   20 miles

N

CARIBBEAN SEA

Glovers Reef
Marine Reserve

Glovers
Reef
Long Caye • Northeast Caye
Middle Caye
Southwest Caye

Southern
Long Cayes

Colson Cayes

Mosquito
Caye
Columbus Caye
Cross Caye

Sandfly
Cayes
Man-O'-War Caye
Tobacco
Caye
Tobacco
Range

South Water Caye
Marine Reserve

South Water
Caye
Carrie Bow Caye

Coco
Plum
Caye
Wee Wee Caye
Crow's Nest Caye

Silk Cayes

Laughing Bird Caye
Marine Reserve

Laughing Bird
Caye
Little
Water
Caye

Long Coco
Caye

Bugle Cayes
Colson Caye

Ranguana Caye

Sapodilla Caye
Marine Reserve

Sapodilla
Cayes
Nicholas Caye
Lime Caye
Hunting Caye

Biotopo Punta
de Manabique

Golfo de Honduras

Tobacco
Reef

Saddle Caye

Riversdale

Maya Centre
Maya Beach
Seine Bight Village
Sapodilla
Lagoon
Placencia
Lagoon
Placencia
Mango Creek
Big Creek
Independence
Harvest
Caye

Lark
Caye
Sittee
Point
Sittee
Point

False Sittee
Point
Twin Cayes

Palmetto Caye

Rocky Point South
Great Monkey Caye
Monkey River Town

Punta Ycacos
Lagoon
Port
Honduras
Punta Negra

Mullins River
Colson Point

Melinda
Forest
Reserve
Pomona Melinda Forest Station
Sarawina
Dangriga

Commerce Bight
Commerce Bight
Village Bight
Hopkins

Silk Grass

Gales Point

S
Reserve

Mullins
Hummingbird Highway

Sittee
Middlesex
River Mt Margaret
940
Baldy Sibun

Blackwater Branch

Cocoa Branch
Victoria Peak
1120

Stann Creek
District

Jaguar
Reserve

Cockscomb
Basin
Wildlife Sanctuary

Alabama
Georgetown

Savannah
Forest
Reserve

Swasey Bladen
Forest Reserve

Deep River
Forest Reserve

Monkey
River

Bedford Cayes
Wild Cane Caye
Snake Cayes
Mangrove
Cayes

Punta
Manabique

Bahía de Amatique

Punta Gorda
Punta Cocoli

Orange
Point
Mother Point

San Juan

Puerto Barrios

Hidden Valley Falls
(Thousand Foot Falls)
St Herman's Cave

Mountain Pine Ridge
Forest Reserve

Seven Sisters Falls
Rio On Falls
Augustine
(Douglas d'Silva)
Rio Frio Cave

San Luis

Las Cuevas Forest
Research Station

Millionario

Maya Mountain
Forest Reserve

Richardson Peak
1000
Bladen Branch

Bladen River
Nature Reserve

Hellgate

Cayo
District

Cahal Pech
Barton
Creek
San José
San Antonio
Buenavista del Cayo
Sucotz
Benque Viejo
del Carmen
Xunantunich

Caracol
Caracol
Natural Monument
Reserve

Vaca Plateau

Chiquibui National Park

Columbia
Forest Reserve

San José
Naj Tunich
Río Blanco
Pueblo Viejo
Aguacate

Uxbentun
Lubaantun
San
Antonio
Santa Cruz

San Miguel
San Pedro Columbia
Mafredi

Machaca
Forest Reserve

Toledo
District

Cattle Landing
Toledo

San Pedro

Pusilhá
San Lucas

Blue Creek
Village

Sarstoon-Temash
National Park

Barranco

Modesto
Arenales
Izabal

Sarstoon

Mopán
Chaché

San Pedro
Cárdenas
Poptún

G U A T E M A L A

El Naranjo
Yaxjá
Laguna
de Mencos
Sacnab
Sosjagudnas
Ciddaberqás
Melchor
de Mencos
El Naranjo

Uañal

Flores
13
Ixtun
Sacul

Mopan

CA13
San Pedro
Méndez

Puerto Barrios

PLACES

A detailed guide to the entire country, with principal sites
clearly cross-referenced by number to the maps

Belizeans like to tell you that that once you have drunk fresh Belize creek water and tasted rice and beans, their staple diet, you are certain to come back. Even if you don't succumb to these particular culinary temptations, once you have dived the rainbow-colored water world around Belize's spectacular coral reef, traced the ancient footsteps of Maya priests to the top of great pyramids, and swum in crystal clear pools in the rainforest, it's still more than likely you will want to return for a second helping.

Belize City is the hub, the whole nation under one roof, distilled down into this bustling, ramshackle port town by the Caribbean Sea. It's no surprise the locals often refer to their true capital simply as "Belize" because it seems like everyone in the country has crammed in here, leaving the rest of the country for the birds.

North of the City, riverside Creole communities left slumbering since the end of the logging industry in the 1960s are waking up to help unlock Belize's environmental treasure-chest. Situated in vast wetlands and pristine rainforest, you can see more wildlife here in one day than in most other parts of the world in a year.

In the forested northwest, Maya cities hidden for centuries by the jungle are coming back to life, their mysteries painstakingly being unraveled by teams of archeologists from around the world.

Heading west into the hills around San Ignacio, a welcome drop in temperature is accompanied by a booming network of comfortable jungle lodges, and it's possible to adventure here in style. Capped by the Mountain Pine Ridge, home of the great Maya city of Caracol, the region has become Belize's main inland ecotourism center.

In the south, years of splendid isolation are coming to an end with the arrival of paved roads. The fascinating communities of the afro-indigenous Garífuna people dominate nearly the entire southern coastline, from Dangriga all the way down to Punta Gorda.

In Placencia, one of the fastest developing of all Belize's holiday destinations, the locals retain a defiantly laid-back lifestyle. More adventurous souls can head for the interior of the deep south and Belize's only true tropical rainforest, where Maya villages coexist with nature in a way that hasn't changed in thousands of years.

Finally, and the highlight for most visitors to Belize, are the cayes (pronounced keys), a necklace of islands strung the length of the coral reef that offer probably the best diving, snorkeling and fishing in the world. Unforgettable islands, the cayes range from upbeat tourist spots to stranded desert isles, where the only other life you are likely to see will be the pelicans, palm trees and crabs. ❑

PRECEDING PAGES: the tranquil beauty of Belize's southern coast, at Jaguar Reef Lodge, near Placencia.
LEFT: Belize's cayes offer the ultimate tropical paradise experience.

BELIZE CITY

The hidden charms of Belize's largest and shambolically ramshackle city are all in its non-stop street life: chaotic but laid-back and unmistakeably Caribbean

Maps:
Area 206
City 212

U nlike the debauched pirate town of Port Royal in Jamaica, which fell into the sea following an earthquake, **Belize City ❶**, which was equally uninhibited in its buccaneer heyday, was literally raised from the sea on top of empty rum bottles. Built on a swamp, divided in two by the Haulover Creek, and surrounded on three sides by the Caribbean Sea, Belize City often seems to be more water than land and is fighting an ongoing battle against drowning – fortunes are spent every year keeping it out of the mud. Yet its 60,000-strong population drawn from just about every ethnic group under the sun manages to keep the city afloat, combining to create a metropolis all of its own.

History

The city was founded in the early 1700s by the British "Baymen" – former pirates who had settled in the Bay of Honduras in the 17th century *(see page 181.)* The Baymen made their first Belizean settlement on St George's Caye, a few miles off the coast of Belize, succeeded by a settlement at the mouth of the Belize River, which developed into Belize City, the country's commercial capital. The city grew with the development of the timber trade – first logwood, which grew nearer the coast, and then mahogany, found further inland.

Belize City was the country's capital until another in a regular series of devastating hurricanes in 1961 killed hundreds of people and flattened many of its buildings. The seat of government was subsequently moved inland to a purpose-built site at Belmopan.

Visitors usually only stay in the City begrudgingly, put off by its bad reputation, shabby and neglected appearance and the lure of the cayes and the interior. The reputation was mainly based on the old foul-smelling open drains, and a gang problem which got out of hand. Yet Belize City is worth a visit, if only for a day or two. It remains the commercial and cultural center of the country, and has some excellent museums on the country's rich marine ecology and archaeology. Throughout a turbulent history of hurricanes, fires, disease and violence, the capital has retained a friendly Caribbean charm, which always shines through.

The city center

At the heart of the city is the **Swing Bridge ❹**, the most popular crossing point across the Haulover Creek, so named because cows and other large objects had literally to be hauled over the creek by the original settlers. The Swing Bridge is the world's oldest operational manual swing bridge, assembled in 1923 from parts shipped from Liverpool, England. Cranked open at dawn and dusk (5.30am and 5.30pm) so tall

LEFT: Belize City from the air.
BELOW: people-watching is a favorite city pastime.

Belize City

↑ Municipal Airport
Moho Caye

University College Belize

National
Ⓜ Stadium

St John's College

New Library

National Library

Karl Heusner Memorial Hospital

San Cas Plaza

Fire Station

Belcan Bridge

Haulover Creek

Mopan Street

Mahogany Street

Nargusta Street

Ebony Street

Vernon Street

Logwood Street

Banak Street

Cemetery Road

Novelo's Bus Station

Roger's Stadium

Gibnut Street

Hiccatee Street

Queen's Square Market

Racoon Street

Seagull Street

Curassow Street

Central American Boulevard

Neal's Pen Road

Fairweather Street

Caesar Rd

Princess Margaret Drive

St Matthew Street

St Charles Street

19th St
18th St
17th Street
15th St

St Thomas Street

8th St
6th Street
4th Street
3rd Street
1st Peter Street
St Joseph Street

7th St
5th Street
Hopkins Street
Landivar Street

Baymen Avenue

Newtown Barracks Road

Barracks Road

Lindbergh's Landing

Pickwick Club

FIESTA PARK

MCC Grounds

Fiesta Inn

Simon Lamb Street
Nurse Seay Street

Freetown Road

Mexico-Belize Cultural Institute Ⓛ

Wilson Street

Cran Street

Cleghorn Street

Cinderella Plaza

Kelly Street

Eve Street

Castle St

Douglas Jones St

Victoria Street

Barracks Road

North Front Street

Belchina Bridge

New Road

Pickstock Street

Hydes Lane

Museum of Belize Ⓒ

Central Bank Building

Sarstoon Street

Lakeview Street

Magazine Road

Venus and Z-Line Bus Station

James and Transportes del Carmen Bus Station

Batty Brothers Bus Station

Regent Street West

Mortuary Lane

Queen Street

US Embassy

Hutson St

Mexican Embassy

LORD'S RIDGE CEMETERY

Orange Street

Glyn St

Commercial Center/ Municipal Market

Swing Bridge

Ⓐ

Marine Terminal

Ⓑ ⓘ Tourist Board

Maritime Museum

MEMORIAL PARK

North Park Street

Cork Street

Chateau Caribbean Hotel

Radisson Fort George Hotel and Marina

Fort George Lighthou

Dolphin

West Collet Canal Street

East Collet Canal Street

Amara Avenue

Euphrates Avenue

Tigris Street

George Street

West Street

West Canal Street

Church St

BATTLEFIELD PARK

Ⓕ

Ⓖ Court House and Treasury

Ⓗ Bliss Institute

King Street

Prince Street

Regent Street

Police Headquarters

Dean St

Southern Foreshore

Belize Harbour

Ⓔ ⓘ

Baron Bliss Memorial

Fort George

Basra Street

South St

Allenby St

Rectory Lane

Albert Street

YARBOROUGH CEMETERY

Ⓚ

Racecourse Street

Queen Charlotte Street

Ⓘ

Government House (Museum)

✝ St John's Cathedral

Bird's Isle

Belmopan and Western Highway

Haulover Bridge, Northern Highway and Bella Vista

C A R I B B E A N

S E A

0   500 m
0   500 yds

N

Karl Heusner Memorial Hospital

boats can sail up the river, traffic and pedestrians have to wait patiently the 15 minutes or so it takes before normal service resumes.

By the north side of the Swing Bridge on North Front Street, the harbor-front **Maritime Museum** ❸ (open Mon–Sat, 8am–5pm; entry fee) is devoted to the history of Belize's long-standing marriage with the sea. The continuing strength of this bond can be seen in the dozens of brightly colored fishing skiffs moored up on the river outside, and speed boats lined up at the Marine Terminal, adjacent to the museum, to take passengers to the cayes. The museum, which is built on the site of a former fire station, houses a collection of antique boats and maritime memorabilia, as well as an aquarium and displays on marine life and coastal geography, with an impressive 3-D model of the entire Belize Barrier Reef. It also has a small café and shop.

Still together after all these years: Belizean and British flags.

The **Museum of Belize** ❹ (Open Mon–Fri, 9am–5pm; entry fee) on Gaol Lane at its corner with Queen Street (in the Central Bank Compound) is housed in a former prison building. The brick structure dates to the early 19th century and remained Belize's only correctional facility until as recently as 1993. One of the original prison cells has been preserved as part of the restoration and there are displays with photographs of the gallows used for hanging people convicted of capital offences.

The Museum contains two permanent exhibitions: "Maya Masterpieces," a collection of artifacts found at ancient Maya sites throughout the country and "Historical Belize City," featuring photographs of old Belize City and the ravages of the 1931 and 1961 hurricanes, and various antiques. There is also an extensive collection of preserved insects and butterflies, old coins and bottles, antiques and a display of Belizean stamps.

BELOW:
the Court House,
one of the city's
finest old buildings.

A short walk east of the Marine Terminal, brings you to the riverside **Image Factory**, at 91 North Front Street, an art gallery run by Yasser Musa, one of a group of popular Belizean poets. The gallery is worth checking out as it often runs shows by some of Belize's most talented modern artists, who sometimes drop in and are glad to discuss their work. The gallery is open Mon–Fri, 9am–6pm, free entry.

Colonial Quarter

Continuing down North Front Street, you'll soon come to a junction, where a left turn along North Park Street will bring you to **Memorial Park** ❶, in a pretty, seafront location, amidst a cluster of grand edifices. The park, with its stage and bandstand, has been at the center of many historic occasions. Music concerts and other events are held here, especially during the September holiday period. The surrounding wooden colonial buildings, including the old Mexican Embassy building, lit up at night in Mexico's national colors, contribute to make this the City's most graceful quarter.

Another elegant mansion nearby is the Chateau Caribbean Hotel, at 6 Marine Parade, on the seafront side of Memorial Park. This former hospital, which stands in contrast to the towering modern opulence of the neighboring Radisson Fort George Hotel, was the favorite haunt of Harrison Ford during the shooting of the 1986 movie *The Mosquito Coast*.

The Harbor entrance

A few blocks south of Memorial Park brings you to where the Fort George Lighthouse dominates the sea wall at the entrance to the harbor. Beneath the lighthouse, the **Baron Bliss Memorial** Ⓔ commemorates a wealthy British yachtsman and fisherman who fell in love with Belize from the sea and became its generous benefactor (*see box on facing page.*)

Down the street from the Baron Bliss Memorial and commanding a large strip of land along the harbor entrance is the Tourism Village, a terminal for arriving cruise ship passengers lined with small gift and duty free shops and restaurants. However, access is restricted to people with valid ship passes.

Dozens of tour companies and taxis operate just outside the village and provide packages for Belize City tours or trips to the Zoo, Altun Ha, Baboon Sanctuary and other destinations in the Belize or Cayo districts. Be sure to negotiate fares and prices of trips before setting off. All tour guides are required to have certification from the Tourism Board so ask to see their credentials.

South of the river

Across the Swing Bridge, pedestrians, cyclists and cars fight noisily for space along the narrow streets and walkways which characterize the Southside. This part of town is regularly gridlocked – when the offices and shops open and shut at 8am and 5pm, and at either end of the lunch hour. Lunch is the big meal of the day so don't expect anything to be open between noon and 1pm.

Downstairs at the modern **Municipal Market** Ⓕ, at the foot of the Swing Bridge, the stubborn survivors of the site's old market, which was dismantled and taken away around their ears, remain to give the place its character. Here

BELOW: speedboat ferries to the Cayes are always buzzing around the city's river mouth.

there's everything the denizens of Belize City need for their favorite meals of rice and beans and cowfoot soup, as well as a range of bush medicines, including the ever popular cleansing bitters.

A couple of blocks south down Regent Street is Belize's **Court House G**. With its elaborate wrought ironwork capped off by the town clock, the building is a reconstruction of the wooden original destroyed by fire in 1926. Next to the Court House, the Treasury Building marks the commercial center of town, where most of the banks, as well as Belize's only department store, Brodie's, are located.

Behind the Court House and Treasury, the walk along the Southern Foreshore beside the river gives the best view of the harbor, and has a boat service to the Cayes from Court House Wharf. The modern **Bliss Institute H**, 2 Southern Foreshore, is Belize's main cultural venue and home to the National Arts Council. You can see a good range of theater, music and dance productions here – it is worth checking with the box office to find out what is on. The institute also houses the National Art Collection (open Mon–Fri, 8.30–noon, 2–8pm.)

Map on page 212

Getting some shade from the heat: crowds crossing the Swing Bridge in the rush hour.

Government House

At the end of Regent Street, in an idyllic seashore setting, is **Government House I**, the city's grandest building, with its wide sweeping staircases and panelled oak interior (open daily, 8am–4pm; entry fee.) When the Governor General, the Crown's representative in Belize, moved to Belmopan in 1981, Government House was converted into a museum and opened to the public. The museum's displays include collections of silver and glassware and colonial furniture, and, in keeping with the regal theme, photographs of the winners of the annual Belize Queen of the Bay beauty pageant.

BELOW: the Fort George Lighthouse.

THE BOUNTIFUL BARON BLISS

Visiting Belize in 1926 in order to recuperate from a serious bout of food poisoning caught in Trinidad, Henry Edward Ernest Victor Bliss, a wealthy businessman and sailor from Buckingham in England with a Portuguese title, discovered a passion for the country that kept him here for the rest of his life.

He spent several months in Belize's coastal waters, living aboard his yacht, the Sea King, fishing and hoping for his health to improve, while enjoying the calm, unspoiled surroundings and Belizean hospitality.

However, his health eventually failed him, and on March 9, 1927 he died peacefully aboard his yacht. So impressed had the Baron been by the beauty of the Belizean coast and cayes, and the kindness shown to him by the people during these difficult months, that he left in his will a trust fund of $2 million established for the benefit of the people of Belize.

Without once being well enough to step ashore, the Baron endowed the people of Belize with a legacy from which health clinics, libraries and museums continue to benefit. In recognition of this generosity, 9 March, the anniversary of his death, is a national holiday celebrated every year with a regatta in the harbor.

Map on page 212

Opposite Government House, on Albert Street, **St John's Cathedral ❶** is famous for being the oldest Anglican Cathedral in Central America. It was built by slaves in the 1800s from English bricks brought to Belize as ballast in the hulls of sailing ships. Nowadays St John's competes with the Holy Redeemer Catholic Church on North Front Street as the dominant place of worship, though the City's religious life is just as diverse as its people and all major religions and denominations are well represented.

Further attractions

To the west of St John's Cathedral is Yarborough, once a wealthy neighborhood, but now the gateway into the poorer parts of town. Running along the Southside Canal, just west of the cathedral, **Yarborough Cemetery ❸** is famous for tales of old Belize now secreted away in the illegible inscriptions of headstones dating from centuries past. Named for the magistrate James Yarborough who owned the land, it was used as a cemetery between 1781 and 1882, first as a burial ground for the colony's prominent personages and later opened up to the masses. Close by the cemetery is a statue of Belize's first self-made millionaire, Emmanuel Isaiah Morter, a follower of Marcus Garvey, and owner of much of Barracks Road, who left a great deal of his fortune to the United Negro Improvement Association. The monument also marks the entrance to what was Eboe Town in the 19th century.

The newer areas of Belize City are more spread out, and you'd be advised to take a car to visit them. Taking a taxi ride can be quite an adventure here with the cabs racing through the streets, narrowly missing pedestrians, and rocketing across bridges. (On the plus side, cab drivers – as everywhere – like talking and can be a good source of recommendations for the latest restaurants and sightseeing.)

BELOW: laid-back friendliness is the city's style.

Newtown Barracks, a short taxi ride north from the city center, is the place to enjoy some sea breeze after the heat and hustle of downtown, with a good selection of parks, restaurants and night clubs. To get acquainted with things Mexican before journeying north, it is worth looking in at the **Mexico-Belize Cultural Institute ❶** which often has art and photographic exhibitions featuring Mexican culture and traditional Mexican music concerts. It is open daily 8am–5pm and entrance is usually free, except for certain events such as concerts when a ticket may need to be purchased in advance.

A drive past the Newtown Barracks, which eventually become Princess Margaret Drive, takes you past the **National Stadium ❻**, a sports arena built by the Marylebone Cricket Club of Great Britain and where all the big cricket matches were once played. Today, cricket is rarely played here (although it is still popular in villages) and soccer has taken over as the crowd-pulling Sunday afternoon event. The National Stadium is also sometimes used for concerts or cultural events.

The area around Princess Margaret Drive is where the more prosperous Belizeans live and where many of the city's schools are located, including St John's College, established by Jesuits in 1887. The exclusive Belize Pickwick Club is a members-only sporting facility featuring tennis courts and one of the city's very few swimming pools. ❑

Belize Zoo

There is one place in Belize where you can be sure of seeing a jaguar or a tapir in a natural setting. The Belize Zoo is an oasis of ponds, forests, and flowers among the sprawling savannas 47 km (29 miles) west of Belize City. More than 60 indigenous Belizean animals live here in large, naturally vegetated enclosures.

In fact, at the height of the midday sun, many of the animals are difficult to see through the dense green foliage in which they lazily shade away from the heat and your prying eyes. Here, the animals come first, taking precedence over visitors' needs, and this makes the experience unlike visiting any other zoo in the world.

You will often feel that you are in the forest, peering through a tangle of vines and shrubs to catch a glimpse of a puma, jaguarundi or ocelot, and just like in the rainforest, patience and persistence are necessary to view the beautiful creatures here. But here your patience will always be rewarded; a glimpse of a jaguar staking out his dominion, time in the company of curious and lively kinkajous, or eye-to-eye contact with the towering jabiru stork; any or all will make the visit more than worthwhile.

The animals and grounds are meticulously cared for, and fun and folksy signs all around the zoo spell out the natural habits of each animal and its endangered status, reminding Belizeans and visitors that "Belize is my home too!".

Raised gravel paths lead from exhibit to exhibit through natural savanna and pine ridge vegetation, as well as transplanted rainforest. The Belize Zoo is as much a botanical garden as it is a zoological park, and it is a focal point for environmental awareness in Belize. The message: we need to save the habitat to save the animals.

Sharon Matola, the North American founder and driving force behind the zoo, arrived in Belize after a colorful career that included time as a lion-tamer in Romania, and a circus tour in Mexico. Today, she often recounts an incident that helped convince her that she was on the right track during the zoo's difficult years of the early 1980s.

A very old man showed up at the gate after closing, and Matola let him in and gave him a personal guided tour. At first the old man commented freely at each cage about well-entrenched Belizean myths – how ant-eaters kill dogs with their tongues, or that boa constrictors are poisonous during the day.

Soon he grew silent. Finally, as they stood in front of a jaguar, basking in the setting sun light, Matola noticed tears in the old man's eyes. "I'm very sorry, Miss," she recalls him saying. "I have lived in Belize all my life and this is the first time I have seen the animals of my country. They are so beautiful."

That was in 1983, when the zoo consisted of just a few animals in temporary chicken wire cages, left behind by a natural history film. Today, the Belize Zoo covers 12 hectares (30 acres), and is part of a larger complex that includes a Tropical Education and Research Center. An unmissable visit. The zoo is open daily, 9am–4.30pm; entry fee. ❑

RIGHT: the jaguar, Central America's largest, and the most elusive, wild cat.

NORTHERN DISTRICTS

*Wide open spaces – vast forests, wetlands, fields of sugar cane –
and the magical mix of environmental and archeological treasures
make Northern Belize a rewarding destination*

Map
on page
206

Belize
City●
Belmopan
●

The North of Belize is the most agriculturally developed region of the country but also, somewhat ironically, the least attractive for visitors. Probably the main reason the people here have been slow to promote the attractions of their part of the country is because they are too busy growing sugar cane, Belize's main crop. Beyond sugar, though, there's plenty to see and do and the North is Belize's ecotourism HQ, home to the country's most successful conservation projects.

North of Belize City, the Northern Highway winds between the Belize river and the deep blue sea, to Ladyville, a village dominated by the International Airport, and Airport Camp, home of the Belize Defence Force, and the remaining British army presence in Belize (they still run jungle training courses here.)

Nine km (5 miles) past Ladyville, a left turn signposted to Burrell Boom and Bermudian Landing is the start of a paved road which winds through quiet Creole villages created and then abandoned by the logging industry.

Community Baboon Sanctuary

Bermudian Landing hosts the **Community Baboon Sanctuary ❷**, a conservation project established in 1985 by an American zoologist backed by the Worldwide Fund for Nature. Persuading local farmers to sign to a plan protecting the broadleaf forest habitat of local black howler monkeys (known in Belize as "baboons"), the project has spread to eight neighboring riverside villages and reversed an alarming fall in monkey numbers.

Tours of the sanctuary can be arranged from the visitors' center (open 8am–5pm; US$10 for entry and tour.) Led by local guides, the tours explore the forest with the highlight being the chance to hear a howler's howl, a frighteningly loud noise which sounds more like what you might expect from a jaguar's roar.

Altun Há

Back on the Northern Highway, past the village of Sand Hill, a turning on the right is signposted to Maskall and Orange Walk. This is the Old Northern Highway, and 19 km (12 miles) along this one-track pot-holed lane, is a left turnoff which leads to the Maya ruins of **Altun Há ❸**, the closest archeological site to Belize City.

Altun Há, Mayan for "stone water", was first excavated in 1957, but extensive work didn't start until the discovery of a jade pendant in 1963 which excited a great deal more interest. Archeological excavations unearthed a jade replica of the head of the Maya sun god Kinich Ahau, found in the Temple of the Masonry Altars. At 15 cm (6 inches) high and weighing 4.4 kg

LEFT: vast swathes of lush rainforest.
BELOW: mask of Kinich Ahau, sun god, in Lamanai.

Making friends: Mestizo girl with pet coati-mundi.

(9¾ pounds), it is the largest carved jade object ever found in the Maya world. The discoveries at Altun Há have pointed to its importance as a coastal trading base and ceremonial center, though the final fate of the settlement, which was suddenly and mysteriously abandoned, has never been discovered. The site is open daily, 8am–4pm; entry fee.

Crooked Tree Wildlife Sanctuary

At Mile 33 (52 km) on the Northern Highway is a left turn sign-posted to the village of Crooked Tree and the **Crooked Tree Wildlife Sanctuary** ❹. Crooked Tree, built on a freshwater island, is the largest of Belize's Creole villages, and the growing popularity of its developing Wildlife Sanctuary has given it a new lease of life. However as most of the 800 people who live here rely on either their feet or their horse to get around, it is in no danger of getting busy.

The 1,200-hectare (3,000-acre) sanctuary opened in late 1984 and is run by local volunteers with support from the Belize Audubon Society. The Sanctuary's lagoons, rivers and wetlands provide perfect habitats for more than 300 species of birds and waterfowl, including ospreys, snail kites, and kingfishers, as well as other wildlife including crocodiles and turtles. The rarest of all is the jabiru stork, a tall, prehistoric-looking monster of a bird, which makes an unnerving rattle with its long beak if it becomes agitated.

RIGHT: Temple of the Masonry Altars, Altun Há.

To help you get the most from the Sanctuary there is a Visitors' Center at the end of the 5-km (3-mile) causeway linking the Northern Highway to Crooked Tree village, which has displays and maps, and can advise on lodgings and tours. Crooked Tree also hosts the annual Crooked Tree Cashew Festival. Held in May, this has grown into one of the area's biggest annual events, showcasing

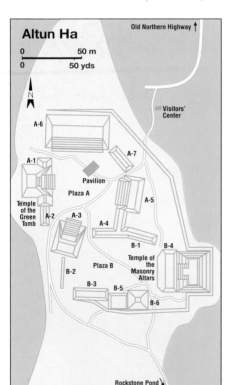

Altun Ha

0 ——— 50 m
0 ——— 50 yds

N

Old Northern Highway ↑

Visitors' Center

A-6

A-7

A-1

Pavilion

Plaza A

A-5

Temple of the Green Tomb

A-2 A-3

A-4

B-1 B-4

Temple of the Masonry Altars

Plaza B

B-2

B-3 B-5

B-6

Rockstone Pond ↘

Belize's culture, products and above all the ability of locals to have a good time. Ostensibly to celebrate the cashew harvest the festival is really just a good opportunity to eat, drink and make merry on homemade Creole food and wine.

Map on page 206

Lamanai

Approaching Orange Walk town on the Northern Highway, some 35 km (22 miles) from from Crooked Tree is the Tower Hill Toll Bridge. On the banks of the New River, by the bridge, a taxi rank of boats ply their trade, waiting to take you along the scenic river journey to Lamanai. This one-hour boat journey is worth making even without the lure of these important Maya ruins. Plants, birds and the occasional crocodile give the expert tour guides plenty to talk about, as the river slowly drifts through the Mennonite colony at Shipyard, past old deserted logging camps, before opening out onto the New River Lagoon.

On the west shore of the New River Lagoon, **Lamanai** ❺, which translates as "submerged crocodile" (though "place of the mosquito swarm" would be an equally appropriate name), was one of the longest continually inhabited settlements anywhere in the Maya world. As well as the Maya ruins, excavations have uncovered the remains of two 16th-century Spanish missions destroyed by the Maya, who apparently rejected this attempt to convert them to Christianity.

Most of the stelae, relating the lives of the city's Maya rulers, were found scattered, burnt and broken amongst the ruins. One of the most elaborate in the country, depicting the Lord Smoking Shell was discovered intact, however, and is now on display under a thatched canopy, near to the site's main temple. An impressive visitors' center and museum contains pottery and other artefacts dug from the site as well as details of plant and animal life around Lamanai,

BELOW:
the old market
house, in Corozal.

A typical Creole dish of fried fish, plantain and rice.

which doubles as a wildlife and botanical reserve with rare untouched tracts of jungle and savanna. The site is open daily, 8am–4pm; entry fee.

Orange Walk Town

Back on the Northern Highway, **Orange Walk ❻**, 92 km (57 miles) north of Belize City, is Belize's second commercial center, and the working-class heart of the sugar industry. Nearby is the Tower Hill Sugar Refinery which handles all Belize's sugar cane, and at harvest time the rumble of trucks can be heard from dawn to dusk, pulling the precious cane to the factory.

From Orange Walk and beyond the culture perceptibly changes from Creole to Hispanic – this part of the country was settled by Mestizos fleeing the Yucatán Caste Wars in the 1860s, and for a long time, until the Northern Highways were built, the people here had closer ties with Mexico than with the rest of Belize. The route west of the town passes by the small Cuello Maya ruin which is on land owned by the Cuello brothers' Distillery, whose permission is needed to visit the site (ask to speak to Oswaldo or Hilberto, or tel: 22141.) While there is not much for the casual observer to see (excavations are filled in after research has been completed), the site has become of pivotal importance in understanding the history of the Maya.

Cuello has been systematically explored and researched from 1973 to the present day, led by Norman Hammond of Cambridge University, who found the site had been continuously occupied since at least 1000 BC until AD 1500. The findings were startling for historians because the earliest known Maya civilization before then had only dated from 600 BC. Compounding this discovery, previously unknown trade artefacts (probably obtained in exchange for local bird feathers and animal skins) found at Cuello have led Hammond to suggest the Maya may have had other unknown influences independent of the Mexican Olmec peoples from whose culture the Maya way of life is usually believed to descend.

There is no visitors' center, nor any other source of information at the site, but background information can be obtained from the Department of Archeology in Belmopan. The site is open every day except Sunday and visits can also usually be combined with a worthwhile tour of the Distillery, where Caribbean Rum (Belize's most famous brand) is produced.

BELOW: taking care of baby brother.

Río Bravo Conservation Area

Further southwest is the Mennonite settlement at Blue Creek, famed for having built its own hydroelectric plant out of parts salvaged from an airplane wreck. South of Blue Creek is one of Belize's most successful environmental conservation projects. The **Programme for Belize** was launched in 1988 by the Massachusetts Audubon Society and has established the 93,000-hectare (230,000-acre) **Río Bravo Conservation Area ❼**. The lands were acquired through donations inspired by its distinctive "sponsor an acre of rainforest" fund-raising appeal.

With over 240 species of trees, 390 species of birds and 70 known species of mammals, Rio Bravo represents one of Belize's highest concentrations of biodiversity. To generate further income, the Programme has entered the tourism industry and offers on-site accommodation, including modern conservation technology, for tourists interested in conservation and research.

Map on page 206

Corozal

Some 145 km (90 miles) north of Belize City, Corozal is a seaside town (no beach) with a quiet and welcoming character. The name derives from the Spanish for the cohune palm tree, a Maya symbol of fertility, and reflects Corozal's fertile soils and benign climate. The town's history is told through the colorful mural by Manuel Villamor Reyes, on a wall inside the Corozal Town Hall, which traces events from the original settlement in 1849 by refugees fleeing a massacre in the town of Bacalar in Mexico's Yucatán Peninsula.

TIP

For information on visiting the Shipstern Nature Reserve, check before setting off with the Belize Audubon Society in Belize City, who manage the reserve.

Shipstern Nature Reserve

About 24 km (15 miles) southeast from Corozal is the **Shipstern Nature Reserve ❽**. The trees on the Shipstern Peninsula were flattened by Hurricane Janet in 1955 but, thanks to the assistance of the International Tropical Conservation Foundation, a large tract has been set aside as a designated nature reserve and the forest is making a remarkable recovery. It is one of the most remote and untouched areas in Belize and native mammals to be found here include tapirs, peccaries, coati-mundi, wild cats and a wide variety of birds. The reserve can be reached by boat or plane from Corozal (via the village of Sarteneja.) Alternatively, there is a rough road from Orange Walk, via Little Belize and then on to Chunox and Sarteneja. The reserve headquarters is 5 km (3 miles) before Sarteneja, and tours can be arranged from here. ❑

BELOW: typical countryside house, built on stilts.

THE SOUTH

The south of Belize is blossoming after years of isolation. From archeological revelations, to new lifeforms discovered in vast caves and plants found deep in the forest, it is a region full of surprises

Ýou can always expect to find the unexpected in Belize's southern regions. Having become readily accessible only in the last few years, the south contains three diverse districts; Cayo, which dominates the center-west of the country, and Stann Creek and Toledo respectively, which cover the coastal strip south from Belize City to Belize's southern border with Guatemala.

The journey south begins on the 122-km (76-mile) Western Highway which slices Belize in half, soon leaving Belize District behind for Cayo, where the monotony of the flat coastal plain is quickly transformed into a luscious landscape of hills and rivers. Cayo is the heart of Belize, embracing all the country's landscapes and cultures and a perfect antidote to the heat and bustle of Belize City; the air is cooler, the people calmer, the pace gentler. And a short journey south from western Cayo into the Mountain Pine Ridge opens a world of environmental treasures here in the foothills of the majestic Maya Mountains.

Venturing further south, the newly paved Hummingbird Highway cuts a spectacular route back east through the mountains to reach the southern coast. Alternatively the unpaved Coastal Road takes a more direct route south starting near Belize Zoo, driving along the coast and through some stunning savanna scenery. Either way the destination is Stann Creek District, where citrus and banana plantations squeeze onto the slopes and fringes of the Maya Mountains, and Garífuna fishing communities "ketch and kill" a living from the sea. South of Stann Creek, Toledo District is Belize's last frontier where the "real world" gets left behind for something even more real.

LEFT: the peaceful waters of Placencia.
BELOW: a boy from Cayo District.

Burrell Boom

The Western Highway leaves Belize City through the Lord's Ridge Cemetery, follows the swampy coastline for a few miles before turning sharply inland into a landscape alternating between palmetto scrub and grasslands. Hattieville, 26 km (16 miles) out of Belize City, is of little interest but it is possible to venture off the beaten track here by turning either north along the dirt road to the village of Burrell Boom, from where you can take a short cut to the Northern Highway. **Burrell Boom ❾**, is an historic village on the bank of the Old Belize River. The name Boom derives from the old logging term for the area in which mahogany logs were caught on their way downstream by a chain stretched across the river. Today Boom is one of the main overnight stops on La Ruta Maya River Challenge canoe race, held in March, and is famous for its cashew and berry wines, horse racing and cricket matches. **Hilltop Winery** offers wine tasting, but many small shops sell the sweet, yet potent, local product. There are also horse races held around major holidays; check local press for cricket match schedules.

Mennonite girls wearing traditional handmade dresses.

Belize Zoo

At Mile 30 (48 km), the road passes one of Belize's major tourist attractions, the **Belize Zoo 10** (*see page 217*.) The zoo was founded as a home for animals abandoned after the making of a natural wildlife film, *Path of the Raingods*. With its sister Tropical Education Centre, it plays an important role in environmental education in Belize (open daily, 10am–4.30pm; entry fee.)

The **Caves Branch Archaeological Reserve** (open daily, 8am–5pm), near Frank's Eddy Village (turn off at Jaguar Paw on the Western Highway), is part of a spectacular four-mile (6-km) underground cave system. Visitors can rent rubber inner tubes and travel downriver exploring what the ancient Maya considered to be the entrance to the sacred underworld. Although the river is shallow through the caves participants should be be able swimmers, since tubing occurs in total darkness and the river moves swiftly in places. Expect long lines; this is the most popular cruise ship visitor site in the country.

Another 30 km (20 miles) along the Western Highway is the intersection with the Hummingbird Highway. Sitting on this junction is the entrance to the small **Guanacaste National Park 11** run by the Belize Audubon Society and named after the ancient Guanacaste tree near the entrance. The 21-hectare (52-acre) park is packed with birdlife, orchids, bromeliads, ferns, lizards and small mammals such as gibnut, agouti and kinkajou. A network of nature trails are mapped out on a leaflet available from the visitors' center (open daily, 8.30am–5pm.)

Spanish Lookout

A right turn shortly after the village of Unitedville leads to the Mennonite settlement at **Spanish Lookout 12**. The dirt track first crosses the Belize River and

BELOW: rustic luxury of Maya Mountain Lodge, Cayo District.

then Iguana Creek, and ploughs on through Mennonite farmland before reaching the outskirts of Spanish Lookout. Here, the most modern of Belize's Mennonites have created a surreal-looking American Mid West-style farming community (*see page 185.*) The town's paved main strip has a hardware store, diner, gas station, grain silos, John Deere tractor showroom – nothing out of the ordinary except to find it all here in the middle of nowhere in Belize. People in Spanish Lookout are very friendly, although quite reserved. The town is self-contained, running its own churches and schools, and is also incredibly productive, supplying Belize with much of its corn, chicken and dairy produce.

The road emerges onto the Western Highway between Central Farm and Esperanza Village, and the highlight is the ride back across the Belize River on the ancient wooden ferry. Three cars at a time can squeeze on, before the ferry is slowly hand-winched by its "driver" back across the river.

Mountain Pine Ridge

The main access road to the **Mountain Pine Ridge Forest Reserve** ⓭ runs south from Georgeville, on the Western Highway, 16 km (10 miles) west of Belmopan. This hilly region is named for the expanses of temperate pine forest which dominate what was once an ecological "island" raised above the rest of Belize. The landscape is still mainly unspoiled, and the vast reserve includes tracts of pristine pine and hardwood forest liberally sprinkled with bromeliads and orchids; rivers, waterfalls and extensive, little-explored limestone cave systems. The ongoing excavations at the enormous Caracol Maya site deep in the Mountain Pine Ridge have led to road improvements, making the area more accessible.

An entrance checkpoint at the top of the climb into the mountains marks the beginning of the reserve. A couple of kilometers further is the Baldy Beacon junction, and the main road continues south parallel to the Guatemalan border, reaching the Rio On Falls, marked on the left some 29 km (18 miles) from the Western Highway. Here the road crosses the **Rio On Falls** ⓮, a tributary of the Macal River, where clear waters cascade over smooth-as-glass boulders and granite slabs, creating water slides and chutes, and jacuzzi-sized pools of bubbling water. East at the junction towards Baldy Beacon, on the northern side of the ridge, are the equally awesome **Hidden Valley Falls** (or "Thousand Foot Falls".) The waterfalls are actually 1600 ft (490 meters) high, and are the tallest in Central America. A viewing platform has been built nearby at the end of a short track, leading north off the main road.

An interesting side trip from Georgeville can be made to the spectacular **Barton Creek Cave**, near to the traditional Mennonite farming community of Upper Barton Creek, *en route* to the Mountain Pine Ridge Forest Reserve. The limestone cave, in which Maya artefacts have been found, is only accessible by river, boat trips are organized in San Ignacio (*see Travel Tips, page 358.*)

A short drive beyond the Rio On Falls is the Douglas Da Silva Forest Station based in **Augustine** ⓯. Augustine remains the only settlement in the Mountain Pine Ridge, with about 100 people living in wooden houses amongst the trees. You can pick up a (free) permit here to visit Caracol and the Chiquibul National Park.

Map on page 206

TIP

Roaring Creek flows into the Belize River at Guanacaste National Park's western boundary, making it an excellent spot for relaxation, swimming and picnics.

BELOW: selling johnny cakes (Garífuna-style bread rolls.)

The national animal, the national drink, and, for some, the national pastime.

Shortly after Augustine and 8 km (5 miles) after the Rio On Falls, signs point to the **Rio Frio Cave**, once used by the Maya as a ceremonial center, and the largest of several caves in the immediate vicinity. The cave can easily be reached along a 2-km (1-mile) track off the main road, or alternatively by taking the 45-minute Rio Frio Nature Trail. A 280-meter (300-yard) long tunnel carved through solid limestone, the cave is light enough to be accessible without flashlights and suitable for inexperienced spelunkers wanting to experience the awesome shapes and colors sculpted into the rock by centuries of erosion and mineral deposits.

Caracol

Beyond Rio Frio, the road drives ever deeper into the forest with few signposts. It eventually forks, with the right turn leading to **Caracol ⑯**, some 2 hours' drive from Augustine village. Uncovered in 1937, the ancient Maya city of Caracol ("snail" in Spanish), was one of the most powerful in the Maya world. Caracol's 42-meter (138-ft) tall *Caana* or "sky-house" remains the tallest man-made structure in the country. The site is immense – 142 sq. km (55 sq. miles) – with an estimated 35,000 buildings in total though only a small fraction have so far been excavated. At the center are five plazas, 32 large structures and an astronomical observatory with main plazas linked by causeways to the outlying ruins. There was no reliable water supply – only the ingenuity of the Maya engineers' reservoir and irrigation systems kept Caracol alive during the long dry seasons each spring.

BELOW:
roadside sign for handicrafts center, near Lubantuun, Toledo District.

There are few facilities at the site, so bring your own refreshments (open daily, 9am–5pm; entry fee, which includes a compulsory guided tour.) There have been some hold-ups along the Caracol Road so exercise caution if you are in a rental car, travel in a caravan with other drivers whenever possible.

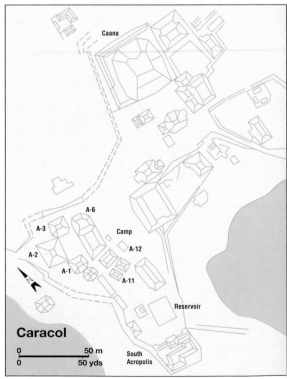

Map on page 206

The left fork leads into the Chiquibul National Park, and the British Natural History Museum's **Las Cuevas Forest Research Station** at the end of the road. In the grounds of the station is a cave entrance into the Chiquibul cave network, but the area is still largely inaccessible.

San Ignacio and Santa Elena

Continuing on the Western Highway from Georgeville, the road runs 10 km (6 miles) into Santa Elena and San Ignacio. These twin towns are separated by the Macal River which flows under the Hawksworth Bridge, a single lane suspension bridge across which vehicles are marshalled by the only set of traffic lights in the region. **San Ignacio ⑰** is a lively town with a single main street, Burn's Avenue, with all its shops and eating places. Unforgettable caving, horseback riding, canoeing and hiking experiences can be arranged either through the resorts or hotels or through one of the tour guides in San Ignacio.

On the hills overlooking San Ignacio are the haunting ruins of Cahal Pech, or "Place of the Ticks". Cahal Pech was once the home of a Maya royal family and although there are no pyramids, the collection of rooms and small courtyards paint an intimate portrait of the lifestyle of the Maya elite.

Xunantunich

Heading west toward the Guatemalan border, 11 km (7 miles) outside San Ignacio is the village of San José Succotz. Here is the crossing point over the river to reach the road which continues for about 3 km (2 miles) on to Xunantunich. The Xunantunich road is steep and very rough, so only 4WD vehicles will be able to make it up to the car park a few hundred meters climb from the ruin.

Caracol's 250,000-strong population – more than the whole of modern-day Belize – once famously defeated rival Tikal 100 km (60 miles) to the west in present-day Guatemala

BELOW: the Classic Maya site of Xunantunich.

TOLEDO ECOTOURISM PROGRAMS

One especially rewarding way of visiting Toledo district is through several village projects offering accommodation and guided visits to local attractions. The projects provide villagers with a livelihood, and an alternative to the timber industry that is causing deforestation in the region at an alarming rate.

The **Toledo Guesthouse and Eco-Trail Program** is run by a grassroots organization of Mopan, Q'eqchi' Maya and Garífuna leaders: the Toledo Ecotourism Association, 65 Front Street, Punta Gorda; tel: 722 2096. Guesthouses sleeping eight people in bunk beds or hammocks have been constructed in six villages, where families chosen on a rotating basis host visitors. Nature trails, planned and constructed by the villagers, lead to local sites of interest. These can be found in the communities of **San Miguel** (bat cave and a river walk), **San Pedro Columbia** (river trip), **Santa Cruz** (waterfall and ruins), **Laguna** (wetland and caves), **San José** (forest walk), and **Barranco** (Garífuna village and Temash River.)

The villagers have a wealth of knowledge in herbal medicine, flora and fauna, and Maya folklore, which they are proud to share with visitors, enabling you to gain a unique experience of this traditional way of life.

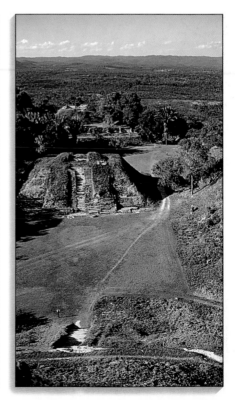

Maya artefacts on view by arrangement in Belmopan's government offices.

The highlight of **Xunantunich** ("**Stone Maiden**") ⓲, once an important ceremonial center, is the view from the top of the 40-meter (130-ft) tall El Castillo temple, from where a jungle landscape spreads out for miles around over the Mopán River Valley and into Guatemala. El Castillo dominates the three adjacent plazas at the heart of Xunantunich, which were flanked by many temples and a ball court. Little is known about the site despite extensive excavations in 1959–60, which have yielded up objects of stone, obsidian, shells and jade, and a jeweller's workshop with flint hammers and stone chisels. Wrapped around the eastern wall of El Castillo is a reproduction of a spectacular carved frieze depicting astronomical symbols, human faces and jaguars' heads. Also on display are three well-preserved stelae. Archeologists believe damage to some of the buildings may have been caused by an earthquake and possibly led to the abandonment of the site in around AD 850.

Visitors' facilities on site include a museum, part of a project covering all archeological sites in Belize, which is being funded by the Inter-American Development Bank. There is a small visitors' center and shop (open daily 8am–5pm, weekends 8am–4pm; entry fee.)

Benque Viejo

BELOW:
Xunantunich,
dominated by
the multi-layered
El Castillo.

On 3 km (2 miles) from San José Succotz, **Benque Viejo del Carmen** ⓳ is the last town before the border. Benque is a quiet town except during fiesta days and Easter when its streets throng with crowds. The Durán family, Spanish expatriates have established Cubola (Belize's main book publishers) and Stonetree Records (Belize's main music producers), tucked away in this corner of the country. There is also a small art gallery and monthly lectures and classes.

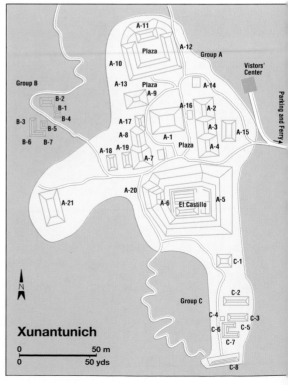

Xunantunich

Belmopan to Dangriga

Map on page 206

The tiny, modern capital of Belize is reached from the junction on the Western Highway opposite Guanacaste National Park. **Belmopan ⑳** was born when the Government and part of the diplomatic community relocated from Belize City following Hurricane Hattie. Belmopan has few facilities for tourists and the town is dominated by government offices, arranged in the style of a Maya plaza. The Department of Archeology houses a collection of Maya artefacts. If you want to see these you will need to call in advance.

Heading south on the Hummingbird Highway, 19 km (12 miles) past Belmopan is the **Blue Hole National Park ㉑**. Within the park are the entrances to both the St Herman's Cave and Mountain Cow Cave, as well as Petroglyph Cave, which contains ancient rock drawings. While St Herman's Cave is open to the public, both Mountain Cow and Petroglyph require Department of Archeology approval to visit. The centerpiece of the park is the Blue Hole, a brilliantly clear pool created as mountain streams rise to fill a sink hole before flowing off back into the earth and eventually into the Sibun River. While there are no overnight facilities, it makes an excellent location for birdwatching. and swimming, though beware the fast-moving waters (open daily 8am–4pm; entrance free.)

The journey from here is spectacular, as the road carves its way over and through the Maya Mountains. Just over 80 km (50 miles) out of Belmopan the road ends at the Garífuna town of **Dangriga ㉒**. In a beautiful location and with a fascinating Garífuna heartbeat. The best time to be in Dangriga is on and around Garífuna Settlement Day (November 19) when the first coming ashore of the Garífuna people is re-enacted amidst great festivity.

TIP

Take extra care when visiting Blue Hole National Park since there have been a number of vehicle break-ins and even muggings reported around the area.

BELOW: a quiet day at Eva's Restaurant, San Ignacio's main street social hub.

Map
on page
206

The black orchid,
national flower
of Belize.

BELOW: old Church
near Punta Gorda.

Southern sights

The Southern Highway begins 9.5 km (6 miles) before Dangriga. 10 miles (16 km) along this road a left turn leads to the village of **Hopkins** ㉓, the best place to enjoy traditional Garífuna hospitality. Six km (4 miles) further south along the Southern Highway, the village of Maya Centre marks the entrance to the **Cockscomb Basin Wildlife Sanctuary** ㉔, the world's only designated jaguar reserve. A rough 8-km (5-mile) road leads off the highway to the visitors' center, which contains details of numerous well-marked trails through the rainforest.

At Mile 23 (37 km) on the Southern Highway is the left turn to Placencia village. The route branches east a little further along, hits the coast and then runs south to **Placencia** ㉕, which is second only to Ambergris Caye as a tourist hotspot. Sparkling sandy beaches, vibrant social life, and a budding art scene attract both holidaymakers and an increasing number of retirees. With its wooden houses on stilts and its main road a sidewalk through the sand, the place is about as relaxed as you can get. But it's still a working fishing village and the annual Lobsterfest in July celebrates both a bountiful harvest and fishing as a way of life.

About 60 km (40 miles) along the Southern Highway, the road branches sharply right to continue for another 60 km through the only rainforest in Belize, and into **Punta Gorda** ㉖, a quiet place with beautiful views out to sea. Most visitors come through here to catch the ferry boats to Puerto Barrios and Lívingston in Guatemala.

Hidden in the hills around Punta Gorda are numerous Maya villages. It's possible to stay in these villages *(see box on page 229)* and there are Maya sites in the area, including **Lubaantun** ("Fallen Stones"), the most important site in southern Belize – built from crystalline limestone blocks with no visible mortar – and **Uxbentun** ("Ancient Stones"), a largely unexcavated site to the northwest. ❑

The Garífuna

The Garífuna story begins on the island of St Vincent, where, years before the Europeans arrived, Carib Indians had sailed north from South America to explore the Caribbean territories of the peaceful Arawak tribes. The Caribs raided Arawak territories, killing the men and taking the women for wives and over time a language evolved with a female Arawak version and a male Carib version, understood by both sexes.

English and French sailors first ventured into the Caribbean in 1625. A treaty between the British and the Caribs guaranteeing the latter perpetual possession of the islands of St Vincent and Dominica was broken by the British a few years later. As the British began to settle the islands, the independent Caribs grew closer to the French military who saw them as a useful ally in their colonial wars with the British. French words found their way into the Carib language, and the Caribs gradually converted to Roman Catholicism

Meanwhile, in 1635, two Spanish ships carrying captured Nigerian slaves were shipwrecked off the St Vincent coast. Some of the captives managed to swim ashore and found shelter in Carib settlements. The relationship between the indigenous Caribs and marooned Africans followed a stormy course over the next century and a half, from reluctant acceptance to intermittent warfare and, finally, wholesale fusion of the two cultures.

By 1773, this hybrid people, the Garinagu (whose culture is "Garífuna") was the dominant population of St Vincent. Yet more and more British settlers landed on St Vincent, until it was clear the colonial forces would never tolerate a free black community at the very heart of their own slave plantations.

Following repeated raids to remove the British settlers, in 1795 the Black Caribs attempted one final all-out attack, led by Chief Joseph Chatoyer. His fatal wounding by a British soldier in a sword duel eventually led to the Garinagu surrender in June 1796.

Less than a year later, fearful of a resurgence of the Black Carib power, Britain deported 2,000 Garinagu to the island of Roatan off the northern coast of Honduras. While many died of disease on the journey, and the rest were abandoned with supplies for only three months, this marooned population not only survived but flourished as fishing and farming communities along the coast.

An abortive takeover by royalists against the republican government of Honduras in 1823 found the Garinagu siding with the losing faction and facing continued persecution. They began to move up the coast to British Honduras (now Belize) and, in 1832, led by Alejo Benji, a large group of Garinagu landed at Stann Creek. Today, they are a thriving community along the southern coast, and Garífuna Settlement Day on November 19 each year commemorates this landing. Nearly all Garinagu are tri-lingual, speaking English and Spanish along with their own language. Traditional activities such as the *dugu*, a sacred ceremony involving ancestral spirit worship, are reminders of a distinctive heritage, while modern Garífuna culture has created "Punta Rock" a lively dance music based on Garífuna drum rhythms. ❑

RIGHT: Garífuna children from Seine Bight.

THE CAYES

Nearly everyone's main reason for visiting Belize, the cayes are unsurpassed destinations for that diving adventure of a lifetime, or just kicking back on the beach with a book and a rum punch

Map on page 206

Belize has the world's biggest and best aquarium, encompassing hundreds of square miles of the Caribbean Sea around the 300-km (200-mile) long coral reef which skirts her coastline. Here you can swim in clear waters packed with a kaleidoscope of flirting tropical fish, dive vast underwater walls spun through with tunnels and caves, sail alongside playful schools of inquisitive dolphins, kayak in coral lagoons flocked with pelicans, egrets and herons, and catch the blue marlin of your dreams.

Exploring this wonderful aquarium is becoming easier as more and more of Belize's cayes, the sand and palm islands which dot the perfect blues and greens of the sea around the reef, provide springboards to the underwater world. From simple campsites with basic facilities to luxurious resorts offering full-service diving and fishing packages, the cayes are perfect places from which to base your adventures.

Previously bases for Maya traders, Spanish conquistadors and British pirates, the cayes were until recently either sleepy fishing villages, or uninhabited patches of mangrove, sand and coconut palms – places for fishermen to set lobster traps, or to rest up and count their catch. Then word caught on that this was one of the world's most exciting diving and sports fishing locations. The late French filmmaker and marine biologist Jacques Cousteau popularized the diving at Lighthouse Reef's Blue Hole in a 1972 documentary, and more and more people began to arrive packing wetsuits and fins. The rest is yet another episode in the history of this remarkable part of the world.

Two cayes, Ambergris Caye and Caye Caulker, have gone on to develop into Belize's only "commercial" tourist resorts, but by most yardsticks they remain quiet and genuine, and are totally absorbing. They retain the essential ingredients of Belize – warm and hospitable people, things tending not to happen quite "on time" or "as planned", and an experience guaranteed to be the real deal.

LEFT: admiring the view in the Barrier Reef National Park.
BELOW: Journey's End Resort, Ambergris Caye.

Ambergris

The northernmost and largest of Belize's cayes, **Ambergris ㉗** is a strip of land and lagoons 40 km long by 2.5-km wide (25 miles by 4 miles) which would be in Mexico but for a sliver of a channel which sets it adrift. The island is in two parts separated by "the Cut", an 18-meter (60-ft) wide channel about 2 km (1 mile) north of San Pedro. Most of the 3,000-strong population live in San Pedro, a few streets of colorful wooden clapperboard houses on the south-east corner of the island. The locals are nearly all *mestizos*, so Spanish is the local language, though English is widely spoken.

The Maya and their ancestors were the first settlers of the cayes, using many of the islands as trans-shipment centers for their extensive regional trade network.

San Pedro only has three main streets, Barrier Reef Drive, Pescador Drive and Angel Coral Street – more commonly known to locals by their pre-tourism names, Front, Middle and Back Streets – so finding your way around is easy. Arriving by scheduled plane (15 minutes) or water taxi (1 hour) from Belize City, puts you right in the center of town, and most resorts are within easy walking distance. If you are staying out of town, a short boat or taxi ride will take you on to your destination.

The soft sand streets of San Pedro town encourage most people to go barefoot, while, for exploring further afield, electric golf carts, bicycles and horses are available for a price. Sea kayaks can be rented for exploring the coastline, and the island's 13 lagoons are ideal paddling spots. Most other water sports can easily be organized through tour operators and resorts including surfing, water-skiing, fishing, snorkeling and, of course, scuba-diving. There are also nearly all the basic amenities you'll need on the island – banks, post office, pharmacy, library and stores.

Onshore sights include the **Ambergris Museum and Cultural Center** in the central Island Plaza Mall, which has a collection of artefacts from the caye's recent past. Amongst the more unusual items on display are a collection of tools fashioned from deer horns – made before deer-hunting was outlawed in the 1960s (open daily, 2–6pm; entry fee).

On the lagoon (west) side of the island, even the most inexperienced birdwatcher is likely to see flamingos, pelicans, herons, egrets and frigate birds. However, be sure to take plenty of mosquito repellent and sunscreen, and be prepared for some adventures as signposts are few and far between once you stray from the well-beaten tracks around San Pedro.

BELOW:
many hotels on the cayes are rustic but spotless *cabañas*.

Beach life

Beach lovers will appreciate Belizean laws which insist all beaches are open to the public. The best beaches are to the south of San Pedro town, so simply stroll down along the shore until you find somewhere you like. For added comfort, most beach front resorts have their own supply of hammocks and sun loungers for resident guests, and will usually be more than happy to lend or rent these out to you. For fueling up, there is no shortage of restaurants – San Pedro is a festival of culinary delights compared to the rest of Belize. A good way to start a day in the sun and on the sea is with a traditional cayes breakfast of fry jacks (fried dough), eggs and bacon, washed down with a freshly squeezed fruit juice – try soursop or watermelon, which are both delicious.

Hol Chan

San Pedro's main attraction, though, is its ability to launch you off into the world of the reef. While the best diving is further out at the atolls, there's excellent diving close to Ambergris. Most takes place in and around the 13 sq. km (5 sq. miles) of the **Hol Chan** (Maya for "little channel") **Marine Reserve** 28, established in 1987 and the first of its kind in Central America.

The reserve is based on a 9-meter (30-ft) deep cut in the reef, the sides of which are lined with caves and sinkholes, including the incredible Boca Ciega, an underwater cave and fresh spring crammed full of tropical fish, including parrot fish, horse-eye jacks, blue-striped grunts, gray angels and yellowtail snapper. Because there's so much here, Hol Chan is equally rewarding for inexperienced snorkelers and veteran divers alike. It's also possible to ride over the reef in a glass bottom boat to see spectacular sights without ever getting wet.

Daily trips to Hol Chan are run by most of the tour operators in San Pedro, normally in small skiffs – twin-engined speed boats – or sailboats. Tours leave only when the boat is full so expect some waiting around if the captain has to hustle up extra passengers.

For more independent-minded snorkelers and explorers, hiring a sea kayak is worth considering because it provides an alternative mode of transport for do-it-yourself trips around the island and the reef. Whichever way you go, check out the Hol Chan Visitors' Center on San Pedro's Barrier Reef Drive for brochures and other information on Belize's marine life (tel: 226 2247).

Trips to Hol Chan also usually take in Shark Ray Alley – a spot where locals have bribed rays and nurse sharks with fish feeds to gather in a convenient spot. There are other good sites around Ambergris – Mexican Rocks on the windward side of the reef is recommended, as is Coral Garden – and a full day snorkeling or diving trip will also normally take in lunch at the neighboring island of Caye Caulker.

Caye Caulker

Only 45 minutes by boat from Belize City, **Caye Caulker** 29 is a smaller less developed version of Ambergris, 6.5 km (4 miles) long by 600 meters wide at its broadest point. It is also split in two along a channel called "The Cut", this one created by the fierce

Map on page 206

The toucan – national bird of Belize – enjoying a martini on the rocks; shaken, not stirred.

BELOW: bird-watching at Man O'War Caye.

Here's looking at you; keeping a close eye on the sharks.

winds of Hurricane Hattie in 1961. The majority of the 750 or so population live in the southern part of the island, in the mile or so stretch from the southern tip to the Cut. Here is altogether less busy than Ambergris, prices are a little lower, and accommodation more homely. Many resorts are between the airstrip on the island's southern tip and the main settlement just to the north, on sandy beaches looking straight out through tall coconut palms onto the Caribbean Sea.

Caulker is often referred to by the locals by its original Spanish name Hicaco, which British pirates and settlers anglicized to Caulker. It has a simple street arrangement – Front Street, Centre Street and Back Street – with the front of the island closest to the reef. Basic amenities include a bank, phone office, grocery, souvenir stalls and laundromat.

The Split of sand, a pier and a bar, is the only place to swim, but currents are strong here so, while it's not deep, you need to be careful. On the island, it's worth checking out Sea-ing is Belizing on Front Street, where local photographer and reef expert Jim Beveridge displays underwater and wildlife works, and runs regular slide-shows.

The sea-based activities available on Caye Caulker are similar to those on San Pedro, though because the island is that much smaller there is correspondingly less choice. The best known of the diving operations are Frenchie's Diving Services (tel: 226 0234), and Belize Diving Services (tel: 226 0143), but several others also come recommended.

BELOW:
cargo sailing boats off San Pedro.

Caye Chapel and St George's Caye

South of Caye Caulker, the beautiful **Caye Chapel** ㉚ is private property and not accessible unless you are guests of the island's owners. Further south, only

14 km (9 miles) out from Belize City, **St George's Caye** , and was once home base to pirate Edward "Blackbeard" Trench. It is also famous for being Belize's first capital, being the scene of a sea battle in 1798 which finally put paid to Spanish claims on Belize. British soldiers continue to use St George's for recreation, and like Caye Chapel it's not publicly accessible unless you're staying at one of its two upmarket resorts.

A popular day-trip destination from Belize City is **Goff's Caye** ㉜, a patch of sand and coconut palms perched on the edge of the reef. Snorkeling and fishing in the area is excellent, and there are several equally attractive cayes nearby including Gallows, Sergeant's and English Cayes. Buccaneers used to spy on Spanish Galleons from tiny Spanish Lookout Caye, 16 km (10 miles) southeast of Belize City. Now free from pirates, the island is a highly recommended destination for divers with a keen interest in environmental conservation.

The Turneffe Islands

The largest of Belize's three atolls (the same size as Ambergris Caye), the **Turneffe Islands** ㉝ are also the easiest to get to – only about 90 minutes by boat from Belize City. In the early 20th century, small groups of settlers made their living on Turneffe from trading sponges and coconuts, but now, after a succession of hurricanes and plant diseases, only a few fishermen, coconut collectors and resort operators survive. The largest and most visited resort is Blackbird Caye which has become a renowned international marine science facility as well as offering the usual facilities you'd expect at a cayes resort.

The main attraction at Turneffe is sports fishing, while for divers the southern tip of the atoll has one of the best wall dives around – "The Elbow".

Map on page 206

BELOW: Mata Chica Resort, San Pedro.

Taking time out; little blue herons enjoy a rest on the mangrove.

Considered an advanced dive because of strong currents, the drop-off is sensational, as are the rippling herds of eagle rays who gather together here. The reef on the western side of Turneffe is wide and gently sloping, ideal for snorkeling and shallow dives. Also on this side is the wreck of the Sayonara, a cargo boat which sank in 1985, and which is a good place to practice wreck diving.

Lighthouse Reef

Lying some 100 km (60 miles) east of Belize City, **Lighthouse Reef ㉞**, can be reached in about 6 hours by boat from Belize City or San Pedro, or in under one hour by plane landing at Lighthouse Reef Resort's private airstrip. At the center of Lighthouse Reef is one of Belize's most well-known "landmarks", the Blue Hole, now protected as a Natural Monument. From the air the Blue Hole can be clearly seen as a dark blue circle fringed by the lighter blue of shallow waters. This 120-meter (400-ft) deep circular sinkhole was created by the collapse of an underwater cavern some 12,000 years ago and since Jaques Cousteau's visit in 1972 has become one of the world's most famous dive-sites. While there is not much marine life in this vivid blue shaft of water, the geological formations and encircling coral are spectacular. You can visit Lighthouse Reef from San Pedro or Caye Caulker; for a day or overnight stay, with a range of all-inclusive fishing and diving packages on offer.

One of the two lighthouses at Lighthouse Reef is in Sandbore Caye, close to the Blue Hole. The waters in this area are especially treacherous for shipping, as the many wrecks on the seabed testify. On one such doomed voyage, the Spanish trade ship *Juan Bautista* went down off Sandbore Caye in 1822, and is said to have taken with it a cargo of still unrecovered gold and silver bullion.

Map on page 206

Half Moon Caye

Belize's first national reserve, **Half Moon Caye Natural Monument** (35) was created back in 1982 to protect the nearly extinct red-footed booby bird. Now a thriving nature colony, loggerhead turtles and mangrove warblers, amongst others, keep the booby birds company. Diving and snorkeling here are particularly enjoyable because of better-than-average visibility. The Half Moon Caye dropoff is a classic wall dive plunging from a coral ridge 9 meters (30 ft) below the surface, the drop broken by an ever changing seascape of mysterious caves and tunnels. For more information on Half Moon Caye contact the Belize Audubon Society in Belize City.

South of Lighthouse Reef, Glover's Reef, off the coast of Dangriga, is named after pirate John Glover who "traded" from its southeast cayes. As well as sports fishing, Glover's has several good snorkeling and diving spots. Emerald Forest Reef is a shallow spot suitable for novices, while Southwest Caye and Long Caye both have excellent wall dives. For longer stays on the atolls, Glover's has the most reasonably priced accommodation.

Tobacco Caye

A few kilometers offshore at Dangriga are a number of cayes where tourism is only just beginning to take off. If you want to know what Caye Caulker was like a few years back try visiting **Tobacco Caye** (36), the largest of the cayes in Tobacco Range. Despite the late entry into the tourism market, the cayes of Tobacco Range have been well used over the years by both fishermen and traders. Puritans, for example, set up shop here over 300 years ago to trade tobacco and other goods with visiting mariners. The resorts on Tobacco Caye

BELOW: snorkeling off Tobacco Caye.

Map on page 206

Kayaking is one of the best ways to enjoy Belize's calm, clear waters.

BELOW: Coco Plum Caye.
RIGHT: Laughing Bird Caye National Park, off Placencia.

are typically rustic, usually run by local fishing families to supplement their fisherman's wage. As prices tend to be lower than elsewhere, the camping facilities make Tobacco a favorite of budget travellers. The absence here of the sort of luxury you might expect at upmarket resorts is well compensated for by reasonably priced boat trips and some excellent tour guides who have an intimate knowledge of the sea and the reef.

South Water Caye

Nearby **South Water Caye** ③, 5 hectares (12 acres) of desert island sitting right on the reef, is another first-rate diving and fishing location, and the center of local and international marine research. The British-based organization, Coral Caye Conservation Ltd, recruits volunteers to participate in ongoing studies of the marine environment here, and across the South Water Cut on Carrie Bow Caye, Washington DC's Smithsonian Institute operates a major marine research station (*see Travel Tips, page 358, for contact details of both organizations*).

Carrie Bow used to be twice its current 0.4-hectare (1-acre) size, but storms and mangrove clearing have taken their toll. The reef around Carrie Bow gives some of the best snorkeling in the entire Caribbean. It has also been used by the Smithsonian's scientists to track how Belize's fragile reef is reacting to the chemicals washed into the sea from the citrus and banana industries, overfishing and tourism. The Smithsonian lease the caye from its owners, Tony Rath – the brains behind some of the best Belize websites – and Therese Bowman-Rath, who also own part of South Water Caye and run Dangriga's best known resort, Pelican Beach, from where trips to South Water can be organised.

The Southern Cayes

The cayes further south are quieter still with only a few offering accommodation. The atoll-like "faro" of **Laughing Bird Caye** ③ is a favorite destination for local and visiting day-trippers from Placencia, and this tiny island can get very busy. Partly in response to this and to try and prevent the resident laughing gulls from being frightened away again it has been declared a National Park. The gulls abandoned their rookery here once before, back in the 1980s, and have only begun to return since 1990. They share the caye with flocks of green herons, brown pelicans and melodious blackbirds, but increasing numbers of visitors make it more than likely that they'll fly the roost again.

Instead of bothering the gulls, try the other equally beautiful cayes in this area – favorites include Colson, Silk, Bugle, and Lark Cayes. It's possible to stay overnight on Ranguana Caye, which has basic accommodation and sea kayaks for rent, or at nearby Wippari and Little Water Cayes. Beyond this, the Sapodilla Cayes off Punta Gorda remain little explored except by local fishermen, scientists and Guatemalan holidaymakers, for whom the few resorts that operate here predominantly cater. Nicholas and Lime Cayes both have some facilities, while Wild Cane Caye, just off the coast of Punta Gorda, was once a major Maya ceremonial site and is in the process of being excavated. ❑

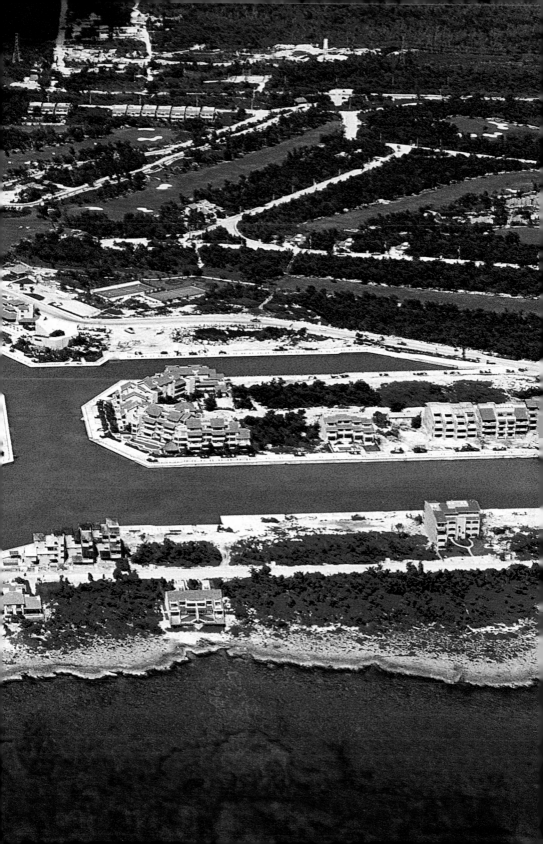

THE YUCATAN

The Yucatán Peninsula contains a wealth of cultural and ecological treasures – and, of course, its beaches

Believed to be an island by the first Spanish conquistadors in early 16th century, the Yucatán Peninsula has always been a distinctly different, detached region of Mexico. The three states of the peninsula – Campeche, Yucatán and Quintana Roo – are primarily composed of flat limestone plains, sometimes not much more than a meter or two above sea level, a terrain honeycombed with caves and sinkholes (*cenotes*). Dense sub-tropical dry forest covers the south of the peninsula, while in the north the environment is even drier and the forest more sparse and scrub-like.

Water has always been in short supply. In much of the country the shortage has been alleviated by *cenotes*, formed when the limestone surface collapses exposing water beneath. Associated with the cult of the rain god Chac, *cenotes* have been discovered half-filled with offerings thrown in to appease the god, alongside the skeletons of many sacrificial victims. At his first sight of a *cenote*, early explorer John L. Stephens raved about "a spectacle of extraordinary beauty... the very creation of romance; a bathing place for Diana and her nymphs. Grecian poets never imagined so beautiful a scene."

In the north-central Chenes region (the suffix -*chen* indicates a well) water was stored in underground cisterns, *chultunes*, for the dry season. The ancient Maya cultivated basic crops of corn, beans and squash and these same staples, supplemented by pigs and chickens, are still grown by their descendents today.

The modern economy

The characteristic Yucatecan landscape today is of whitewashed thatch-roofed houses, oversized Franciscan monasteries and crumbling *haciendas*, once the homes of henequen (agave fibre) planters who supplied most of the world's sisal rope until the advent of synthetics. Henequen is still grown, albeit on a smaller scale, with the fibrous leaves also used to make such items as bags and carpets. But the era when the industry's millions paid for mansions along Mérida's Paseo de Montejo and for their owners' children to attend European schools are long gone.

The Yucatán's income today comes from two incompatible sources: oil and tourism, with the former fortunately restricted to the offshore oil rigs south of Campeche and the latter starting to overrun parts the Caribbean coast. Cancún is the mighty modern-day temple of of the sun, a resort that was selected by government bureaucrats, literally hacked out of the jungle and which now attracts more than 2 million visitors every year. But as interest

PRECEDING PAGES: Chac-Mool turning his back on the beach at Cancún; the landscape-designed Fiesta Americana Condesa resort in Cancún.
LEFT: the magnificent symmetry of Chichén Itzá.

grows over the achievements of the ancient Maya civilization, more and more hitherto-ignored jungle ruins have been attracting attention while the better known sites such as Uxmal, Chichén Itzá and Tulum can barely cope with the growing hordes of visitors.

Meanwhile, back at the farm, hi-tech agribusiness is replacing traditional agriculture, with wider markets being developed for chilli peppers, tomatoes and cantaloupes. The Yucatán is one of Mexico's top pork producers. Honey is also a major product. To the east of Progreso, with its large industrial park, is the region's main fishing port Yukalpeten, which has huge seafood-processing facilities.

The Yucatán is surrounded by the sea to the north, east and west and the coastline of the peninsula has been an important trade route since Classic Maya times or earlier. Christopher Columbus first encountered Yucatec Maya traders in 1502, their large canoes loaded with textiles, obsidian and jade. Today much of the coastline is devoted to tourism, especially in Quintana Roo, but though there has been intensive development of the infrastructure in recent years to serve this boom, vast areas of the coast remain protected, such as the Sian Ka'an Biosphere Reserve, Río Lagartos and Celestún.

Environmental treasures

Perhaps the continent's greatest living treasure is the Great Maya Reef, which stretches from north of Cancún to the Bay Islands of Honduras. The reef is host to thousands of species of coral creatures (plus 18 sunken galleons) and visiting pelagics: dolphins, whales, tarpon, tuna, turtles and even whale sharks. It's easy to plunge into this sub aqua paradise with the help of the dive schools of Cozumel, Cancún and Playa del Carmen.

Fortunately, the jungles that have always characterized the peninsula are still relatively pristine; if you're lucky you might spot animals here such as cougars, jaguars, wildcats, coati-mundi, armadillo, opossum and spider monkeys as well as such smaller creatures as rabbits, lizards, raccoons and birds of every kind. Buried deep in the interior are also enough uncovered ancient sites to keep archeologists busy for several lifetimes. Perhaps the greatest Maya city of the early Classic era, Calakmul has barely been touched and investigation and restoration will take many more decades.

Local conservation groups are getting increasingly well organized. In the Sian Ka'an Biosphere Reserve, environmental groups are working in partnership with the World Wildlife Fund to introduce crop rotation experiments, limit commercial fishing and demonstrate drip irrigation methods that can maintain a self-supporting farm.

"The idea of a biosphere reserve is new in conservation," says the bulletin of the Amigos de Sian Ka'an. "It promotes the protection of different natural ecosystems of the world and at the same time allows the presence of human activities through the rational use and development of natural resources." ❑

RIGHT: skimming the surface, along the Yucatán's superb coastline.

THE MAYA IN THE YUCATAN

Some of the Maya's greatest cities were built in the Yucatán,
despites the obstacles of isolation and lack of water

The Maya settlements in the Yucatán Peninsula of Mexico are thought to have begun later than those in Guatemala and other regions of southern Mexico. The dry limestone peninsula, with few readily available sources of fresh water, made the area less attractive for village communities. From early times, the Maya established themselves near the *cenotes* – the pools or caves with springs where the rainfall collected. Some of the first ceramic evidence of human habitation has been found at the caves of Loltun, in the center of the peninsula, which is thought to have been inhabited since soon after the last Ice Age.

Ancient origins

There were also scattered settlements around the coasts of the peninsula, and it is plain from these sites that trade and cultural exchange with the Caribbean and the rest of Mexico's Atlantic seaboard was another important feature of Maya life in the peninsula. One of the earliest of these influences was from the Olmec people who lived further north on the Caribbean coast from about 1000 to 400 BC. The amazing sight of the vast centers in the midst of this isolated and sparsely populated region of southern Mexico led the explorers of the 18th and 19th centuries who rediscovered them to imagine that the Maya must have been in contact by sea with the ancient civilizations of the Middle East – with Egypt, Assyria or even the Greeks. It was even thought for some time that they must be the lost people of Atlantis.

Now, however, there is much greater understanding of how the Maya evolved over the centuries. Like the Olmecs, the early Maya gradually changed from living in small villages dedicated to agriculture to a more complex society centered on ceremonial complexes, and

PRECEDING PAGES: detail from a mural inside the Governor's Palace, Mérida, by Fernando Castro Pacheco.
LEFT: traditional dress is still worn by Maya women in the Yucatán, though mainly on special occasions.
RIGHT: a ten-gallon hat on a two-pint head.

ruled by hereditary dynasties. In the Yucatán, the need to save water led to the construction of complicated irrigation canals and the use of terracing to increase the efficiency of agricultural production. The Maya farmers grew maize and other vegetables as staples, but also cultivated cotton for trading, and are known to have been

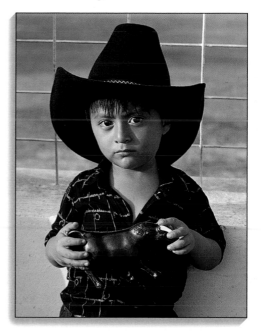

expert beekeepers, as Yucatecan honey became prized throughout the region. The salt deposits harvested on the northern coast were also greatly valued, and the salt was traded for jade, obsidian and other precious commodities throughout the Maya world.

Centers of civilization

There were several main areas for Maya development: around the River Bec in the south of the peninsula, along the low ridge of hills known as the Puuc mountains in the center, and at individual sites such as Chichén Itzá or Dzibilchaltun that grew up close to a *cenote*.

The principal Classic Maya center in the

region was Uxmal, which flourished between the 7th and 10th centuries (*see page 297*). Uxmal dominates the Puuc area, together with Kabah, Sayil and other smaller sites.

One of Uxmal's distinguishing features are the *chultunes* or man-made cisterns used to store rainfall during the dry months, as elsewhere in the Yucatán, the site lacks either rivers or other natural water sources. Native historians say the builders of Uxmal were a group known as the Xiu, who are thought to have arrived from the south in the 7th century, gradually extending their rule over the Puuc region, but ultimately collaborating with the Spanish.

of the local sculptors in carving the soft limestones of the region. At the same time, the elaborate abstract lattice-work designs are thought to imitate the patterns in the woven cotton textiles that were also a characteristic of the Yucatán. Some of the site's architectural styles hint at other influences from Mexico, particularly from the Totonacs, based in Veracruz.

Ceremonial causeways

Another common feature of Maya life in the Yucatán were the *sacbeob* or causeways that linked each of the great centers. Built from limestone raised above ground level and sur-

Elaborate architecture

As their power grew, so did the splendor of their ceremonial buildings. The Maya architects at Uxmal used finely cut stone, built delicate arches and slender columns, and covered the exterior of their buildings with lively washes of stucco and riotous ornamentation.

The best examples of this architecture are what are known as the "Governor's Palace" and the "Nunnery Quadrangle", considered as two of the finest buildings in ancient America. Here, naturalistic sculptures as well as the typical "hooknose" motif thought to represent the rain god Chac, and which is placed at the corner of many of the buildings, demonstrate the prowess

faced with white cement, their function is unknown; but since they linked important sacred sites, it is thought more likely that *sacbeob* were used for ceremonial purposes rather than just for transportation. A *sacbe* 18 km (11 miles) long runs from Uxmal to Nohpat and Kabah. At Kabah, one of the most impressive features is the huge arch at the point where the *sacbe* enters the site, which gives some idea of its size and importance during the Classic Maya period.

Although it is difficult to say how many people lived in each of these centers, a recent calculation puts the number of inhabitants at Sayil, a slightly smaller site in the Puuc region, at close to 10,000 people living in an area of no more than 4 sq. km (1½ sq. miles). Sayil was organized around a north-south internal path of more than 1 km (½ mile) in length. At the northern end of this *sacbe* was the main palace, where it is thought the dynastic rulers lived, while at the southern end are to be found various temples and the ballcourt.

Peak and decline

By the end of the 9th century AD, Uxmal was at the heart of a powerful empire covering the

center of the Itzaes, who worshiped the god Kukulcan or Quetzalcoatl. So great was the importance of their capital from the 10th century onwards, that when the Spaniards conquered the region six centuries later, they thought of founding their own regional capital there, as Hernan Cortés had done in Mexico City.

The name Chichén Itzá in fact means "beside the pool of the Itzae", and the sacred pool or *cenote* around which it was built was a place of pilgrimage – and sacrifice – for several hundred years. In the

> ### ITZAES' JUST DEITY
>
> Bishop Landa spoke favorably of Quetzalcoatl: "He was regarded in Mexico as one of their gods… [and] a god in Yucatán on account of his being a just statesman."

Puuc region and the lowlands around it. Over following generations, the number of people in this area of the Yucatán seems to have exceeded the capacity of the land to support them. Gradually, sites such as Uxmal and Sayil appear to have been abandoned in favour of smaller places, which came under the rule of the next great center, at Chichén Itzá.

As its name indicates, Chichén was the main

LEFT: a traditional thatched Maya home, near Cozumel, defying the spread of the ultra-modern mega-resorts.
ABOVE: an artist makes a traditional jade mosaic mask, preserving an ancient tradition.

16th century, Bishop Landa related how the local Maya of his time still spoke of this pool: "It was the custom to throw live persons into this pool at times of drought; these people were thought not to die, although they were never seen again. They also threw in many valuable objects and things they valued highly."

Powerful people

This and other pools provided Chichén Itzá with a good supply of water, to support almost 15,000 people living in an area of 30 sq. km (11 sq. miles). Most archeologists agree that the Itzaes were more warlike than the Maya at Uxmal. They used the central position of their city in the north of the Yucatán Peninsula to control populations as far north as the coast and the Puuc hills in the south, and to dominate trade in important commodities such as salt, honey, cotton, jade and obsidian.

The sculptures at Chichén show that they had deities like the jaguar and the eagle, both of them identified with the sun. They shared other gods with the Toltecs further north in Mexico, who are also thought to have been responsible for the introduction of the cult of human sacrifice, and the "platforms of

skulls" or *tzompantli,* as well as the importance of Venus for astronomical calculations.

Violent decline

Chichén Itzá too fell into decline. By the end of the 13th century the site had been largely abandoned, following battles between its leader Chac Xib Chac, and the victorious ruler of the Cocom dynasty of Mayapan, closer to the coast of northern Yucatán.

Architecturally, Mayapan has little of the splendor of Chichén, and its rule was limited to the northwestern corner of the peninsula. The political organization at the time seems to have been less hierarchical, with different centers

LITERALLY NAMED
The name of Tulum refers to the walls that surround the site on three sides; *tulum* is Mayan for fence or enclosure.

existing in a federation centered on Mayapan. After more than a century of dominance, Mayapan too seems to have fallen as the result of a violent uprising, so that by the time the Spaniards arrived in the 16th century, the Maya in Yucatán were split up into as many as 16 different groups.

Several of these groups were concentrated on the coasts of Yucatán. The most impressive center of this late period is undoubtedly Tulum, on the northeastern side of the peninsula *(see page 319).*

Built upon a scarp rising from the Caribbean, Tulum was an important trading center for the islands of Cozumel and Isla Mujeres, and a link to the other Maya settlements further south in what is now Belize and Guatemala. Its ruins – which stretch along the coast for almost four miles – show evidence of cultural influences from these places and from further north in Mexico, yet its social organization and influence in the region remain a mystery. The Tulum archeological site is now a National Park covering more than 650 hectares (1,600 acres).

The Spanish arrive

The first Spaniards to penetrate the Maya world of the Yucatán were two shipwrecked sailors, the survivors of Valdivia's expedition which went down off Jamaica. One of them spent the rest of his life among the Maya; the other, Gerónimo de Aguilar, became Hernan Cortés's interpreter and went with him on the conquest of central Mexico.

The first proper expedition to the Yucatán by the Spanish arrived in 1517, led by Francisco Hernandez de Cordoba. And in 1518, Juan de Grijalva became the first European to see the splendor of Maya civilization at Tulum. In 1519, it was the turn of Hernan Cortés. He landed on the island of Cozumel, where he was warmly received by the indigenous people, and where he celebrated the first Mass. By 1527, exploration of the Maya world of the Yucatán Peninsula had begun in earnest, led by Francisco de Montejo. The era of colonization, integration and resistance had begun. ❑

LEFT: Maya woman from Valladolid, center of the bloody Caste Wars (1847–51).
RIGHT: Izamel Convent, where the Spanish converted thousands of Maya to Christianity.

MODERN HISTORY OF THE YUCATAN

Independence brought freedom from the Spanish to the Yucatán, but it also led to a bloody war and continued hardship for the Maya

When Mexico won independence from Spain early in the 19th century, the Yucatán, with the Chiapas region, tried at first to become part of the Central American federation. Guatemala City was much closer geographically and in spirit to the Maya lands of the Yucatán, and local politicians hoped that the peninsula could be an independent province within the federation. By 1823, however, after the emperor Iturbide had been thrown out and Mexico had become a federal republic, the Yucatán decided to join the federation. It was not until 1848 that it fully became part of the Mexican federal state.

This decision to become an integral part of the Mexican union followed the most serious revolt of the indigenous Maya people in many years. The situation for the local Maya population in the Yucatán had changed for the worse over the previous hundred years. Reforms which the Spanish colonial authorities began in the late 18th century meant that lands previously owned communally by the Maya had been taken over by the state.

In addition, for almost the first time since the Spanish conquest, the Maya elders who exercised great authority over their fellow Maya in villages and towns were ousted by colonial officials. Fresh taxes made life even more difficult. The emergence of the Mexican republic only served on the one hand to increase this trend towards greater control by the state, and on the other to concentrate land ownership in fewer and fewer hands.

War of the Castes

So it was that in 1847, the Maya in the east of the Yucatán Peninsula rose up against the whites, or *dzules* as they called them. What became known as the War of the Castes began in the town of Valladolid, a place considered

---

PRECEDING PAGES: a 19th-century view of Uxmal, prior to excavation, by Frederick Catherwood.
LEFT: detail of mural in Mérida's Governor's Palace.
RIGHT: Casa de Montejo, Mérida.

one of the bastions of racism and exploitation, where indians and *mestizos* were banned from the main plaza and the smarter streets. When one of the Maya leaders, Manuel Antonio Ay, was shot on suspicion of plotting a rebellion, his death sparked off reprisals such as the massacre of non-Maya in the small town of Tepich.

Soon, a fierce war was raging between the majority Maya population and the *mestizo* Mexicans, who were mostly concentrated in the towns and cities of the Yucatán. It was when the Maya rebels advanced on Mérida – which had been the main city in the region since Spanish times – that the white politicians called on the central government for support. In return, they agreed to accept rule from Mexico City. Federal troops helped defend Mérida, and the city was saved, although historians argue that it was only a victory of sorts; most of the Maya, still dependent on farming for their livelihoods, halted their attack and went off to sow their crops at the start of the maize planting season.

The federal troops went on to help drive the Maya rebels back to the south of what is now Quintana Roo state. There they established their own city, called Chan Santa Cruz. It was here in 1850 that a Maya leader, Jose Maria Barrera (with the help of a ventriloquist) saw a vision of a small cross which appeared in a tree and began talking to him.

MAYA TEASER

An ancient Maya riddle reflects their deep-rooted stoicism. "What do you call a man on the road?" it asks. "Time," comes the reply.

This "talking cross"– and three others which appeared subsequently and were known as the "daughters" of the first one – won thousands of Maya to the rebel cause. These "Cruzobs", as

was based on the *henequen* plant. This had been used for centuries by the Maya for making rope known as sisal, but it was not until the 19th century that its commercial possibilities were realized by white landowners. Such was the demand from Europe and the United States for sisal that around the turn of century Mérida could boast more millionaires *per capita* than any other city in the world. Mérida became a beautiful city with broad avenues flanked by splendid palaces in the latest European styles. Railways were built

they were known, even took their war tactics from what the crosses told them, and continued the fight against domination for more than a generation.

In the end, it was an outbreak of smallpox around the turn of the 20th century that did as much as the government to defeat the Maya rebels. In 1901, federal troops were able to enter Chan Santa Cruz without resistance. All told, by the end of the Caste War the population of the Yucatán fell from some half a million to just over 200,000.

Despite this threat in the interior of the Yucatán, the end of the 19th century was a boom time for the region. The era of prosperity

for exporting the rope and other products, and once again, the white politicians hailed the sisal boom as the triumph of progress.

Slave conditions

But at the same time, the Maya peasants employed on the big henequen plantations were cruelly abused in near-slave status. They were forced to work long hours in miserable conditions, and were often paid in tokens that could be exchanged only in stores also owned by the landowners. The situation in rural Mexico during the early 20th century was exposed by the North American journalist John Kenneth Turner in articles and the book *Barbarous Mexico*.

Turner's attacks on the lack of political freedoms and the slave conditions in many parts of the country even led the London *Daily Mail* to protest: "If Mexico is half as bad as she is painted by Mr Turner, she is covered with the leprosy of a slavery worse than that of San Thomé or Peru, and should be regarded as unclean by all the free peoples of the world."

Violence flares

Turner predicted that the tide of opposition to this situation was rising quickly, and that radical change must soon come. In the Yucatán, as in other parts of Mexico, the revolution broke

In 1915, however, President Carranza stepped up efforts at reform. The governor he appointed, Toribio de los Santos, tried to end forced labor and to increase taxes on the landowners. This led the rich leaders of the Yucatán to attempt one last time to make the region independent of Mexico. They drove out the federal governor, declared the Yucatán a sovereign state, and sent representatives to the United States to see if that country would back their struggle for independence – or even annex the region on their behalf.

In March of the same year, however, the federal army under one of its most senior leaders,

out in 1910. Once again, the flash point in the region was the town of Valladolid, and once again the Maya population was in the forefront of fighting for new freedoms, and in particular a fairer share of the land.

In the first years of the revolution, the local landowners or *hacendados* managed to keep a tight rein on the situation. They continued to employ the mainly Maya laborers in highly exploitative conditions, and resisted any attempts at land re-distribution.

LEFT: during the War of the Castes, many colonial churches were fortified against rebel attacks.
ABOVE: a 19th-century view of the plaza at Izamal.

PAINTING THE RUINS

Miss Adela Catherine Breton, the daughter of an English officer, was one of the most intrepid early recorders of the Maya sites in the Yucatán Peninsula.

Born in 1849, she was already well into her forties when she first visited the site of Chichén Itzá. She returned many times up to 1907, painting delicate and extremely accurate watercolors of the mural paintings and making plastercasts. Miss Breton also carried out an important full-color drawing of the elaborate stucco relief at Acancéh, to the southeast of Mérida. She was never to visit the Yucatán again after 1908, and died at the age of 73 in Barbados.

General Salvador Alvarado, routed the motley forces pushing for independence, and brought the Yucatán firmly under federal control. He helped to pacify the region by corralling the local revolutionary groups into a centralized organization, and encouraged the formation of the first real trade unions in Mérida. Alvarado also created almost a thousand regional schools, many of which for the first time brought the Spanish language and the idea of Mexico beyond the Yucatán to scattered Maya villages.

LETHAL EPIDEMIC

Several smallpox outbreaks struck the Yucatán in the early 20th century, reducing the Maya population to a fraction of what it had been in the mid-19th century.

In 1918, Alvarado was succeeded by Felipe Carrillo Puerto, who continued with political and social reforms. By 1923, after several years of fighting, a left-wing revolutionary government was in power in the Yucatán. Led by the socialist governor Felipe Carrillo Puerto, women were given the vote for the first time, rural schools were set up to teach the remote Maya villagers to read and write, and birth control programmes were introduced. In 1924, Carrillo Puerto was murdered by local landowners, and the attempts to change the lives of the Maya majority came to an abrupt end.

It was not until the second half of the 1930s, during the reforming nationalist government of Lázaro Cárdenas, that any new effort was made to bring more social justice to the region. In 1937, President Cardenas redistributed almost half of the large henequen plantations among peasant farmers. But by this time the international market for sisal had slumped, and although land ownership was now more equal, the move did little to increase the region's wealth. The Yucatán continued to be one of the poorest areas of Mexico, with the majority of its 300,000 inhabitants – most of them Maya in origin – living in great hardship.

Arrival of tourism

This situation changed dramatically in the 1970s. It was at this time that the Mexican government decided to begin actively promoting tourism as a foreign currency earner. The beaches of the eastern Yucatán, and what was

MAYA RELIGIOUS FESTIVALS

In the Yucatán, the two main festivals are related to rain and fire. The rain ceremony is known as *Cha-Chaac* and takes place at the start of the maize-growing season in February. The ceremony is led by a shaman or Ha-men who prepares the traditional drink of *balche*, a mixture of honey, water and secret plant roots that the participants consume before ritual dancing and chants.

The *Tumbul Kak* or New Fire ceremony has also been performed since the beginning of Maya civilization. According to the Maya calendar, each historical period came to an end after 52 years. This was a very dangerous moment, when the sun might be extinguished, ending life

on earth. In order to prevent this, when the planet Venus appears in the heavens, the shaman lights a new fire, which is then taken out to each of the houses, underlining that fire and life are shared by all in the community.

As with many other Maya religious practices, the ritual has been adapted to Christian beliefs brought by Spanish missionaries. It now takes place on Easter Saturday, during the hours when, according to Christian tradition, Jesus had died on the Cross and not yet been resurrected. In this, as in many other ways, Maya culture has learned to borrow from sources outside itself, but has transformed them into something meaningful for its own people.

then the small fishing port of Cancún, were chosen as ideal sites for tourist development. Since then, Cancún has become a world resort that welcomes millions of international tourists each year. The beaches at Cancún and neighboring resorts have been baptized the "Maya Riviera". The great Classic Maya sites at Chichén Itzá, Uxmal, Tulum and elsewhere have also been made accessible for mass tourism *(see page 279)*.

Yet close by the tourist resorts, many Yucatán Maya live in much the same way – and often in as much neglect – as they have for centuries. There are almost half a million Maya in the region, most of whom speak the Mayan peninsular language, which is often also used by many of the non-indigenous population. In the more remote areas, Maya villagers still own and farm the land communally. They cultivate maize, chili peppers, and beans as they have always done, and most families have beehives for the honey that for centuries has been famous in the region.

Spiritual life

The Maya of today still have a profound religious spirit and religion continues to play an important role in bringing communities together. This has been channeled into Catholicism and in recent years into evangelical Protestant sects, but often, the Maya continue rites that their people have practiced for hundreds if not thousands of years. As well as strong Catholic elements, the rites are interwoven with many traditional Maya beliefs and practices. There is often still a belief that holy crosses talk to people, and the men who understand these messages are given special authority in the Maya communities. Special feast days are celebrated throughout the year, and often these too would be recognizable to the ancient Maya, as they are closely related to the seasons and the gods of rain and fertility.

Nevertheless, the Maya still have to struggle to survive; population increase, the poor quality of the soils, and the possibility of much greater earnings from the tourist industry, have led many young Maya in the Yucatán to abandon their traditional way of life. As a new millennium begins, the Maya are faced with the same problems as they have encountered since the arrival of the Spaniards.

Perennial problems

The Maya's right to own and farm land communally is still constantly threatened by people who want to "develop" the area. The Maya's independent cultural traditions and way of life are often denied, or seen only as a picturesque part of the tourist industry. And although they are the most Mexican of the inhabitants of Mexico, they are still excluded socially and regarded as outcasts in their own land.

In the neighboring state of Chiapas, this situation led to a revolt by the highly traditional Lacandón Maya and the so-called Zapatista National Liberation Army in 1994. As so often in the past, the Maya emerged from the remote jungle areas and took over some towns under "Mexican" control to press their claims for more land and other social demands. More than 150 people were killed when government troops retook the town. In spite of mediation the two sides have yet to reach a peace agreement. However, the demands for independence have generally been peaceful since 1994, and it is possible the Zapatistas may decide to enter legitimate politics. ❑

LEFT: Maya fruit sellers, from a 19th-century photograph by Desiré Charnay.
RIGHT: abandoned machinery at the Yaxcopoil henequen hacienda, near Mérida.

The Zapatistas

Until December 31, 1993, Chiapas state in Mexico was best known for the magnificent Maya ruins of Palenque, set deep in the jungle, and the charming, if somewhat chilly, colonial city of San Cristobal de las Casas.

Apart from San Cristobal, this part of Chiapas is one of the least populated regions of Mexico, with a variety of different indigenous groups living in scattered villages. Further into the jungle areas of the center of the state, the Lacandón Maya live much as they have done for centuries.

These present-day indigenous inhabitants of Chiapas, who make up roughly one-third of the state's three million inhabitants, were seen mostly as a colorful backdrop by the many Mexican and foreign tourists who came to see the ruins of Palenque, or to spend a night or two in San Cristobal. The tourists could visit the indigenous markets, and the Catholic churches where they continued to practise their age-old beliefs, only thinly disguised under a veneer of Catholicism. Unseen by the tourists, the indigenous people of Chiapas lived short, impoverished lives, largely ignored by the Mexican government except at election time, when they were offered gifts and other inducements to vote for the governing party.

Armed uprising

Then came January 1, 1994. This was the day when, more than a 1000 km (621 miles) away in Mexico City, president Carlos Salinas de Gortari was celebrating the fact that Mexico had joined the US and Canada in NATO. This, according to the president, would bring benefits to all Mexico, and prove that it had finally entered the modern, capitalist world, where it could compete as an equal with its two northern partners. On that same day, several thousand armed Amerindians emerged from the forests of Chiapas and took over San Cristóbal and another half dozen smaller towns. They drove out the local authorities, the police and the Mexican army troops stationed there, and announced to the world that they were the Zapatista National Liberation Army (EZLN). The fact that they chose the name of Emiliano Zapata, the hero of the Mexican revolution who had led peasants from the south of Mexico in a crusade to gain more land and freedom, showed what their main demands were.

The rebellion took central government completely by surprise. At first, there was an attempt to retake the occupied towns by force. More than 150 people died in a week's fighting, nearly all of them Amerindian peasants. By now, however, the indigenous revolt in Chiapas had become news all over the world, and the Mexican Government could not afford to be seen as repressive, just at the moment when it was seeking to prove it was part of the modern, democratic world. So, after 12 days of fighting and tension, President Salinas declared a truce. He appointed a former mayor of Mexico City as the government negotiator. The bishop of San Cristobal, Samuel Ruiz, who had worked with Maya communities for over 20 years, was brought in as mediator. And from the Zapatista side, about twenty indigenous peasants, dressed in traditional clothing, but wearing balaclavas to avoid identification, sat down at the negotiating table.

But the star of the show was the one Zapatista who was clearly not of indian origin. He was "subcomandante Marcos", who said he was only deputy commander of the EZLN because the commander of the Zapatista army was the Lacandón people. Marcos' trademark cap and balaclava mask, through which he incongruously smoked a pipe, quickly became the international symbol for the Zapatistas. It was he who spoke on behalf of the Lacandón; their demands were for guarantees to the lands they were living on, which were being increasingly infringed by timber companies, cattle ranchers and other non-indigenous farmers.

Stop-start negotiations

Despite their armed uprising, the Zapatistas soon declared they were interested only in sparking a peaceful revolution by Mexican "civil society". Then, although the talks with Camacho had apparently produced a workable solution that included many of their demands, the EZLN rejected the terms of the agreement, arguing they did not go far enough.

In early 1996, resumed negotiations produced another agreement, which the EZLN backed. This time, the Mexican government failed to make the agreement legally binding, and the EZLN once more broke off talks.

The government began a campaign to undermine the Zapatistas. They "unmasked" Marcos as a former university teacher called Rafael Sebastian Guillén, and claimed he was a "professional" revolutionary who was merely using the indigenous groups of Chiapas for his own ends.

After the breakdown of the 1996 talks, an uneasy standoff was reached. The Zapatistas and their supporters still controlled towns and villages in the Lacandón jungle. Facing them were several thousand Mexican federal troops. To make their voice heard, the Zapatistas called on Mexican and international intellectuals to come to the jungle to show their support. A great convention was held at the poetically named village of La Realidad (Reality), where once again subcomandante Marcos captivated his audience with his self-deprecatory rhetoric. The government used its control of the media to counter this message, and to cast doubt on Marcos and the other EZLN leaders.

At the same time, on the ground in Chiapas, the government at best permitted – and at worst promoted – the proliferation of anti-Zapatista paramilitary groups. The federal army and the local police tightened their grip on the "conflict zone", but did nothing to prevent violence between communities, which as ever was provoked by disputes over land or by religious strife.

Then on December 22, 1997, a paramilitary group calling itself "Red Mask" attacked a group of unarmed civilians sympathetic to the EZLN in the hamlet of Acteal, in the Chiapas jungle; 45 people, including 14 children, were killed. Federal police later arrested dozens of suspects, among them a retired army general who had been acting as an adviser to the Chiapas police. But senior officials who allowed the paramilitary gangs to

roam unchecked, still faced no charges. The Acteal massacre did, however, appear to convince the federal authorities that the Chiapas problem must be solved. A new Interior Minister, Francisco Labastida, was brought in, who promised the EZLN that indigenous rights would become legal, as had originally been demanded, but the EZLN was wary of the new offer, considering it to be a travesty of the original agreement.

In Chiapas, the standoff continued. Tourists were advised not to travel in the "conflict zone", where armed troops patroled the indigenous villages while the inhabitants went about their daily lives. Priests, foreign observers, and volunteers

were harassed and some even expelled for alleged interference in Mexican politics. There was also a stepped-up campaign to dismantle the EZLN's network of "autonomous municipalities" and supposed "ringleaders" were jailed.

Isolated and surrounded, the Zapatistas attempted to break out by using modern technology to show that their rebellion was continuing. Marcos' texts appeared on the Internet, and a worldwide network of supporters helped guarantee that the Chiapas region and the protests of its first inhabitants, were not stifled by silence. More recently, the Zapatistas indicated that they may enter legitimate politics, a move that was welcomed by the Mexican Government. ❑

LEFT: Izamal, a Yucatán village in the 19th century.
RIGHT: Zapatistas dolls for sale in San Cristobal.

THE COAST OF THE YUCATAN

Coral reefs, white sand beaches, fascinating fauna and simple fishing villages:
these are the highlights of the Yucatán coastline

The Yucatán Peninsula is famous for many reasons, not least its indigenous Maya culture, unique geological formations of *petenes* and *cenotes* (hardwood hammocks and sinkholes), prehistoric caves and subterranean rivers. It is also known as a major stop for millions of nearctic and neotropical migratory birds. But what catches the attention of most first-time visitors is its still mostly pristine and extensive coastline, stretching for 1,830 km (1,140 miles). Bordered on the west and north by the tranquil, green waters of the Gulf of Mexico, and on the east by the turquoise blue of the Caribbean Sea, much of the coastline features broad, uninterrupted expanses of magnificent white sand.

Large areas of these superb natural habitats within the coastal zone have been established as protected reserves. The conservation strategy being used is one which promotes rational use rather than a "hands off" policy. By putting coastal wetlands, forests and coral reefs under protection, rules can be established for the use of natural resources between competing economic activities – for the most part, fisheries and tourism.

The reserves fall under diverse authorities, including federal, state and municipal governments. Private non-governmental conservation organizations have aligned themselves with most of the reserves, to ensure their long-term viability. Starting from the west, they include the areas of Laguna de Términos and Los Petenes in the state of Campeche; Celestún, El Palmar, Dzilam de Bravo and Río Lagartos along the northern Yucatán coast, with Alacrán Reef located offshore; Yum Balam, which includes Isla Holbox on the northern tip of the peninsula; Isla Contoy; the Marine Reserve of Isla Mujeres, Punta Cancún and Punta Nizuc; the Marine Reserve of Puerto Morelos; and Cozumel Reefs and Laguna Columbia reserves

PRECEDING PAGES: basking iguana at Tulum.
LEFT: Laguna de Nichupté, Cancún.
RIGHT: brown pelican, one of the coast's many birds.

on Cozumel Island. Sian Ka'an and Banco Chinchorro, off the southern coast of Quintana Roo, conclude the list.

Deep impact

In recent years, the modern fishing village of Chixchulub, on the north coast of the penin-

sula, has been put under scrutiny by the international scientific community. It has been determined that it was here that a meteor – more than 10 km (6 miles) in diameter – impacted upon the Earth some 65 million years ago, creating a crater over 250 km (160 miles) across. It has been argued that when the dust cleared, several million years later, the dinosaurs were extinct and in their place birds and mammals prospered, along with plants and trees. However, there are problems with this explanation as fossil plankton found near the rim of the crater put its formation earlier than the required period. The north-south divide created by the rim of the ancient crater is what today causes the subterranean rivers of the peninsula to deposit their water in either the Gulf of Mexico or the Caribbean Sea. The brackish mixture of fresh and salt water is responsible for carving out the picturesque inlets, or *caletas*, found just beyond coral sand beaches at points along the Caribbean coast.

The steeper shelf of the east coast, in comparison to that of the Gulf, makes it possible to easily distinguish variations of ancient coastlines. Prior to the last Ice Age, the sea stood at

A GIANT ATTRACTION

The east coast coral reef is second in size only to the Great Barrier Reef of Australia and is a prime reason why 2½ million people pass through Cancún every year.

from northern Quintana Roo to Honduras. The offshore islands of Isla Contoy and Isla Mujeres in the north, Cozumel off the central coast, and Banco Chinchorro in the south, are all part of this unique system. The north coast of the peninsula is not entirely void of reef formations either. One in particular, Arrecife Alacrán, 60 km (38 miles) north of Progreso, is actually an atoll composed of five separate islands. Its flora and fauna are so valuable that it has been declared a biosphere reserve.

least 6 meters (20 ft) above the present level. This caused the shoreline to move approximately 1 km (½ mile) from its present position – coinciding with the present day coastal highway. The last glacial period caused a retraction, with the sea dropping 100 meters (330 ft) below its present level. There it remained for 80,000 years. For the past 18,000 years, the glaciers have been melting, moving the coastline inland once more. The shallowness of the shelf along the Gulf coast, on the other side of the peninsula, caused the shoreline to move as much as 20 km (12 miles).

The east coast also hosts a magnificent coral reef, stretching a total of 300 km (190 miles).

The other islands of the outer Campeche Bank, south of the continental shelf, are enormous sandbars, used both by nesting seabirds and as bases for oil exploration. Along the mainland coast, winds from the north have created large extensions of sandbars parallel to the coast, varying from a few meters to a half a kilometer (540 yards) in width. They function as limits to coastal lagoons and salt flats.

Ancient industries

Coastal fishermen, going back at least 2,000 years to the time of the early Maya settlements, have used these locations for fishing and saltmaking. Not a whole lot has changed – fishing and saltworks are still the primary economic activities of the zone. At the turn of the century, dyewood was extracted by the English from both Campeche and Belize, to the south. During the first half of the 20th century, coconut plantations replaced native vegetation along large extensions of the coast from Veracruz to Belize as a result of the copra trade, and chicle was exported from inland forests prior to the development of synthetic gum. Tourism, however, is the latest industry, coinciding with the depletion of forest products and fish populations, and the destruction of coconut palms by a lethal yellowing disease.

region. Government and private organizations are actively working to conserve them.

Of major importance to science – as well as local fishermen – are the lagoons. Besides serving as natural nurseries for an abundance of fish, crab and mollusk species, the lagoons are used as shelters by fishermen for their boats, just as the ancient Maya used them, when they plied the coastal waters in dugout canoes, trading goods from the shores of the Gulf of Mexico all the way to Central America. Indeed, present day settlements on both sides of the peninsula trace their origins back to ancient times. The original choice of location was

Natural villages

The natural, unimposing atmosphere of the fishing villages along the Gulf coast – such as Isla Aguada, Celestún, Telchac Puerto, Rìa Lagartos and El Cuyo, which have not been corrupted by tourism – are favored destinations for independent travelers who seek the cultural interexchange that occurs in such towns. The abundance of endemic species of flora and fauna, as well as the importance of the coastal habitat to commercial activities, has given rise to a number of natural protected areas in the

based on various criteria, from a good site for fishing or saltmaking to natural openings through the reef, which provided safe harbors.

The mangrove-lined Laguna de Términos, a natural protected area behind Isla del Carmen, Campeche, is the largest bay on Mexico's Gulf Coast. It is a natural nursery for shrimp larva, the basis for the area's enormous shrimping industry. It also harbors fish species sought by saltwater flyfishermen, who have practiced their sport at the village of Isla Aguada, at the southern mouth of the lagoon, for many years. The zone sees oil exploitation, too.

Turning north along the coast, one comes to the village of Champotón, which sits on a

---

LEFT: mangroves, favorite sites for birdwatchers.
RIGHT: green turtle laying its eggs at Akumal.

lagoon formed behind a beach by the only surface-flowing river on the west coast of the peninsula. In the early 16th century, it boasted as many as 8,000 stone houses with thatched roofs. Its size has shrunk, and grown, since, vacillating in relation to the health of the local fisheries. This is true of many coastal villages. Some have been revived, but in recent years it has been tourism, rather than fishing, which has brought life back to these communities. The reserve of Los Petenes – whose name refers to the formation of hardwood hammocks (islands of forest trees located on higher ground in seasonally inundated wetlands) – harbors a wealth

of fauna, from jaguars to the rare Jabiru stork.

On the northwest coast of the peninsula is the sand-street village of Celestún. It is located on a beachhead between the Gulf and an extensive coastal lagoon system and is an example of the effects of increasing visitor numbers. Fishing is still the major economic activity, as the saltworks were abandoned long ago. But now tourism is moving in quickly, taking advantage of the beauty of the mangrove-lined estuary and its colorful inhabitants. The main attraction is the nonbreeding colony of some 3,000 American flamingos, which can be seen in the estuary almost any time of year. They and the abundant migratory waterfowl in the adjacent wetlands,

along with endangered reptile and mammal species occupying the petenes beyond, are the major reasons for the establishment of the Celestún Special Biosphere Reserve and the two state reserves of El Palmar and Dzilam de Bravo to the north. Kayaking and birdwatching boat tours are specialties of the area.

Northeast of Celestún is the port town of Progreso, which hosts the migration of Merideños each summer, when they seek relief from the heat of the state capital 36 km (22 miles) inland. Canadians, looking for warmth, settle into the same homes during the winter months. But the real charm of the coast is found in modest fishing villages such as San Felipe, at the mouth of the Ría Lagartos estuary. It is not far from the old port of Isla El Cerrito, once used by the Itzas of Chichén Itzá. The major export in ancient times was the same as today's – salt, produced in the extensive flats behind Las Coloradas, within the Río Lagartos Biosphere Reserve on the north coast, east of Progreso.

Flamingos and turtles

The primary nesting site of Mexico's population of the American flamingo is located within this extensive coastal reserve, near the fishing village of El Cuyo. Equally outstanding in this area is the near pristine coastal vegetation, which mixes Gulf coast and Caribbean species, so important to the endemic Yucatán wren and millions of migrating landbirds. The shorebirds fill the estuaries behind the coastal sandbar during their spring and fall passages. The village of El Cuyo, on the border with the state of Quintana Roo, is still small and quaint, yet has opened its gates to tourism. Actually, it has

A NEW KIND OF WORSHIP

Unknown to most visitors to the self-proclaimed "eco-archeological park" of Xcaret, just south of Playa del Carmen, is the fact that it is believed to have been the ancient seaport of Pole, before the arrival of the Spaniards in the 16th century. It was the departure point for pilgrims traveling under sail to Cozumel to worship Ixchel, the goddess of fertility.

Today, Cozumel welcomes "reef worshipers," who want nothing more than to scuba and snorkel. Xcaret is a multi-faceted theme park, offering a wide range of activities for day-visitors, including museum, aquarium, aviary, botanical garden and a "Maya village."

received visitors for years, as green and tor-toiseshell sea turtles come ashore each summer to bury their eggs in the soft, white sand.

Isla Holbox, at the northeastern tip of the peninsula, within the Yum Balam Biosphere Reserve, also still hosts nesting sea turtles, as well as large concentrations of migratory shore and landbirds. It, too, has opened up its unpaved village to ecotourists, providing opportunities to view colonial marine and wad-ing birds on islands in the adjacent Yalahau Lagoon. Kayaking is a popular activity here.

Around Cancún

Rounding the northeastern tip of the peninsula, full of mangrove islands, bays and lagoons, the Isla Contoy National Park – a bird sanctuary – becomes visible. It is visited by a limited num-ber of boats from Isla Mujeres and Cancún. Now the major tourist destination in Mexico, the island of Cancún – separated from the main-land by two natural canals and Nichupté Lagoon – was the site of an ancient Maya fish-ing camp 2,000 years ago. Its conversion to a modern resort has been complete, as has the transformation of the former fishing village of Playa del Carmen to the south.

The important ports of Playa and Puerto Morelos, between Cancún and Playa del Carmen, were popular with fishermen due to the existence of natural *quebradas*, or reef openings, offshore. Puerto Morelos is still home to fishermen, though some are turning in their boats to become waiters and dive masters in the growing tourism trade. A marine reserve has been set up offshore, to ensure sustainable use by both activities.

The central coast of Quintana Roo, south of the ancient site of Tulum (110 km/70 miles south of Cancún), is a massive wetland of inter-national importance, with an adjoining coral reef to the east and important extensions of tropical forest inland. It has been incorporated into the Sian Ka'an Biosphere Reserve, a UNESCO Natural World Heritage Site. Its for-mer coconut plantations are now gone, as well as the port facilities that once exported chicle.

Instead, sportfishing lodges (the area is pop-ular in the Americas for saltwater flyfishing) and private homes dot the narrow strip of land that borders the sea and the interior wetlands.

LEFT: Xcaret, near Playa del Carmen.
RIGHT: iguanas can move very quickly, if they want to.

Two large, shallow bays are found within the protected area containing important sea and wading bird colonies. The local lobster fishery supports the three small communities at the entrances to the large bays of Ascenciòn and Espiritú Santo. Tourism within the reserve is limited to low impact activities – such as a locally run boat trip through the wetlands.

The southern coast of the Sian Ka'an Bios-phere Reserve is sparsely populated with private properties and a few diving resorts, but change is already coming further south. A cruise ship pier is under construction in front of the small com-munity of Majahual, reached via an east-west

road an hour's ride south of Felipe Carrillo Puerto in the Maya zone of central Quintana Roo. South again, on the Belize border, the tiny fishing community of Xcalak is now connected by paved road. The fishermen here depend upon the recently established, offshore Biosphere Reserve of Banco Chinchorro, capturing lobster and fish around its abundant coral reef. Tourism in the zone is geared towards scuba diving, though the locals accommodate birdwatchers and trips through the mangroves.

Tourism has brought change – both favor-able and negative – but it is hoped that the pro-tected areas will limit economic activities and tourists will be better informed. ❑

TOURIST TRAP – OR PARADISE?

The introduction of tourism to the region may have brought
much-needed wealth – but at what cost?

The two visitors waved goodbye at the gate to the only house on the island – not counting the handful of thatched huts belonging to the fishermen and the two-room ranch house in the coconut grove. They headed down the winding sand road through a mixture of thick coastal vegetation and mangrove before passing through a coconut palm grove, eventually reaching the small Maya archeological site of San Miguelito. After investigating the ancient stone structures, overgrown with grasses, vines and trees, they continued on to the larger site of El Rey, where the caretaker showed them around. A dense deciduous forest flanked the enormous dunes to the east. They could hear the waves breaking on the beach beyond. The Laguna de Nichupté lay a short distance to the west, past the watery mangrove, where a family of coati-mundi ducked into the underbrush, their long, furry tails held erect.

Few people today share the author's memory of what Isla Cancún was like some 40 years ago. In fact, present day visitors would probably have trouble even imagining such a scene – without the 26,000 hotel rooms, restaurants, marinas, golf courses, shopping malls and entertainment centers that cover almost every inch of the island. How did such a phenomenon occur? And is it bad or good? These are questions asked by international tourism developers and by their Mexican counterparts, as they contemplate increasing investment in the area.

Unforeseen success

Even with all the initial enthusiasm, none of the planners directly involved imagined the impact that Cancún would make on the country's tourism industry – contributing 15–20 percent of the annual gross income derived from the activity. In fact, FONATUR, the government agency responsible for promoting tourism

---

LEFT: some of Cancún's resorts combine traditional styles with modern architectural designs.
RIGHT: some souvenir shops, on the other hand, settle for eye-catching kitsch.

development throughout the country, wisely inaugurated two other planned tourist destinations – Loreto in Baja California and Ixtapa in Guerrero, west of Acapulco – in the 1970s in order to disperse the industry's growth. This is always an important consideration: tourism is a labor intensive industry and Mexicans, on the

whole, are not a highly mobile society. For the head of the household to change his or her base in order to work implies moving not only the immediate family, but the extended family as well. But the success of Cancún in the early 1980s coincided with an economic recession resulting in a continual stream of families moving into the area from all over the country. The movement continues even today.

Cancún's magnificent white sand beaches, lining the transparent turquoise Caribbean Sea, are only one reason that increasing numbers of tourists flock to the resort each year. What pulled Cancún far ahead of Loreto and Ixtapa, and later Huatulco on the Oaxaca coast, were the direct flights from major US population centers. Once there, Americans found the beaches, water and accommodations superb. Even the hamburgers tasted like home. You did not even have to worry about speaking Spanish, since everyone spoke enough English.

The resort has been so successful that between 1982 and 1992 the permanent population of Cancún grew at an unprecedented 25 percent per year. Today, there are more than half a million permanent residents, contrasting with less than 210,900 in the entire state in 1980.

But is all this growth in one location good? Certainly, you don't need to be an economist

Concentrating the infrastructure in one area has other benefits. Building one large, international airport to handle all sizes of planes, for example, is much less costly than building several regional airports. The cost of duplicating the basic infrastructure – from cargo handling to customs and immigration – for a reduced volume of plane movement just doesn't justify the investment. Besides, people who land at Cancún airport do not have to vacation only in Cancún. They have an infinite variety of choices, from scuba diving along the sparsely developed southern coast of Quintana Roo, to visiting Tikal in Guatemala, or a fishing village on the coast of

to recognize the benefits of doing volume business. In countries such as Mexico, where unemployment abounds, tourism is the ideal industry to take up the slack, with more tourists translating immediately into more jobs. It is the nature of the modern world to seek profitablity, and industrialized countries have demonstrated the advantage of gearing their production to volume, rather than niche, sales. For tourism, it is much the same. It is more cost-effective to sell what's easy – the beach and sun – to hundreds of thousands of potential visitors, rather than targeting specialty markets, which attract independent travelers who tend to make their own vacation plans.

Yucatán. They can even hop on a commuter plane to the multicultural highlands of Chiapas. Small ecotourism operators don't have the budget for widespread advertising. Instead, they successfully rely on their Internet pages.

The bigger picture

In attempting to judge the merits of Cancún's success, one must also look at the social, cultural and environmental impact on local inhabitants. Certainly, the original planners of Cancún were very aware of the potential damage mismanaged tourism could cause in all three of these areas. In the 1980s, as if to prove their concern, Acapulco, the country's number one tourist resort at the time, began to show serious signs of stress. Like Cancún, Acapulco had received a helping hand to make it one of the world's most popular winter playgrounds. From 1946 to 1952, Mexican president Miguel Alemán encouraged foreign investment in hotel construction, and offered up the broad beaches surrounding Acapulco Bay as an enticement. Acapulco grew and grew, but without any thought to planning. The highway from Mexico City kept improving, thereby

PRESIDENT OF TOURISM

Even after he left office, President Alemàn continued to support the development of the hotel industry throughout the country as President of the National Tourism Board.

nated as a result of the lack of drainage infrastructure amid the growing slums. It was years before there was a major effort to make amends. Today, Acapulco, second only to Cancún, remains popular with national and international visitors.

No-risk strategy

The architects working for FONATUR in the early 1970s weren't going to take any risks with their new creation – Cancún. Their solution was a masterplan which would limit

shortening the travel time to the coast, and the local airport developed to support the increased air traffic. However, improved transportation not only brought an increase in visitors but also swelled the resident population of Acapulco. Shanty towns expanded, covering the hillsides above the bay. Those who could not find jobs, spent their days selling trinkets to tourists or begging. Eventually, the "success" of the resort brought ecological disaster. Drinking water became unsafe and the bay became contami-

---

LEFT: souvenir dolls in traditional Yucatecan costume.
ABOVE: crowds gather for the equinox spectacle at the foot of El Castillo pyramid, Chichén Itzá.

growth and separate the town from the tourist zone. It all sounded great on paper, and even worked for a number of years. But then too much success – and too much greed – took its toll. The first "limit" on hotel rooms was rumored to be 12,000. Today, the island is pushing 27,000 rooms, while the permanent population is up to more than 500,000. The government is trying to incorporate more land into the already stretched city in order to provide homes for thousands of residents who lack the basics of water and electricity, not to mention paved streets, transportation, schools and health care.

Such challenges for planners are widespread. It appears that all of northern Quintana Roo, from Isla Mujeres to Tulum, is affected by the movement of mass tourism through its villages and archeological zones, and on its reefs and beaches. The construction of a cruise ship pier near the Sian Ka'an Biosphere Reserve in southern Quintana Roo, for example, has forced local inhabitants and government officials to review future development projects.

For one thing, developers are now consulting with conservation groups, such as Amigos de Sian Ka'an, with regard to precautions they should take prior to construction of coastal infrastructure. In addition, Amigos, along with its counterpart, Pronatura Yucatán in Mérida,

and national and international funding sources, have been training fishermen from coastal communities to be naturalist guides. Some work as scuba divers, while others have taken to bird observation. This has allowed them to benefit directly from the growing ecotourist market. It also makes them jealous guardians of the natural resources surrounding their communities.

The previous model for tourism development resulted in putting local inhabitants at a disadvantage, due to their lack of appropriate education and training. Outsiders from Mexico City and Acapulco claimed the well-paid jobs in Cancún, while the local Maya were hired as unskilled laborers on construction sites, and later as chamber maids and gardeners. Yes, they earned more than living off the land, but moving into a tourist resort such as Cancún meant dealing with high inflation. Food prices were the first to rise, and not just in Cancún itself. The effect was felt almost immediately in the Maya zone, around the agricultural town of Felipe Carrillo Puerto, 200 km (125 miles) to the south. Local food prices reflected the elevated demand in Cancún, creating greater poverty. This inflation also drove up prices on the so-called "low cost" housing projects, to the point that investors, rather than low-income workers, bought multiple dwellings at reduced interest rates, and then rented them out to locals at a nice profit.

A fairer share

Increased local participation in the benefits of tourism is also reaching forest communities in central and southern Quintana Roo. Rather than open their villages to curiosity seekers, the Maya inhabitants are being trained to produce such goods as wood carvings of native fauna, hand-embroidered garments, and even furniture. The mass tourism of Cancún is making a major contribution to these people by providing a market place for their products.

Interestingly, among the more than 2 million visitors that enter Cancún each year, a growing proportion are seeking additional experiences, which take them away for a couple of days from the sun and fun of Cancún itself. They want to be independent and to experience the local culture, flora and fauna. Some arrange a day tour to the Sian Ka'an Biosphere Reserve, while others go kayaking at Isla Holbox, or visit the flamingo colony in the Rio Lagartos or Celestún Reserves in Yucatán. Most locations can be visited independently, though many tourists prefer to join a small group organized by ecotourism operators.

Cancún's commercial success is a fact, in spite of natural disasters such as Hurricane Wilma, which struck the Yucatán Coast in 2005. Its future is tied to its ability to recover and disperse the traveler so that native inhabitants may also share in the benefits, without sacrificing either their rich cultural heritage or their ability to live in harmony with their natural environment. ❑

LEFT: sun, sand and sea are still the main attractions.
RIGHT: Cancún's dazzling resorts line the coast.

PLACES

*A detailed guide to the entire region, with principal sites
clearly cross-referenced by number to the maps*

With seemingly endless sunshine, a glittering coastline and all the luxurious allure that modern resorts can dream up to entice visitors, the Yucatán is now a globally important travel destination, attracting visitors from North and South America and from many different European nations. Away from the resorts, inland Yucatán is little changed, and the Yucatecan Maya that haven't been attracted to the coast for work continue to farm the *milpa* fields, planting the maize and beans that have been harvested here for perhaps five millennia. The land they farm is not especially productive, and for many Maya it's an annual struggle to work the harsh conditions – arid lowlands and scrub bush – under the relentless sun.

Cultural sights

The Yucatán's Maya ruins can be found all over the peninsula, hundreds of them still unexcavated. Despite their primitive tools, the Maya were great stone builders, using simple obsidian chisels to shape the huge blocks which were then carved and dated, commemorating the priests, warriors and events through the various periods of Maya history. Corbelled vaults in which walls got progressively thicker until meeting at the top or in which cantilevered stones overhung each other – the genuine arch supported by a keystone remained undiscovered – were a major feature of the architecture. The system, noted US historian George Kubler, was "inherently unstable" despite being strengthened with wooden tie rods, cement corners and boot-shaped stones. But, unstable or not, an enormous amount of it has endured.

Between the two cities of Campeche and Mérida is perhaps the region's greatest concentration of superb sites; including Uxmal, with its stunning Pyramid of the Magician and Nunnery Quadrangle *(see page 298)* and the other Puuc sites of Kabáh, Sayil and Labná, with many more minor ruins close by.

No visit to the Yucatán is complete without a good look at Chichén Itzá, perhaps the most famous ruin in the Maya world *(see page 304)*. Chichén is certainly not remote any more, but its Castillo temple, sacred *cenote* sacrificial pool and the group of a Thousand Columns are still inspirational, unforgettable sights.

More wonders abound elsewhere in the peninsula, away from Chichén Itzá and the Puuc sites. Edzná, in the west, to the south of Campeche, has a remarkable five-story temple. Tulúm, a minor site in every sense, has an incomparable location: framed with white sand Caribbean beaches and turquoise waters. In the far south of the

PRECEDING PAGES: Tulum, the Yucatán Peninsula's most picturesque site, standing on a cliff-top overlooking the Caribbean coast.
LEFT: Chac-Mool surveys the El Castillo temple-pyramid, Chichén Itzá.

The Yucatán

0   50 km
0   50 miles

N

GULF OF MEXICO

Parque Na
de San F

Telchac   Boca de Dzilam
Puerto
Chuburna   **Progreso**   Chabihau   Dzilam
Chicxulub   de Brav
Xcambo
Punta Baz   Sisal   Chicxulub   Dzidzantún
Puerto   Baca   Cansahcab
Parque Natural   261   Temax
del Flamenco Méxicano   Dzibilchaltún   Tepakán
de Celestún   Motúl
Punta Boxchuo   **Hunucmá**   **Mérida**   Aké   **Izamal**
Kinchil   Umán   Seyé   Hóctun
Celestún   Bella Flor   Acancéh   Kantunil
281   Chocholá   Yaxcopoil   Tecoh   Libre
180   Y   Mayapán   Telchaquillo   Unión
Maxcanú   Muna   Mama   Tekit   **Chichén**
Tankuché   Oxkintoc   Lázaro   Mama   Mayapán
Halacho   Cárdenas   Teabo
Becal   Calkiní   Uxmal   Ticul   Mani
Pochoc   Kabáh   Oxkutzcab   Grutas de Loltún
Jainá   Hecelchakán   Sáyil   Tekax de A.O.
(Zac-Pol)   Xcalumkin   Xlapak   Labná   Ticum   Peto
Punta Nitún   Pomuch   Kihuic   Tzucacab
Bahía de Campeche   Tenabó   261   184
Boxol   Nocuchich   Xkichmook
Campeche   24   Chumul   Dzuiché
Lerma   Chencoyi   Hopelchén   Hunto Chac   José María
Cayal   Morelos
180   Seybaplaya   Tixmucuy   Nohyaxché   Iturbide   Dzibilnocac
Balneario Acapulco   261   Edzná   Pich   Chenko   Chunh
Haltunchén   Ruíz   Dzibalchén
Champotón   Moquel   Cortínes   Hochob   Q
San Enrique   Pustunich   M   E   X   I
Chencán   Pustunich
Huayahaca   Pixoyal   Reserva de la
180   261   250   Meseta
Puerto   Biósfera de
Isla del   Real   de Zohlaguna
Ciudad del   Carmen   Calakmul
Carmen   Dieciocho   Ponte   Francisco   Tzibanche
Zacatal   Laguna   de Marzo   Díaz Ordaz   Escárcega   Lechugal   Conhuas   Becán   Xpujil
de Términos   Mamantal   186   Lago   Dzinapara   Francisco
Coyoc   Fuco Villa   Sivituc   Chicanná   Xpujil   Villa
Buenavista   Río Bec   186
El Ramonal   Tortuga   Kohunlich
Candelária   Reserva de la
El Tigre   Maruchín   365   Biósfera de   Azúl
Cuauhtémoc   Calakmul   Tomás   Or
Chiapas   El Triunfo   Nueva   Calakmul   Garrido
Coahuila
Chablé   Balakbal
GUATEMALA

Palenque   Bonampak   Yaxchilán

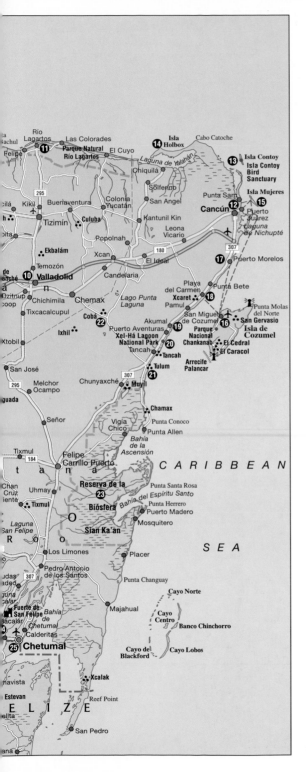

Yucatán, beyond the Río Bec ruins, are the remains of Calakmul, one of the two superpowers of the Classic Maya era (along with Tikal), with a population of some 70,000 and a network of subsidiary cities. The archaeological site at Calakmul is in a biosphere reserve, so if you visit now there's still a real sense of discovery to be had in scrambling over the roots and shoots that still choke the mighty temples.

Aside from the great Maya ruins, there is a generous slice of Spanish colonial charm on offer here too, especially in the cities of Mérida and Campeche. Also, some of the Yucatán's finest colonial mansions are now being converted into comfortable hotels in the tranquil countryside. A few of the former henequen plantations are still operating today, many were abandoned and have become empty ruins *(see page 296)*, but others have been resurrected as luxury hotels, the airy, high-ceilinged rooms remaining cool even in the searing heat of the Yucatecan summer.

The coast and countryside

The Yucatán's Caribbean coastline is stunning, although Cancun was struck by Hurricane Wilma in 2005. The white beaches and azure waters between Cancún and Tulum attract the most visitors and there are many fascinating beaches and lagoons down this way including Xcacel and Akumal. Offshore is the island of Cozumel, its coral walls the talk of dive magazines the world over, and the glorious beaches of tiny Isla Mujeres, where development has been restricted. Laguna Bacalar is another jewel, a lovely lake just to the north of Chetumal.

The Yucatán's national parks and reserves are extensive and varied. Most impressive is the colossal Calakmul Biosphere Reserve with its blanket of jungle. The Sian Ka'an Biosphere Reserve is another vast protected territory, whose boundaries also include the offshore reef. The Río Lagartos National Park and Celestún wetlands are superb for birders, especially for the huge flocks of flamingos. Finally, there are hundreds of atmospheric (and refreshing) *cenotes* to cool off in wherever you are. ❑

NORTHERN YUCATAN

This is Mexico's Maya heartland, centered on two of its greatest cities, Chichén Itzá and Uxmal, both within a short hop from Mérida, the elegant colonial state capital of Yucatán

Maps:
Area 288
City 293

The northern section of the Yucatán Peninsula is occupied largely by the wedge-shaped state of Yucatán. The landscape up here is flat, dry and covered in tangled scrub. The sacred *cenotes* of the Maya are the deep wells formed in the limestone that provided the only access to fresh water. Second to the peninsula's Caribbean beach resorts, this is the region that draws the most visitors for its sheer quantity of superb archeological sites, crowned by the magnificent Chichén Itzá and Uxmal. The nature reserves at Celestún and Río Lagartos offer rich pickings for birders in a tranquil setting that contrasts with the glitz of Cancún.

Mérida

The ideal base for exploring Yucatán is its elegant colonial capital, **Mérida ❶**. Formerly the home of numerous millionaires grown rich during the henequen heydays *(see page 296)*, today this thriving city is visited by almost all of the 1.7 million people – just under half of them Mexicans – who come to the state of Yucatán annually.

In spite of all this year-round human traffic, Mérida remains a relaxing and pleasant city for visitors. Once enclosed by walls, Mérida's downtown area is compact, its narrow streets and closely packed buildings originally laid out in the era of the horse and buggy, and now filled by motor traffic. It operates on a grid plan with numbered streets: even numbers run north-south, odd numbers east-west.

At the heart of the city center, the wonderfully shady **Plaza Mayor ⓐ** is bound by Calles 61 and 63, and by Calles 60 and 62. On its northern side, the Pasaje Pichata leads to an internal plaza where central tables under a glass roof are surrounded by self-service food counters. In the bustling streets between here and the **Mercado**, two blocks to the southeast, are the *correo* (post office), two supermarkets and the typical street stalls and little shops to be found in any local *barrio*. On Sundays the streets around the plaza are closed to traffic and vendors set up their stalls here and in Hidalgo and Santa Lucía parks.

Casa de Montejo

On the south side of the laurel-shaded plaza is the **Casa de Montejo ⓑ,** built in 1549 by one of Cortés' soldiers who founded the city, Francisco de Montejo. It has been transformed into a bank but still displays on its fortress-like walls busts of family and carvings of armed warriors standing on the heads of vanquished demons. Montejo himself lived in his mansion only for eight years after which, disillusioned with his surroundings, he left.

LEFT: the pyramid of the magician, Uxmal. **BELOW:** a leisurely business in Mérida.

The shady patio of the Governor's Palace in Mérida.

The cathedral

The Maya name for the city on the site, Tihó, means "the Place of the Five Temples", and its impressive appearance reminded the conquistadors of the Roman ruins of Mérida in Spain. Their admiration for the buildings, however, did not extend to preserving them. Once dismantled, the stones were used to erect the **Catedral de San Ildefonso ⓒ**, built 1561–98, diagonally opposite the Montejo mansion, on the northeast corner of the plaza. The cathedral's interior was stripped during the 1915 revolution apart from a sculpture known as Cristo de las Ampollas (Christ of the Blisters), supposedly carved from a tree that burned unharmed all night, after being struck by lightning in the village of Ichmul. The 20-meter (66-ft) wooden Christ above the altar was a gift from Spain.

Next to the cathedral, housed in the former archbishop's palace, is the **Museo de Arte Contemporáneo de Yucatán ⓓ**, Mérida's major modern art museum, containing the state's largest and most important collection of works from local and national artists, and well worth a visit (open Wed–Mon 10am–6pm; entry fee; tel: 999 928 3258).

On the plaza's northern side is the **Palacio del Gobierno ⓔ** (Governor's Palace), built in 1892, on whose murals Fernando Castro Pacheco worked for 25 years, including one which recalls the infamous destruction of the Maya codices by Bishop Diego de Landa at Maní in 1562. The restored **Teatro Mérida**, in an art deco building behind the palace, has a piano bar and a cinema. A few blocks east at Calles 50 & 59 is the **Museo de Arte Popular ⓕ** (open Tues–Sat 9am–8pm, Sun 9am–2pm) in the former Monasterio La Mejorada. It displays indigenous costumes, musical instruments and ceremonial masks. The **Arco de los Dragones**, one of the only three remaining Moorish arches – once

BELOW: foodstall in Mérida selling corn on the cob.

Map below

there were 13 – which stood at the entrance to the city, is just south of the museum on Calle 61. (Another arch is further up Calle 60 at the **Parque de Santa Ana**.) The history of Mérida in photographs can be seen in the **Museo de la Ciudad** , housed in the former church of San Juan de Dios at the corner of Calle 58. One block north of the cathedral, the **Parque Hidalgo** is dominated by the Jesuit-built church, **La Tercera Orden** (built in 1618), containing a painting which depicts the meeting in 1546 of Montejo and Tutul Xiú, the Maya ruler, who became a convert to Christianity thus inducing most other local chiefs to follow his lead. The sparsely equipped **tourist office** (open daily 8am–8pm; tel: 999 281 966/999 247 381) is here in the domed **Teatro Peón Contreras** (built in 1900), whose ornate marble staircase was designed by the Italian architect Enrico Deserti, also responsible for the city's Anthropology Museum. Next to the tourist office is a pleasant sidewalk café, and Yucatecan artists are featured in the **Juan Gamboa Guzmán Pinacoteca** (open Tues–Sat 8am–8pm, Sun 8am–2pm; entry fee).

Opposite the theater, the University of Yucatan has another gallery displaying the work of Yucatecan painters and has an indoor mural depicting its founding in the 19th century by General Cepeda. A block further north is leafy **Parque Santa Lucia**, once the city's stagecoach terminus, and where on Sunday mornings a crafts market is held. Tour buses depart from this little park, which on Thursday evenings hosts folk dancing. When Mérida was still walled-in, Santa Lucia marked the northern city limits with the neighborhood designated for blacks and mulatos; downtown was for Spaniards, and the Santiago section – where the Santa Isabel hermitage was the last stop of travelers setting out on the Royal Road to Campeche – was designated for the Maya. At the corner of

Mérida has long been known as the White City, possibly because of the many white buildings once here, or the white clothes worn by the inhabitants, or even from the white lime used to make the rooftops watertight.

BELOW: vivid historical mural by Fernando Castro Pacheco in the Governor's Palace.

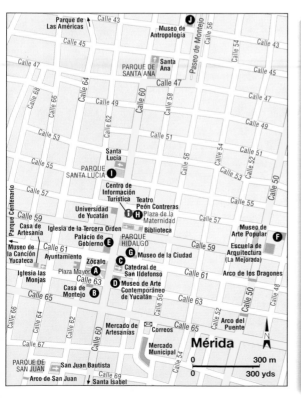

Yucatecan Architecture

The legacy of the past is never far away on the Yucatán Peninsula. Ancient pyramids co-exist with Christian monasteries and ruined *haciendas*. The Spanish Conquest was followed by a campaign of religious conversion. Missionary friars were the most prolific builders of the 16th century. In the Yucatán, the Franciscans used Maya labor to build severely simple monasteries. Immense and majestic, with few carvings or moldings to distract the eye, they conformed to Franciscan principles of asceticism. Big timbers were scarce, but there was a plentiful supply of stone. Often, the friars re-used the "pagan" temple-platforms and cutstones.

By 1560, six Franciscan monasteries had been completed at Mérida, Campeche, Mani, Izamal, Dzidzantun and Valladolid. Of these, the most imposing and spacious is the monastery at Izamal (*see page 303*). Here,

as at other centers of Christian worship, Maya converts gathered in great numbers inside the large walled atrium. A thatched and open-sided shelter, called a *ramada*, offered protection from strong sun and rain. In each corner of the atrium was a small, chapel-like sanctuary where Mass was said and the sacrament given. Often referred to as *capillas de indios*, these "chapels for indians" accommodated vast congregations.

The Spanish population of the Yucatán, greatly outnumbered by the Maya, created few large urban centers. The city of Mérida, founded in 1542, retains a rare and celebrated example of civil Plateresque (ornate baroque) architecture. Facing the main plaza, the Casa Montejo was completed in 1549. The entrance, surmounted by a coat of arms, is flanked on either side by a conquistador in full armor. In Mérida and in the neighborhood of Valladolid, some fine churches were built with elaborate *retablos* (altarpieces) to meet the spiritual needs of Spanish families. At Izamal, during the 17th century, arcades were added round the edge of the atrium for the benefit of worshipers.

Geographically and culturally, however, the peninsula remained isolated from changing architectural fashions. Only the rise of sisal exports in the 19th century brought conspicuous consumption to the region. With profits won from vast henequen plantations, landowners built opulent and eclectically designed villas in Mérida, giving it a European aura that it retains today. The decorative style incorporated rococo, neo-classical and neo-Baroque traits. Meanwhile, in the countryside, Moorish-style double archways like that at Yaxcopoil *(see page 296)* marked the entrance to huge estates. Autonomous and self-sufficient *haciendas* operated along feudal lines. Included in the *hacienda* complex was the *casa grande* (main house), the processing plant, warehouses and work yards, a church, the *tienda de raya* (estate shop), and the humble dwellings of the laborers. After 1910, many *hacienda* buildings were sacked or destroyed by revolutionaries. Today, once imposing structures stand roofless and abandoned. ❑

LEFT: the ornate façade of the Casa Montejo in Mérida, which is now occupied by a bank.

the arcade leading off the park, a poets' corner contains busts of some of the musicians and writers who ennobled Yucatán's artistic past.

Four blocks further north, starting at Calles 56 and 47, is **Paseo de Montejo**, a wide, shady boulevard created in the early 20th century as Mérida's answer to Mexico City's Paseo de la Reforma and the Champs Elysées of Paris. President Porfirio Diaz attended the boulevard's grand opening in 1906 and many of the impressive mansions still stand, among them the identical twin palaces of the Barbachano family who virtually created the Yucatán tourist industry in the 1930s. At the corner of the Paseo and Calle 43, the **Museo de Antropología ①**, (open Tues–Sat, 9am–8pm; Sun, 9am–2pm) is worth seeing. In a splendid former palace built in 1911, it contains panels, photographs and some impressive Maya artefacts, including a jadeite mask brought from the sacred *cenote* at Chichén Itzá. It also has a well-stocked bookshop.

It's a lengthy walk from the central plaza to the Paseo, providing the ideal opportunity to ride a *calesa* (buggy) and study the mansions and the statues. One such statue is of Felipe Carillo Puerto – tagged as the Red Governor – who was assassinated by political enemies because of the 1920s reforms he tried to introduce to improve the lives of the Maya. Although married, he fell in love with US journalist Alma Reed, leaving his family to live openly with her, a tremendous social scandal at the time. One of the most famous love songs in Mexico, *La Peregrina* (The Wanderer), was written at his request in her honor. He's still remembered as a romantic figure, whose wide-ranging reforms were ahead of their time.

Another statue is to **Justo Sierra**, the father of Yucatecan literature and admired educator. The boulevard ends with the **Monumento a la Patria** (Monument to the Nation), created by Colombian sculptor Romulo Rozo in 1946, from stone brought from the town of Ticul. The circular composition portrays the history of Mexico, from the days of the Maya to the Spanish conquest.

If you're on a tour you'll find it ends several blocks to the west at **Parque de Las Américas**, planted with trees from every country on the continent. Divided into four sections, it includes an open air theater (the Rozo mural around the stage depicts the Maya fine arts) now used for children's festivals; a playground, a fountain and library, all with beautifully conceived and executed pre-hispanic motifs. Another big park, **El Centenario**, at the southwestern edge of the city (bus along Calles 61 or 65) houses the city's zoo.

Mérida to the west coast

The main attraction on the west coast is a wildlife reserve devoted to flamingos. Take Ruta 281 for 92 km (57 miles) to the fishing port of **Celestún ②**, perched on a narrow peninsula connected to the mainland by causeway across a lagoon. The lagoon is part of the Parque Natural del Flamenco Mexicano, where flamingos, herons and other wildlife are under official protection. Flamingos, males and females virtually identical in appearance, form monogamous couples, and live as long as 30 years or even more. They obtain food by filtering plankton through the sensitive hairs

Maps:
Area 288
City 293

Detail on the modernistic Monumento a la Patria.

BELOW:
Monumento a la Patria.

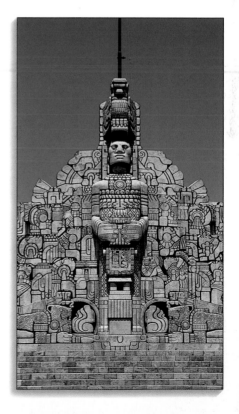

Snowy egret, one of the many waterbirds seen at Celestún.

on their tongue. The lagoon is also a wintering place for ducks from Canada. A tour boat leaves from the dock in front of the Edificio Cultur, on the road leading into the town, to explore the mangrove-fringed lagoon and estuaries of the Rio Esperanza, offering possible sightings of turtles, crocodiles, pelicans, egrets and sometimes spider monkeys. You can swim and scuba dive at freshwater Baldiosera Springs. The beaches here and *en route* to **Sisal**, 40 km (25 miles) further north are fine for swimming but fierce winds sometimes fill the area with dust. At the southern end of Celestún's lagoon, visited by the tour, is Real de Salinas where salt is still mined and shipped out.

Southern Routes

Two popular tour itineraries to the south of Mérida are The Puuc Route and The Route of the Convents. To some degree they overlap, both going through the village of **Umán** and past **Yaxcopoil ❸**, a preserved *hacienda* about 40 km (25 miles) from Mérida, which demonstrates how wealthy henequen tycoons lived a century ago (open Mon–Sat, 8am–6pm; Sun, 9am–1pm; entry fee; 999 900 1193/999 910 4469).

The Puuc Route (the name refers to the low-lying hills of the region) goes via **Muna** before heading southeast on Ruta 184 through a region of citrus groves, banana trees and coconut plantations as well as the *milpas* on which the country dweller survives. Having first cleared the ground with his axe and machete and burned the pile of scrub to create earth-nourishing ashes, the farmer plants seeds for squashes, corn, melons, peppers. The rain comes in late May or early June and the *milpa* is ready to harvest in September. (After three years, the soil is exhausted and a new site must be found.)

BELOW:
carved figure at Yaxcopoil henequen *hacienda*.

THE HENEQUEN BOOM

At the turn of the 20th century a dizzying economic boom swept Yucatán, based on the cultivation of henequen. The spiky relative of the agave plant was grown on huge plantations in the countryside to the south of Mérida, and harvested for the sisal fiber to make rope.

This was the oil of another era, creating scores of millionaires. Henequen plantation owners lived like kings, their children educated at the best schools in Europe, their wives dressed in the latest Parisian finery – all attained, however, at the expense of their Maya laborers, who were practically slaves. Henequen was exported and the French bricks and tiles that came back as ballast were used to build mansions for the tycoons in Mérida.

Today, most of the plantation *haciendas* lie abandoned and crumbling, but some, such as the one at Yaxcopoil, are open to visitors. A giant brown, Moorish-style double arch on the highway leads to the main house, a series of large, airy rooms full of period furniture. Next to the private chapel with its shiny marble floor, an ancient kitchen opens onto a garden of citrus trees and banana plants. Hundreds of Maya laborers operated the now-rusting machinery on a terrace at the rear, living in squalor in the surrounding huts still occupied by their descendants.

Loltún Caves and the Puuc Sites

Continuing south, turn left at Muna onto Ruta 184 for about 30 km (18 miles), to **Oxkutzcab** ("land rich in turkeys"), today known as "The Garden of Yucatán" for the exotic fruits which are sold in the busy market. This is the jumping-off point for the **Grutas de Loltún ❹**, which stretch underground for almost a mile, reaching heights of up to 45 meters (125ft). Guided tours take about one hour and lights are pointed at such phenomena as the natural simalcrum of the Virgin of Guadalupe, the smoke-blackened portions where early residents did their cooking, the *choltunes* (water tanks) and the occasional nest of bats. Rebel Maya sheltered here during the 19th-century War of the Castes.

Just to the south of Loltún are a quartet of ancient sites bearing "Puuc" architectural features: carved stone designs, what are known as roof combs (walls perforated with narrow perpendicular slits like narrow doors) and masks of Chac, the god of rain. The first site, **Labná,** whose palace with its dozens of rooms and virtually unweathered Chac masks, is connected by a series of *sacbeob* ("white causeways") to other buildings deep in the woods including an observatory and a magnificent corbeled red sandstone arch adorned with a stone frieze representing typical Maya thatched huts.

Much of **Sayil** remains unexcavated but its major attraction is its three-level Great Palace, the upper portion punctuated with short, Greek-style columns, which towers over a large open space. Many more Chac masks and a carved stone sky serpent peer from above and paths lead to the ruins of the observatory. Nearby **Xlapak** is a small site with one building whose restoration is evident from the different colored blocks of stone. A short distance to the north, **Kabáh** is set majestically above two grassy *plazas* at different levels. The main building, a rectangular palace with 30 rooms, dominates the site but equally important is the Codz Poop ("rolled straw mat") whose west façade is covered with Chac masks. Dozens of other grinning stone faces are jumbled at the foot of the steps. Kabáh's Triumphal Arch, restored in the 1950s, marked the start of what was once a *sacbe* to Uxmal. These highly durable roads were prepared from a type of white earth, *sahcab*, found in thick layers below the ground but, when wetted and spread out, quickly solidified.

Uxmal

Continuing a few kilometers/miles north from Kabáh, you come to **Uxmal ❺** (open daily 8am–5pm; entry fee), first excavated in 1929 by Danish archeologist Frans Blom. Uxmal was the most important Puuc ceremonial center and its architecture is striking. In 1840, the US explorer John Lloyd Stephens compared the **Palacio del Gobernador ❹** (Governor's Palace) favorably with Grecian, Roman and Egyptian art. "The designs are strange and incomprehensible, very elaborate, sometimes grotesque, but often simple, tasteful, beautiful," he wrote. The palace, 100 meters (330 ft) wide, sits atop a hill with an impressive façade. The Puuc style of building was to face rubble-filled walls with cement and cover the whole with limestone mosaic panels, in this case 20,000 of them.

The North of the palace is the 39-meter (128-ft)

TIP

The town of Tlcul, near to Oxkutzcab, is famed for the quality of its embroidered *huipiles*; shoes, hats and ceramics are also made here.

BELOW: Yaxcopoil *hacienda* still retains the atmosphere of its past grandeur.

Maps:
Area 288
Site 299

Maya expert Sylvanus Morley called the Governor's Palace at Uxmal simply "the most magnificent, the most spectacular single building in all pre-Columbian America."

BELOW: the pyramid at Uxmal.

high Pyramid of the Magician, legendarily built in one night by the son of a witch, but actually the product of several generations of builders (Uxmal means "three times built"). The steps are steep and intimidating to climb even with the aid of the heavy chain handrail, but there are terrific views from the top where apparently another structure was planned but never completed. Some wooden lintels have endured through the centuries because they were made from the sapodilla tree, valued for its hardness and durability. The unusual soft contours of this rounded pyramid, according to one story, were created so that Ehécatl, the god of the wind, would not hurt himself on any sharp edges when he blew over the structure.

Immediately west is the 74-room quadrangle, possibly a palace complex or military academy but referred to as the **Nunnery Quadrangle ❸** because its form reminded its discoverer, Father Diego Lopez de Cogolludo, of a Spanish convent. The entire complex is built on an elevated man-made platform and typifies the Puuc architectural style, which is based on the Maya hut, the *na*, with its smooth walls and high-peaked thatch roof. Although the nunnery's original purpose is not known, one rumor is that sacrifical victims spent their last few months there in debauchery. On the south side is a ruined ballcourt. Just beyond is the **House of the Turtles ❸**, which gets its name from the turtle carvings on the cornice, an animal associated with Chac in Maya legend and whose tears were believed to bring rain. Chac was of course significant in this area where water was scarce, and his image in stucco masks is ubiquitous, at one point even taking the form of a doorway.

West of the pyramid is **El Palamar** (the Dovecote) **❸**, its name derived from the Spanish for the nine projecting roof-cones with lattices like a dovecote.

ERASING MAYA HISTORY

Northeast of Oxkutzcab is the small town of **Maní**, whose sorrowful name in Maya means "the place where everything has stopped."

On a day of infamy in July 1562 it was at Mani that Father Diego de Landa gathered together hundreds of "idols" and all he could find – but could not read – of the Maya scriptures and publicly burned them as "works of the devil", thus destroying virtually all Maya recorded history in a single misguided act. As they had become more aware of the Maya's bloody sacrificial practices, the Spanish invaders resolved to stamp out what they believed to be evil heresy and convert the inhabitants to Christianity.

As first bishop of Yucatán, Diego de Landa (1524–79) mercilessly hunted down and punished participants in native rites. Nevertheless Landa admired the virtues of courage, temperance and willpower which the Maya shared with Christianity and he was awed with their earlier accomplishments. "This country, although it is a good land is not at present such as it appears to have been in the prosperous time, when so many and such remarkable buildings were built." He went on to write the *Yucatán, Before and After the Conquest*, which, ironically remains the most reliable account we have of Maya history.

Away to one side, southeast of the Governor's Palace, is the **Casa de la Vieja** (House of the Old Woman) **E**, now a ruin, which Maya legend avers was the house of a sorcerer, the mother of the dwarf magician who built the pyramid.

The **Visitors' Center F** at the entrance to the ruins includes a shop, museum, and a restaurant that stays open till 10pm. The 45-minute Sound & Light Show is at 8pm; an English translation is provided through headphones. Buses from Mérida leave earlier but there is a daily tour bus from Mérida's 2nd-class bus station at 8.30am which visits this and several Puuc area sites.

Tragic Maní

The Puuc route and the Ruta de los Conventos overlap at Oxkutzcab with the latter itinerary heading north to **Maní 6**, where, in 1562 the bishop of Yucatán, Father Diego de Landa ceremoniously burned a pile of Maya sacred texts and idols *(see box below)*. Landa's house still sits among Yaache (cedar) trees near Maní's church of San Miguel Archangel in whose chapel are a series of reliefs depicting the battles fought by the conquistadors for the territory. A stone depicts the legend of an early Maya chief, Tutul Xiu, a convert to Christianity.

Northwest, on the same minor road, is **Mayapán**, one of the last strongholds of the ancient Maya with its Temple of Kukulcan (copied from Chichén Itzá with which Uxmal and Mayapán formed an alliance). The confederation ruled the region peacefully (AD 987–1185) but the partnership ended when the Mayápan leader, a Toltec named Hunac Ceel Canuch, took sole control. He was succeeded by other members of his Comom dynasty until overthrown by Ah Xupan Xiu from Uxmal. The *Chilam Balam* – the Maya "Bible" – dates Mayapán's destruction as occurring in (the equivalent of) 1441.

Maps:
Area 288
Site 299

TIP

The Tutul Xiu restaurant in Maní (named after a Maya chief) specializes in a local delicacy: Pocchuc, a tasty pork loin cooked with tomatoes and onions.

BELOW: climbing Uxmal's steep-sided pyramids demands a good head for heights.

Map labels: Mérida; North Group; Hotel Hacienda Uxmal; 261; Campeche; Platform of the Stelae; Nunnery Quadrangle (Cuadranglo de las Monjas) B; Museum; Cemetery Group; Group of the Columns; Main Entrance; F; Pyramid of the Magician; Visitors' Center; Ball Court; House of the Turtles (Casa de las Tortugas) C; Dovecote (El Palamor) D; Governor's Palace (Palacio del Gobernador) A; Great Pyramid (El Gran Pirámide); South Temple; House of the Old Woman (Casa de la Vieja) E; Temple of the Centipede (Chimez Temple); San Simon Road; N; Uxmal; 0 200 m; 0 200 yds

Inter-tribal struggles and the broken alliance were largely responsible for the ease with which Maya Yucatán fell prey to the invading Spaniards in the following century when Francisco de Montejo founded Mérida. Excavations at Mayapán are unexciting and, wrote one visitor, yielded proof that it "sheltered a society in decline." Mayapán once had 3,500 buildings but has now been almost totally reclaimed by the jungle.

Heading north on Carretera 18, a few other stops along the route are worth the pilgrim's time. At **Telchaquillo** a staircase in the town park leads to an attractive *cenote* and the Franciscan temple whose façade was worked by Maya artisans. There's another *cenote* with fascinating caves at **Tecoh**, where a former convent, the Virgin of the Ascension, is based on what may have been a Maya pyramid. And at **Acanceh** the 16th-century Franciscan temple of Nuestra Señora de la Navidad adjoins the Plaza de las Tres Culturas, which has pre-Hispanic, colonial and modern structures.

From Mérida to the North Coast

Heading north from Mérida on Ruta 16, about halfway to Progreso is a junction at Taxché, leading 3 km (2 miles) to the ruins of **Dzibilchaltún** – meaning "where there is writing on flat rocks" – an important Preclassic site, continually occupied from as early as 500 BC until the Spanish Conquest. Thousands of structures, all joined by broad *sacbeob,* have been mapped including the widest Maya palace so far discovered, stretching 130 meters (400 ft) across one side of the central square. Even from the top it is hard to see over the dense jungle that covers most of the 13 sq. km/25-hectare site, yet once 20,000 people lived here, with an economy based on salt mining.

BELOW: the ruins of Dzibilchaltún.

Near the palace is the **Cenote Xlacah**, dredged by a team from the *National Geographic* in 1958, which has yielded thousands of Maya sacrificial offerings including human skeletons, but which centuries ago became a watering hole for farm livestock. The cenote is open to the public for swimming until 4pm and can get very busy at weekends.

To the right of the entrance is a 9.5-meter (30-ft) pyramid with stairs on two sides; to the left is a *palapa* (thatch)-covered walkway lined with statues from Chichén Itzá, Uxmal and other sites leading to an excellent museum. Inside, the central exhibit is a colorful panorama of jungle and seashore, profuse with jaguars, herons, turtles, cenotes and pyramids. Beyond the elaborately carved stones from a ballcourt and other Maya artefacts is another gallery, dedicated to the European technology that followed the conquest. Follow the path from the museum to the **Templo de las Siete Muñecas** (Temple of the Seven Dolls), a low structure with an impressive temple, at the east end of the site. The seven clay dolls for which it was named currently reside in a museum in Mexico City.

Contemporary visitors might marvel at such ruins spread over immense areas but, as an exhibit at the museum explains: "Maya communities are today thought to have been garden cities with large plantings in the interior to sustain a large concentration of inhabitants."

Glowing smile from a Maya girl.

Progreso

Continuing north, the formerly bustling port of **Progreso** ❼ (pop: 50,000) lies 36 km (22 miles) from Mérida. The highway into town becomes Calle 78, just east of the famous shipping wharf, Puerto de Altura (a lengthy concrete pier to compensate for the shallow sea). Near El Faro, the 40-meter (130-ft) lighthouse

BELOW: painted buggy at Izamal.

145 km (78 nautical miles) north of Progreso are five islets, bordered by cliffs, the Arrecifes Alacranes, which are a nesting place for turtles and many seabirds including frigate birds. Boats can be hired on the Progreso seafront.

BELOW: Maya woman in traditional dress in a religious parade.

which replaced one built on the site in 1885, are the market and the bus station. At weekends Mexican visitors hit the scorchingly hot beachfront, lined with several of the town's best hotels and good seafood restaurants.

East of Progreso, along Ruta 27, are a string of resorts known locally as La Costa Esmeralda. The first are some classy places near to the grubby little fishing village of **Chicxulub** (thought to be the location of a crater left by a meteorite some 65 million years ago, which may have led to the extinction of the dinosaurs).

You'll spot signs all along the coast for beachside holiday complexes. It's best to wait for **Telchac Puerto**, a seaside village with thatched bungalows – *cabañas* – on the beach. Next along the coast is Chabihau and finally Dzilam de Bravo where the road ends. Expensive boats can be rented here to visit Boca de Dzilam**,** a swampy coastal region of dunes and marshes, for wildlife watching (a huge variety of reptiles, birds and monkeys) in the **Parque Natural de San Felipe**. Spartan rooms can be located by asking at the shop named La Herradura in the village of San Felipe.

Inland to Tizimin and Izamal

From Telchac, Ruta 172 heads inland for 3.7 km (2 miles) past salt flats to the lesser-known **Xcambo** or X'tampu as the signs say (the Maya X is pronounced "sh") pyramids and other structures at each side of a square. A Catholic church built from Mayan stones is among the ruins. It's a further 60 km (27 miles) in countryside dotted with the tall metal columns bearing wind-power mills to **Motúl**, a neat and tidy little town. Horse-drawn *calesas* roam the streets and the tower of the convent (adjoining the distinctive church) offers fine views. In the market, women wearing long *huipiles* sell bags of *nanzes*, a grape-sized yellow

fruit that tastes like a soft apple and is used for jams and desserts. In season you'll find fruit drinks of *pitahaya,* a red peach-sized fruit that ripens midsummer on the spiky cerreus cactus. Pitahaya juice is mixed with fresh lime and mineral water and drinking it is reputed to stain the urine red.

Ruta 176 heads east from here to the state's second largest city, **Tizimin** (pop: 62,000), a livestock center with a small zoo and a colonial convent. Ubiquitous here, as in every small town in the Yucatán, are the three-wheeled *bici-taxis* which are used to transport everything from construction supplies and vegetable stands to entire families.

One mile from Motúl past spiky henequen fields under puffy Rorchsach clouds on the road to Izamal is a **cenote** which, 80 steps down in a cave, serves as the local swimming hole (admission 3 pesos). There's a café/bar there.

At **Izamal**, are plazas on two sides of the vibrantly painted convent. At the top of the steps porticos surround a grassy plaza fronting the cathedral; at the foot, a plaque commemorates the visit of "Papa Juan Pablo II" on 11 August 1993. The 16th-century Franciscans subsumed this sacred city early in their conquest, destroying the Popul Chac pyramid where Itzamna, the goddess of creation, was worshiped to build the St Anthony of Padua convent. The Kinich Kakmo pyramid is one of several Maya pyramids that have survived in the town.

East from Mérida

Turn off the Mérida to Valladolid highway, Ruta 180, after 26 km (16 miles) near the village of Tixcobob, to **Aké** ❽, already an important site in the era before AD 300 where regional leaders met to plan alliances. Aké was occupied until the 15th century and is notable for a huge palace ascended by 27 steps and topped

Map on page 288

TIP

Near to Aké is the luxurious hotel Hacienda Katanchel, a former henequen plantation converted by Seville-born architect Anabel González.

BELOW: drawing of the center at Valladolid, from a photograph by Desiré Charnay.

DESIRÉ CHARNAY

One of the most influential early explorers of Maya sites was the Frenchman Desiré Charnay. It was he who first photographed Palenque, Uxmal and Chichén Itzá, and these superb photographs and lithographs led the way for the first scientific archeological expeditions.

Charnay first became interested in the Maya ruins when he heard of Stephens' and Catherwood's trips to the region while he was teaching in New Orleans. A few years later, in 1857, he succeeded in persuading the French education ministry to pay for a lengthy trip to take photographs and papier-mâché casts of the Maya civilization. By 1860, using the immensely cumbersome collodion wet plate method, he managed to complete a volume of 47 plates published as *Cités et ruines américaines,* which became famous in France and throughout Europe.

It was only 20 years later, in 1880, that Charnay returned to the Maya region. By now, the photographic process had been simplified, and he was able to take many photographs, not only of monuments but of the local people and scenes of the exuberant jungles of southern Mexico. These were published as engravings in magazines and books back in France, and were a great contribution to spreading knowledge of the region.

Quetzalcoatl, the Plumed Serpent.

BELOW: age-worn features of Chac-Mool at Chichén Itzá's temple of the warriors.

with 30 stone pillars which once supported a wooden roof. Adjoining is a still-operating henequen factory churning out reels of straw-colored rope and twine. About one-third of Yucatán's workforce is still employed in the industry.

Chichén Itzá

Continuing east along Ruta 180, about 116 km (72 miles) from Mérida, you'll come to **Chichén Itzá ❾** (from the Maya *chi* = mouths; *chen* = wells; *Itza* = the tribe that settled here), the best known and most spectacular Maya site in the whole of the Yucatán Peninsula.

Founded around the 5th century, Chichén Itzá flourished for some 500 years until it was apparently conquered by the Toltecs under their leader, Topiltzin. He took the name of the deity Quetzalcoatl – god of the arts and the wind – and added it to his own. Toltec styles range from types of clothing and weapons to the plumed serpent motif of Quetzalcoatl (plumed head, rattlesnake's tail) also known by the Maya as Kukulcán. Aztecs believed him to be the only god to have taken human form; to the Maya he was the fountain of wisdom. Kukulcán's significance varied between civilizations.

In the 13th century, after provoking war with a neighboring tribe, Chac Xib Chac, the ruler, presided over Chichén Itzá's decline, and by the time the Spaniards arrived in the 16th century the site had been long abandoned. Maya had occupied the region since around 1500 BC, but Chichén Itzá is an anomaly because it resembles Tula, the 10th–12th-century Toltec capital in central Mexico with nothing similar in between. By the time the Spaniards arrived in the 16th century most of the sites had been abandoned

The site was first brought to the attention of the outside world by the US

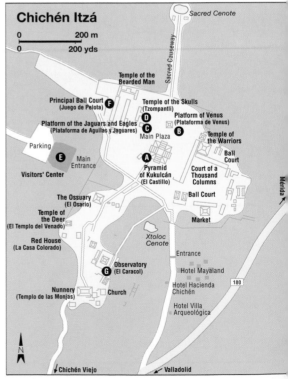

Chichén Itzá

0   200 m
0   200 yds

Sacred Cenote

Sacred Causeway

Temple of the Bearded Man

Principal Ball Court (Juego de Pelota) **F**

Temple of the Skulls (Tzompantli) **D**

Platform of Venus (Plataforma de Venus) **B**

Platform of the Jaguars and Eagles (Plataforma de Aguilas y Jaguares) **C**

Main Plaza

Temple of the Warriors

Parking

E Main Entrance

A

Ball Court

Pyramid of Kukulcán (El Castillo)

Court of a Thousand Columns

Visitors' Center

The Ossuary (El Osario)

Ball Court

Temple of the Deer (El Templo del Venado)

Market

Red House (La Casa Colorada)

Xtoloc Cenote

Entrance

Observatory **G** (El Caracol)

Hotel Mayaland

Nunnery (Templo de las Monjas)

Church

Hotel Hacienda Chichén

180

Hotel Villa Arqueológica

N

Chichén Viejo

Valladolid

Mérida

Maps:
Area 288
Site 304

explorer Benjamin Norman in 1839, and John Lloyd Stephens in 1840. Their accounts and detailed sketches (provided for Stephens by Frederick Catherwood) prompted further explorations. The American consul in Mérida, Edward Herbert Thompson, a Harvard professor, bought the site in 1904 and more thorough excavations began soon after. He described Chichén Itzá as having "scattered carved and square stones in countless thousands and fallen columns by the hundreds… Facades, though gray and haggard with age and seamed by time, sustain the claim that Chichén Itzá is one of the world's greatest monuments of antiquity."

Thompson imported dredging equipment and drained the sacred cenote (60-meter/197-ft diameter; 35 meters/ 115 ft deep) which yielded a vast collection of offerings: incense statues, jade, amber, gold, engraved metal discs and sacrificed human skeletons. People who survived being thus sacrificed were presumed to have spoken to the gods and endowed with the gift of prophecy. Today a pleasant café with a well-stocked bookshop overlooks the murky, green water.

The site's dominant structure, the 24-meter (80-ft) high **Pyramid of Kukulcán** (El Castillo) Ⓐ, represents the Maya calendar, with four 91-step staircases plus a single step at the main entrance (or the one at the top, say some) adding up to 365. Eighteen terraces divide the nine levels which represent the eighteen 20-day months. The nine terraces symbolize the nine underground worlds. Each side has 52 panels representing the 52-year cosmic cycle, the point at which their two calendars, the religious and the secular, coincided and they considered that cycle ended, only to begin anew.

The carved snakes' heads and tails are joined at sunset during the spring equinox by undulating shadows, interpreted as a time to sow the crops just as

The ancient Maya fasted and abstained from sex during the crucial equinox periods, still celebrated today at Chichén Itzá.

BELOW: El Castillo, Chichén Itzá's dominant structure.

the snake's apparent ascension of the pyramid at the fall equinox signified harvest time. Thousands of visitors attend here on March 21 and September 22 every year, when the serpent's slithering up or down the north stairs still takes place. The illusion, which lasts more than 3 hours, is imitated during the nightly 35-minute *Sonido y Luz* (Sound & Light) performance (visitors should check times on arrival).

Inside the pyramid, open only for a couple of hours in the middle of the day, is an earlier one atop which, in an inner sanctuary, is an altar or throne in the shape of a bright red jaguar with jade spots and eyes and real jaguar teeth. There is also a reclining Chac-Mool holding up a shallow sacrificial bowl, which held the heart of many a human victim.

Statues and carved faces of Chac-Mool, messenger of the gods and provider of rain, were ubiquitous because water was in short supply. (Most of the old *cenotes* have since been filled in because they were breeding grounds for mosquitoes.) The Chac rain gods were believed to create lightning by hurling stone axes at the earth and then pouring rain by emptying their gourds. The croaking of frogs was thought to announce an imminent rain shower.

Offerings to the gods

By the middle of the 20th century, decipherment of Maya scripts had revealed more about the race's warlike tendencies, a society in which dynastic rulers waged war with their neighbors, apparently with the main purpose of capturing victims who could be tortured and mutilated before being sacrificed.

There were specialized duties for these bloody rituals: the *chacs* held the victim's arms and legs while the *nacoms* split open the breast and the *chilan*

BELOW: a carved mask detail.

interpreted the sacred books possibly under the influence of hallucinatory drugs. It was believed that the gods could be appeased or nourished by these sanguinary gifts, supplemented by personal blood offerings obtained by jabbing manta ray spines through the ear or genitals, or by drawing a thorn-studded cord through the tongue. Paper used to soak up the blood was burned and tossed into the sky.

To the north of the pyramid are three small platforms; the **Plataforma de Venus ❸** (stairway at each side guarded by feathered serpents); and the **Plataforma de Aguilas y Jaguares ❹** (the base has relief carvings of eagles and jaguars holding human hearts, also jaguar and eagle symbols of Toltec warrior classes, one of whose duties was to capture sacrificial victims).

The third platform, the **Tzompantli ❺**, from which human heads were hung, displays carved stone grinning skulls in horizontal rows all around its sides. "This shocking custom", says a sign, "was derived from the need to create lasting memorials to acts of war and sacrifices as well as acting as an effective psychological deterrent for quarrelsome neighbors and would-be rebellious subjects."

At the entrance to the ruins (open daily, 8am–5pm; entry fee) is a large **Visitors' Center ❻**, with shops selling maps, books and film; cloakroom, cafeteria, small museum and free audiovisual show.

The ball-game

The enormous **Juego de Pelota** (146 meters/480 ft long, 36 meters/118 ft wide), the biggest of half a dozen ball courts around the site, has stone rings high on the walls through which a solid latex ball was propelled, usually under rules prohibiting the players from using their hands. "They struck (the ball) with any part of their body, as it happened, or they could most conveniently," recorded one 16th-century observer quoted by Totten in his *Maya Architecture*, "and sometimes he touched it with any other part but his hip, which was looked upon among them as the greatest Dexterity; and to this effect that the ball might rebound the better, they fastened a piece of stiff leather on their Hips."

But that was a report of a game played for the entertainment of Montezuma and a sign beside the ballcourt today speculates that the size of this court and the height of the rings made it unlikely that play was according to the rules governing the "hip movements game known at the time of the Conquest." One thing about which historians seem to be agreed is that the faded panels depicting the game show one player (the winning captain?) holding a ritual knife and a decapitated head (the losing captain?).

There are numerous other structures around this vast site, the earliest buildings in the Puuc architectural style but displaying dates from circa AD 900–1200, a period following the Toltec arrival. In **Chichén Viejo** (Old Chichén), the southern, pre-Toltec section are **El Osuario**, a 10-meter (33-ft) tall pyramid containing crypts with skeletons discovered a century ago; **El Templo del Venado** (the Temple of the Deer); **La Casa Colorada**, the Red House, named for the red paint on the doorway mural; **El Caracol** , a domed, circular tower shaped like a snail with stone latticework roof facade, resembling an observa-

Map on page 304

TIP

Allow yourself at least one whole day to see around all of Chichén Itzá; it is an enormous site and gets very hot and crowded by midday, but your entry ticket allows you to go in and out as often as you want.

BELOW: the Observatory at Chichén Itzá.

tory with roof slits through which certain stars appeared at certain times and enabled priests to dictate times for planting, harvesting and various rituals; and the **Templo de las Monjas** (the Nunnery), a partly collapsed palace complex 35 meters (115 ft) wide, 65 meters (213 ft) long, 20 meters (66 ft) high, probably housing Maya royalty but named by the Spanish conquistadors for its resembance to a convent. Adjoining buildings are adorned with carved stone masks of Chac and mythological *bacabs* (deities) resembling snails, turtles, armadillos and crabs reputed to hold up the sky.

Chichén Itzá is inundated with tourist buses every day of the year but regular buses from Mérida and Valladolid also pass the site. Buses may drop you off at the junction of old and new roads or go straight to site (8am–5pm). In addition to the main entrance, there is another entrance beside the Hotel Mayaland. Just beyond this is the charming Hacienda Chichén, converted from Edward Thompson's old home. Budget accommodations are available at **Piste**, a village on the highway 3 km (2 miles) before the site, about US$2 by taxi.

The Caves of Balankanché

Beyond Chichén Itzá and halfway to Valladolid, just off the (expensive) tollroad, Ruta 180, are the **Grutas de Balankanché**, in which the ancient worshipers left offerings to the rain god Tlaloc, the Toltec equivalent of Chac. A guide with flashlight accompanies visitors through the caves, up and down 320 irregular steps over a distance of some 900 meters (3,000 ft). It's a hot and sweaty route past stalactites, stalagmites and dank pools, the ceiling sometimes closing in, forcing you to crouch, and at other times soaring up to cathedral-like heights (open daily, 9am–5pm; guided tours in Spanish at 9am, noon, 2pm and 4pm, and English at 11am, 1pm and 3pm).

BELOW: ceramics found inside the Balankanché caves.

Discovered accidentally in 1959, the caves – believed by the Maya to be a sacred entrance to Xibalbá, the underworld – were re-opened with a special ceremony *"Tzicult'an ti yunti yunts'loob"* – a respectful message to the gods."

Catholicism notwithstanding, in rural Yucatán the traditional Chac Rain Ceremony still takes place in time of drought. A wooden altar is constructed with an arch of leaves and baked bread and other food offerings are placed on beds of sacred ceiba leaves, arranged in specific patterns. The shaman faces east while offering prayers and food to the gods. This is then distributed and eaten, along with a drink made fom *balche* bark, water, honey, cinnammon or anise. Small boys squat at each table leg making croaking sounds to imitate frogs.

A number of small villages, each with multiple sets of *topes* (speed bumps), punctuate the otherwise monotonous landscape along the back road between the caves and Valladolid. The countryside is dotted with *milpas*, the fecund plots in which Maya farmers raise their crops of corn, beans, chilies, sweet potato and melons. First comes Xcalacoop, then Kaua with its circular thatched-roof church and bundles of coconuts hanging from roadside stalls. Savvy peddlers with fruit or figurines hang out beside *topes* to solicit slowed-down drivers.

Valladolid

Continuing along the back road, you'll come to **Valladolid ❿** (population 52,000), some 40 km (25 miles) east of Chichén Itzá. Previously a Maya ceremonial center called Zaci, this attractive city was the scene of the historic massacre of its white citizens during the War of the Castes, the 1847 uprising by the Maya inhabitants who had been discriminated against for centuries *(see page 263)*. After months of violence and most of the region falling to the rebels (Campeche and Mérida held out) the war ended abruptly at planting time when the Maya – reminded of their rural obligations by the annual sighting of the winged ant – returned to their fields to plant the year's corn. The Federal government sent troops and supplies and, with the help of 1,000 mercenaries from the US, the whites regained control. In retaliation over the next few years the Maya population was partially wiped out.

The city's colonial atmosphere is maintained by its many well-preserved churches and mansions. The church of **San Bernardino de Siena**, next to the fortified Convento de Sisal, on Calle 41 on the western outskirts, is one of the the oldest churches in the Yucatán (1552), and has some interesting murals. Visit the San Roque City Museum and the *Mercado de Artesanías*, on Calle 39 between Calles 42 & 44, and admire the houses along Calzada de los Frailes (Street of the Friars). Most guidebooks recommend Valladolid's two local *cenotes*, the **Zaci** (Calles 36 & 39) and the out-of-town **Dzitnup**, 7 km (4½ miles) west. Both are somewhat tawdry, with multitudes of beggars and tacky souvenir stands; but Dzitnup, with its own museum and open-air restaurant, is the more attractive. The water here is much cleaner, and you can swim in the icy blue water (the caverns are electrically lit, but it is definitely worth taking your own torch).

Río Lagartos

Further beyond Valladolid, the other main attraction is up on the north coast. A morning bus leaves daily for **Río Lagartos ⓫**, 107 km (66½ miles) to the north via Tizimín on Ruta 295. The coastal region here is a nationally-protected wildlife refuge, famous for the thousands of flamingos that nest there. Named "Crocodile River", by the Spaniards for the alligators that once infested the area, but which are now rare, Río Lagartos is a rather scruffy fishing village with narrow streets and multihued houses on an estuary rife with egrets, herons, white ibis, spoonbills and flamingos.

The narrow peninsula offshore provides shelter from the ocean in the lagoon between San Felipe in the west and El Cayo in the east. Flamingos arrive in April in the lagoon to make nests, lay eggs in June and depart in September for Celestún and other estuaries. Turtles also use the beaches annually for laying their eggs. Boat trips leave Río Lagartos early in the mornings to visit the flamingos (cheaper at weekends when there are more people around to split the cost). There is also good tarpon fishing off the coast here.

If you are traveling on from Rio Lagartos to the Caribbean coast, you will need to return to Valladolid to catch an eastbound bus. ❑

Map on page 288

TIP

A sign outside the cathedral at Valladolid asks visitors to "Avoid child exploitation. Do not buy anything from them. Do not give them money. Encourage them to go to school. They deserve a better future."

BELOW: spoonbills can be seen at Río Lagartos.

THE CARIBBEAN COAST

Map on page 288

Dominated by the mega-resort of Cancún, the Yucatán's Caribbean coastline also contains tranquil island retreats, spectacular diving and snorkeling off the coral reef, and yet more Maya ruins

Mexico's Caribbean coast is best known for Cancún, the country's purpose-built answer to Spain's Costa del Sol, with its enormous hotel chain resorts lining otherwise perfect beaches. Tourists flood to Cancún year round, drawn by its clear waters and white sands, the range of outdoor leisure activities, and glitzy nightlife. The area was hit by Hurricane Wilma in 2005, however, recovery was quick and the sun-soaked coastline continues to offer numerous other attractions: tranquil islands such as Isla Mujeres, the fascinating archeological sites of Tulum, Cobá, and Kohunlich, and pristine wildlife reserves, such as Sian Ka'an in the far south.

Cancún's historical roots

In the early 1840s, US writer and explorer John Lloyd Stephens (*see page 333*) noted: "In the afternoon we steered for the mainland, passing the island of Kancune, a barren strip of land with sand hills and stone buildings visible upon it."

The buildings were some Maya sites which, against all odds, have survived: the major one, **El Rey**, now stands on the golf course of the Hilton Cancún Beach and Golf Resort. Believed to date from the 13th century, El Rey owes its (Spanish) name to the belief that it was a burial site for the nobility. Today, it is frequented more by iguanas than tourists; exotic wading birds, and sometimes crocodiles can be spotted in shallow waters offshore.

Cancún was created during the administration of President Luis Echeverría (1968–76) after the government agency FONATUR was set up to identify potential new tourist sites, draw master plans and solicit investment. The agency's pilot project, however, has faced criticism over the rapid commercialization of Cancún. Yet wildlife is still abundant, with wading birds, foxes, weasels and raccoons residing in the surrounding mangrove swamps.

At first there was only jungle and a narrow sandstrip enclosing the brackish Laguna Nichupté. What was a village at the northwestern end of the 7-shaped island was transformed into a modern town to house workers at the big hotels, of which there are now more than 70. The first hotels opened in 1972, bridges connected the island to the mainland at both ends and the building boom still continues. The population is now around 500,000 and more than 2 million visitors arrive every year, three-quarters of them from the US.

Cancún's hotel strip

For those in search of a lazily luxurious vacation, sunbathing on a pristine beach and swimming in glorious turquoise waters (or in your own miniscule pool), **Cancún ⓬** is tailor made. Honeymoners are not the

LEFT: the calm waters of Cancún's coastline.
BELOW: a big catch at Playa del Carmen.

Cancún's souvenir shops offer something for all tastes (except perhaps good taste).

BELOW:
the gleaming towers of Cancún's beach hotel zone.

only people who check into a world-class hotel and rarely leave it. All the hotels on the Bulevar Kukulcán are huge and, although next to each other, so far apart because of lengthy driveways it hardly seems worthwhile to go visiting. Most hotels are self-contained with restaurants, pools, beachfront, discos, lobby bars with futuristic glass atriums, shopping arcades, even postal facilities.

These monumental resort hotels have been built in every conceivable architectural style, from the verdant lobby of the **Gran Meliá Cancún**, whose leafy plant tendrils drift over the balconies to create a lush tropical atmosphere, to the sophisticated urban ambience of the **Ritz Carlton**. There are domed Mexican neo-colonial complexes and even a number of buildings clearly inspired by the sloping walls of Maya pyramids.

Just before the halfway point where the boulevard turns sharp right is the **Centro de Convenciones**, scene of major concerts and other activities. Behind the center is the **Museo Arqueológico** (open Tues–Fri, 9am–8pm, Sat–Sun 10am–8pm; entry fee, free on Sun; tel: 998 883 0305), with displays of Maya artefacts and deformed human skulls – the ancient Maya went in for forcibly shaping the cranium by means of wooden devices. At the **Marina** (Km 15.2) are facilities for deep-sea fishing, snorkeling, diving and other aquatic activities; and from here tours are arranged respectively on or under the enticing waters of Laguna de Nichupté by paddlewheeler or miniature submarine *(see pages 366–7)*.

Shopping plazas

The hotel strip has no street numbers but rather indicators of the approximate distance in kilometers between hotels. It is dotted at intervals by shopping malls called plazas, offering a range of souvenir shops, bars, restaurants, cinemas and

tourist activities, including a bungee jump. Some of these plazas are upscale, such as **Flamingo Plaza**, with its Maya flavor (Km.10.5; tel: 998 883 0599) and the huge, 350-shop **Kukulcán Plaza** (Km.13; tel: 998 885 2200) but others are frankly tacky, such as **Plaza La Fiesta**, opposite the Centro de Convenciones, where tuneless mariachi bands play outside all-purpose stores selling over-priced souvenirs and garish T-shirts .

Opposite, the narrow lane Playa Gaviota Azul leads to the **Rainforest Café** (tel: 1-800 552 6379), which has thick foliage (fake and real), mist machines, tubular fish tanks and giant plastic butterflies flapping their wings. Waiters wearing big hats and bandoliers of cartridges dispense $8 hamburgers and other gringo food to the accompaniment of *música ranchera* – Mexican country, and a soundtrack of chirping birds. Outside the restaurant the balcony overlooks a plaza where folk dancers perform and a glass elevator connects to the fast-food counters on the third floor. The classiest plaza, **La Isla Shopping Village** (Km. 12.5; tel: 998 883 5025), with upscale shops, sits on an artificial island with a food court, "river walk," aquarium and restaurants.

Map on page 288

Downtown Cancún

Travelers less addicted to glitz, or maybe on a budget, stay in Ciudad Cancún (downtown), establishing a base in one of the inexpensive hotels near reliable Sanborns and the bus station where Avenida Uxmal meets the main drag: tree-shaded Avenida Tulum. Explore the side streets for offbeat, little restaurants. Between the **Monumento a la Historia de Mexico** (Mexican History Monument) at the bus station end and the **Monumento Diálogo Norte-Sur** (dedicated to North-South dialog) is everything a visitor might need: markets, shops, money-changers, hotels, bars, tourist offices, a vast supermarket and – a block away from the southern end where Bulevar Kukulcán leads to the hotel zone – airline offices and the US consulate. Buses marked Hotel Zone run continually from downtown along the wide boulevard emerging at the southern end near the Club Med. Unmetered taxis are everywhere but, because of the distances involved, expensive.

BELOW: a Cancun hotel overlooks ruins.

Just to the north of Cancún is **Isla Contoy ⑬**, a sanctuary for pelicans, egrets, boobies, cormorants and sea turtles. Carefully monitored and guided eco-friendly boat excursions are run from the main pier on Isla Mujeres or from Cancún by a cooperative (Amigos de Isla Contoy; tel: 998 884 7483). There are no accommodations on the island. Similar, and ideal for camping and swimming, is **Isla Holbox ⑭**, reached by a short ferry ride from Chiquila, which is about 160 km (110 miles) from Cancún. There are a handful of thatched-roof bungalows for rent and sea-food restaurants. A bus from Valladolid or Puerto Juárez connects with the last ferry from Chiquilá at 3pm.

Isla Mujeres

A more accessible island than Holbox and Contoy is **Isla Mujeres ⑮**, about 8-km (5-mile) long, with only two roads and nowhere more than 1 km (½ mile) wide. Some have suggested that the island's name derives from the 17th-century pirates who kept their women

BELOW: making a
reproduction of
ancient Maya
carving for
handicraft shops.

sequestered here but it is more likely to have come from the female idols discovered in the temples honoring Ixchel, the Maya goddess of fertility. At the island's southern tip are the ruins (reconstructed after a devastating hurricane) of the astronomically oriented Temple of Ixchel. Usually identified as the benefactor of weavers and doctors as well as women, her counterpart was Itzamna, the sun god who was patron of the arts and sciences. While Itzamna was considered to be entirely benevolent, Ixchel had unfavorable aspects and was often depicted as an evil old lady. An ancient clifftop temple/observatory was destroyed by Hurricane Gilbert in 1988.

Many of today's visitors spend their time either on the undersized town beach, **Playa Los Cocos**, where the water is very shallow, or snorkeling a couple of miles south in the clear waters of **El Garrafón**, which is usually teeming with people. Buses run only as far as Playa Lancheros and nearby Hacienda Gomar but they finish early and there might be difficulty finding a taxi after sunset. Excursions can be taken by boat to visit the turtle sanctuary at **Sac Bajo** (open 9am– 5pm; entry fee; tel: 988 877 0595) or **El Garrafón Natural Reef Eco Park** (open 8.30am–5pm in winter, until 6pm in summer; entry fee; tel: 998 984 9422). Of interest to divers here is the sunken wreck of a pirate ship. On **Los Manchones**, a reef off the southern tip, crystal-clear waters flow around a 3 meter (10 ft) bronze crucifix, placed there in 1994 to mark the 140th anniversary of the island becoming a township. It was sponsored by ecologists hoping to inspire conservation. "In other words," wryly notes writer Pancho Shiell, "they don't want tourists to batter and ruin Los Manchones like they did El Garrafón."

Further back up the island's east coast are the lighthouse and what remains of **Hacienda Mundaca** (entry fee), the former mansion of Fermín Mundaca, a 19th-century slave trader who is said to have been spurned by a local *señorita* and left the house he had built for her unattended to fall into disrepair. Mundaca's unoccupied tomb in the island cemetery is decorated with a skull and crossbones and bears the enigmatic inscription: "Como eres, yo fui. Como soy, tu serás" (*What you are, I was. What I am, you will be).*

The **Reef and Cave of the Sleeping Sharks**, in deep waters off the northeast coast, was the subject of a *National Geographic* feature (April 1975), which explained that immobile sharks are a rare phenonemon because sharks must be in constant motion in order to breathe. Nurse sharks are harmless and you can snorkel above them.

Car ferries run to Isla Mujeres, a 45-minute trip, at 8am, 11am, 2.45pm, 5.30pm, and 8.15pm from **Punta Sam**, about 8 km (5 miles) north of Cancún. There are more frequent passenger boats from both **Puerto Juárez** and Punta Sam, and catamarans from Playa Linda pier next to the Hotel Casa Maya in the hotel zone. Call Dolphin Express (tel: 988 849 4621).

Cozumel

South of Isla Mujeres is the much larger island of **Cozumel 16** 47 km (30 miles) long with a lighthouse at each end, and 16 km (10 miles) wide. Cozumel was another sacred island dedicated to Ixchel, the ruins of whose sanctuary can still be seen at the

Map on page 288

mostly overgrown site of **San Gervasio** (entry fee). According to legend, Ixchel acknowledged the shrines and temples built in her honor by sending her favorite bird, a swallow. Thus the island was named "Land of the Swallows".

In the days before Cancún's development, Cozumel was a sleepy backwater: today it welcomes more than 300,000 visitors a year. 19 km (12 miles) from the charming coastal town of Playa del Carmen, from which there are regular ferries (and a car ferry service operating from Calica, further down the coast), it is also on numerous tour itineraries from Cancún.

Laguna Chankanaab

It was predicted in the *Chilam Balam* – Maya history books – that bearded conquerors would come from the east, and thus early 16th-century locals were barely surprised when Hernan Cortés and fellow Spanish conquistadors landed on Cozumel, before heading up the coast of Mexico. In the century that followed, most of the remaining inhabitants were driven away by Jean Lafitte, Henry Morgan and other pirates who holed up in the coves and bays of the east coast, refilling their water tanks at Laguna Chankanaab on the west coast of the island. Morgan was much feared in the region long before he looted Panama in 1671 and carried away an astonishing $100 million fortune in gold, silver and gems. Like every landfall in the Caribbean, Cozumel offered a prime base from which to prey on the stream of merchant vessels carrying slaves and staples to the New World as well as Spanish treasure galleons en route from Central America back to Europe. Cozumel was abandoned by the middle of the 19th century but underwent a revival with the newfound popularity of chewing gum from the sap of the zapote tree; the Ixchel ruins in the jungle were discovered as a result.

Colorful wooden fish recreate the underwater splendors around Cozumel.

BELOW: scuba divers at Laguna Chankanaab, Cozumel

Today at **Laguna Chankanaab**, connected by a narrow channel to the sea, schools of brightly colored fish dart among the enormous yellow sponges and dangling sea anemones. There is a small aquarium and botanical garden with 350 types of tropical plants (open daily 7am–6pm; entry fee; tel: 987 872 0914), and, for a larger sum, you can swim with dolphins. Scuba divers favor the bay and the clear waters of the adjoining coral reef where underwater visibility can be as much as 61 meters (200 ft), or you can observe the underwater wonderland from the comfort of glass-bottomed boats. Further south is popular **Playa San Francisco**, which stretches for almost 3 km (2 miles). The most easily accessible Maya ruins are **El Cedral**, although they are small and not particularly special. In the 1800s, one of the structures was used as a jail.

The island's only town, **San Miguel de Cozumel** on the western coast, is spread alongside the 14-block waterfront Avenida Rafael Melgar. In the central Plaza del Sol where local musicians perform on Sunday evenings, are statues to revolutionary leader Senito Juarez and General Andres Quintana Roo. The **Museo de la Isla Cozumel** (open daily 9am–5pm; entry fee), on the waterfront in a former hotel, features native plants, stuffed animals and Maya artefacts.

The east side of the island is deserted apart from beaches and, at the southern tip, the Celarain lighthouse and **El Caracol** ruins. Bird watching is popular

TIP

Public buses around Cozumel are scarce, but jeeps, bicycles and motorcycles can be rented in San Miguel.

in the swampy areas, especially just south of where the only road crossing the island meets the scenic road on the east shore. There the beaches are often hammered by treacherous surf and the waters are subject to riptides and undertow. The coconut palms once prevalent on this exposed coast were long ago swept away by hurricanes. There is no road to the Molas lighthouse at the northeast point. In the central (jungle) areas are iguanas, deer, foxes and coati.

Further south

Ruta 307, the "coastal highway" south of Cancún, actually runs about 2 km (1 mile) inland with occasional unpaved side roads heading to coastal communities. The first of these is sleepy **Puerto Morelos** ⓱, with a few inexpensive hotels and where an expat American named Goyo operates jungle tours (and finds visitors inexpensive accommodation: tel: 988 710 189) from his information center on the corner of the town plaza. Car ferries (tel: 984 872 0827; at 8am, 1.30pm and 7pm) run from here to Cozumel. Diving excursions are made from here to **Palancar Reef** where Jacques Cousteau, famous French oceanographer, filmed in the 1960s. Only Australia's Great Barrier Reef is longer than the Great Maya Reef which stretches for 350 km (220 miles) south through Belize and Honduras. Apart from being the nemesis of dozens of ships over the centuries, the reef, which rises from 900 meters (3,000 feet) in depth to 4 or 5 meters (12 or 15 ft) from the surface, shelters hundreds of species of fish in addition to mollusks, crustaceans and sponges.

Back on the highway, stop at the Information Center next to the Pemex station to pick up a map of "The Maya Riviera" and have a drink of ice-cold water. The first of this string of white-sand beaches are the little-visited Playa del Secreto and Playa Paraiso (which has a large hotel on the beach), with such basic services as water, electricity and telephones. Next come Punta Marama, Punta Bete and Xcalacoco ("twin coconuts") with fish restaurants and rustic lodgings.

BELOW: Aztec calendar of brightly colored threads.

Playa del Carmen

About 50 km (22 miles) south, a side road leads inland to the trendy resort of **Playa del Carmen** ⓲ (pop: 30,000) with its espresso cafés and shops incongruously offering fashionable clothes. There are numerous nightclubs and discos. Although highly Americanized, it's a charming place whose pedestrian walkway running close to the sea calls itself 5th Avenue (heading inland the parallel streets are respectively 10th, 15th, 20th and 25th avenues; the cross streets numbered as 2, 4, 6, 8 etc). Newcomers might well head for Calle 8, where the block nearest the beach houses mid-range hotels as well as restaurants. Ferries run to Cozumel every hour from the dock (5am–11pm), only four blocks away. There's a taxi stand outside the bus station and you can rent scooters and bicycles at Alemaya (Calle 12 & 5). Divers can rent equipment at The Abyss (Calle 12 & beach; tel: 984 873 2164).

Adjoining Playacar has an 18-hole golf course, condos and some archeological sites representing what were once the departure points for pilgrimages to

Map on page 288

Cozumel to worship Ixchel. The Xaman-ha Aviary is here, home to 200 birds in a protected area of tropical forest. Just down the coast is **Xcaret** (open 9am–9pm winter, until 10pm summer; entry fee; tel: 998 883 8470), once a Maya ceremonial center, and now a well-publicized ecological park with an orchid farm, butterfly pavilion, Maya village, aquarium, bat cave, flamingos, underground rivers, an open air theater and several restaurants. You can ride horses, swim with dolphins, snorkel or just lie on the beach. Buses make the one-hour trip daily from Cancún (call for times, tel: 998 883 3143) and most visitors stay until night when traditional songs and dances are performed.

Shipwrecks and manatees

Continuing south along the coast, nearby Paamul is a beach with a small reef close to the shore, which is popular with campers; it also has a few comfortable chalets, a restaurant and dive shops. **Puerto Aventuras**, 20 km (12 miles) from Playa del Carmen, has a beautiful beach, is centered on a marina and features the Museo Cedam, a shipwreck museum containing articles recovered from the numerous 16th-century galleons wrecked along the reef (open Mon–Fri, 10am–5pm; entry fee). Between here and Akumal is the delightful bay of **Xpu-Ha**, on which stands the Xpu Ha Palace Resort. Lucky kayakers may glimpse a manatee in the estuary, the endangered sea mammal that frequents these parts.

Akumal

The clear waters of the Yal-Ku lagoon (where the Spanish ship *Matancero* sank in 1741) flow into the sea just north of **Akumal ⑲**, a little resort town set around twin bays, 36 km (20 miles) south of Playa del Carmen. Legendary

Sit at La Tequilana, the colorful bar at Calle 6, and watch the crowds go by.

BELOW: fishing boats at Playa del Carmen

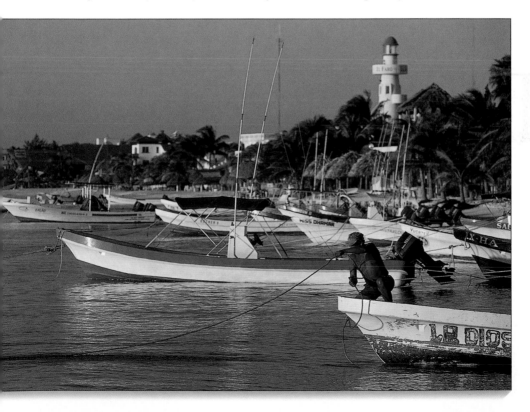

Cabañas, rustic huts, can be rented on the beach all along the coast south of Cancún.

BELOW: the glowing emerald waters at Xel-Há.

"place of the turtles" – Akumal is the home of **Centro Ecológico Akumal** (tel: 984 875 9095), an environmental research center where, from May to August, green, hawksbill and loggerhead turtles crawl up onto the sands to lay their eggs. The town also has diving and windsurfing schools where equipment can be rented and bicycles are also available.

The clear, shallow waters of nearby **Chemuyil** make it a favorite for families, while the adjoining Xcacel is another of the turtles' preferred breeding grounds. Tours can be taken from Chemuyil west of the highway to jungle *cenotes* (natural wells) which riddle the region. Near the coast, *cenotes* tend to be as near as two or three meters (7–10 ft) below the surface whereas comparable aquifers can be at depths of 130 meters (425 ft) in the southern part of the state.

Xel-Há ecological park

Swimming with dolphins is one of the main attractions at **Xel-Há** ⓴ (open daily 9am–6pm; entry fee; tel: 984 875 6000), just beyond Akumal, where freshwater underground rivers mingle with the ocean in a carefully managed ecological national park. Before entering the water, visitors are requested to remove all suntan lotions and skin creams (as they can wash off and poison the wildlife), or to use biodegradable creams. An expensive daily admission ticket includes rental of snorkel, a wet journey through the underground *cenote* network and lunch.

Multi-colored fish dart among sprawling mangrove roots at the edge of the lagoon and a variety of birds can be seen around the *cenotes*. On a wooded peninsula are the vestiges of an altar devoted to Yum Chac, god of *cenotes*, lagoons and bays. In ancient times, Maya believed the *cenotes* were all connected by underground tunnels, with what was said at one heard at another.

Map on page 288

Tulum

Some 27 km (17 miles) south of Akumal is the cliff-top site of **Tulum ㉑**. Originally called Zama, which means "dawn", due to its easternmost location watching the sun rise, **Tulum** was a provincial outpost whose function some scholars believe was to protect sea trade routes. "Long distance trade provided the nobility with products of great variety, quality or rarity," observed one museum curator, "all symbols of rank." The patron deity of Tulum was Ek Chuah, the god of trade, and cacao beans served as currency.

Prior to the Spanish Conquest, Tulum is estimated to have had a population of only about 600. Already in decline when the Spaniards arrived in 1518, it was conquered by Francisco de Montejo in 1530. The priestly and noble classes perhaps resided within the stone walls which still surround the 6½-hectare (16-acre) site on three sides, with the rest of the population outside. The only times commoners were allowed inside the walled city were to see government officials or to attend religious ceremonies. In the Maya world, it was the warrior class that was held in great esteem, answerable only to the supreme leader *Halach Uinich* who headed a council of chiefs, which collected taxes, raised armies and negotiated alliances with neighboring city-states.

Tulum's fortress, if such it was, sits on dramatic white limestone cliffs above attractive powdery white beaches. The perimeter wall has five entrances and the remains of what may have been watchtowers. The **Temple of the Frescos**, a two story structure with columns on the bottom level and a much smaller room on top, has one fresco of human figures in style that suggests Toltec influence. Masks of Chac, Maya god of rain, extend around the corners of the façade.

To the left of the platform in front of El Castillo, used as a stage for ceremonial dances, is the **Temple of the Swooping God**, which has a relief of this personage in a relatively good state of preservation over the barred door. He may have represented the Maya god of honey, Ab Muxen Cab. The Maya carvings above doorways are now protected with *palapa* (thatched) canopies.

El Castillo

The tallest building in the complex is **El Castillo** (the castle), fronted by serpent columns, which was built on top of two earlier pyramids, and which might have been a lighthouse. It was from here that defenders saw the Spaniards sail in, and it can still be climbed for excellent views. Michael Creamer, funded by the National Geographic Society, placed lanterns on shelves behind two windows and found that their beams met at an opening in the reef.

John Lloyd Stephens and his companion, artist Frederick Catherwood, spent one night in the Castillo, at first lamenting the lack of a sea view but then concluding that the experience had "wrought a great change in our feelings. An easterly storm came on, and the rain beat heavily against the sea wall. We were obliged to stop up the oblong openings, and congratulated ourselves upon the wisdom of the ancient builders. The darkness, the howling of the winds, the cracking of branches in the forest, and the dashing of angry waves against the cliff, gave a romantic interest,

BELOW: cliff-top Tulum has the most spectacular setting of all the Yucatán's Maya sites..

almost a sublimity to our occupation of this desolate building, but we were rather too hackneyed travellers to enjoy it, and were much annoyed by *moschetoes*."

Back on the main highway, an almost straight monotonous road leads to Coba, 54 km (34 miles) to the northwest, toward Valladolid. There are a few villages, one supermarket and several *cenotes* on the way. There are no gas stations en route and it is advisable to bring your own drinking water. Numerous examples of Maya homes can be seen, constructed in the traditional way on a base of stone with upright poles (Y-shaped at the top) supporting branches covered with palm leaves. These roofs shift and shake during hurricanes but, unlike some more solid structures, usually stay in place. Maya houses stay cool, too, aided by always-open front and back doorways and a breeze blowing between the poles.

Cobá

The problem with *moschetoes* is, if anything, magnified at **Cobá ㉒**, some 43 km (27 miles) inland, northwest of Tulum, surrounded as it is by tropical jungle. Watching Frederick Catherwood sketching away on their first visit, John Lloyd Stephens observed that "nothing could be finer than his position, the picturesque effect being greatly heightened by his manner of keeping one hand in his pocket, to save it from the attack of moschetoes, and by his expedient of tying his pantaloons around his legs to keep ants and other insects from running up."

It's a long walk, hemmed in by greenery and the sounds of tropical birds, to the actual site but *en route* you might be able to admire the delicate flights of butterflies and a possible rare sighting of tapirs, herons, toucans or snakes. A pair of Yucatecans, José Peon Contreras and Elizalde, were the first modern-day

BELOW: Nohoc Mul Temple at Coba.

Map
on page
288

exlorers to visit this Classic site back in 1886 and five years later the 42-meter (138-ft) high pyramid ("big hill") – the tallest pyramid in the north of the Yucatán Peninsula – was photographed by Teobert Maler. Eventually, the Maya expert Sylvanus G. Morley persuaded the Carnegie Institute to include Cobá in its research program and assigned the British archeologist J. Eric Thompson to lead an expedition. On that first trip to the site, Thompson and his three companions took the train to Valladolid from where they rode horseback for eight hours.

Sacbeob causeways

About the same time, the Carnegie Institute commissioned Professor Alfonso Villa Rojas along with 15 Maya laborers equiped with axes and machetes to uncover the 100 km (62 miles) of *sacbeob*, joining Coba to Yaxuna. The road, wrote Eric Thompson in the 1920s, "averages 32 feet in width. For the greater part of its length it is a little over two feet high, but in crossing swampy depressions its height increases, in one case slightly more than eight feet. Walls of roughly dressed stones form the sides, large boulders topped with smaller stones laid in cement compose the bed, and the surface, now badly disintegrated was of cement and stucco." This *sacbe* was wider than the Great Wall of China.

And yet today, the magnificent site – less than 10 percent of which has so far been excavated – seems isolated and relatively unvisited. Cobá ("water stirred by the wind") is between lakes which provided the water so rare elsewhere in the Yucatán and allowed the community to thrive for a thousand years. The 70-acre (28-hectare) site reached a population of 55,000 at its peak in the 9th century and many of the 34 huge stelae found at the site bear dates from around that period. Scientists expressed admiration for the clarity with which they had been carved without metal or what today would be considered adequate tools.

Because the soaring heights of the pyramids here, along with their narrow proportions, resemble the architectural style of such cities as Tikal in Guatemala, there have been suggestions that there was extensive trade between them. However, the temples on top which may have been added much later are quite different, resembling the flat and low profile of the one atop El Castillo at Chichén Itzá. Those at Tikal are topped with high sculptured crests adorning and enhancing them like the tall tortoiseshell combs used in the famous Spanish women's headdress.

South of Tulum, a narrow peninsula – the only access to which is an execrable dirt road with basin-sized potholes – heads south beside the ocean for 60 km (37 miles) or so to the lobster-fishing village of **Punta Allen** (population 600), where you can sleep on the beach in a hammock. On the way are a score of tiny, seafront bungalow colonies.

The Talking Cross

Ruta 307 south of Tulum is a long, mononotous road with no villages, no Pemex stations and no reason to stop until **Felipe Carrillo Puerto** where Ruta 184 heads west. This was the site of the Maya oracle the "Talking Cross" which inspired the 19th-century

BELOW:
Xel-Há Lagoon.

rebellion of native Maya and had its precedent in the earlier talking idols of their religion. After the War of the Castes in 1850 *(see page 263)*, the Maya rebels were rallied by José María Barrera who manipulated a wooden cross near a *cenote* at Chan Santa Cruz (which this town was then called) as a ventriloquist, persuading his followers that they were the chosen people *(crucobs)* and inciting them to battle against the Mexican army.

Ear and nose piercing for personal beautification were popular practices with the ancient Maya, as explained in the excellent Museo de la Cultura Maya in Chetumal.

To the east of Felipe Carrillo Puerto is the vast region of the 500,000-hectare (1¼ million-acre) **Reserva de la Biosfera Sian Ka'an** ㉓, a pristine area of tropical forest and mangrove swamps, which nurtures 300 species of birds and an abundance of such animals as jaguars, pumas, white tail deer, crocodiles and monkeys. Turtles lay eggs in May which hatch eight weeks later and then are mostly eaten by seabirds. More than 100 km (60 miles) of the Great Maya Reef are included in the reserve as well as 30 known Maya sites. All-day treks include three-hour boat trips (Centro Ecológico Sian Ka'an; tel: 984 871 2499). At the bottom of the peninsula, remote **Xcalak** is served by electricity generators and local *cenotes*. There is access from here to the diving paradise of **Banco Chinchorro**, a sheltered reef housing many shipwrecks.

Laguna de Bacalar

BELOW: marriage ceremony combining western and Maya dress.

Continuing south along Ruta 307, some 40 km (25 miles) before Chetumal, you'll come to **Bacalar** ㉔, known for the deep *laguna* (scuba divers have descended to 130 meters/427 ft) of the same name whose varying hues in sunlight have caused it to be tagged the Lake of Seven Colors. On a hilltop beside the lake is the **Fuerte de San Felipe**, built by the Spaniards in 1729 to protect the region from pirates and still-rebellious Mayas. A five-minute drive further

on, a restaurant sits beside the Cenote Azul, 90 meters (300 ft) deep and separated from the lake by a thin strip of forest.

Chetumal

At the southernmost base of the peninsula, bordering Belize, is Quintana Roo's state capital **Chetumal ㉕**, a modern port with wide avenues, and a frequent unwelcoming host to visiting hurricanes. Bulevar Bahía winds attractively along the seafront all the way north to the palm-fringed fishing village of Calderitas with its minor Maya site. Where the wide Avenida Héroes meets the coast are government offices and the Muelle Fiscal (Maritime Pier) and between here and the Universidad de Quintana Roo to the north where the road becomes a dual highway are some of the nicest restaurants.

There are two main museums, close to each other by the junction of Avenida Héroes and Lázaro Cárdenas. **The Museo de la Ciudad**, on Héroes at Chapultepec (open daily except Mon, 9am to 7pm; free entry), has some interesting 19th-century memorabilia, including old coins, a cash register, an old-fashioned telephone in a wooden box and a phonograph. There's also a photographic section on hurricanes as well as old black and white pictures of local celebrations.

The imposing face of Chac, from Kohunlich.

Much bigger and more significant is the superb **Museo de la Cultura Maya** (open Tues–Sun 9am–7pm; entry fee; tel: 983 832 6838), near the corner with Avenida Mahatma Gandhi, with video displays of the Yucatán, and reconstructed Maya cities in miniature set under a glass floor. A diagram illustrates the skull-deforming devices employed by the ancient Maya (in order to create a distinct, high, sloping brow – considered a feature of nobility), and a method producing crossed eyes by hanging a ball between a child's eyes.

BELOW: wells and *cenotes* are still the Yucatán's only sources of water

There are copies of two stelae from Cobá, a panel delineating the different kind of Maya arches and a display of the crops that the Maya farmer grows on his *milpa,* as well as such forest products as animal skins, resin from trees, feathers, and rubber and bark for making paper. Touch screens demonstrate the uses of various herbs and plants and a fascinating device which enables visitors to move a series of balls and bars to add up in the Maya manner. "With the count we know when the great star will return from the underworld, and when the moon will hide from us the face of the sun," declares the accompanying text.

About one hour's drive west of Chetumal, down a side road off Ruta 186 are the largely unexplored, early Classic ruins of **Kohunlich**, once noted for its sophisticated drainage system which diverted rainwater into *aguadas* for storage.

The **Palace of the Masks**, left of the Acropolis on the main plaza, was once covered with wonderful, painted effigies of the rain god and the sun god, although almost all of them have been looted (open daily, 9am–5pm; entry fee).

Back on Ruta 186, continuing further west toward the western coast of the Yucatán, takes you through the **Calakmul Biosphere Reserve**, a vast archeological site in the rainforest, spanning neighboring Guatemala and Belize *(see pages 325–6).* ❑

CAMPECHE AND CHIAPAS

Map on page 288

Most visitors pass through Campeche en route to better known destinations, but this state has its hidden gems too, and the jungles of neighboring Chiapas reveal yet more Maya ruins

Tucked into the southwestern corner of the Yucatán, the state of Campeche is the least-known region of the peninsula, devoting more energy to its fishing and oil industries than tourism. It doesn't have the beaches to rival those of the Caribbean coast. But it does have a clutch of fascinating Maya sites, some of which still lie undiscovered in the jungle interior of the state. And Champotón marks the site of the Spaniards' first landing on Mexican soil (after their brief landing on Isla Mujeres), under Francisco Hernández de Córdoba, on March 20, 1517.

The adjacent state of Chiapas to the south does not lie within the Yucatán Peninsula at all, but ranks high on the Maya "circuit" for many travelers, lured by its superb sites Bonampak, Yaxchilán and, above all, Palenque, with its beautiful temple pyramids nestled on jungle-clad hilltops. In contrast to the pancake-flat Yucatán, much of Chiapas is covered in forested mountains, with crystalline rivers and sparkling waterfalls gushing down steep gorges.

With its rugged landscape, Chiapas is home to around 1.5 million Maya, from eight different tribal groups, each of whom retain their own culture and language. The Tzotzil and Tzeltal Maya (each numbering around 500,000) are the most numerous of these, inhabiting the high-altitude region around San Cristóbal de Las Casas. There are estimated to be just 600 or so surviving Lacandón Maya (who refer to themselves as the Hach Winik, "True People"), some of whom still adopt traditional customs, wearing their hair long and dressing in long white smocks.

Leftist Zapatista rebels have challenged the authorities' control of Chiapas since 1994, leading to sporadic confrontations and violent incidents, but the situation has generally been calmer in recent years and travelers to the region are unlikely to be affected. That said, the Mexican military maintains checkpoints on highways throughout the state, where they will inspect your passport.

LEFT: escape from the crowds on the Gulf Coast beaches.
BELOW: henequen is cultivated in the Yucatán.

CAMPECHE

Heading west into Campeche from Chetumal, Ruta 186 traverses the base of the Yucatán peninsula. It's a hot, humid and scarcely populated region now, and relatively few tourists pass this way, but 2,000 years ago this area was part of the heartland of the ancient Maya civilization. Some of the sites, such as **Xpujil** and **Becán**, are just off the road, while **Río Bec** and **Calakmul** lie hidden in the forest far from the highway.

The Mexican government has built roads to the more remote sites, and much of southern Campeche state is within the **Calakmul Biosphere Reserve**, increasing your chances of seeing wildlife on a jungle trip. Although the new roads make the sites and the reserve more accessible you'll still need a 4-wheel drive vehicle to visit them and it's best to have a guide as well. North and south of Chicanná, UNESCO's biosphere reserve conserves the Calakmul rainforest, with at least 60 archeological sites, connecting up with Guatemala's Maya Biosphere Reserve and Belize's Río Bravo Conservation Area.

The Río Bec sites

The Río Bec style characterizes buildings of well cut stone blocks covered with stucco, their corners rounded, with high towers and often temples embedded in the major structures. Such structures tend to be covered in deep relief carvings, with steep steps leading to small, enclosed rooms.

The first of the Río Bec sites you'll come to from the east is **Xpujil**, some 118 km (73 miles) west of Chetumal, right by the roadside. The main attraction at these small ruins are the three, almost vertical towers on the south side of the road, with decorated stairways (open daily; entry fee). The village of Xpujil, with basic lodgings and gas station, is 1 km (½ mile) to the east.

Becán, just to the west of Xpujil, also by the side of Ruta 186, was one such place, the political, economic and religious capital of this region. It is still impressive, with a passageway beside the main structure ending in a series of corbelled or false archways. In the adjoining clearing an immense palace topped with roof combs contains a temple dedicated to Itzamna, the sun god.

Río Bec itself is a scattered collection of buildings, down an unmade track to the south of the main highway, and you'll need to join a private tour to see them all. Similar to Xpujil, there are twin steep-sided towers at these partially excavated ruins. Guides to the site are available at the museum in the nearby village of 20 de Noviembre.

Calakmul

The most important Río Bec site, **Calakmul** ㉖, is in the southern portion of the Calakmul Biosphere Reserve, 54 kms (33 miles) down a minor branch road south of the main highway, at the junction with Conhuás, 98 km (61 miles) from Chetumal. It is accessed through a gate outside a café on the highway where admission must be paid. The way there is a long (3-hour), lonely drive and you're not likely to encounter any distractions on the way – except the occasional flock of wild turkeys – so it is advisable to take some drinking water, and set off early as the site closes at 5pm (open daily).

The immense site of Calakmul is the largest known city in the Maya world, comprising over 6,000 structures including the most massive Maya pyramid, 50 meters (165 ft) high. In the power politics of the Classic period the regional "superstates" of Calakmul and Tikal were locked into deadly rivalry over control of the Maya lowlands. Through networks of alliances and vassal states these giants wielded enormous influence over an area stretching from Palenque in the south, to the Motagua Valley in the east, in present-day Guatemala. Eventually, Tikal defeated Calakmul in AD 695, almost certainly reinforcing the triumph by sacrificing Calakmul's king, Jaguar Paw.

BELOW: elegant *Campechana* in local costume.

Between the 5th and 9th centuries the Lords of Calakmul ordered more than 150 great stelae to be sculpted, and they are everywhere to be seen. Many still bear dates, one corresponding to December 4, 810, and another to the year 410. Structure 6 is part of an astronomical complex which experts have said is similar to those found in Tikal and Central Petén. Extensive as the site is, if you climb to the top of the highest building you will note that the city stretches far into the jungle in every direction even though relatively little has been excavated.

Returning to the main road, the biggest town before the west coast is **Francisco Escárcega**, which has no attractions for visitors, but has a gas station, bus terminal, and a reasonable selection of hotels and restaurants if you need to break your journey. From here, Ruta 261 heads north to Champotón and Campeche; alternatively, Ruta 186 winds southward into the state of Chiapas, leading to the major Maya sites of Palenque, Bonampak and Yaxchilán (see pages 331–335).

Campeche

Traveling north 146 km (91 miles) from Francisco Escárcega brings you to the state capital, also called Campeche. Founded in 1540 by Francisco de Montejo on the site of a former Maya trading village called Ah Kim Pech, which may have been there as many as 1,000 years earlier, **Campeche ㉗** suffered from attacks from pirates attracted by the galleons laden with gold and silver which set sail from here for Spain. The beleaguered people of Campeche suffered the worst assault of all in 1663 when the buccaneers of several nations joined together in a ferocious onslaught, raping the women, slaughtering the populace and destroying buildings in an attack of unprecedented savagery.

Maps:
Area 288
City 327

The Baluarte de San Carlos, part of Campeche's colonial defence against the English and French pirates.

BELOW: Fuerte de San Miguel, outside Campeche.

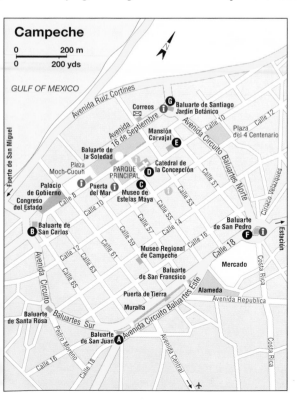

This finally led the Spanish crown to encircle the city with massive fortress walls, constructed between 1668 and 1704. Nearly 3.5 meters (8 ft) thick in places, the walls were originally 2,536 meters (8,320 ft) long and stretched along today's Avenida Circuito de los Baluartes, making Campeche one of the few fortress cities in the Americas, a hexagonal stronghold guarded by eight towers. Faced with the now impregnable port, where shipping was forced to enter between the daunting walls, the pirates redirected their energies elsewhere. The walls also protected the city during the 1847 War of the Castes (*see page 263*).

After beginning to dismantle the bastions to install trolley lines, the city had second thoughts and the **Puerta del Mar** (Sea Gate) was rebuilt when its value as a tourist attraction was realized. The 18th-century **Puerta de Tierra** (Land Gate; open Tues–Sat 8am–2pm, 4–9pm, Sun 8am–2pm) across the city, with its gun emplacements still intact, is still connected to the bastion, **Baluarte de San Juan Ⓐ**. The old bastions, or *baluartes*, seven of which still define the shape of the old town today, are open mornings and evenings and have been adapted in various ways. They can be encircled on a 45-minute tour called **Tranvía de la Ciudad** which runs four times each day. There are city tourist offices in the **Baluarte de San Pedro** (Calle 51) and the **Baluarte de Santa Rosa** (Calle 14).

Nearby Balaurte de San Juan are the **Baluarte de San Carlos Ⓑ** (dungeons and a city museum that includes a model of the fortifications and arms collection; open Tues–Sat 8am–10pm, Sun 9am–1pm; entry fee) and the State Congress, which is housed in a squat concrete building that is known locally as the Flying Saucer.

BELOW: fishing is still one of the major industries in Campeche.

The Plaza Principal

Three blocks north of Baluarte San Carlos, between Calles 55 and 57, is the town's **Plaza Principal**. The **Museo de Estelas Mayas** ◉, facing the plaza, houses some hieroglyph-covered stelae (open Tues–Sat 8am–8pm, Sun 8am–1pm). All explanations in the museum are in Spanish but often accompanied by clear reproductions of the carved inscriptions. Some are from Edzná, an important Preclassic site. Also on the plaza, the **Casa de Cultura** (open daily 9am–7pm) preserves the interior of a 19th-century house with the original stone fireplace, carved mahogany bed and rocking chairs.

On the north side of the plaza, the **Catedral de la Concepción** ◉, the peninsula's oldest cathedral (1540) is topped with twin towers, flying buttresses and dome. Campeche's other interesting architecture includes the church of **San Francisquito**, some 20 minutes' walk from the center northeast along the seafront; and the **Mansión Carvajal** ◉, on Calles 10 & 53, which once belonged to a wealthy *hacienda* owner, has undulating Moorish arches, checkered floors and a sweeping staircase.

Painted colonial tiles in Campeche.

City market

The lively market at Calles 18 & 51, where Av. Gobernadores begins, is near the **Baluarte de San Pedro** ◉, which houses a regional crafts exhibition (open Mon–Fri 9am–1pm, 5–8pm; free). The **mercado** is like a combination red-light district and Moroccan souk with women hovering in dimly lit doorways amidst stores and stalls so close to each other that one's pile of gilt sandals overflows into her neighbor's canned hams and cheeses. Not far away, the rebuilt **Baluarte de Santiago** ◉ encircles the Jardín Botánico, filled with tropical plants.

BELOW: fruit stall in Ciudad del Carmen.

TIP

The Marina Yacht Club in Campeche runs 90-minute tours of the bay (Avenida Resurgimiento 120; tel: 981 816 1990).

On a hill at the southern end of town, **Fuerte de San Miguel** offers a panoramic view from behind the Colonial-era cannons of its battlements. The fort's grim rooms have been transformed into an interesting museum displaying stone masks, decorative pieces from Edzná, figurines from Jainá and 2,400-year-old jugs with sophisticated designs, all described with bilingual signs (open Tues–Sat 8am–8pm, Sun 8am–3pm; entry fee). The "El Guapo" trolley (Tues–Sun) runs from the main plaza to the town's fort – and to Fuerte de San José in the north.

Beyond Campeche

Out in the ocean, 32 km (20 miles) to the north, are the ruins of the tiny twin islands of **Jaina**, the burial site of high-ranking people from all over the Maya world and famous for the clay figurines that were interred with the dead. The small scale sculptures have been invaluable for their realistic portrayal of costumes and the implications of how people once lived (and some are on display at the Museo Regional de Campeche at Fuerte de San Miguel on Calle 59). At present, Jaina is not accessible to the public, but it is being restored with a view to opening it in the future, so check the progress at Campeche's tourist office.

Edzná

BELOW: the Temple of the Five Stories at Edzna.

Some 61 km (38 miles) southeast of Campeche, off Ruta 261, **Edzná** ㉘ was an important Preclassic city, now partly excavated. Standing at the center of an extensive series of canals that were probably used for irrigation but wide enough for boat traffic, Edzná was already thriving by AD 100, thanks to its location on

major Maya overland and sea trading routes. The city continued to evolve for almost one thousand years but was finally abandoned around 900 AD.

Some carved stelae with Maya glyphs sit by the entrance of the ruins (most of the others being in Campeche museums). Beside the expansive main plaza, is the site's central, dominant structure, **The Temple of the Five Stories**, a stepped palace pyramid almost 30 meters (100 ft) high on a huge base from which a central staircase (65 steps) rises through five levels to a three-roomed temple. On May 3 (and August 8) the sun alights on a stela in the center of the temple, marking the start of the Maya agricultural year. Each door is illuminated directly by the sun on a different date once a year.

Arranged around this central area are various lesser buildings, only some of which have been excavated. **The Temple of the Masks** is lined with stuccoed masks representing the Sun God. **The Great Tribune**, an amphitheater, has 15 tiers of steps as seats for 5,000 people. **The Palace of the Knives** (in which many offertory knives were found) is divided into rooms which may have been reserved for royalty or priests.

There are many other less accessible sites in the region: **Hochob** (a three-room temple covered with carved snakes and masks) near Chenko, and **Dzibilnocac** (temple pyramid) near Iturbide.

Map on page 288

CHIAPAS

Leaving the Yucatán Peninsula proper now, the strongly indigenous state of Chiapas to the south provides an adventurous extension to many visitors' itineraries, to explore some fascinating Maya settlements and ancient ruins buried deep in the jungle.

BELOW: Bolonchén de Rejón, near Campeche; lithograph by Federick Catherwood, 1843.

STEPHENS AND CATHERWOOD

John L. Stephens, North American explorer and travel writer, and his colleague, the English architect Frederick Catherwood, came to Central America in 1839, inspired by some books they had just read in New York, about the ruins of ancient cities here, which in Stephens' blunt prose "roused our curiosity."

Over the next three years, the two men traveled throughout the region, overcoming illnesses and the threats posed by ongoing civil wars. They visited dozens of Maya cities, including Chichén Itzá, Palenque, Quiriguá and Copán, describing some places never before seen by outsiders and others no longer in existence today. Stephens and Catherwood were captivated by these fabulous sites and they were driven to discover the origins of the Maya, and the meaning of their intricate glyphs.

In 1841, Stephens published *Incidents of Travel in Central America, Chiapas and Yucatán*, beautifully illustrated with Catherwood's finely detailed lithographs, still in print today as a true travel "classic". They never did manage to decipher the glyphs however, or find out exactly who the Maya were, but they did bring the culture to the attention of the outside world, attracting further study that continues unabated today *(see page 33)*.

Colorful coffee shop sign from San Cristobal de Las Casas, Chiapas.

BELOW: Palenque, looking toward the temples of the Cross (left) and the Sun (right).

Palenque

Looming out of the dense, jungly undergrowth of Chiapas, 355 km (220 miles) from Campeche, the Maya ruins at **Palenque ㉙** are, for many visitors, the highlight of their trip to Mexico (open daily 9am–5pm; entry fee). The complex site inspires awe, and yet what one sees today represents a fraction of the incredible complex of chambers, terraces, staircases, temples, palaces and other structures that graced Palenque at its peak in the 7th century AD. At this time, when the city was a lively metropolis and an important religious center, the stucco and limestone relief panels would have been polychromed, and the effect of the colors and the white plaster – set off against the backdrop of dark green foliage – must have been truly dazzling. Stucco, plaster or lime mixed with water and a vegetable glue, was commonly used by the Maya as a decorative material because of its resemblance to polished marble when set. Originally as hard as stone, it gradually deteriorates in a humid climate.

Palenque was an inland trading city where the highlands and coastal plain meet, near the Río Usumacinta, which flows into the Gulf of Mexico. Father Antonio de Solis arrived in 1746, sent by his bishop to investigate the ruins, which in 1784 were more fully explored by José Antonio Calderón, who had listed 220 buildings, including 18 palace buildings. Incredibly, even today, less than one quarter of the site has been excavated.

In 1786, nearly 1,000 years after the sudden decline and abandonment of Palenque (meaning palisade in Spanish; the original Mayan name was Lakamhá or big water) in about AD 810, Captain Antonio del Rio was sufficiently impressed by the site to conclude that other cultures must have helped in their construction. "I do not take upon myself to assert that (the Romans) did actually land in this country, but there is reasonable ground (for suspecting that) some inhabitants of that polished nation did visit these regions."

The ruins

Concealing its treasures almost until you stumble into them, the wall of jungle divides just beyond the entrance to reveal the two most important and magnificent structures of the site: the pagoda-like tower complex of the **Palace Ⓐ** and, to its right, the **Temple of the Inscriptions Ⓑ**, a superb example of Classic Maya architecture, crowned with the characteristic roof comb.

The temple is in fact a pyramid with a temple on top, at 26 meters (85 ft) high, dominating the whole site. The hieroglyphic inscriptions on the walls, with the date AD 692, give the temple its name. In 1952, Mexican archeologist Alberto Ruz Lhuillier discovered a sealed stone passageway that led to the burial chamber 25 meters (82 ft) down, at the center of the pyramid. It contained the skeleton of the deified King Pacal, greatest of all Palenque's rulers, wearing a mosaic jade death mask with shell and obsidian eye insets, and his body richly adorned with jade jewelry: a piece of jade in his mouth and another in each hand; jade rings on each finger of both hands, jade bracelets, a diadem of jade, jade earplugs, and his favorite necklace.

To descend into Pacal's tomb you must obtain a

permit from the site museum; it is only possible to view the chamber after 3pm. A steep staircase leads from the top to the tomb, 1.5 meters (5 ft) below the plaza floor; the way down is lit up but it can get extremely hot and humid.

Almost directly opposite the pyramid, and in the center of the site, is the **Palace**, a complex of buildings with courtyards, passages and tunnels, arranged around a unique, four-story, square-sided tower. The tower has been reconstructed and its function has attracted much speculation; once thought to have been an astronomical observatory, it was not however clearly aligned with the constellations. It does offer an unrivalled view across the jungle though and its position in relation to Pacal's temple led to the suggestion that it may have been used for viewing the winter solstice sun as it made its journey to the underworld, via his tomb. The juxtaposition of the other major temples around the site reinforces the theory that space and location held a symbolic significance to the Maya architects.

The walls of the palace are embellished with finely detailed stucco panels, and its grassy courtyards have low walls decorated with hieroglyphics, many of which have yet to be deciphered, and impressive sculptures of giant human figures carved on huge stone slabs.

There is a **ballcourt** and another group of lesser temples in a grassy clearing to the north of the Palace, called the **Northern Group**. To the east, across the stream, and on the edge of the encroaching jungle are the three important temples known as the **Group of the Cross**. All were completed in AD 692 during the rule of Kan B'alam II, and were constructed to glorify Palenque's trinity of gods. Towering above Palenque's ceremonial core, the Temple of the Cross is the largest of the three, its interior containing a stela of Kan B'alam II, depicted

Maps:
Area 288
Site 331

BELOW: the beautifully carved sarcophagus lid of Palenque's greatest ruler, Lord Pacal.

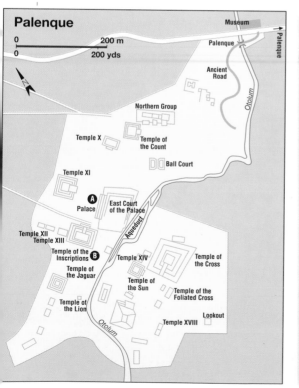

on the left as a prince and on the right as a king wearing full royal robes. Opposite the Temple of the Sun has the finest remaining roof comb at the ruins, while the Temple of the Foliated Cross has another carving of B'alam wearing a quetzal-feather headdress.

Excavation work is underway to restore more of the outlying buildings, but you can easily get around the site in half a day; come early in the morning to avoid the heat and the crowds, but be sure to bring mosquito repellent as there are plenty around.

The site itself lies about 8 km (5 miles) from the town of Palenque, from where there are regular minibuses to the ruins. There is a visitors' center with an adjoining museum about 1 km (½ mile) from the site which also has a restaurant and gift shop. There are a few hotels near the ruins, as well as trailer parks, with space for camping and hammocks for hire.

Ruins in the rainforest

The other two important Maya sites in Chiapas, Bonampak and Yaxchilán, are located deep in the heart of the rainforest near the Río Usumacinta, which marks the international border with Guatemala.

Bonampak ㉚ can be reached from Palenque, 140 km (87 miles) southwest, via a paved road running down the Usumacinta Valley. Take the turning at San Javier for Bonampak (13 km/8 miles), passing the Lacandón village of Lacanjá after 9 km (5½ miles). Archeologists, who only "discovered" the site in 1946, were excited by the vividly colored murals *(see page 20)*, which have taught us so much about the ancient Maya way of life.

BELOW: the ruins of Yaxchilán, on the banks of the Río Usumacinta.

The frescoes cover the walls and ceiling of the Temple of the Frescoes, pre-

Map
on page
288

senting an historical narrative of ceremonial activities, battles, festivals, celebrations and dances, depicted in tiny, fascinating detail. If you cannot reach the remote ruins of Bonampak, there are reproductions of the murals in the anthropology museums in Mexico City, and even in the lobby of the Hotel Bonampak in Tuxtla Gutierrez.

An even stronger spirit of adventure is needed to reach the much larger (and, to many, more wonderful) Maya site of **Yaxchilán** ㉛ on the banks of the Río Usumacinta, most admired for its intricate stucco carvings and roof decorations. Yaxchilán is reached by a side road further down the same highway, continuing 20 km (12½ miles) past San Javier, then 19 km (12 miles) down a side road to Frontera Corozal, a small village on the riverbank, served by buses from Palenque (and with one good hotel, the Escudo Jaguar). The ruins themselves are about an hour by boat downstream, with several temples around a main plaza, more buildings lying in the jungle.

One of Mexico's most enjoyable and picturesque colonial towns, **San Cristóbal de Las Casas** is situated at an altitude of over 2,100 meters (7000 ft) and enjoys a beautifully temperate climate. It is highly popular with visitors, and has a cosmopolitan array of restaurants, cafés and boutiques as well as some wonderful historic hotels. San Cristóbal is especially atmospheric around the central plaza, which is framed by elegant buildings, including a stately baroque cathedral. **Na Blom** (open daily; tours 11.30am and 4.30pm), a beautiful 19th-century house with surrounding gardens 500 meters (547 yds) east of the plaza is another prime attraction. Several tour operators (see Travel Tips, page 366) organise trips to the region's indigenous villages, such as Chamula, and natural places of interest. ❑

Jade mask from Calakmul, now in the Campeche Museum at Fuerte San Miguel.

BELOW: copy of Bonampak murals, from the Museum of Anthropology, Mexico City.

※ INSIGHT GUIDES

Travel Tips

In this ever changing world,
  Singapore Girl, you're a great way to fly.

First to Fly A380 in 2006

SINGAPORE AIRLINES

CONTENTS

Getting Acquainted

Climate

The Maya region is subtropical, and temperatures are governed far less by the seasons than by altitude.

The Rainy Season

Called *invierno* (winter), the rainy season is from May to October, but it very rarely rains all day; often there will be a fairly substantial afternoon downpour and the skies will clear. In most of the region, maximum temperatures are kept to a moderate level (25–30°C), because of cloud cover in *invierno*, and nights are pleasantly warm.

The Dry Season

November–April is the dry season (*verano*) and the skies are usually clear. At this time of year it can get quite chilly at night anywhere in the region, but especially at night in the Guatemalan highlands where frosts are not unknown in high-altitude towns such as Quezaltenango.

Altitude

Altitude is the most important climatic factor. The Yucatán is very flat and low-lying, so it's nearly always hot but never too humid inland around the major ruins. Much of Guatemala enjoys a delightful climate (the tourist board like to call it "Land of the Eternal Spring"), especially Guatemala City, Antigua and Lago de Atitlán which are all around 1,500 meters (5,000 ft) above sea level. Above this altitude at Quezaltanango and in the Cuchumatanes mountains, nights can get very cool between December and February.

In Belize, the Maya mountains have the most pleasant tempera-tures, while the low-altitude forests are the most uncomfortable with humid conditions most of the year.

The central lowland forests in the southern Yucatán and northern Guatemala are hot and pretty humid all year round, but most manage-able in the dry season, which starts a little later, in December.

By the Coasts

There is normally a pleasant breeze off the ocean to cool things down a little by the Pacific and Caribbean coasts; the Belizean cayes are never too sticky. Severe storms can strike during hurricane season (September and October) but warnings are usually excellent locally and it's important to remember that Hurricane Mitch in 1998 was the worst ever recorded in the region. It did not vent its full fury in the Maya region, but to the south. However, Hurricane Wilma hit the Yucatán coast hard in 2005.

When to Visit

There's no bad time to visit the Maya world, but perhaps the very best season is between November and March when temperatures are never oppressive, the skies are clear and the humidity low.

Security and Crime

It's important to take some basic precautions when visiting the Maya countries, but not to adopt a paranoid attitude – crime against tourists is still relatively rare and the majority of visitors will not experience trouble of any kind.

Probably the two cities with the worst reputations are Belize City and Guatemala City, especially the downtown areas. Both are generally perfectly safe in the day, but after dark it's best to take taxis to get around. There are hustlers in Belize City who will try to intimidate you into parting with a dollar, but the threats are seldom serious. Walk on, or speak to the tourist police if you are persistently harrassed.

You should take care in markets and bus terminals anywhere in the region; the hustle and crowds mean

Dos and Don'ts

A few sensible measures will help you enjoy your stay:
● Don't drive or take buses after dark. Avoid fanny packs (bum bags). Use a concealed money belt.
● Adopt an air of confidence: this is excellent protection.
● Downtown in big cities, enter a café or restaurant to check your map rather than looking lost on the street.
● Avoid wearing jewelry or an expensive-looking watch.
● Conceal cameras in a daypack when you're not using them.
● Don't walk down quiet streets after dark.

that bags can easily be snatched or pockets picked. While traveling on local buses, it's very rare for your luggage to go missing from roof rack or baggage compartments – there is nearly always an *ayudante* (conductor-helper) whose job it is to ensure that his passengers' goods arrive safely.

Hikers will feel safe in most parts of the Maya world. In Guatemala, although the mountain areas of the Western highlands are remote, the indigenous communi-ties are very insular and attacks are extremely rare. Volcanoes can be the exception to this rule, so take a tour if you are climbing Volcán de Pacaya (*see pages 348–9*).

Marijuana (*ganja*) is illegal throughout the region, as are other drugs. If you get into any trouble with the police, the first thing to do is to contact your embassy.

Health

Hygiene standards are much better than in many other parts of the developing world, but diarrhea may still strike no matter how careful you are. Tummy upsets are likely to be your main concern, but you should also be inoculated against polio, cholera, tetanus, typhoid, and hepatitis. None of these diseases are at all common in the Maya countries, immunization is not a mandatory requirement, and the risk is very low; but every year there are cases. Getting bitten by a rabid animal is also statistically extremely unlikely, but if you are bitten begin immunization shots immediately.

Mosquitoes are likely to be much more of a concern, and it's imperative to minimize the chances that you'll be bitten, especially in remote, lowland areas. Diligently apply repellent (*repelente*) to all exposed areas of skin, especially around your ankles. You may want to buy your own mosquito net, though they are often provided by hotels in lowland areas. Burn mosquito coils (available locally) and leave a fan on at night while you sleep.

Malaria is present but not at all common in the Maya countries. There have been no reports of chloroquine-resistant strains of mosquito in the region but check with your health clinic before you go for the latest information. There's no malaria above 1,500 meters (5,000 ft) in the region, so if you're just visiting highland Guatemala you may choose not to take the course.

Dengue fever, carried by a daytime mosquito, is on the increase all over the world and there have been a few outbreaks in the Maya region. The symptoms are fever, severe headache and usually a skin rash. There's one rare strain, **dengue hemorrhagic**, that can be very serious but in most cases the body heals itself within a few days. There's no vaccine for any strain of dengue, so you should take great precaution against being bitten.

Take high-factor sunscreen, a hat for protection against the sun, and drink plenty of water (bottled) to avoid dehydration, especially at high altitudes.

DRINKING WATER

Don't drink the tap water. In the cities, drinking water is heavily chlorinated but should still be avoided. It's sometimes difficult to avoid, but make sure all drinks are served without ice (*sin hielo*), and

it's better not to try *refrescos* or "fresca" water-based drinks.

Ask for *agua purificada* (*agua pura*) or *agua mineral* or stick to bottled drinks like Coca Cola, beer etc. Juices (*jugos*) should be safe, but watch out for added ice. *Licuados* (shakes) are safe if made with milk (*con leche*), not water.

If you plan to spend much time camping, either buy a water filter and purification tablets or boil water for 20 minutes to be safe. Brush your teeth with *agua pura*.

Money Matters

The safest and most convenient way to carry money in the Maya countries is by using travelers' checks and credit and debit cards. **Travelers' checks** can be cashed in most banks. Make sure you get your travelers' checks issued in US dollars (other currencies are rarely accepted) and from an established name such as Thomas Cook or American Express.

Credit cards are also an excellent and safe way to carry money. Visa and MasterCard are widely recognized. Most towns will have a ATM machine or two for 24-hour withdrawals; in smaller places it usually possible to arrange a cash advance on your card, though this is often a little time-consuming. Only large hotels and expensive restaurants accept credit cards; anywhere else you'll have to settle the bill in cash – check if there's an additional charge.

Debit cards are slowly becoming more useful throughout the region, but should be regarded as a reserve facility.

Generally, **US dollar bills** are not widely accepted, except in Belize and Cancún. It's worth having a few bills for emergencies, however, since some shopkeepers and hotels will change dollars (usually for a poor rate) if the banks are closed.

Costs

Guatemala is an extremely cheap country to travel in, but Belize and Mexico, while still reasonable by

Insurance

It's essential to have a comprehensive insurance policy, so don't leave home without one. Cover should include accidental death, emergency medical treatment, trip cancelation, and cash and baggage loss. If you plan to scuba dive, rockclimb, go caving or rafting, or partake in any other sport that may be considered risky, make sure you have cover.

North American standards, are about 50 percent more expensive. In Guatemala, backpackers can budget on $20 a day or less (hotel, *comedor*/market stall food and travel); "mid-range" travelers perhaps $40–50 per person a day; to travel in real comfort it'll cost $80–120 a day per person. If you've a taste for exclusive jungle lodges and dive resorts in Belize, rates can run up to $2,000 a week.

Photography

The Maya world is an extremely exciting photographic destination – the scenery, ruins, buildings, and people are all astoundingly picturesque and the fiestas and markets unleash a riot of color.

Equipment

Print and slide film are available in most towns (though the choice is limited), and black and white film can be found in the cities. Many photographic stores and internet cafés will transfer digital images to discs. Video tape (mainly Hi 8 and VHS-C) is also sold in the larger towns, but it's better to bring your own supply.

What to Photograph

Be sensitive about photographing Maya people (and anyone else, for that matter). Many people object to intrusive camera-toting, so it's best to ask permission before you start snapping. Be extremely sensitive if you visit highland Chiapas – the Maya there object strongly to being photographed.

Occasionally, some locals may ask for money in exchange for a photograph; agree on a moderate sum before you take any pictures. Similarly, be very careful not to offend local customs in religious or spiritual places including churches (photography inside the Santo Tomás church, Chichicastenango, is completely taboo). Markets and fiestas are often ideal places to photograph people from a distance.

The lowland jungle ruins (especially Tikal) can be difficult to capture well. The acute humidity that cloaks the temples in thick mist at all times of the year can steam up your lenses. Normally, professional photographers love the "golden hours" just after sunrise and before sunset when the harsh tropical sun is tempered by longer shadows, but in the rainforest you'll often have to wait for the morning sun to burn off the mist. Conversely, if you plan to climb a volcano, it's best to start as early as possible, even before dawn, in order to reach the summit before the clouds sweep in.

Underwater Photography

If you plan to snorkel, consider buying a disposable camera that's waterproof to 3 meters (10 ft) or so. The larger scuba schools will often have underwater cameras available for rent, and some will even video your dive for a price.

Traveling with Kids

Guatemala, Belize, and Mexico are superb countries for children to visit. Critically, the locals love kids and you'll find that by traveling with children cultural barriers are immediately broken as waiters, shop assistants, bank managers, *mestizos*, and *indígenas* fuss over, feed, and spoil your kids rotten. In general, you'll find that hotels and restaurants are far more accommodating towards children than their counterparts in Northern Europe or North America, and will go out of their way to provide an extra bed or a child's portion.

Health

Health concerns are obviously paramount (*see page 340*); contact your doctor before you go. You'll have to weigh up whether to take malaria pills, and you'll also have to decide on behalf of your kids. Getting young children to swallow malaria tablets is troublesome, so you might have to grind the pills up and add the powder to a drink or food. Breast-feeding babies will be protected with their mother's milk. A baby mosquito net is a sound investment.

Where to Go

With young children, you'll have to choose your destination carefully. The highland market towns of Guatemala may be culturally fascinating, but trying to keep an eye on your children among the crowds and commotion could be a nightmare. Anywhere by the sea, or if you can find a hotel with a pool, will quickly cool capricious young tempers.

Touring

If you plan to travel independently with your children, don't set an ambitious itinerary or the heat and hours on the road will exhaust you and your kids. Think about how you plan to travel around: it's far easier to stop and change a diaper or go to the restroom if you're in a hire car than if you're packed on a chicken bus. Remember to order a baby seat for kids too young to wear a seatbelt from the hire company. The occasional bus journey in Mexico, where the buses are much more comfortable and air-conditioned, should be tolerable, but in Belize (and especially Guatemala) it's a different story.

Flying

Aeroplanes can also be problematic with very young children, who find the whole exercise uncomfortable and even painful (on their ears). Ideally you'll want a bassinet (hanging cradle) for your baby – order one from the airline in advance and confirm before you fly.

Entertainment

Relieving boredom is another crucial consideration (one small tip for whiling away hot afternoons is to take a small selection of Lego or Duplo pieces). Unfortunately most children are going to suffer in the lowland humidity and heat of the jungle (where many of the best

Etiquette

Politeness, a smile, and an effort to speak a little Spanish will help you get more out of the Maya countries. Avoid being openly critical of the region's problems, including corruption, inefficiency and poverty – Mexicans, Guatemalans, and Belizeans recognize their countries' difficulties, but some are sensitive to criticism.

If you have an appointment, get there on time, but don't be too surprised if you have to wait around a little while – punctuality is not generally considered a great virtue. Try not to talk too loudly; the Maya in particular find Westerners overbearingly loud. If you visit one of the smaller highland markets in Guatemala (ie. not Chichicastenango or San Francisco El Alto), one of the most interesting aspects is how quiet the whole affair is, with business being conducted in sotto voce.

If you add some flexibility to your travel plans, and expect the odd delay, you'll have a far less frustrating time if you get held up. Perhaps the biggest mistake inexperienced travelers make is to try to see too much in too short a time. With the inevitable delays, by setting a punishing itinerary you'll spend most of your time on buses and in bus stations. Sometimes less is more!

Public nudity is offensive throughout the region. It's also essential to cover your legs when you visit churches; short shorts are usually frowned upon.

ruins are). They may not be too impressed by the stones anyway. If you're going to Tikal, and your hotel has child-minding facilities, try to visit on a day-trip excursion.

What to Bring
Disposable diapers are available throughout the region, but bring your own changing mat. You may want to invest in a child-carrying backpack – this will save a lot of grief as most of the roads are far too bumpy for a pushchair.

The local food is rarely very spicy and most children find it delicious.

Tummy troubles are another concern, so bring children's diarrhea pills with you. Powdered milk is everywhere. The other main hazards are the sun (hats and waterproof sunblock are essential), dogs (keep them away), and traffic.

Gay Travelers

The Maya world presents no serious difficulties for gay travelers, but the scene in all three countries is very underground, with very few gay bars and almost no meeting places for lesbians. Though Mexico's reputation as an overtly macho society is well deserved, the Maya states are among the least homophobic in the country – indigenous Mexicans are much less concerned with crude machista postures than the mestizos of the cities and desert states in the north.

Mexico
Homosexuality is legal in Mexico, since there are no federal laws forbidding it, but cruising zones are occasionally targeted by police in campaigns to protect "public morality" – discretion is wise. Cancún is the exception; it's much more in tune with US resorts than rural Mexico.

Guatemala
Guatemala has a small gay scene, centered in the capital where there are a few gay clubs and bars. While it's best to be discreet (holding hands in public is unwise), most gays and lesbians find little local hostility. Exercise some common

sense and avoid the more macho men-only cantinas.

Belize
Homosexuality is illegal in Belize and there are no openly gay bars and clubs. Generally, gay travelers shouldn't have any trouble, but some subtlety is essential. Caribbean attitudes towards gays can be radically homophobic, so holding hands is out, but you'll get much less vitriol than in Jamaica, or some of the other islands.

Travelers with Disabilities

Disabled travelers will have a hard time in the Maya region, except in Cancún where the sidewalks are smooth and the hotels have elevators. Access for wheelchair users is usually non-existent everywhere else, and mobility is compounded by pot-holed sidewalks and roads, cobblestones and an almost complete absence of elevators outside the five-star city-center hotels.

Travel by public transport is another challenge. In **Mexico**, traveling by long-distance bus need not be too much of a problem since wheelchairs can be stored in the luggage compartment, there's a conductor at hand to assist passengers, and you'll be assigned your own seat. Traveling by "chicken bus" in **Guatemala** is not worth thinking about, though there are a number of privately run shuttles that ply the main tourism towns. In **Belize**, travel is also difficult, though the massive, period-piece sedan taxis present a possible but pricey option.

Obviously, if you can travel with an able-bodied friend to help you get around, all these difficulties are going to be reduced.

There are organizations that will direct you to tour operators that are well set up for disabled travelers. Try **Twin Peaks**, Press Box 129, Vancouver, WA 98666 (tel: 360/694 2462). A good travel agent is **Directions Unlimited**, 720 North Bedford Rd, Bedford Hills, New York 10507 (tel: 914/241 1700).

Planning the Trip

Getting There

The main gateways to the Maya region are Cancún and Mérida in Mexico, Guatemala City, and Belize City. Most flights from North America are routed via Miami, Houston, and Los Angeles, often with a stopover in Mexico City. Flying from Canada, you'll probably have to travel via one of the US gateway cities. If you want a holiday in the North American winter, consider a charter flight – there are plenty to Cancún and a few to Belize City, and they're usually direct and cheaper.

Traveling from Europe, most flights are routed through the US gateway cities (listed above). The only direct scheduled flights are to

Airlines

Aeroméxico: (USA) 1-800 237 6639; (UK) 020 7355 2233.
American: (USA) 1-800 624 6262; (UK) 0345 789789.
Aviateca: (USA) 1-800 327 9832; (UK) see Taca.
Canada 3000: (Canada) 416 674 2661.
Continental: (USA) 1-800 231 0856; (UK) 0800 776464.
Delta: (USA) 1-800 241 4141; (UK) 0800 414767.
Iberia: (USA) 1-800 772 2272; (UK) 020 7830 0011.
Mexicana: (USA) 1-800 531-7921; (UK) 020 7267 3787.
Taca: (USA) 1-800 535-8780; (UK) 01293 23330.
United: (USA) 1-800 622 1015; (UK) 0845 844 4777.
US Airways: (USA) 1-800 428 4322.

Useful Addresses

USA

Caribbean Resource Center, Medgar Evers College, 1150 Bedford Avenue, Brooklyn, New York, NY 11225; www.dynatech.com.crc Research and publications center linked to New York City University. Publishes a vast range of titles covering politics, health, economics and cultural issues of all latin American countries.
Interlink Publishing Group, 99 Seventh Ave, New York 11215 (tel: 413/582 7054). Publish the "In Focus" series in the USA.

UK

Maya: The Guatemalan Maya Centre, 94a Wandsworth Bridge Rd, London SW6 2TF, tel/fax: 020 7371 5291; www.maya.org.uk. An incredible library of over 2,000 books on the Maya, plus an amazing textiles collection.
Latin American Bureau (tel: 020 7278 2829) www.lab.org.uk. Excellent library and publishers of the authoritative "In Focus" series of country guides.

Maya World

Belize Aubudon Society, PO Box 1001, 12 Fort St, Belize City (tel: 02-34987). Information about protected areas from Belize's oldest conservation organization.
Defensores de la Naturaleza, 7 Av. 7–09, Zona 13, Guatemala City, tel: 2440-8138; www. defensores.org.gt). Help to manage the Sierra de las Minas and Bocas del Polochic reserves.
ProPetén Calle Central, Flores, Petén, Guatemala (tel: 7926 1370; www.propeten.org). Conservation group fighting to protect the Petén environment. Also organizes trips into the forest.
Pronatura Península de Yucatán, Calle 32, 269 col, Pinzón II, Mérida, CP 97207, Mexico (tel: 999-988 4436/7; www.pronatura-ppy.org.mx). Nonprofit organisation looking at alternative ways to use resources.

plus rafting, volcano climbing. Will organize independent itineraries.
International Expeditions
Tel: 1-800 633-4734.
Archeological and ecotourism tours throughout the Maya countries.
Journeys
Tel: 1-800 255 8735,
e-mail: info@journeys-intl.com
Ecotourism and culture tours in Belize and Guatemala.
Slickrock Adventures
Tel: 1-800 390-5715,
e-mail: slickrock@slickrock.com
Sea kayaking, rafting, snorkeling, and caving trips. Recommended.
Toucan Adventure Tours
Tel: 805 927 5885,
www.toucanadventures.com
Well-priced camping 'ruin and rainforest' tours.
Tread Lightly Limited
Tel: 1-800 643 0060,
e-mail: info@treadlightly.com
Cultural and natural history tours of the Maya region.

Canada

Adventures Abroad
Tel: 1-800 321 2121.
Quality low-impact tours of the main ruins and natural sites.
Gap Adventures
Tel: 1-800 465 5600,
e-mail: adventure@gap.org
Good variety of trips, with camping and kayaking options, especially in Belize.
Island Expeditions
Tel: 1-800 667 1630
e-mail: info@island.expeditions.com
Excellent diving, river- and sea-kayaking trips.

UK

Cathy Mattos Mexican Tours
Tel: 020 7284 2550.
Archeological and cultural trips with a personal touch.
Journey Latin America
Tel: 020 8747 8315,
www.journeylatinamerica.co.uk
Long-established company with bespoke trips plus the Quetzal escorted tour.
Reef and Rainforest Tours
Tel: 01803 866965, e-mail: reefrain@btinternet.com. Nature and scuba diving orientated trips.

Cancún with British Airways. A number of charter flights also fly to Cancún from Europe, with some very cheap deals available, though there's no ticket flexibility.

Reservations from North America and Europe need to be booked as far ahead as possible, especially in high season (Dec–Feb and August).

AIRPASSES

It's well worth looking at airpasses if you plan to travel around the region. The **TACA airpass** is valid for 18 days and involves a minimum purchase of three flights. The pass links the US gateway cities with all the Central American capitals, and offers savings and an opportunity to combine scuba diving in Belize with jungle trekking in Costa Rica. The **Mexipass International** utilizes the extensive connections of AeroMexico, Mexicana, and AeroPeru – ideal if you want to combine a Maya-Inca

vacation. The third pass is the **Mexipass Domestic**, a good deal if you want to fly internally within Mexico. Purchase passes outside Mexico and Central America.

Tour Operators

There are a number of excellent specialist companies that offer tours to the Maya region, often specializing in archeology, ecotourism, adventure activities, and scuba diving. Many will allow you to create your own bespoke trip and sort out flights and hotel reservations for you.

USA

Far Horizons
Tel: 1-800 552-4575,
e-mail: journey@farhorizon.com
Specialize in archeological expeditions throughout the Maya region, with expert guides.
Guatemala Unlimited
Tel: 1-800 733-3350.
Excellent trips to main Maya ruins,

South American Experience
Tel: 020 7976 5511,
e-mail: sax@mcmail.com
Highly recommended regional
specialists, for competitively priced
flights and tailor-made packages.
Trips Worldwide
Tel: 0117 987 2626,
www.tripsworldwide.co.uk
Specialist company with a selection
of fascinating options in the region.

Information

The "information revolution" is now
fully activated in the Maya countries
and there's been a burgeoning of
websites and online services to add
to the tourist offices (*see page
347, Guatemala; 358, Belize; and
366, Yucatán*), publications and
resource centers.

WEBSITES

Internet resources in the Maya
countries have increased massively
and there are now dozens of useful
sites, some of which are US-based:
www. lanic.utexas.edu is excellent,
and one of the best newsgroups is
**www.news2mail.com/rec/travel/
latin-america.html**.

The following websites in the
Maya region itself also provide a
useful range of travel information
and news.

Mexico
www.mexico-travel.com
www.mexconnected.com
www.mexicanwave.com

Guatemala
www.aroundantigua.com
www.atitlan.com
www.guatemalaweb.com
www.insideguatemala.com
www.mayaparadise.com
www.mayaspirit.com.gt
www.quetzalnet.com
www.revuemag.com

Belize
www.belize.com
www.belizeit.com
www.belizenet.com
www.belizereport.com

www.channel5belize.com
www.turq.com/belizefirst

Maps

All the region's tourist offices will
provide you with a basic map of their
country, which are fine for general
use, but tend to be outdated and
inadequate if you plan to venture off
the beaten track.

The best maps of the Maya
countries are published by
**International Travel Map
Productions of Canada** (736A
Granville St, Vancouver, BC V62
1G3) – they produce maps of the
Guatemala, Yucatán, Belize, and
South East Mexico.

Purchase before you travel, since
they are not that widely available in
the region. In Mexico, the Guía Roja
maps are good for drivers.

Hikers will want larger-scale
maps. In Guatemala, the **Instituto
Geográfico Militar**, Av. Las Américas
5-76, Zona 13, Guatemala City
(Mon–Fri 8am–4pm) is the place to
acquire 1:50,000 maps. In Belize
Ordnance Survey maps (1:50,000)
cover most of the country, you can
buy them at **Stanfords**, Long Acre,
London WC2, tel: 020 7836 1321,
fax: 020 7836 0189, e-mail:
sales@stanfords.co.uk or
alternatively from the **Ministry of
Natural Resources** in Belmopan,
Belize. The best large-scale maps of
Mexico are produced by the state
cartographers INEGI, who have an
office in every state capital.

A Note on Addresses

In Guatemala, the street number
is written first followed by the
building number; 12 Calle 23
means number 23 on 12 Calle
(literally, 12 Street).

In Yucatán however,
addresses are listed as follows:
Calle 60, 23, which means
building number 23 on 60 Street.

GUATEMALA

The Place

Area: 108,889 sq km (42, 031 sq
miles).
Capital: Guatemala City.
Highest Mountain: Volcán Taju-
mulco 4,220 meters (13,850 ft).
Population: 14 million (growth rate
2.7 percent); 49 percent below the
age of 15.
Language: Spanish; 21 Maya
languages (K'iche', Mam, Kaqchikel
and Q'ekchi' are the four most
widely spoken); Garífuna.
Religion: 60 percent Roman
Catholic; 40 percent Protestant and
Evangelical (the highest proportion
in Latin America).
Time Zone: US Central Standard
Time; GMT minus 6 hours.
Currency: the quetzal, which comes
in denominations of Q0.50, Q1, Q5,
Q10, Q20, Q50, Q100. It is divided
into 100 centavos.
Weights and Measures: Generally
metric, though some quirky endemic
measures are still used including
legua (about 6.5 km/4 miles) and
manzana (about 0.7 hectares).
Electricity: 110 volts, flat North
American-style two-pronged plugs.
International Dialing Code: 502.

Geography

Guatemala is extremely mountainous in the south and very flat in the
north. The Pacific Ocean pounds
the southern shores, while in the
east of the country there is a small
Caribbean coastline.

The country's dominant physical
feature is the chain of volcanoes
that rises above the Pacific
coastline; the largest is Volcán
Tajumulco (4,220 meters/4,616
yds). To the north of this barrier are

the delightful Western Highlands, Lago de Atitlán, and the non-volcanic Cuchumatanes mountains. To the south of the volcanoes is the Pacific littoral, which is Guatemala's most productive farmland.

The east of the country is extremely varied, from the near desert of the mid-Motagua valley around Zacapa to the hot steamy lowlands around Lago de Izabal near the Caribbean coast.

The northern third of the country, covering the department of Petén, is generally flat and covered with a mix of tropical forests, savannas and swamps.

Economy

The Guatemalan economy is fired by agriculture with 51 percent of the population employed in this sector. The country's vast coffee, sugar and banana plantations earn the big export bucks, while subsistence farmers survive on small plots and increasingly marginal land. Very little of significance is manufactured in Guatemala, except garments for export to Korea and the US.

Even by normal Latin American standards, Guatemala's wealth distribution figures are some of the worst on the planet – the richest 10 percent of the population own half of the nation's wealth. Unemployment is officially 5 percent, but nearer 40 percent are underemployed. Tourism is one boom sector of the economy, with over 900,000 visiting in 2004, and this has overtaken coffee as the nation's main export earner.

Government

Guatemala is a republic whose head of state and government is the president, who holds office for a four-year term. The country is made up of 22 administrative departments. The present constitution dates from 1985. The president is the head of state.

After the CIA-backed coup of 1954, which evicted the demo-cratically elected government of Jácobo Arbenz, there were 32 years of military dictatorship. Since 1986,

democracy has tentatively been established (despite an attempted self-coup by a president in 1993) and the military have largely avoided obviously overt interference.

Visa & Passports

For citizens of the USA, EU, Canada, Australia and New Zealand, all you need to enter Guatemala is a valid passport to stay up to 90 days. If you need the full 90 days, make sure you ask for it as immigration officials can also give out 30- or 60-day permits. There is no charge if you enter overland at one of the more remote border crossings, though officials often demand a small fee. The initial 90-day period can be extended by a further 90 days by visiting Migración in Guatemala City (in the same building as the Inguat HQ; *see Tourist Offices, page 347*). This costs Q100.
Other requirements: the immigration official can also ask for proof of sufficient finances to fund your stay, though this is rare. A credit card or travelers' checks should be adequate.

Customs

Duty Free: 80 cigarettes or 100g of tobacco; 1.5 liters of alcohol; two bottles of perfume; camera and film for personal use
Restricted Items: fresh food

Business Hours

Businesses and offices are generally open between 9am and 5pm, but they often close for an hour or two between 12 noon and 2pm. Many banks stay open until 7pm (and even 8pm), especially in tourism-orientated towns. Archeo-logical sites are usually open daily from 8am to 5pm; and nature reserves (like the Quetzal Reserve and Cerro Cahui) are usually open from 6am to 5pm.

Media

NEWSPAPERS AND MAGAZINES

The main daily newspapers are *Prensa Libre*, *Siglo XXI*, *El Gráfico*, *El Periódico*, and *La Hora*. All the above are published in Spanish. There is also a good free monthly English-language magazine, *The Revue* (www.revuemag.com), produced in Antigua. *The Revue* deals with tourism and cultural issues of interest to an ex-pat and tourist readership. It's well worth consulting for its informative features and listings. There's a page or two devoted to different regions in Guatemala, and also Belize, Honduras and El Salvador.

RADIO AND TELEVISION

There are hundreds of radio stations, devoted to everything from merengue to evangelical worship. La Marca (94.1 FM) is a popular rock station, while Prisma (89.7 FM) plays jazz and pop classics.

There are 25 television stations in Guatemala, and several foreign channels (including CNN) are broadcast on cable, which is available in most of the main towns.

Postal Services

There are post offices *(correos)* in every town; air mail takes between three days and a week to reach North America, but between one and two weeks to get to Europe. The postal service is quite reliable, but many people choose to use a courier company to send anything important overseas.

The poste-restante system is no longer operational in Guatemala. If you need a secure address to send items to, use a language school.

To send home souvenirs such as handicrafts or carvings, you can dispatch small parcels from any post office, though large parcels are very expensive to send overseas. It's better to use a specialist shipping company: **Get Guated Out**,

Calle de Los Árboles in Panajachel (tel: 7762 2015) is one that is recommended.

Telecommunications

Guatemala's telecommunications network has improved greatly in recent years and can be considered reliable and pretty efficient. Cellular coverage is extensive across most of the nation, and compatible with many North American cellphones.

However, try to avoid using the Telgua offices found in most towns as their rates are punishingly high. Fortunately, a plethora of internet cafés, travel agents and many businesses offer much cheaper rates. The cheapest method of phoning home is via a webcall (at around US$0.20 per minute to North America, or US$0.30 a minute to the EU) but line quality can be poor and delay-prone. Conventional phone calls abroad typically cost about double these rates.
To make a collect-call (reverse charge) home from Guatemala, tel: 147120 from a Telgua phone.

Local calls in Guatemala are very cheap, at around US$0.10 per minute; national calls work out at around US$0.35 per minute.

Calling cards
Using a phone card is another option. All the main North American telecoms companies issue these including AT&T, Canada Direct, MCI and Sprint; get in touch with your phone company before you leave.

Internet
Guatemala has an extraordinary number of internet cafés, which are abundant throughout the country. Rates are around US$1.25–US$3 an hour. Connection speeds are usually rapid in the main centres, much less so once you get off the beaten track.

Health

You must have medical insurance before coming to Guatemala. Public hospitals are not good, and should be avoided if at all possible; the private sector is generally much more efficient and better equipped. Your embassy will have a list of English-speaking doctors and dentists. In remote areas, it may be best to get to a city as soon as possible if you can travel. Keep all receipts and contact your insurance company immediately if you do need medical treatment.

Alerta Médica is a private medical emergency assistance service; contact them by phoning **1711**.

Hospitals
Centro Médico, 6 Av 3-47 Zona 10, Guatemala City (tel: 2332 3555).
Santa Lucía Hospital, Santa Lucía Sur 7, Antigua (tel: 7832 3122).
Centro Médico Galeno, 2C 2-08 Zona 3, Cobán (tel: 7952 1315).

Dentists
Central de Dentistas Especialistas, 20C 11-17, Zona 10, Guatemala City (tel: 2337 1773).
Dr Leonel Rodriquez Lara, 4 Av Norte, Antigua (tel: 7832 0431).

Public Holidays & Festivals

January 1 New Year's Day.
January 15 Greatest pilgrimage in Central America as thousands of pilgrims descend on the basilica of the black Christ at Esquipulas.
March Huge pilgrimage to remote Chajul in the Ixil Triangle on the second Friday in Lent.
Semana Santa (Easter week) The most spectacular place in the world to witness Easter is Antigua, Guatemala. There are four days of huge processions, sawdust carpets fill the streets, and the whole town seems to dress up and re-enact the last days of Christ.
Good Friday In Guatemala City, this day is marked with political satire from the city's students in Zona 1, an event called Huelga de Dolores. There is also a famous confrontation between Maximón and Christ in Santiago Atitlán.
May 1 Labor Day. Union-led marches, especially in the capital.
June 30 Army Day.

Centro Dentro Cristal, 5 Av 1-55, Zona 3, Cobán (tel: 7952 1777).

Tourist Offices

Inguat (www.mayaspirit.com.gt), the Guatemalan tourist board, have offices in five locations. The staff are generally very helpful and will provide you with myriad glossy color brochures, which tend to be visual rather than useful. All the offices will try to point you in the right direction and solve any difficulties but the Antigua, Guatemala City and Quezaltenango offices are probably the most efficient.
Guatemala City: 7 Av 1-17, Zona 4 (tel: 2331 1333, fax 2331 8893). Also a kiosk at the airport.
Antigua: Parque Central (tel: 7832 0763).
Quezaltenango: Parque Central (tel: 7761 4931).
Panajachel: Calle Santander (tel: 7762 1571).
Flores: Plaza Central (tel: 7926 0669). Also a kiosk at the airport.

August 15 Spectacular fiesta in Joyabaj, Western Highlands, with ceremonies that include the *palo volador* – men swinging upside down attached to a pole.
September 15 Independence Day.
October 12 Discovery of Americas anniversary. A controversial bank holiday, celebrated by many ladinos, but many of the politically-active indigenous population use "Columbus Day" to protest against racial discrimination.
October 21 Revolution Day.
November 1 & 2 All Saint's Day and Day of the Dead. Wild alcohol-charged horse race in Todos Santos Cuchumatán on the 1st. Flying of giant kites in Santiago Sacatépequez and Comalapa. "Day of the Dead" on the 1st, when families remember their dead in cemeteries.
December 21 Culmination of the Chichicastenango fiesta with firecrackers and the palo volador.
December 25 Christmas Day.

Antigua has tourist police (corner of 4 Calle Norte and the plaza), who can help with security problems.

Useful Numbers

Directory Assistance **124**
International Call Operator **171**

Emergencies
Police **120**
Fire **123**
Ambulance **125**
Tourism Police **110**

Getting Around

Though Guatemala is a small country, the mountainous terrain and ancient buses mean that travel can be time-consuming and uncomfortable. Stick to the main highways and things move reasonably well, but many of the minor routes are unpaved and the going can be tediously slow. Thankfully, the scenery is usually spectacular.

BY BUS

The regular Guatemalan bus, called a *camioneta*, is an old North American school bus. It's three to a seat, and as many as possible standing in the aisle. Progress is always pretty slow, but never dull, as ranchero and merengue music blares from tinny speakers, children wail, and chickens cluck. Travelling on a "chicken" bus is one of the quintessential Guatemalan experiences; just make sure you get a more comfortable bus for long journeys. A camioneta will stop just about anywhere, and, as the joke goes, a "chicken" bus can never be full. Expect to pay about Q5 an hour.

There are also first-class buses (*pullmanes*) that connect the major towns along the main highways and into Mexico and the other Central American countries. They are a little quicker, don't stop so frequently, and you'll have a seat reservation. Expect to pay Q7 an hour.

Shuttle buses, usually modern Japanese minibuses, provide a useful and comfortable alternative. They mainly cover the prime tourist destinations, such as Antigua–Chichicastenango– Panajachel, but are increasingly common throughout the country. Expect to pay about US$5 per hour.

BY AIR

The only internal flight that's worth considering is the 50-minute Guatemala City–Flores flight (to visit Tikal) which saves a 16–20-hour round trip by road. Expect to pay $110–150 for a return ticket. You'll probably get a better deal by booking your ticket from a travel agent, rather than the airline. If you want to visit Copán, Honduras, and don't have too much time to spare, consider using Jungle Flying *(see below)*. Try to make reservations well in advance for all flights.

Domestic Airlines
Jungle Flying
Tel: 2339 0502.
Taca
Tel: 2361 5784.
www.taca.com
Tikal Jets
Tel: 2334 6855.
www.tikaljets.com
RACSA
Tel: 2361 5704.
www.racsair.com

BY BOAT

Boats connect the villages around Lago de Atitlán; Puerto Barrios and Lívingston, and Lívingston and Río Dulce town. These routes all have daily services, and it's not possible or necessary to book in advance.

BY TRAIN

There are currently no passenger train services at all in Guatemala.

Specialist Attractions & Tours

Adrenalina Tours, Pasaje Enríquez, Quezaltenango (tel: 7761 4509; www.adrenalinatours.com). Volcano climbs including Santa María, and tours of the Xela region. The branch at Huehuetenango, 4 Calle 6–38 (tel: 7736 2615) covers the Cuchumatanes mountains.
Antigua Tours, Casa Santo Domingo, 3C Oriente, 28, Antigua (tel: 7832 0140; www.antiguatours.net). Elizabeth Bell leads exceptional guided tours of the old capital, focusing on the history and colonial architecture.
Arcos Iris, 7 Av Sur 8, Antigua (tel: 7832 4202; www.guatemala reservations.com). Reliable tour and travel agent offering trips around the Antigua area.
Asociación de Vuelo Libre, 12 Calle, 1-25, Zona 10, Oficina 1601, Edif Géminis 10, Guatemala City (tel: 2335 3215). Hang-gliding over lakes Atitlán and Amatlitán; best times Nov–May.
ATI Divers, Iguana Perdida Hotel, in Santa Cruz La Laguna, Lake Atitlán (tel: 7762 2621; www.laiguanaperdida.com). Freshwater, high-altitude dives, and excellent instruction; PADI courses.
Clark Tours, Diagonal 6, 10-01, 7th floor, Torre II, Las Margaritas, Zona 10, G City (tel: 2470 4700; www.clarktours.com.gt). Organizes tours of Guatemala City and more.
Exotic Travel, Calle Principal, Lívingston (tel: 7747 0049). Trips to Playa Blanca and around Lívingston.
Explore, 4 Calle, Santa Elena (tel: 7926 2375). Tours to Ceibal, Aguateca and Lago de Petexbatún.
Hostal d'Acuña, 4 Calle 3–17, Cobán (tel: 7952 1547). For tours of Semuc Champey and Lanquín, in the Verapaces. Also organize shuttle buses.
Martsam Travel, Calle Centro América, Flores (tel: 7926 3225; www.martsam.com). Daily trips to Yaxhá and other ruins in Petén.
Maya Expeditions, 15 Calle A 14-07, Zona 10, Guatemala City (tel: 2363 4955; www.mayaexpeditions. com). If you want to explore the

isolated ruins of Petén, or white-water rafting trips.

Mayan Mountain Bike Tours, 1 Av Sur 15, Antigua (tel: 7832 3383). For an escorted mountain bike tour of the beautiful countryside around Antigua.

Miguel Morales, 4C Diag 3-67, Quezaltenango (tel: 7761 4673). Rock climbing on Guatemala's volcanoes.

Monarcas Travel, Alameda Santa Lucía 7 (tel: 7832 1939). Fascinating ecological and historical walking tours of Antigua and daily shuttle buses to Copán.

Monkey Eco tours, based at the Ni'tun Ecolodge in Flores, Petén (tel: 5201 0759). This agency specializes in customized jungle and ruin trips.

Old Town Outfitters, 5 Av Sur 12, Antigua (tel: 7832 4243; www.bikeguatemala.com). Terrific mountain bike tours, plus volcano- and rock-climbing trips.

Pablo's Tours, 3 Calle 3-20, Nebaj (tel: 7755 8287). Hiking trips and horseback-riding excursions in the Ixil region.

Posada Belén, 13 Calle A 10-30, Guatemala City (tel: 2253 4530; www.guateweb.com). Guided walking tours of the historic capital, and museum day tours.

Proyecto Eco-Quetzal, 2 Calle 14-36, Zona 1, Cobán (tel: 7952 1047; www.ecoquetzal.org). Superb trips to remote Maya villages and the cloudforests in the Verapaces.

Quetzaltrekkers, Casa Argentina, 12 Diagonal 8–37, Quezaltenango (tel: 7761 5865; www.quetzal ventures.com). A superb organization that arranges trips to Volcán Tajumulco, the highest peak in Central America, as well as amazing three-day hikes from Quezaltenango to Lago de Atitlán. All the profits benefit a local charity for street children.

Ravenscroft Stables, 2 Av Sur 3, San Juan del Obispo (tel: 7832 6229). Horseback riding in the Antigua area.

Trekking Ixil, 3 Calle 3-18, Nebaj (tel: 7755 3678; www.nebaj.org). Guided walks in the Nebaj area to remote villages.

Where to Stay

Hotels in the capital are listed first, in alphabetical order, then the regions are listed, likewise in alphabetical order.

GUATEMALA CITY

Hotel Camino Real
14C 0-20
Tel: 2333 3000
www.caminoreal.com.gt
Long established as the most prestigious five-star hotel in the capital. Located in the heart of the Zona Viva with over 400 rooms, swimming pools, nightclub, and full international facilities. **$$$**

Hotel Chalet Suizo
14 Calle 6-82, Zona 1
Tel: 2251 3786
Fax: 2232 0429
Very well run and maintained hotel, with 47 rooms and a small café. **$$**

Dos Lunas
21 Calle 10-92, Zona 13
Tel: 2334 5264
Excellent, inexpensive guesthouse run by a fluent English-speaking Guatemalteca. **$**

Holiday Inn
1 Av 13-22, Zona 10
Tel: 2332 2555
www.holidayinn.com.gt
Competitively priced luxury inn, well sited for the nightlife in Zona Viva or the main business districts. **$$$**

Hotel Posada Belén
13 Calle A 10-30, Zona 1
Tel: 2253 4530
www.guateweb.com
A very pleasant and atmospheric hotel in a converted colonial mansion with rooms situated around a central courtyard. **$$**

Hotel Spring
8 Av 12-65, Zona 1
Tel: 2232 6637
Fax: 2232 0107
Popular budget hotel with a variety of well-priced rooms and a café. **$**

Hotel Prices

The following categories are based on two people sharing a room, including breakfast:

$$$	US$70 and over
$$	US$40–70
$	under US$40

THE EAST

Cobán
Hotel la Posada
1 Calle 4–12
Tel: 7952 1495
The finest hotel in Cobán, whose rooms have real period charm. Fine restaurant and café. **$$$**

Hostal d'Acuña
4 Calle 3–17
Tel: 7952 1547
Superb budget hotel, with a sump-tuous restaurant, and a travel agency. **$**

Lívingston
Villa Caribe Tucán Dugú
Tel: 7947 0072
www.villasdeguatemala.com
The most luxurious hotel in Lívings-ton, on the main street just up from the jetty, with nice rooms and a big pool. **$$$**

Puerto Barrios
Hotel del Norte
Corner of 7 Calle and 1 Av
Tel: 7948 0087
Amazing, all-wooden, colonial period piece, right on the Bahía de Amatique, though the restaurant is mediocre. **$$**

Río Dulce
Hacienda Tijax
Near bridge
Tel: 5902 7825
Working teak and rubber farm with very pleasant accommodation, a pool, and an excellent range of activities including a canopy jungle walk. **$$**

Hotel Prices

The following categories are based on two people sharing a room, including breakfast:

$$$	US$70 and over
$$	US$40–70
$	under US$40

PACIFIC COAST

Las Lisas
Isleta de Gaia
Tel: 7885 0044
www.isleta-de-gaia.com
Beautiful, luxurious beach hotel, with 12 delightful cabins and fine European-style food. **$$$**

Monterrico
Dulce y Salado
Tel: 5817 9046
www.ducleysalado.dk
The complex enjoys a prime beachside location and has attractive thatched bungalows, a pool and a restaurant.
$

PETEN

Flores
Hotel la Casona de la Isla
Calle 30 de Junio
Tel: 7926 0593
Very comfortable lakeside hotel with attractive rooms, good service, and tasty snacks available. **$$**
Mirador del Lago
Calle 15 de Septiembre
Tel: 7926 3276
Excellent budget hotel, where all rooms have hot-water bathrooms and fans. Restaurant and lake-front terrace. **$**

El Remate
La Casa de Don David
Tel: 7928 8469
www.lacasadedondavid.com
Efficiently managed hotel, with clean rooms (some with air-conditioning), hearty meals, plus excellent travel information available from the American-Guatemalan owners. **$$**

La Lancha
Tel: 7928 8331
www.lalancha.com
Stylish boutique-style hotel, with rooms perched on the cliffs above Lago de Petén Itzá. With gourmet cuisine and a pool. **$$$**

Tikal
There are three hotels right by the wonderful ruins of Tikal; all of them are somewhat overpriced but have the obvious advantage of allowing you to get into the site early before group tours arrive, and when the wildlife is at its most active.
Jungle Lodge
Tel: 2476 8775
www.junglelodge.guate.com
34 comfortable bungalows and a pool – the best of the bunch. **$$**
Tikal Inn
Tel: 7926 1917
Thatched rooms and cabins and a pool. **$$**
Jaguar Inn
Tel: 7926 0002
www.jaguartikal.com
Nine reasonable rooms with fans; budget rooms also available. **$$**

WESTERN HIGHLANDS

Antigua
Hotel Aurora
4C Oriente 16
Tel/fax: 7832 0217
www.hotelauroraantigua.com
Pleasant if old-fashioned hotel where all rooms are set around a grassy courtyard. **$$**
Casa Encantada
9C Poniente 1
Tel: 7832 7903
www.casaencantada-antigua.com
Boutique hotel with 10 wonderful rooms, all with stylish bathrooms. Small pool, and a rooftop bar. **$$$**
La Casa de Santa Lucía
Alameda 4, Santa Lucía Sur 5
Tel: 7832 6133
Very spacious, comfortable and well-priced rooms. **$**
Mesón Panza Verde
15 Av Sur 19
Tel: 7832 2925
www.panzaverde.com
Immaculate small hotel, with a

selection of beautiful rooms, and a lap pool. Has one of the finest restaurants in Antigua. **$$$**
Posada La Merced
7 Av Norte 43a
Tel: 7832 3197
www.merced-landivar.com
Bright, cheery rooms with spotless private bathrooms. Children are made very welcome. **$$**
Posada San Sebastián
3 Av Norte 4
Tel: 7832 2621
Rooms are decorated with imagination and taste, and it's just off the main plaza. **$$**
Hotel Santo Domingo
3 Calle Oriente 28
Tel: 7832 0140
www.casasantodomingo.com
Breathtakingly stylish and luxurious hotel, in a converted monastery, with full facilities including a huge pool. **$$$**
La Tatuana
7 Av Sur 3
Tel: 7832 1223
Good value, with attractive bedrooms that all have private bath. **$**
Sky Hotel
1 Av Sur 15
Tel/fax: 7832 3383
Small and pleasant with good communal facilities and bicycle hire. **$**

Chichicastenango
Hospedaje Girón
6 Calle 4–52
Tel: 7756 1329
Very clean, basic, but reasonably priced rooms. **$**
Mayan Inn
Corner of 8 Calle and 3 Av
Tel: 7756 1176
www.mayaninn.com.gt
One of Guatemala's most famous hotels, very comfortable and traditional. **$$$**
Posada El Arco
4 C 4-36
Tel: 7756 1255
Welcoming guesthouse with seven spacious, attractive rooms and a beautiful garden. **$**
Hotel Santo Tomás
7 Av 5–32
Tel: 7756 1061
Luxury hotel with full modern

amenities, including a heated swimming pool. **$$$**

Huehuetenango
Hotel Mary
2 C 3-52
Tel: 7764 1618
Fax: 7764 7412
Small, but pleasant rooms all with TV and shower. **$**
Hotel Zaculeu
5 Av 1–14
Tel: 7764 1086
The best hotel in town. **$$**

Jaibalito
La Casa del Mundo
Lago de Atitlán
Tel: 5218 5332
www.lacasadelmundo.com
Tremendous views over Lake Atitlán, very comfortable rooms, and friendly owners. **$$**

Panajachel
Hotel Atitlán
Atitlán
Tel: 7762 1441
www.hotelatitlan.com
Tasteful luxury hotel, though it's a 20-minute walk from the center of town; by the lakeside. Pool. **$$$**
Hospedaje Villa Lupita
Callejón El Tino
Tel: 7762 1201
Superb family-run hotel with pleasant rooms, some with private bath. **$**
Hotel Dos Mundos
Calle Santander
Tel: 7762 2078
Attractive bungalows, a pool, and a good Italian restaurant. **$$**
Hotel Posada de Don Rodrigo
Calle Santander
Tel: 7762 2322
www.hotelposadadedonrodrigo.com
Colonial-style hotel in a good position close to the lakeside. **$$$**
Rancho Grande Inn
Calle Rancho Grande
Tel: 7762 1554
www.ranchograndeinn.com
Very comfortable bungalows, good service, and pretty gardens. **$$**

Quezaltenango
Casa Kaehler
13 Av 3-33
Tel: 7761 2091
Comfortable, dependable budget hotel; but be sure to book ahead. **$**
Casa Mañen
9 Av 4–11, Zona 1
Tel: 7765 0786
www.comeseeit.com
Very tasteful and well-run B & B with a great roof terrace. **$$**
Pensión Bonifaz
4 C, 10–50
Tel: 7761 2182
Fax: 7761 2850
The city's best-known hotel, old-fashioned but classy, and just off the plaza. **$$$**

Santa Cruz La Laguna
La Iguana Perdida
Next to Arca de Noé
Tel: 5706 4117
www.laiguanaperdida.com
Great budget hotel, with atmosphere and character. Also home to ATI Divers. (*See page 348.*) **$**

San Pedro la Laguna
Hotel Mansión del Lago
above the dock
Tel: 5811 8172
www.hotelmansiondellago.com
San Pedro's most comfortable hotel with excellent-value rooms. Rooftop Jacuzzi. **$**

Santiago Atitlán
Posada de Santiago
On the lakeside, 1 km south of town.
Tel/fax: 7721 7167
www.posadadesantiago.com
Plenty of character here; the accommodation is in stone lodges, all with fireplaces. **$$**

Where to Eat

In Guatemala most people only ever eat out at cheap restaurants called *comedores*, which are the rough equivalent of a North American diner. There will be a daily special or two and a basic menu of four or five standard dishes, usually grilled or fried meat *(carne asada o frita)* and vegetables *(verduras)*, or a

Restaurant Prices

The following categories are based on the price of a meal for two, including drinks:

$$$	over US$40
$$	US$20–40
$	under US$20

broth *(caldo)*. Eggs *(huevos)* beans *(frijoles)* and tortillas are always available and make a useful vegetarian option. Anything with grander pretensions is a restaurant *(restaurante)*, which will offer a more varied selection of food and perhaps a set menu of three courses *(menú del día)* – these are especially good value at lunchtime and start from $2.50. Finally there is a plethora of street food, from tacos and tamales to pupusas and tostadas *(see Gastronomic Guidelines, page 49)*. Hygiene standards can be variable, but most of these snacks are fine. The capital's restaurants are listed first, followed by the regions, in alphabetical order.

GUATEMALA CITY

Altuna
5 Av 12–31
One of the finest restaurants in the old town, an oasis of civilization in the chaos of Zona 1. Spanish menu, majoring in fish. **$$$**
Olivadda
12 Calle 4–5, 1 Zona 10
Quality Mediterranean food in leafy surroundings. **$$**
El Gran Pavo
13 Calle 4–41, Zona 1; also at 12 Calle 5–54, Zona 9
"The Big Turkey" is the place for Mexican food, with an expansive, reasonably priced menu. **$$**
Margarita's
4 Av 13-20, Zona 10
One of the capital's most fashionable and contemporary restaurants, serving modern Italian cuisine. **$$$**

Restaurant Prices

The following categories are based on the price of a meal for two, including drinks:

$$$ over $40
$$ $20–40
$ under $20

Piccadilly
Plaza España
7 Av 12-00, Zona 9; also at corner of 6 Av and 11 Calle, Zona 1
Eclectic menu of international dishes, very popular with Guatemalans and overseas visitors. **$**
Tamarindos
11 C 2-19 A, Zona 10
Terrific Asian fusion cooking; the décor has a strong Japanese influence. **$$**

THE EAST

Puerto Barrios
Rincón Uruguayo
Corner of 7 Av and 16 Calle
Excellent South American-style barbecue meat feast. **$**
Safari
5 Av
Open-air seafood restaurant overlooking Bahía de Amatique. **$$**

Río Dulce
Río Bravo
Lakeside, by the bridge
Popular for pizza and pasta, also has a lively bar. **$**

Lívingston
Bahía Azul
Main St
Simple, informal café-restaurant, great for breakfast. **$**
Casa Rosada
About 10 minutes' walk west of the dock, in Hotel Casa Rosada. Fine vegetarian cooking; eat overlooking the Lívingston bay. **$$**

Cobán
Bistro d'Acuña
4 Calle 3–17
Extremely civilized bastion of European cooking, with good European dishes on the menu, fine coffee, and an amazing dessert cabinet. **$$**
Cafe Tirol
North side of plaza, 1 Calle
Epic line-up of coffees, plus decent snacks. **$**

PETÉN

Flores
La Luna
Calle 30 de Junio.
Elegant place in a historic wooden building, with an eclectic menu that includes pasta and fish. **$$**
El Tucán
On the lakeside, by the causeway
Tel: 7926 0677
An extensive menu of salads and fish dishes; huge portions. **$**

WESTERN HIGHLANDS

Antigua
Fernando's Kaffee
7 Av Norte 43.
Modest-looking place that serves the finest coffee in Antigua, plus to-die-for homemade cakes. **$**
La Fonda de la Calle Real
5 Av Norte; also at 3 Calle Poniente 7
Long-established Guatemalan restaurant with a delicious selection of local specialties, especially grilled meats, broths, and sausages. **$$**
El Mesón Panza Verde
5 Av Sur 19
Extremely tasteful and atmospheric European-style restaurant, proper service and relaxed atmosphere. **$$$**
Nicolas
4 Calle Oriente 20
Antigua's grandest restaurant, with gourmet European cuisine and a wallet-busting wine list. **$$$**
La Escudilla
4 Av Norte 4
Delightful courtyard restaurant, with a very well-priced menu. **$**
Rainbow Café
7 Av Sur 8
Good mainly vegetarian menu, best for a casual lunch or an afternoon smoothie or coffee. **$**

Frida's
5 Av Norte 29
Antigua's finest Mexican restaurant, though the décor is pure Americana. **$$**
Doña Luisa's
4 Calle Oriente 12
An Antiguan institution and popular meeting place, with cakes, snacks, and meals served in a converted colonial mansion. **$**

Chichicastenango
La Fonda del Tzijolaj
Centro Comercial Santo Tomás (north side of market)
Above the indoor vegetable market. Economical local menu and a fine view of the hubbub below. **$**
Restaurant La Villa de Los Cofrades
Corner of 6 Calle and 5 Calle
Simple but well-executed Guatemalan menu. **$$**

Nebaj
Maya-Inca
5 Calle
Very simple but charming joint Andean-Guatemalan restaurant. **$**

Panajachel
Las Chinitas
Calle Santander
Stylish Malaysian-owned restaurant with a creative menu full of Chinese, Malay, and Thai favorites. **$**
La Terraza
Calle Santander
Fine continental food and tasteful decor. **$$**
Deli
Calle Principal
Very classy cafe with home-baked cakes, healthy sandwiches, and uplifting classical music. **$$**
Chez Alex
Calle Santander
Arguably the most elegant place in Pana, with fine European cuisine including lobster and lamb. **$$$**

San Pedro La Laguna
Pinocchio
On the lakeside between the two jetties.
Good-value, simple Italian food, great for pizza and pasta. **$**

Quezaltenango

Baviera
5 Calle 12–50, Zona 1
Good selection of coffees plus great cakes in stylish wood-panelled dining room/café. **$**

Cardinali's
14 Av 3–41, Zona 1
Recommended for authentic Italian cooking; the pizzas are a real treat. **$$**

Restaurante Bonifaz
4 C, 10–50 (inside Pensión Bonifaz)
Good people-watching venue and a reliable, if not exciting, menu. **$$**

Dos Tejanos
Pasaje Enríquez
Wonderful Tex Mex food in historic surrounds. **$$**

Huehuetenango

Mi Tierra
4 Calle 6–46
Popular café with friendly service, and healthy, interesting eating. **$**

La Fonda de Don Juan
2 Calle 5–35
Attractive pizza/pasta parlor, although it is slightly overpriced,and the portions are on the small side. **$$**

La Cabaña del Café
2 Calle
Wonderful coffee shack with good cakes and nice atmosphere. **$**

Nightlife

Most Guatemalan towns are extremely quiet after nightfall, and generally the country is not known for its hip clubs and bars. The capital, Guatemala City, is the exception, though it's divided sharply on class lines – the rich have their fun in the Zona Viva in Zone 10 and Cuatro Grados Norte in Zona 4, while the rest head to the highly atmospheric but run-down bars of Zona 1.

Antigua has a varied and exciting bar scene, though it's definitely geared to Western tastes; there are also two nightclubs. In Panajachel you'll find plenty of good bars, and a few nightclubs. Quezaltenago has a couple of clubs and a few good bars.

One of the most lively places in the country is tiny Lívingston (population 5,000), where the Garífuna really know how to party. There's a beach disco and a number of busy bars.

Elsewhere in the provinces, the ladino towns will certainly have a few bars and even a nightclub, but in most indigenous villages there may be only a liquor shop with a couple of stools propped up against the counter for their hard-drinking regulars.

Generally cantinas are a male preserve, and women may feel much more comfortable enjoying a drink or two in a restaurant.

Shopping

Cigars

Honduran cigars are among the very best in the world and are far cheaper in Guatemala than in the West. Try the **Los Próceras Mall**, Guatemala City.

Jade

Guatemala is one of the world's most important producers of jade, (pronounced "ha-day" in Spanish). Antigua again has the best selection of stores: try **Jade S.A.**, 4 Calle Oriente 34, or **The Jade Kingdom**, 4 Av Norte 10.

Jewelry

There is a number of smart stores in Antigua selling silver and gold. Try the silver factory **La Antigüeña**, Callejón Los Horcones, San Felipe de Jesús, just outside Antigua.

Textiles

Guatemala's unique weavings are justifiably world-famous, and are the country's premier handicrafts. The most authentic weavings are huipiles – women's blouses, but in recent years a massive textile

industry geared to Western tastes has developed. Called típica, these weavings encompass everything from trousers and dungarees to waistcoats made from colorful Guatemalan fabric. Tablecloths, napkins, purses, wallets, and bedspreads are also woven. The típica industry is an important part of the Guatemala economy, which exports all over the world, and a vital income source for many indigenous women.

To get an idea of the quality and variety of Guatemalan weavings, there's no better place than **Museo Ixchel** in Guatemala City (see page 112). You'll find another amazing collection of textiles at **Nim Po't** in Antigua (5 Av Norte 29); here the weavings are for sale. You'll find weaving co-operatives throughout the country; the best one are in the villages of Todos Santos Cuchumatán, Nebaj, Zunil, San Antonio Palopó, San Juan la Laguna, and San Antonio Aguas Calientes. One of the best places to find weavings is **Panaja-chel**, where there is an amazing

number of stalls and weavers. Other markets include Chichicaste-nango, San Francisco El Alto, Antigua, and Sololá. There is also a good selection in the mercado in Zona 1, Guatemala City.

Wooden Masks

Ceremonial wooden masks, called máscaras, are another superb Guatemalan craft and have been used since Preclassic Maya times. They are used in fiestas through-out the highlands, especially in Maya dances. You'll find maseareros (mask-makers) in **Chichicastenango**; there are two stores on the path to the hilltop site of Pascual Abaj. There are also some interesting pieces in the **Chichicastenango Museum** and in Guatemala City in the **Popul Vuh Museum**.

Wool

By far the best place to buy woolen blankets is the highland Maya village of **Momostenango**; ideally you should try to make it for the Sunday market.

GUATEMALA CITY

Kahlua
Corner of 15 Calle and 1 Calle,
Zona 10
Hip club with Latin and Western
dance music.
Konga
Corner of 13 Calle and 3 Av, Zona 10
The Latin pop and salsa attracts a
rich, young crowd.
Renato's
Corner of 13 C & Av La Reforma,
Zona 9.
Informal bar with live rock music.

Gay Clubs

Ephebus
4 C 5-30
Small club; mainly house music.
Genetic
Corner of Via 3 and Ruta 3, Zona 4
The biggest gay club in Guatemala.

Antigua

No Sé
1 Av Norte 11C
Intimate place with some live music
and a tequila/mescal bar at the rear.
La Casbah
5 Av Norte 30
One of the best clubs in the
country, house music and latin pop.
Spectacularly set in the ruins of a
baroque church. Expensive.

Panajachel

Chapiteau
Calle de los Arboles
Salsa, rock, and pop for tourists,
both local and foreign.
El Aleph and **Circus Bar**
Both Calle de los Arboles
Two live music venues. Often good,
occasionally awful.

Quezaltenango

Bar Tecún
Paisaje Enriquez, Parque Central
A lively drinking den, popular with
Europeans and North Americans.
El Duende
14 Av A
Bar-club with Latin house, salsa and
merengue.
Hektisch
15 Av
Hip club with techno, hip hop, and
drum 'n' bass.

BELIZE

Area: 23,300 sq km (9,000 sq
miles).
Capital: Belmopan.
Population: 280,000.
Language: English.
Religion: Roman Catholic, Anglican,
Methodist, Mennonite, Bah'ai,
Hindu, Muslim, Presbyterian, and
Seventh Day Adventist. The
Garífuna people have their own
unique religion.
Time Zone: US Central standard
time; GMT minus 6 hours.
Currency: Belizean dollars.
Weights and Measures: The
English Imperial system is generally
used, with speed and road signs in
miles, not kilometers; however, fuel
is sold by the American gallon, and
some imported goods are weighed
using the metric system.
Electricity: 110 volts, flat two-
pronged plugs.
International Dialing Code: 501.

Geography

Belize's most striking natural feature
is clearly visible from the air. As you
fly into Belize City, the view of the
seemingly endless coral reef is
breathtaking. At almost 300 km (185
miles) long, it is second only to
Australia's Great Barrier Reef.
(Belizeans will point out, however,
that it is the longest *unbroken* reef in
the world.) Three of the four major
atolls in the Western Hemisphere are
located here, including Lighthouse
Reef with its nearly perfectly circular
and highly photographed Blue Hole.
The Hole itself is 55–90 meters
(180–300 ft) deep.

Back on the mainland, the coastal
and northern areas of Belize are flat
and hot, mostly made up of
mangrove swamps and lagoons that
provide the spawning environment for
marine life. Further inland, rising to
around 915 meters (3,000 ft) above
sea level, the vast central and
southern regions are covered by
tropical pine, hardwood forests, and
rainforests. These largely uninhabited
regions are rich in flora. The
limestone formation of the country
has left it riddled with cave systems,
which rival the largest in the world.

Economy

Traditionally based on logging, the
Belizean economy is currently
supported by tourism, broader-based
agricultural exports, which include
sugar cane, citrus fruits, bananas,
honey maize, beans, rice, and an
increasing array of exotic tropical
fruits. Timber is still a major export,
although most of it is now pine
rather than hardwood.

Over the last couple of years
tourism has emerged as the top
foreign-exchange earner for the
economy, and is the twin pillar
along with agriculture in terms of
industry. It has also become a
major contributor to employment
and foreign revenue. Tourism now
contributes 30 percent to the Gross
National Product of Belize.

Belize is still reliant on foreign
aid, particularly for major capital
projects such as tourism infrastructure, hurricane protection,
roads, and so on.

Government

In 1964, the British colony of British
Honduras was granted an internal,
elected self-government. The
Peoples United Party (PUP) remained
in power for nearly 20 years, guiding
the colony's name change to Belize
in 1973 and finally to the declaration
of its independence on September
21, 1981. Britain remained in
charge of foreign relations, defense,
and internal security; a 3,000-strong
military defense was maintained to
deter the neighboring Guatemalans
from pressing their 150-year-old
claim to Belize. Guatemala and

Belize forged agreements over boundaries and access by the seas in the early 1990s, and so the British Military defense was removed in early 1993 leaving only a very small number of soldiers as a symbolic deterrent to possible Guatemalan invasions.

Belize inherited the principles of parliamentary democracy after the Westminster system in Britain – the Prime Minister and cabinet make up the executive branch, while a 28-member elected House of Representatives and eight-member appointed Senate make up the legislative branch.

Politics is very much in evidence in Belize, if only because the major political parties own the national newspapers. Since independence there have been predominantly two parties wrestling for power. PUP regained power in the 1998 General Election and won again in 2003.

Customs

Removal, sale, and exportation of the following are prohibited by law in Belize: any kind of coral without a license; archeological artifacts; orchids; shells; fish and crustaceans; turtles and materials from turtles.

Business Hours

Most stores and offices are open Monday to Friday, 8am–noon, with afternoon hours varying from 1–5pm to 3–8pm. Banks are open Monday to Thursday, 8am–1pm; Friday, 8am–1pm and 3–6pm. Almost everything is closed on public holidays.

Media

NEWSPAPERS

Newspapers in Belize are all weekly and are either owned by, or connected to, political parties, and thus often dwell on bad-mouthing the opposition. The main mastheads are the *Belize Times*, the *Guardian*, the *Reporter*, and the *Amandala*.

RADIO AND TELEVISION

The most popular TV is from cable (mostly pirated from satellite) and is full of American soaps, sport, and chat. Radio is a big favorite in Belize. **Love FM** at 89.1FM has English and Spanish programmes – tune in for a mix of local and BBC world news, weather reports interspersed with chat shows, and a selection of rock and reggae. The other popular channel is **KREM FM** at 91.1FM.

Postal Services

Belize City Post Office is based in an old colonial building on the north side of the Swing Bridge (near the intersection of Queen and North Front streets). Belizean stamps are beautiful, with depictions of native flora and fauna, and are highly prized by collectors. Belize provides one of the most economical and reliable postal systems in Central America. Allow around 4–7 days for mail to arrive in the US and around two weeks (often less) to Europe, Asia, or Australia. The post office is open 8am–noon and 1–5pm (4.30pm on Fridays).

Visas & Passports

Visas are not required by most nationalities, including citizens of the United States, the United Kingdom, and British Commonwealth countries, as well as most members of the European Union; however, it is advisable to check with your nearest consulate or embassy before travel as requirements do change. All people from these countries need an international passport which is valid for at least six months and an onward or round-trip air ticket.

All visitors are permitted to stay up to 30 days. To apply for an extension contact the **Immigration Office**, 115 Barrack Road, Belize City. A moderate fee is charged and applicants must demonstrate sufficient funds for the remainder of their stay as well as an onward ticket.

Telecommunications

Public telephones are available throughout Belize, except in the more remote areas where you will only find a community phone often in someone's private house. Your hotel will also have fixed rates for national and international calls. Check the rate before you make the call (international calls are expensive, and watch out for the service charge some hotels may add to your bill). The more expensive hotels have fax and e-mail facilities available.

Telephone, telegraph, telex, and e-mail/internet services are also available at **Belizean Telecommunications Ltd.**, 1 Church Street (just off Central Park), 8am–9pm on weekdays, 8am–noon on Sundays. International direct dialing is available from most places in Belize. For international calls assistance tel: **115** and Belize directory assistance tel: **113**. Internet cafes are found in all major towns and some villages.

Health

No **vaccinations** are required if traveling to Belize, except a yellow fever certificate if you are arriving in Belize within six days of visiting an infected area. However, typhoid, polio and hepatitis A jabs are recommended by most doctors.

There is **malaria** in some parts of Belize and if you are planning to spend extended stays in jungle areas it is advisable to take a course of anti-malaria tablets.

It is important to be extremely careful in the strong sun and to drink plenty of water, especially on walking trips. Like the Belizeans, it is best to avoid much activity between 11am and 4pm on hot days. Pack sunscreen and strong insect repellent, twice as much as you think you'll need. It is often not that easy to purchase outside of tourist areas.

If you're going diving or snorkeling be very careful to avoid touching the coral, both to protect the reef and yourself. Disturbances to live outcroppings can destroy the coral's fragile ecosystem, while cuts and abrasions from the reef often become painfully infected and take a long time to heal.

The quality of food preparation is generally good in Belize, so there is not such a risk of stomach problems as in neighboring countries. Although tap water is potable in some towns and resort areas, it is recommended that you drink bottled or sterilized water, especially on the cayes or in the south.

Medical Services

It is uncommon for visitors to contract any serious health problems, but should you require a physician your hotel should be able to recommend one; in an emergency contact one of the following:

Belize Medical Associates
St Thomas Street, Belize City
Tel: 223 0303.
Karl Heusner Memorial Hospital
Princess Margaret Drive, Belize City
Tel: 223 1543.
Universal Health Services
Blue Marlin/Chancellor Ave,
Belize City
Tel: 223 7866.
Corozal Hospital
Tel: 422 2076.
Health Center, Caye Caulkner
Tel: 226 0168.
Loma Luz Hospital (Santa Elena, Cayo)
Tel: 804 2985.
Mopan Clinic (Benque Viego Del Carmen)
Tel: 823 2079.
Northern Regional Hospital (Orange Walk)
Tel: 322 2072.
Public Health Center, San Pedro
Tel: 226 2536.
Punta Gorda Hospital
Tel: 722 2026.
San Ignacio Hospital
Tel: 824 2066.
Southern Regional Hospital (Dangriga)
Tel: 522 2078.
Western Regional Hospital (Belmopan)
Tel: 822 2264.

Public Holidays & Festivals

January 1 New Year's Day
March 9 Baron Bliss Day
Easter weekend
May 1 Labor Day
May 24 Commonwealth Day
September 10 St George's Caye Day

September 21 Independence Day
October 12 Columbus Day
November 19 Garifuna Settlement Day
December 25 Christmas Day
December 26 Boxing Day

Getting Around

FROM THE AIRPORT

Most visitors' first vision of Belize is the quaint and possibly frustrating **Phillip Goldson International Airport**. Immigration can be entertaining or infuriating, depending on your attitude! There is a currency exchange window near the exit (if this is closed, you can get by on US dollars without any problems), as well as a tourist information booth.

Most tour operators put visitors straight on to connecting flights or provide a minibus service to out-of-town hotels or jungle lodges.

Independent travelers will find a taxi rank outside the airport doors. Rates into Belize City are fixed by a cartel and are fairly hefty for the 20–25-minute ride. Rates to other parts of Belize can be negotiated (get into the habit of confirming the price before you get into the taxi).

There is an airport shuttle bus that departs at various times during the day but the times often do not connect with incoming flights.

BY BUS

Buses run hourly between Belize City and the major towns to the north and the west, less frequently to the south. The sole bus station in use in Belize City is Novelo's, found at the Northern Transport headquarters. Contact the bus company for schedule information.
Northern Transport
West Collet Canal
Belize City
Tel: 227 4924.

BY TAXI

Downtown Belize is small enough to handle on foot, and during the cool of the day this is the best way to get around. At night, you should travel by private car or taxi, even for short distances, just to be on the safe side. Hotels and restaurants are used to calling for taxis, which arrive almost immediately; always remember to confirm the price with the driver before setting off.

Transfers between hotels are often pre-arranged for tourists by their tour operator. It is also possible to hire taxis to get between towns or to explore the countryside (in San Ignacio, for example, the taxi cartel has fixed rates to various jungle lodges and ruins).

BY CAR

One way to start your trip is to pick up a hire car (or preferably jeep) from the airport. Your own transport comes in very handy in the interior of Belize. Lodges tend to be in isolated areas, and having your own transport allows you to come and go as you please; you are free to visit wildlife reserves and archeological sites at your own pace, and make trips into town whenever you want to.

Driving is on the right-hand side of the road. Speeds and distances are measured in miles, and although signposting is rare surprisingly you don't get lost.

Unfortunately, there are some drawbacks. Renting a car in Belize is expensive and a large damage deposit is required. The other drawback is the bad condition of the roads; if you are driving south some hire companies will only hire you a four-wheel drive vehicle which increases the cost. There is a wide choice of car rental companies in Belize City. Listed below are just a few of the better known.

Avis Rent A Car
Municipal Airstrip, Belize City
Tel: 203 4619.

Budget
771 Bella Vista, Belize City
Tel: 223 2435
Fax: 223 3986
e-mail: reservations@budget-belize.com

Safari/Hertz
11a Cork Street, Belize St., Belize City
Tel: 223 0886
e-mail: safahz@btl.net

BY AIR

With roads being so rough, small propeller plane services have been set up to cover most of Belize. This is by far the most common and convenient form of getting around.

Most of the flights run on time and few of them take longer than half an hour. The most popular destinations are from Belize International Airport to San Pedro, on Ambergris Caye (which takes 20 minutes, and gives you spectacular views of the coral reef) and to Placencia and Dangriga, both in the south. If leaving from Belize City, make sure you know whether the flight you are taking will be departing from the International Airport, or the smaller but more commonly used (and cheaper) Municipal Airport in Belize City.

Scheduled Air Services
Maya Island Air, Municipal Airstrip, Belize City, tel: 223 1403, fax: 227 713; Barrier Reef Drive, San Pedro, Ambergris Caye, tel: 226 2435, fax: 226 2192, e-mail: mayair@btl.net.
Tropic Air: Municipal Airstrip, Belize City, tel: 224 5671, fax: 223 2814; PO Box 20, San Pedro, Ambergris Caye, tel: 226 2012, fax: 226 2338, e-mail: tropicair@btl.net.

BY BOAT

The alternative to flying to Caye Caulker, Ambergris Caye, or St George's Caye is taking one of the boat services from Belize City (next to the swing bridge). For Caye Caulker, and San Pedro boats depart from the Marine terminal and the Courthouse Wharf. Both services stop off at St George's Caye on request.

Specialist Attractions & Tours

Caves Branch Lodge, tel: 822 2800; e-mail:info@cavesbranch.com. Caving expeditions.
Clarissa Falls Resort, tel: 824 3916, e-mail: clarifalls@btl.net; off the Banque road, down a track just before the turning to Chaa Creek, near San Ignacio. Rafting and kayaking on Belize's Mopan River.
Tanisha Tours, Ambergris Caye, tel: 226 2314. Snorkeling trips and expeditions to the Maya sites on the north of the caye.
Eva's Restaurant, 22 Burns Ave, near San Ignacio, tel: 804 2267; www.evasonline.com. Mountain bike hire, good for Mountain Pine Ridge.
Monkey River Magic, Point Placencia (tel: 842 2164; fax: 23291; e-mail: plaind@btl.net). For diving, natural history and sailing trips, contact Dave Dial.
Maya Mountain Lodge, 9 Cristo Rey Rd, Santa Elena, near San Ignacio, Belize (tel: 824 2164. Hiking, riding, canoeing and fishing.
Mountain Equestrian Trails, Mile 8, Mountain Pine Ridge Rd, Central Farm PO, Cayo District, near San Ignacio (tel: 820 4041; www.metbelize.com). Horse-riding for the adventurous, tours of up to four days. "Turf & Surf" expeditions.
Ocean Motion Guides, Placencia (tel: 523 3363). Bernard Leslie organises boat trips.
Toadal Adventure
Placencia Village (tel: 523 3207; fax: 523 3334; e-mail: mail@toadaladventure.com). Dave Vernon is an excellent guide for sea-kayaking, mountain biking, natural history and archaeology trips.

Toledo Ecotourism Association c/o Nature's Way Guesthouse, 65 Front Street, Punta Gorda (tel: 722 2096). Here, they will arrange tours to the Maya villages, waterfalls and archeological sites in the lush hills of the Maya Mountains.

Conservation

Conservation Corridors
Richard Wotton, 183 Saltram Crescent, London W9 3JU
Tel: 0181-964 5325.
Specialises in finding placements for people interested in working on conservation projects in Belize.
Smithsonian Institute
Arts and Industries Building 1163 Washington DC 20560–0402
Fax: 202-357 2116;
E-mail: education@soe.si.edu.
Operates a marine research station.
Programme for Belize (PFB)
2 South Park Street,
PO Box 749, Belize City
Tel: 227 5616,
E-mail: pfbel@btl.net.
Manages a huge swathe of land in the Río Bravo Conservation Area, which is open to visitors by prior appointment.
Siwa-ban Foundation (SbF)
contact Ellen McRae,
PO Box 47, Caye Caulker
Tel: 226 0178
E-mail: sbf@btl.net.
Helped to establish of the Caye Caulker Forest and Marine Reserves in 1998, covering an area at the northern tip of the caye and part of the nearby reef. Also works with umbrella group, FAMRACC-Forest and Marine Reserve Association of Caye Caulker, to co-manage reserves.

Tourist Offices & Useful Organizations

Belize Tourism Board, Level 2, Central Bank Building, P.O. Box 325, Gabourel Lane, Belize City (tel: 223 1913; fax: 223 1943; e-mail: info@travelbelize.com; www.travelbelize.org). The office is open 8am–noon and 1–5pm.

For further information on Belize's ecology and ancient culture, contact:

Belize Audubon Society, 12 Fort Street, Belize City (tel: 223 5004; e-mail: base@btl.net).

The Belize Zoo and Tropical Educational Center, PO Box 1787, Belize City, tel: 220 8004; fax: 220 8010; www.belizezoo.org

For more detailed information about Maya archeological sites, or for permission to visit certain sites in the region, visitors should first contact:

Belize Institute of Archeology, Belmopan (tel: 822 2106; fax 822 3345; e-mail: ia@nichbelize.org).

Where to Stay

Belize offers a brilliant choice of accommodation ranging from comfortable budget hotels to luxurious beach resorts, country cottages to jungle lodges with vast tracts of unspoiled wilderness as their grounds.

There are a few large internationally owned chain hotels and plenty of small private lodges, hotels, and guesthouses. Travelers with special interests are well catered for – there are remote dive resorts on the outer cayes, lodges catering for the "ecotourist" and the birdwatcher, and jungle health resorts for those in need of serious pampering. No two lodges or hotels are identical; styles and atmospheres differ wildly. The environment makes a difference, as does the personality of the owners. Many of these places have American and European owners, who make their marks on the feel of the places.

For accommodation in lodges and on some cayes, it is difficult to give price guides as they usually offer deals which include diving or fishing trips, or rainforest treks, etc. The packages are mostly quite expensive, but very convenient and usually worthwhile. There is also a compulsory government sales tax of 7 percent added to hotel prices and most hotels add a service charge of 5–10 percent.

Accommodation is listed by area in alphabetical order, with the exception of Belize City and the outlying district which is listed first.

BELIZE CITY

Bellevue
5 Southern Foreshore
Tel: 227 7051
Fax: 227 3253
E-mail: bellevue@btl.net
The only hotel on the south side with a pool, restaurant, and bar. Converted and expanded colonial house with a variety of rooms of differing standards. Some of the rooms surround the pool. Can get lively at the weekends with bands playing at the Mayan Tavern Disco in the basement. **$$**

Chateau Caribbean
6 Marine Parade, Northside
Tel: 223 0800
Fax: 223 0900
www.chateaucaribbean.com
Another large old colonial mansion converted into a hotel right on the waterfront. It has its own seafood restaurant, which has great sea views and interesting décor. **$$**

Villa Boscardi
6043 Manatee Drive
Tel: 223 1691
www.villaboscardi.com
Private bath, breakfast included and shuttle to and from the international airport. Simple but good.

Great House Inn
13 Cork St
Tel: 223 3400
Fax: 223 3444
www.greathousebelize.com
Once a colonial private house, this has been recently converted and modernized to a six-bedroomed hotel with a recommended res-

taurant. Rooms have TV, phone, and fax lines to cater for the business traveler. **$$$**

North Front Street Guest House
124 North Front Street, North Side
Tel: 227 7595
Basic, but popular with the backpackers. **$**

Radisson Fort George
2 Marine Parade (on the north side)
Tel: 223 3333
Fax: 227 3820
www.radisson.com/belizecitybz
One of the most expensive hotels in Belize City with a longstanding reputation. Colonial and modern club wing rooms available, all with TV, fridge, and minibar; some with great views. All the facilities expected of a luxury hotel, with the emphasis on business travelers. **$$$**

Seaside Guest House
3 Prince St, South Side
Tel: 227 8339
E-mail: seasidebelize@btl.net
Budget accommodation on the South Side with sea views and large sitting area. Another favorite with seasoned travellers. **$**

Princess Hotel and Casino
Newtown Barracks
Tel: 223 2670
www.princessbelize.com
Largest hotel in the city. Includes casino, cinema, bowling alley, fitness center, pool and nightclub. On the water, but no beach. **$$$**

BELIZE DISTRICT

Belize River Lodge
Tel: 225 2002
www.belizeriverlodge.com
Full service fishing lodge with cabins, live-aboard yachts for extended trips on the flats or cayes. Skiffs for day-trips from the lodge. Excellent food, friendly atmosphere. **$$$**

Belize R Us Resort
Burrell Boom Village
Tel: 225 9028
www.belizerus.com
Family-oriented, riverside hotel with good amenities including a pool. River sports such as kayaking available. Restaurant and bar, air-conditioned rooms. Close to Baboon Sanctuary. **$$$**

Birds Eye View Lodge
Crooked Tree Village
Tel: 205 7027
E-mail: birdseyeview@btl.net
Although quite an ugly concrete
block, it is a favorite with birdwatchers owing to its great lakeside
location. Each room has an en-suite
bathroom and some are dormitory-
style with several beds. The
Belizean food and service are also
highly recommended. **$$**

Maruba Resort and Jungle Spa
40.5 Mile Post
Old Northern Highway
Maskall Village
Tel: 322 2199
Fax: 220 1049
www.maruba-spa.com
A jungle spa offering a range of
treatments from mud therapy to sea-
weed or tropical herbal body wraps.
Elegant rooms, decorated with fresh
flower petals. **$$$**

AMBERGRIS CAYE

Belize Yacht Club
PO Box 1
San Pedro
Tel: 226 2777
www.belizeyachtclub.com
Spacious villas in a central location
with air-conditioning, swimming
pool, and club restaurant. Diving
and fishing trips organized. **$$$**

Captain Morgan's Retreat
San Pedro
Tel: 226 2207
Fax: 226 2616
A boat ride out of town, peaceful
accommodation in comfortable
beachfront thatched *cabañas*;
swimming pool and restaurant
offering tasty home cooking.
Great birdwatching from the
observation tower. Fishing trips
organized. **$$$**

Caribbean Villas
San Pedro (south of the airport on
the beach)
Tel: 226 2715
Fax: 226 2885
www.caribbeanvillashotel.com
Warm and friendly owners offering
a very personalized service. They
will meet you from the airstrip in
their golf buggy and give you a

quick tour of San Pedro.
Accommodation is in spacious
suites with cooking facilities. All
suites have air conditioning and
covered verandas with sea views.
Environmentally aware owners
have built an observation tower for
birdwatchers. Free use of bikes to
cycle into town or around the
island. **$$**

Lilys
Tel: 226 2059
Small budget hotel in the center of
San Pedro, to the south of the
dock. **$**

Mata Chica
5 Miles North, San Pedro
Tel: 220 5010
Fax: 220 5012
www.matachica.com
On the beach, a boat ride out of
town, is one of the most beautiful
resorts on the island, perhaps the
whole of Belize. Well worth a trip
for dinner if you can't stay.
Creatively designed by artistic
French and Italian owners, each
cabaña has a different style. Ask
for one of the larger *cabañas* in
the second row in from beach but
still with sea view. **$$$**

Ramon's Village Reef Resort
Coconut Drive (close to the airport
and on the beach)
Tel: 226 2071
Fax: 226 2214
www.ramons.com
The largest resort on the island and
popular with packages from the US.
The two-story thatched *cabañas* are
great, but make sure you request
one near to the sea since those at
the rear can be a bit dreary. Lively
and fun, but staff seem happier at
the beginning of the season rather
than the end. **$$$**

Rubies
Tel: 226 2063
Fax: 226 2434
Close to the airport in San Pedro,
on the seafront. Small, family-run
hotel, with clean, comfortable
rooms. **$**

Victoria House Resort
Tel: 226 2067
Fax: 226 2429
www.victoria-house.com
Located out of town on a spec-
tacular beach. Renowned for its

Hotel Prices

Prices vary greatly depending on
the season. These are high-
season rates, usually charged
between November 15 and May
15 (but may vary between
hotels). Prices may drop quite
dramatically in the low season.
Categories are as follows for a
double room per night:

$$$	over US$150
$$	US$50–150
$	under US$50

super-friendly service, fine dining,
and intimate atmosphere, the
Victoria House offers a range of
accommodation in thatch-roofed
casitas, air-conditioned double
rooms and luxury villas, all in a
peaceful environment. Various
watersports are available including
snorkeling, scuba diving, windsurfing, sailing, and reef trips in
glass-bottomed boats. **$$$**

BELMOPAN AND SURROUNDS

Bull Frog Inn
23 Half Moon Ave, Belmopan
Tel: 822 2111
Fax: 822 3155
Mainstream motel-style
accommodation but a good place to
stay if you are in Belmopan – it has
the best restaurant in town. **$$**

Pooks Hill Jungle Lodge
Teakettle
Tel/fax: 820 2017
www.pookshilllodge.com
Set in pristine rainforest 5 miles
(9 km) from the village of
Teakettle on main western
highway, 5 miles (9 km) to the
west of Belmopan. Lovely rustic
thatched *cabañas* with electricity
and private bathrooms. Warm and
friendly atmosphere with good
home cooking. Owners have also
developed an iguana-breeding
program. Horseback riding and
river-tubing nearby. Best to take
the full-board option; its remote
location means there is nowhere
else to eat anyway. **$$**

Hotel Prices

Prices vary greatly depending on the season. These are high-season rates, usually charged between November 15 and May 15 (but may vary between hotels). Prices may drop quite dramatically in the low season. Categories are as follows for a double room per night:

$$$	over $150
$$	$50–150
$	under $50

Warriehead Ranch and Lodge
c/o Belize Global Travel Services, 41 Albert St, PO Box 244, Belize City
Tel: 227 5317
Fax: 227 1316
Just off the western highway after Guanacaste National Park, and a favorite with birdwatchers. An old logging camp now a working farm. Accommodation in wooden cabins with beautiful mahogany furniture and private bathrooms. 500 acres (200 hectares) of protected forest with howler monkeys, river swimming and walking trails. **$$**

CAYE CAULKER

There are no luxurious hotels on Caye Caulker and this is part of the attraction for many visitors. There are, however, many relaxing places to stay; just wander around the island and take your pick.
Tropical Paradise Hotel
PO Box 1206, Belize City
Tel: 226 0124
Fax: 226 0225
The most developed hotel on the island, but simple in comparison to those in San Pedro. **$$$**

Maxhapan Cabins
55 Pueblo Nuevo, Caye Caulker
Tel: 226 0118
E-mail: maxhapan04@hotmail.com
Not on the beach, but with a beachside feel. Air-conditioned rooms, with sitting area, fridge, and hammocks on the verandas. Terrific place to relax in privacy. **$**

COROZAL

Tony's Inn and Beach Resort
Southern end of Corozal Town
Tel: 422 2055
Fax: 422 2829
E-mail: tonys@btl.net
Comfortable seafront resort in a great location. Offers a good variety of tours throughout the Corozal district. **$$$**

Corozal Bay Inn
Almond Drive, Corozal Bay
Tel: 422 2691
E-mail: relax@corozalbayinn.com
Waterfront inn featuring cabanas and coconut trees. Poolside lounge and private pier on the bay. E-mail and internet access. **$$**

LIGHTHOUSE REEF

Lighthouse Reef Resort
Northern Two Caye, PO Box 26, Belize City
Tel: (Florida, US) 941 439 6600
E-mail: larc1@worldnet.att.net
Provides luxury *cabañas* with air-conditioning, restaurant, bar, and souvenir shop. Offers weekly fishing or diving packages. **$$$**

ST GEORGE'S CAYE

Pleasure Island Resort
PO Box 428, Belize City
Tel: 209 4020 or 610 4700
E-mail: info@stgeorgescaye pleasure.bz
Lovely accommodation in colorful Caribbean wooden *cabañas* on the seafront, with air-conditioning and private bathrooms. Main activities here are fishing, diving and snorkeling, with some good packages available. **$$–$$$**

St George's Lodge
PO Box 625, Belize City
Tel: 220 4444
Catering mainly for divers, this is a highly-rated resort with quality instructors and equipment. It provides comfortable accommodation in thatched *cabañas* on stilts over the sea. Packages are available for both divers and non-divers. **$$$**

SAN IGNACIO AND SURROUNDS

Almost everyone who comes to this region stays not in the San Ignacio township but in the lodges scattered in the surrounding countryside. Most of the hotels in San Ignacio are budget with one up-market exception:
San Ignacio Resort Hotel
Buena Vista Road
Tel: 824 2034
E-mail: sanighot@btl.net
A basic concrete building but centrally located some 10 minutes' walk up hill from the town center; it has all the facilities required to stay comfortably near the forest. Some rooms have air-conditioning and great views; it has a pool, large bar, restaurant, and a long list of different tours available. Friendly service and its restaurant is busy with the locals at lunchtimes. **$$$**

Forest Lodges

Blancaneaux Lodge
Mountain Pine Ridge
Tel: 824 3878
Nestled in the heart of Mountain Pine Ridge Reserve, an incredible lodge owned by Francis Ford Coppola. Rooms with private bathrooms and spacious luxury villas tastefully decorated with Guatemalan and Mexican artifacts. The lodge has its own stable of horses you can hire to explore the countryside. **$$$**

The Lodge at Chaa Creek
Macal River
Tel: 824 2037
www.chaacreek.com
Probably the most popular place in the San Ignacio region. Spectacular location on the banks of the Macal River. Thatched-roof and stucco cottages reflect the traditional architectural elements of this region. The bungalows are decorated with Maya tapestries and lit by kerosene lamps. There are two amazing luxury suites which do have electricity and air-conditioning (one suite has a jacuzzi too); spa. **$$$**

Maya Mountain Lodge
PO Box 174, San Ignacio
Tel: 824 2164
www.mayamountain.com
Nestled in the foothills of the

Mountain Pine Ridge about a mile (0.5 km) from San Ignacio. Simple thatched cabins with private bathrooms. Dormitories also available for groups. Owners are very keen on ecotourism and wildlife and have set up a well-equipped library and some well-marked nature trails. They offer an extensive list of tours and excursions as well as the usual horseback riding and canoeing. **$$**

Mt Pleasant Hidden Valley Inn
Mountain Pine Ridge, Belmopan
Tel: 824 3320
One of the more luxurious choices in the Mountain Pine Ridge area. Large brick bungalows with fireplaces for the chilly nights. In close proximity to all the Mountain Pine Ridge attractions – waterfalls, caves, etc. **$$$**

Windy Hill Resort, Graceland Ranch
San Ignacio
Tel: 824 2017
Fax: 824 3080
E-mail: windyhill@btl.net
Thirty or more self-contained thatched *cabañas* and cottages with air conditioning spread on an open hillside just outside San Ignacio, some with great views, all with color TV and stocked fridges, pool and fitness center. The comfort of staying in a hotel in town with the style of a jungle lodge. Tours of area attractions available. **$$$**

SOUTH WATER CAYE

Blue Marlin Lodge
PO Box 21, Dangriga
Tel: 522 2243
www.bluemarlinlodge.com
Luxury dive resort. Accommodation is in the main building, or in dome-like *cabañas* with air-conditioning. There is a real diving resort atmosphere. Certification courses available, plus other water sports like snorkeling and windsurfing. **$$$**

STANN CREEK DISTRICT

Jaguar Reef Lodge
Tel/fax: 520 7040
www.jaguarreef.com
Located on the beach south of

Hopkins village. 14 beautifully designed and authentic large thatch-roofed *cabañas*, some with air-conditioning. Closest luxury lodge to Cockscomb Jaguar Reserve. The spacious restaurant serves delicious food in a superb setting with both inside and outside dining. Plenty of activities including sea kayaking, fishing, diving, snorkeling, and cycling. Very friendly and personal service. Also has two smart spacious houses to rent nearby with maid service. **$$$**

Kitty's Place
Placencia
Tel: 523 3237
E-mail: kittys@btl.net
Beachside resort close to the airstrip, 10 minutes' walk north of the village. Variety of moderate accommodation from rooms to apartments, some with kitchenettes. Laid-back atmosphere with good local food, and bar with big screen to watch international sports events. Favorite with divers. **$$**

Luba Hati
Seine Bight
Tel: 503 3086
Fax: 523 3403
E-mail: lubahati@btl.net
Two-story hotel on the beach, just to the south of Seine Bight village, with spacious rooms which have simple yet beautiful European décor created by Italian owners. Recommended restaurant where you need to make reservations ahead if you are not staying in the hotel. **$$$**

Pelican Beach Resort
PO Box 2, Dangriga
Tel: 522 2004
Fax: 522 2570
www.pelicanbeachbelize.com
On the beach in the north of the town near the airport. Rooms vary greatly. The best (and most expensive) ones are the wooden beachfront rooms with refreshing sea breezes. Rooms in the back can be stuffy. **$$$**

Rum Point Inn
Seine Bight village
Tel: 523 3239
Fax: 523 3240
www.rumpoint.com
Each room is a huge dome-shaped

Chan Chich Lodge
Tel: 227 5634
Fax: 227 6961
www.chanchich.com
Rated as one of the oldest and most luxurious jungle resorts in Belize. Located in the far west of Orange District, within the plaza of a Classic Maya ruin, Chan Chich provides 12 beautiful *cabañas* constructed of local woods surrounded by pristine forest. Excellent resident wildlife guides. Delightful Mexican-tiled swimming pool and jacuzzi. The hardy could visit here by road, but most travel by air on either the charter flights that depart three days a week, or on a private charter.

Programme for Belize – Rio Bravo Research Station
PFB office, 1 Eyre Street
Belize City
Tel: 227 5616
Fax: 227 5635
E-mail: pfbel@btl.net
True ecotourism. Originally a research center and now converted into a lodge that welcomes tourists, and educational and special interest groups. Accommodation is in two locations and offers very comfortable well-designed dormitories or more luxurious *cabañas* with private bathrooms and hot and cold water. Prices are based on full-board and include lectures and excursions. Well-organized trails into the forest, notably to the famous Maya La Milpa site. A superb holiday experience that really contributes to conservation. You can't get here by public transport, but if you contact PFB, they may be able to make travel arrangements for you. **$$**

whitewashed building on the beach. They are spacious and tastefully decorated with Guatemalan fabrics and tiled floors. There are also super-large air-conditioned double rooms available in a two-story building at the rear. Excellent spot for divers with one of the best dive boats in Belize. **$$$**

Hotel Prices

Prices vary greatly depending on the season. These are high-season rates, usually charged between November 15 and May 15 (but may vary between hotels). Prices may drop quite dramatically in the low season.

Categories are as follows for a double room per night:

$$$	over US$150
$$	US$50–150
$	under US50

Seaspray Hotel
Placencia
Tel/fax: 523 3148
Basic accommodation by the beach, on the north side of Placencia. **$**

Turtle Inn
Placencia
Tel: 824 4912
E-mail: turtleinn@btl.net
North of Placencia village and well established on probably the best beach on the peninsula.
Picturesque thatched *cabañas* with en-suite bathrooms which offer rustic but comfortable accom-modation. There is also a two-bedroomed beach bungalow available for rent. **$$**

TOLEDO DISTRICT

Fallen Stones Butterfly Ranch and Jungle Lodge
PO Box 23, Punta Gorda
Tel/fax: 722 2167
Unusual lodge 1 mile (1.5 km) from Lubaantun and 40 minutes from Punta Gorda, with amazing views of the surrounding rainforest and Maya Mountains. Accommodation is in authentic small thatched cottages. A cozy restaurant serves local *ketchi* food plus an optional Western menu. A butterfly farm which breeds for export is on-site. **$$$**

Nature's Way Guest House
64 Front St, Punta Gorda
Tel/fax: 702 2119
Rambling house in the town, near the sea and very popular with budget travelers. The building is also home

to the office of the Toledo Ecotourism Association, a cooperative involving guesthouses in 13 outlying villages around Punta Gorda. Guests stay in the village-owned guesthouses and eat their meals with alternate families each day to fairly distribute the income derived from tourism. Villagers will also take them on guided trips into the forest and share their knowledge on the medicinal properties of the plants. **$**

TURNEFFE ATOLL

Blackbird Caye Resort
81 W Canal St, Belize City
Tel: 223 0712
www.blackbirdresort.com
Environmentally sensitive ecotourism resort popular with divers and conservationists owing to the beauty of its natural surroundings. Dolphins often swim in the protected lagoons, there are nature trails on the island, and day excursions to the Blue Hole and Half Moon Caye can be arranged. Accommodation is in simple thatched *cabañas*. Five nights or weekly packages available. **$$$**

Turneffe Island Lodge
PO Box 480, Belize City
Tel: (from USA) 1 770 534 3210
Fax: (from USA) 1 770 534 8290
www.turneffelodge.com
Situated on Caye Bokel, a private 12-acre (5-hectare) island. Recognized as one of the finest fishing locations for backcountry and flats fishing. Also a favorite with divers because it is close to some of the best dive sites, including the "Elbow." Accommodation is in 12 double rooms on the water's edge, some with air conditioning. **$$$**

Where to Eat

Many tourists eat at hotels or lodges, either out of convenience or because they are included in a package deal. Even so, try to experience some of the smaller Belizean restaurants. Since many of the resorts have a standard of international style, this is another way to meet Belizeans and appreciate their friendliness.

Restaurants are listed in alphabetical order within each area.

BELIZE CITY

Macy's Café
164 Newtown Barrack Road
Tel: 224 5020
A car ride from the center but worth the trip because this is one of the best restaurants in the city. It is fairly pricey but good value. Mainly an American/European menu with some Caribbean specialties. **$$$**

Chef Bob's Grill
Newtown Barracks
A lunchtime favorite for Creole cooking with business people, the food is cheap and plentiful. Try the fish balls if they are available. **$$**

Restaurant Prices

The following categories indicate the cost of a meal for one person without drinks:

$$$	over US$20
$$	US$10–20
$	under US$10

BELMOPAN AND CAYO

Bull Frog Inn
23 Half Moon Ave, Belmopan
Tel: 822 2111
The best restaurant in Belmopan. **$$$**

Eva's Bar and Restaurant
22 Burns Ave, San Ignacio
E-mail: evas@btl.net
This is the first and only internet café in Belize. Also doubles as a gift shop and tour desk. Eva's Bar is the place where everyone meets each other, both travelers and Belizeans. **$**

The Running W Restaurant
San Ignacio Hotel
18 Buena Vista Street, San Ignacio
Tel: 824 2034
A lively lunchtime scene. Dishes range from rice and beans to kebabs and lobster. **$$**

PLACENCIA

BJ's Restaurant
On the main road
A popular place serving local dishes, specializing in seafood and wonderful juices. **$$**

The Galley
Next to the playing fields
Serves some of the best fish in the village. Try the conch fritters. **$$**

Kitty's Place
Near the airstrip
Tel: 523 3227
Offers great set meals of seafood, chicken, and steaks. **$$**

Luba Hati
South of Seine Bight, near Placencia
Tel: 503 3086
Fine Italian dining in a peaceful atmo-sphere. Reservations required. **$$$**

Tentacles Bar
On the shore, at the southern end of the village
Serves Creole meals, steaks, pasta, and tasty seafood. Good spot to enjoy the stunning sunsets. **$$**

Turtle Inn
Near airstrip and Kitty's
Tel: 523 3244
An idyllic place to stop for seafood sandwiches. **$$**

SAN PEDRO

Nearly all the hotels listed in the "Where to Stay" section have their own restaurants. Any stroll along the beachfront or sandy streets of San Pedro takes you past an endless string of blackboards advertising the daily dining specials. In other words, the competition is high. New places

are opening (and closing) every week, mostly quite decent, but the following are known successes.

Celi's Restaurant
In the Holiday Hotel, on the seafront
Fun beach barbecues and tasty snacks. Closed on Wednesdays. **$**

El Patio
Just south of the center
Tel: 026 3500
Good food at great prices in calm surroundings. **$**

Elvi's Kitchen
Pescador Drive, opposite Martha's Hotel
Tel: 226 3898
This has been open for years and is always popular with the tourists. Serves good, mainly American food, at good prices. **$$**

Jade Garden
Coconut Drive
Tel: 226 2506
Definitely the best Chinese restaurant in town. **$**

Eating and Drinking

Belize's national dish is rice and beans; the tropical reef fish, lobster, and conch are luxurious ingredients that are regularly eaten by all Belizeans. Conch should not be eaten during the out-of-season months of July, August, and September, since it will have been illegally caught. Belize also offers an exotic range of tropical fruits, especially in the interior. Try a "sour-sap" milkshake, and then ask for whatever other unusual produce is the local favorite.

Alcohol
Belizeans are loyal to one of their national brews – either Belikin beer or sugar-cane spirit.

fiestas are held in Corozal at Carnival (the period before Lent begins, a shifting date every year), Columbus Day (October 12), and Christmas, when colorful *posadas* re-enact the Nativity scene.

The Garífuna population in southern Belize feel very strongly about their heritage and they come together with great enthusiasm from November 19 to the end of the year in celebration of the anniversary of their ancestors' arrival in Dangriga in 1823. If you are visiting Dangriga at this time you might see masked Joncunu dancers, drumming, and impromptu music concerts, or hear conch shells blown on Christmas Eve (although the main entertainment at this time is drinking and wild partying). Other Garífuna religious ceremonies are regularly performed, but rarely in view of outsiders. You could ask around but generally visitors are not welcome.

Culture

Belizeans are very culturally diverse but there is not a lot to do in the way of formal musical concerts or the like. The main way of getting to understand the Creole culture is by meeting people informally in bars, restaurants and on the beach; even such celebrations as Settlement Day every September offer little more to the outsider than a chance to get drunk with everyone else.

Spanish-speaking Belizeans in the north and west have a few more Hispanic rituals and holidays, although they are based around the church and family. Mexican-style

Nightlife

There is nothing remotely like the party scene common in other parts of the Caribbean, even in San Pedro. Nevertheless, there is no shortage of bars in any Belizean town, usually with live music (talent can be questionable!). Nearly every town has a dance or two on weekends, where you can try to do the *punta* – a difficult pelvic gyration and foot stomp. Bars and dances don't usually get going before midnight.

In **Belize City**, try the Bellevue Hotel or Princess Hotel or the Radisson. The action starts late even on weekdays.

San Pedro is packed with bars in every resort (try the Purple Parrot at Ramon's) and all around the town – just walk along the docks and pick one that seems lively. Many have different theme nights providing certain drinks for free. See the sharks being fed at the Sharks Bar. Fido's Courtyard in town and Playador offer live music a couple of times a week. On Wednesday nights Celi's has a great beach barbecue, and a local band plays on the beach. Other places to try are Tarzan's disco, Big Daddy's, and the Playador Hotel.

In the smaller places like **Placencia**, the nightlife scene is unscheduled and irregular yet something always seems to be happening somewhere; The Tentacles Bar at the tip of the peninsula is very popular. Bamboo Room in Serenity Resort has occasional live music, as does the Bockside bar in the village.

In **San Ignacio** try out the Cahal Pech Tavern near the ruins above the town – a giant hut where you can punta till dawn and listen to some of the best Belizean bands.

Shopping

Unlike Mexico and Guatemala, Belize has not developed such a strong souvenir industry, although it is improving. A couple of small operations around San Ignacio are teaching old skills such as Maya pottery and slate carving.

Many hotels near **San Ignacio** stock Guatemalan Indian handicrafts. They are of course much cheaper if bought in Guatemala.

In **Belize City**, in the upper levels of the **Central Market Place** there are a number of small souvenir shops and the **National Handicraft Center** also offers a range of souvenirs and Belizean art and music. There are also a few places in **San Pedro** worth glancing at, mainly offering a big selection of T-shirts and sunhats.

More practically, consider a bottle of **Marie Sharps Habanero Sauce**, a chilli sauce that comes in three different strengths; many tourists become addicted to the taste especially on their morning scrambled eggs. Also enjoyable is bringing back a bottle of Belizean rum or cane spirit.

Don't buy black-coral or turtle-shell souvenirs because this encourages their depletion, and it is illegal.

YUCATAN

The Place

Area: 113,000 sq km (43,630 sq miles)
Population: Mérida 1.5 million, Cancún 350,000, Campeche 190,000, Chetumal 133,000,
Capital Cities: Mérida is the capital of Yucatán State; Campeche of Campeche State; Chetumal of Quintana Roo.
Language: Spanish is the national language, but in many parts of the countryside a sort of hybrid Mayan-Spanish is spoken.
Time Zone: US Central standard time; GMT minus 6 hours.
Currency: The Mexican peso has been dropping in value against the dollar since devaluation in 1994 and currently stands around 10 pesos to the dollar. *Casas de Cambio* change money although the exchange rate is sometimes better at a bank. It is better not to keep money from one visit to the next because – as has happened before – it becomes worthless following a devaluation.
Weights & Measures: Metric. There are 2.2 pounds to the kilogram, 2.5 cm to the inch, 0.62 km to the mile.
Electricity: 110 volts, flat two-pronged plugs. Sometimes there are outages or fluctuations.
International Dialing Code: 52.

Geography

Surrounded by the sea on three sides, with the Gulf of Mexico to the west and north and the Caribbean to the east, the Yucatán Peninsula largely consists of flat, porous limestone. Here and there the surface has collapsed exposing deep sinkholes or *cenotes* which

until recent times have been the only source of water. There are few rivers and what few hills exist are mostly in the Puuc region south of Mérida. Much of the peninsula consists of undeveloped jungle, but in several regions, especially along the coast, national parks have been declared "ecospheres" where the flora and fauna and marine life are especially protected. Politically divided into three states – Yucatán in the north, Campeche to the southwest, and Quintana Roo – the population comprises people of Spanish, Spanish-Indian (*mestizo*), and Maya Indian descent.
Temperature: Average annual range is between 25.4 and 26.3°C. May is the hottest month, and January the coldest.

Economy

Tourism, fishing, and assembly plants form the background to the Yucatán economy, with the addition of offshore oilfields south of Campeche on the southwest coast. In the 19th century, fortunes were made from the harvesting of henequen – turned into sisal rope – and the industry still exists although on a much smaller scale. Petroleum products, honey, limes, hammocks, jewelry, concentrated orange juice, chewing gum, sugar cane, and fish are today's main exports.

Government

The Yucatán Peninsula is represented in the Mexican Senate by two senators each from Yucatán, Quintana Roo, and Campeche states. Each senator serves a six-

Visas & Passports

Visitors from most countries will need a tourist card as well as valid passport instead of a visa to enter Mexico. Canadian and US citizens need proof of citizenship and a tourist card which must be retained and presented on leaving the country.

year term. Yucatán is also represented in the Chamber of Deputies whose 400 members each serve for three years.

Customs

Bags are rarely searched, whether incoming or outgoing, and liquor and tobacco allowances are liberal on both sides of the border. Guns and drugs will always court trouble.

Business Hours

Banking hours are usually from 9am to any time between 3 and 7pm. Many shops close at lunchtime for a lengthy break, reopening around 4 or 5pm and remaining open until late evening. Larger shops and malls stay open all day.

Media

NEWSPAPERS

The News from Mexico City, an English-language daily, can be easily found in major resorts as can many American magazines. *Yucatán Today,* a free monthly that when turned upside down becomes *Campeche Today,* is widely available and is very informative about activities and tourist facilities in those two states. In Cancún, a special edition of the *Miami Herald* is distributed to rooms in major hotels free and there are innumerable free booklets and brochures including maps and information about the region.

RADIO & TELEVISION

There are no local TV stations in Yucatán state. There are several FM radio stations broadcasting in English, based in Cancún.

Postal Services

Post offices usually stay open all day (only mornings on Saturdays) but mail deliveries are slow and when receiving mail it is safest to have it sent to your hotel. Mail sent

Useful Numbers

Mérida

In **Mérida** and throughout the state of Yucatán can be found members of the Tourist Police (999 925 2555) wearing brown and white uniforms and patrolling on foot or motorcycles. They are there to help.

Police 999 925 2034
US Consul 999 925 5011
British Consul 998 881 0100
French Consul 999 925 2886

Cancún

Police 060
Highway Police 998 884 1107
Red Cross 998 884 1616
American Express 998 884 1999
US Consul 998 883 0272
Canadian Consul 998 883 3360
German Consul 998 883 5333
British Consul 998 881 0100

Campeche

Police 981 816 3635/816 1640
Red Cross 981 815 2411

to post offices to be picked up (within 10 days) should be addressed to Lista de Correos. Cards and letters to the US cost 2 pesos, to Europe 3 pesos.

Telecommunications

Equip yourself with a phone card to use **Ladatel** pay phones throughout the country and beware of telephones – especially in resort towns – promoting their access to worldwide destinations. Often they will charge exorbitant rates (as do many hotels, by adding a service surcharge to the actual cost). In most towns there is a an office labeled *Caseta de Larga Distancia* which is the best place to make such calls. Within Mexico prefix the area code and number with 01; for the US and Canada use the prefix 00-1; for the rest of the world 00 followed by the country code. Internet cafés are common throughout Mexico.

Health

A sudden change of diet combined with ubiquitous strains of bacteria cause many upset stomachs and the infamous Montezuma's Revenge, but this can be avoided by frequent hand-washing, and avoidance of tapwater and such potentially hazardous dishes as salads (except in top-class hotels and restaurants). An emergency substitute for bottled water is a small bottle of the concentrated

water-purifying chemical sold for about one dollar in most supermarkets to treat vegetables. There are good hospitals in Mérida (999 926 2111); Progreso (969 935 0951); and Cancún (998 884 6133).

Tourist Offices

The **State of Yucatán** has a tourist office in downtown **Mérida** at Centro de Convenciones, Calle 60, tel: 999 930 3760. In **Campeche,** the office is on Av Ruiz Cortinez in the Plaza Moch Cuoch (tel: 981 811 9229; fax: 981 816 6767). For **Cancún** tourist office, tel: 988 884 8073. **Quintana Roo** state tourist office is at Av Tulum 22 (tel: 998 881 9000). For **Chetumal** tourist office, tel: 983 835 0860, fax: 25073. **San Cristóbal de Las Casas** (tel: 967-678 6570).

Getting Around

FROM THE AIRPORT

From Mérida airport you can walk out onto the access road and flag down a cheaper taxi than in the airport itself. 1.5 km (1 mile) away, the 79 bus marked Aviación operates along the highway.

BY AIR

Mérida's International Airport is supplemented by airstrips at Chable (Highway 188, south of Ciudad del

Carmen), Chichén Itzá, and El Cuyo (near Río Lagartos).

Cancún's International Airport is 16km (10 miles) south of the resort, with minibus connections to the adjacent domestic terminal. Colectivo taxis (shared) will take you to the center for about US$12 or private taxi, US$25 approximately.

BY BUS

Click Mexicana (tel: 999 942 1860; www.clickmx.com) connects most of the airports in the peninsula including Mérida, Chichén Itzá, Cancún, Cozumel, Playa del Carmen, and Chetumal and also operates flights to Mexico City, Veracruz, Oaxaca, and Cuba.

   Terminal CAME (Calle 70, 555, tel: 999 924 8391) is the main long-distance 1st class bus terminal in Mérida and **ADO** the biggest of the national bus companies with routes to Mexico City via Campeche and Villahermosa, and also to Cancún, Puebla, Mérida, and Playa del Carmen.

BY RAIL

A 2nd-class passenger service, **Expreso Maya** (tel: 999 944 9393; www.expresomaya.com), operates between Mérida, Izamal, and Valladolid, and also runs to Progreso, Chichen Itzá, Campeche, Palenque, and Uxmal, but it is neither convenient nor particularly pleasant, and is therefore not recommended to anyone but the hardiest train buffs.

CAR RENTAL

It is often cheaper to make arrangements for your car rental from one of the big companies (Avis is favored) before you leave the US. In **Mérida**, Avis (Calle 60, 498, tel: 999 928 0045); Budget (Calle 60, 491, tel: 999 928 6769); Dollar (Calle 60, 491, tel: 999 928

Public Holidays & Festivals

Regular Mexican holidays are celebrated on New Year's Day, Constitution Day (February 5), Day of the Flag (February 24), Benito Juarez birthday (March 21), Good Friday and Easter Sunday (March/April), East, Labor Day (May 1), Victory Day (May 5), Independence Day (September 16) Día de la Raza (October 12), Day of the Dead (November 2), Revolution Day (November 20), Day of Our Lady of Guadelupe (December 12), and Christmas. Yucatán festivals include the following:
January Tizimín: Los Reyes Magos festival.
February Cozumel: Week-long Lenten celebration with parades, floats and group dance contest

6759); Thrift (Calle 60, 446, tel: 999 923 2493); and National (Calle 60, 486, tel: 992 32493) are among the possibilities. Most of these have desks at the airport.

Specialist Attractions & Tours

Campeche
Viajes Campeche (Av. Ruiz Cortines, 108, tel: 981 816 5233; e-mail: viajescampeche@hotmail.com) and **Viajes Programados** (Calle 59 and Av. 16 de Septiembre, tel: 981 811 1010; www.viajesprogramados.com) are centrally located travel agencies. Tours to Edzná leave daily at 9am and 2pm from the Puerta de Tierra.

Caribbean Coast
Akumal Dive Center, Carr. Cancún-Tulum, km 104 (tel: 984 875 9025; www.akumaldivecenter.com). Training in cave diving, with exemplary safety record.
Aquatech Dive Center, Villas De Rosa Resort, PO Box 48, Akumal (tel/fax: 984 875 9020/1; www.cenotes.com). Cave diving center with courses for the unqualified.

Tzucacab and Chicxulub: La Candelaria festival.
April Ticul: Fiesta del Pascua Progeso La Ascension.
May Cozumel: Cedral Fair with cattle exhibitions, races, rides, bullfights.
June Cozumel: Marine Day fishing tournament. San Pedro y San Pablo: Fair, crafts, shows.
August Oxkutzcab: Traditional fiesta. San Felipe: Santo Domingo de Guzmán.
September Cozumel: Fiestas de San Miguel Arcangel. Honoring the island's patron saint. Cozumel Marathon. Mérida: Cristo de las Ampollas (until October).
October Telchac Puerto: San Francisco de Asis.
November Tekax: San Diego fiesta.

Intermar Cancun (IMC), Av Tulum 225 (tel: 998 881 0000; fax: 998 881 0001; www.travel2mexico.com) operates tours for groups and individuals.
Multiviajes, Tulipanes 22, tel: 998 884 1468. General day-trip operator, including tours of Chichén Itzá, Tulum, Isla Mujeres, and a jungle tour.

Chetumal
Tours to archeological sites can be arranged by **Bacalar Tours** (Av. Alvaro Obregón, 167A, tel: 983 832 3875).

Chiapas
Explora, 1 de Marzo, San Cristóbal de Las Casas (tel: 967 678 4295; www.ecochiapas) offers tours to remote regions of Chiapas, while **Viajes Chincultik**, Real de Guadalupe 34 (tel: 967 678 0957) run guided tours of Maya villages.

Mérida
Calesas (horse-drawn buggies) can be hired downtown; arrange the route and price with the driver before setting out. Be wary of freelance amateur guides, and agree the price before starting off. Buses (tel: 999 927 6119) leave at

10am, 1pm, 4pm, and 7pm on two-hour city bus tours of Mérida from the corner of Calles 55 and 60. The company also operates evening tours to the Sound and Light show at Uxmal.

Iluminado Tours , Calle 66, 588A (tel: 999 900 1414; www.iluminado tours.com) offers a variety of tours that range from day trips to Uxmal, Dzibilchaltun and Izamal, to 7- to 10-day tours of the Yucatán.

Mayaland Tours (tel: 998 887 2450; www.mayaland.com) operates daily tours to Chichén Itzá, Balancanche, Uxmal, the Puuc Route, Loltún, Izamal, Valladolid, Campeche, Cancún, and the Caribbean coast. The Mayaland company (fax: 992 50087) also operates resorts at Chichén Itzá, Uxmal, and Mérida*.

On Wednesday evenings, **Rancho Tierra Bonita** (tel: 999 941 0275; fax: 999 941 0287), near the Convention Center, stages a *charro* (cowboy) show with food, mariachis, dancing, and fireworks.

Valladolid

Travel agencies include: **Contoy**, Av Rueda Medina, (tel: 998 877 1367; www.contoyisland.com).

Where to Stay

• Hurricane Wilma struck the Yucatán Peninsula in 2005, causing damage to hotels in Cancun, Cozumel, Isla Mujeres and Puerto Morelos. Recovery was swift and most were open in time for the 2005/06 winter season.

AKUMAL

Hotel Akumal Centre
Tel: 984 875 9010/12
www.hotelakumalcaribe.com
Beachfront hotel and villas; guest rooms have a fan or air-conditioning. Pool, mini-market and Lol-Há restaurant on property. **$$**

Que Onda
Caleta Yalku
Tel/fax: 984 875 9101/2
www.queondaakumal.com
Italian restaurant with seven charming rooms. Located beside lagoon. **$$–$$$**

Vista del Mar
Half Moon Bay, central
Tel: 984 875 9060
www.akumalinfo.com
Rooms have air conditioning and TV; pool. **$$–$$$**

CAMPECHE

Hotel Alhambra
Av Resurgimiento 85
Tel: 981 816 2323/6323
South of town. Air-conditioned rooms, lobby bar, ocean views, restaurant open late. **$–$$**

Hotel America
Calle 10, 252
Tel: 981 816 4588/4567
Fax: 981 811 0056
www.hotelamericacampeche.com
All rooms have either air-conditioning or a fan and are situated around a central patio. **$**

Baluartes
Av 16 de Septiembre 128
Tel: 981 816 3911
Fax: 981 816 2410
E-mail: baluartes@prodigy.net.mx
Facing the sea. All amenities. **$$$**

Chicanná Eco Village Resort
Tel: 981 811 9192
Near the picturesque site of Chicanná where five structures sit around a central plaza is this luxurious but somewhat sterile bungalow complex with pool, restaurant but no TV or telephones. Owned by the same people who own Hotel Del Mar (see below). **$$–$$$**

Colonial Hotel
Calle 14, 122
Tel: 981 816 2222
As old as it sounds; comfortable and stylish. **$$**

Hotel Del Mar
Av Ruiz Cortines 51
Tel: 981 811 9192
Fax: 981 811 1618
Facing the sea. Best in town. Restaurant. **$$$**

Hotels Prices

The following categories are for two people sharing a double room. Hotel rates, especially in resort areas, rise about 10 or 15 percent in the peak season.

$$$	over US$100
$$	US$55–100
$	under US$55

CANCUN (DOWNTOWN)

Hotel Antillano
Av. Tulúm y Claveles SM22
Tel: 998 884 1132
Fax: 998 884 1878
www.hotelantillano.com
Air-conditioned rooms, pool, lobby bar, travel agency. **$–$$**

Best Western Plaza Caribe
Corner of Avs Tulum and Uxmal
Tel: 988 884 1377
Fax: 988 884 6352
A Best Western outpost with pool, restaurant, nightclub. **$$**

Caoba Bonampak
Av Bonampak 225
Tel: 998 884 0280
Property has a laundry; big pool. **$**

Carrillo's
Claveles 35
Tel: 998 884 1227
Fax: 998 884 2371
Cosily tucked away with pool, restaurant, air-conditioned rooms. **$**

Colonial Hotel
Tulipanes 22
Tel: 998 884 1535
Fax: 998 884 1535
Painted sandy brown, colonial-style architecture, rooms around an open patio. **$**

Hotel Kin Mayab
Av Tulum 75
Tel: 998 884 2999
Fax: 998 884 3162
Rooms with air-conditioning or fan, lobby garden and small pool, restaurant, parking. **$**

Maria de Lourdes
Av Yaxchilán 80
Tel: 998 884 1721/4744
Fax: 998 884 1242
www.hotelmariadelourdes.com
Air-conditioning, pool, laundromat, restaurant. **$**

Diving & Snorkeling

At **Cancún,** the generally calm waters of the hotel beaches are great for beginners and children to learn basic snorkel techniques and all have lifeguards, for your peace of mind. Equipment can be rented at the marinas and some hotels provide it free of charge. **Aqua World** (Blvd Kukulcan 15.2, tel: 998 848 8327; www.aquaworld.com.mx) has complete facilities.

The city's many marinas offer snorkeling and scuba excursions: for the more advanced, Belize's barrier reef, among the longest in the world, begins (or ends) near the Club Med at Punta Nizuc.

Since all beaches are open to the public in Cancún, you could head there to enjoy the sights in the clear shallow water. **Cozumel** is the best scenic diving spot on the peninsula and there's another Aqua World here *(for contact details, see above).* **Isla Mujeres** is a nearby diving destination – check with **Scuba Cancún,** Blvd. Kulkulcan Km. 5 (tel: 998 849 7508; www.scubacancun.com. mx), which offers certification courses and has the only decompression chamber in the city. The magazine *Dive Mexico* gives an overview of diving sites along the Caribbean coast in stunning photos.

Hotel Plaza Kokai
Av Uxmal 26
Tel: 998 884 3218
Fax: 998 884 4335
www.hotelkokai.com
Pool, roof garden and a restaurant on site. **$$**

CANCUN (HOTEL STRIP)

Most of the hotels along Cancún's famous beach strip are grand modern resorts, all of which attempt to outdo each other in sheer monumental fantasy. They cater predominantly for the package tour sector, with all-inclusive amenities, saving guests the trek to the main town, with its cheaper offerings.

Club Med
Punta Nizuc
Tel: 998 881 8200
Fax: 998 881 8280
www.clubmed.com
Adult-only hotel tucked away at the extreme southern end of the island with good view of all the others. All Club Med amenities. **$$$**

Condominios Carisa y Palma
Blvd Kukulcan Km. 9.5
Tel: 998 883 0287
Fax: 998 883 0932
www.carisaypalma.com
On the beach. Tennis, gym/sauna, snack bar, supermarket, pool.
$$–$$$

Dreams Cancún Resort and Spa
Km. 9 at Punta Cancún
Tel: 998 848 7000
Fax: 998 848 7009
www.dreamsresorts.com/cancun
Sleek 20th-century pyramid. On the beach with pool, tennis courts, ocean view. **$$$**

Hotelur Beach Paradise
Blvd Kukulcan Km. 19.5
Tel: 998 885 2222
Fax: 998 885 2526
Ocean-side all-inclusive hotel on nice beach. **$$–$$$**

Gran Melía Cancún
Blvd Kukulcam, km 16.5
Tel: 998 881 1100
Fax: 998 881 2740
www.granmeliacancun.solmelia.com
Large luxury coastal resort, but not too far from the center of town and the international airport. Comfy rooms and good hotel amenities.
$$$

Imperial Las Perlas Cancún
Blvd Kukulcan 2.5
Tel: 998 883 0070
Fax: 998 849 4269
www.hotelimperialcancun.com
On ocean beach, nearest to downtown. Pool, restaurant. **$$**

Krystal Cancún
Blvd Kukulcan Km. 8.5
tel: 998 848 9800
E-mail: nhcancun@nh-hoteles.com
Ocean side. Pool, four restaurants, five bars, tennis, gym, disco. **$$$**

Melía Turquesa
Blvd Kukulcan Km. 12
Tel: 998 881 2500
Fax: 998 881 2501
e-mail: melia.turquesa@solmelia.com
All-inclusive, all suite hotel. Ocean or lagoon view rooms, restaurants with music, pool, tennis courts. **$$$**

The Ritz Carlton
Blvd Kukulcan Km. 13.5
Tel: 998 881 0808
Fax: 998 881 0815
www.ritzcarlton.com
Classier than most, on its own stretch of pristine beach. It offers every luxury including 120 tequila varieties in the bar. **$$$**

Solymar
Blvd Kukulcan Km. 18.7
Tel: 998 885 1811
Fax: 998 885 1689
www.solymarcancun.com
Ocean beach, two pools, two restaurants. **$$–$$$**

CELESTUN

Eco Paraíso Xixim
Km 9. Camino Viejo a Sisal
Tel: 988 916 2100/2060
www.ecoparaiso.com
Cabañas on the seafront, hammocks on the porch; pool. **$$$**

CHAMPOTON

Hotel Geminis
Calle 30, 10
Tel: 982 828 0008
A pleasant oasis in an otherwise unappealing town. Air-conditioned rooms, small pool. **$**

CHETUMAL

Hotel Caribe Princess
Obregón 168
Tel: 983 832 0520
Gardens, rooms with air conditioning. **$$$**

Hotel Casa Blanca
Av Alvaro Obregón, 312
Tel: 983 832 1248
www.casablancachetumal.com
Air-conditioning or fan, parking, laundromat. **$**

Hotel El Dorado
5 de Mayo, 42
Tel: 983 832 0315
Rooms with fan or air-conditioning.
Piano bar. **$$**

Holiday Inn
Av Héroes 171
Tel: 983 835 0400
Fax: 983 835 0429
www.ichotelsgroup.com
Situated opposite the main museum,
Maya gardens, pool, restaurant. **$$$**

Hotel Los Cocos
Av Héroes 134
Tel: 983 832 0544
Fax: 983 832 0920
www.hotelloscocos.com.mx
Hotel near the museums, with a
pool and patio restaurant. **$$**

Hotel Marlon
Av Juárez 87
Tel: 983 832 9411/9522
Bright, central, lobby bar, pool,
adjoining restaurant. **$**

Hotel El Marquez
Av Lázaro Cárdenas 121
Tel: 983 832 2955/2888/2998
Fax: 983 832 2866
www.elmarquezhotel.com
Clean, comfortable. Restaurant. **$**

CHIAPAS

San Cristóbal de Las Casas
Casa Dr Felipe Flores
JF Flores 36
Tel: 967-678 3996
www.felipeflores.com
Classy and atmospheric B&B in a
converted colonial mansion, with
excellent service. **$$$**

El Paraíso
5 de Febrero 19
Tel: 967-678 0085
www.sancristobal.podernet.com.mx
Large sumptuous rooms around a
colonial-style courtyard. Good
restaurant too. **$$**

Palenque
Hotel Maya Tulipanes
Cañada 6
Tel: 916-345 0201
www.mayatulipanes.com.mx
Spacious rooms, all with air
conditioning and stylish modern
bathrooms. Pool and restaurant on
the property. **$$**

CHICHEN ITZA

Hacienda Chichén
Mérida
Tel: 999 924 2150
Fax: 999 924 5011
www.haciendachichen.com
Colonial hacienda favored by the
early explorers and owned by
Edward Thompson. 16th-century
style, modern comforts including
restaurant, pool. **$$$**

Hotel Mayaland
Mérida
Tel: 992 50621
Next to the ruins. Three pools,
restaurants, gift shop and room air
conditioning. **$$$**

COZUMEL

Casa del Mar
Costera Sur Km. 4
Tel: 987 872 1900
Fax: 987 872 1855
www.casadelmarcozumel.com
Pool, hot tub, tennis, restaurant.
$$–$$$

Casa Mexicana
Av Rafael E. Melgar 457
Tel: 987 872 9090
Fax: 987 872 9073
www.casamexicanacozumel.com
Refurbished rooms and swimming
pool. Breakfast included in room
rate. **$$$**

Coral Princess
Carr. Costera Norte Km. 2.5
Tel: 987 872 3200
Fax: 987 872 2800
www.coralprincess.com
Four restaurants and bars, dive
store, two pools. **$$$**

Days Inn Villa del Rey
Av 11 Sur, 460
Tel: 987 872 1600
Fax: 987 872 1692
www.daysinn.com
Pool in tropical garden, breakfast
restaurant. **$$**

Hotel Cozumel
Costera Sur Km. 1.7
Tel: 987 872 2900/2855
Fax: 987 872 2154/2976
www.hotelcozumel.us
1.5 km (1 mile) from downtown
near scuba area. Beach club,
tennis, large pool. **$$–$$$**

Hotel Flamingo
Calle 6, 81
Tel/fax: 987 872 1264
www.hotelflamingo.com
Small, clean and family-run hotel. **$$**

FELIPE CARILLO PUERTO

El Faisan y El Venado
Two blocks northeast of main square
Tel: 983 834 0702
Red building with green trim; the best
in this grubby town. Some rooms with
air-conditioning. Restaurant. **$**

ISLA HOLBOX

Villas Delfines
On the beach
Tel/Fax: 984 875 2196/7
E-mail: delfines@holbox.com
Ten comfortable *cabañas*, restaurant
bar; place to get away from it all. **$$**

ISLA MUJERES

Hotel Cabañas Maria del Mar
Av Carlos Lazo
Tel: 998 887 0179
Fax: 998 877 0213
Air-conditioned hotel rooms or
bungalows, pool, restaurant. **$$**

Hotel María José
Av Madero 21
Tel: 998 877 0130
Rooms with fan or air-conditioning,
minisuper, snack bar, cycle rental. **$**

Marina Isla Mujeres
Laguna Mar, 3 km (2 miles) south
of town
Tel/fax: 998 877 0594
A tranquil place, with a restaurant,
palapa bar, pool. **$$**

Hotels Prices

The following categories are for
two people sharing a double
room. Hotel rates, especially in
resort areas, rise about 10 or 15
percent in the peak season.

$$$	over US$100
$$	US$55–100
$	under US$55

Pocná Youth Hostel
Matamoros 15
Tel: 998 877 0090
Dormitory rooms, cafeteria. Internet
access. **$**

Posada del Mar
Av Rueda Medina, 15
Tel: 998 877 0044
Fax: 998 877 0266
www.posadadelmar.com
Seafront hotel near ferry with pool,
palapa bar. **$$**

Hotel Prices

The following categories are for
two people sharing a double
room. Hotel rates, especially in
resort areas, rise about 10 or 15
percent in the peak season.

$$$	over US$100
$$	US$55–100
$	under US$55

MERIDA

Casa de Balam
PO Box 988, Mérida CP 9700
Tel: 999 924 2150; 1-800 624
8451 (US)
Fax: 999 924 5011
www.hotelcasadelbalam.com
Delightful former home of the
Barbachano family who pioneered
Yucatán tourism. Lovely patio
garden, colonial antiques, pool,
restaurant. **$$$**

Casa Mexilio
Corner of Calles 68 and 59, 495
Tel/Fax: 999 928 2505
www.casamexilio.com
Beautifully decorated 10-room B&B.
Sundecks, pool, tropical garden. **$$$**

Gran Hotel
Calle 60, 496
Tel: 999 924 7730/923 6963
Fax: 999 924 7622
www.granhotelmerida.com.mx
19th-century landmark. Restaurant,
bar, jacuzzi, pizzeria. **$$**

Hacienda Katanchel
Km. 26, Mérida–Cancún
Tel: 999 923 4020
Fax: 999 923 4000
www.haciendakatanchel.com
This one-time henequen plantation
has been converted into a gorgeous

hotel by Seville-born architect
Anabel González. The spacious
bungalows are situated in glorious
tropical grounds to which you and
your bags are delivered by a mule-
drawn train. Pool; games room. **$$$**

Hacienda Petac
Tel: 999 911 2600; 1-800 225
4255 (US)
www.haciendapetac.com
Luxurious accommodation on an
80-acre (32-hectare) estate near
Merida. The entire hacienda is
available for rent by private parties.
$$$

Hacienda Santa Cruz
Tel: 999 910 4549
www.haciendasantacruz.com
Classy B&B owned by an American
ex-pat, located 20 minutes outside
Mérida. **$$$**

Hacienda Santa Rosa
Km. 129 Carretera Merida
Campeche
Tel: 999 910 4852
Fax: 999 923 7963
www.haciendasmexico.com
Beautifully restored accommodation
west of Mérida, operated by
Starwood Hotels as part of the
chain's Luxury Collection. **$$$**

Hacienda Temozón
Km. 182 Carretera Merida-Uxmal
Temozon Sur
Tel: 999 923 8089
Fax: 999 923 7963
www.haciendasmexico.com
Another restored Starwood hotel on
the way to Uxmal. Luxurious rooms,
some with terrace. Spa facilities,
pool and restaurant. **$$$**

Hacienda Teya
Km. 12.5, Mérida–Cancún
Tel: 999 928 5000
17th-century henequen plantation.
Pool. Good restaurant. **$$$**

Hotel Ambassador
Calle 59, 546
Tel: 999 924 2100
Fax: 999 924 2701
www.ambassadormerida.com
Restaurant bar, pool in garden,
babysitting available. **$$**

Hotel Aragón
Calle 57, 474
Tel: 999 924 0242
Fax: 999 924 1122
www.hotelaragon.com
Friendly, inexpensive B&B. **$**

Hotel Colón
Calle 62, 483
Tel: 999 923 4355/4508
Fax: 999 924 4919
www.hotelcolonmerida.com
Restaurant, bar, pool, travel agency.
$$

Hotel El Conquistador
Paseo de Montejo 458
Tel: 999 926 9199
Fax: 999 926 2155
Gourmet restaurant, pool with
panoramic view, cafeteria, lobby
bar. **$$$**

Hotel Los Aluxes
Corner of Calles 60, 444 and 49
Tel: 999 924 2199
Fax: 999 923 3858
www.aluxes.com.mx
A businessman's favorite, midway
between central plaza and Paseo de
Montejo. Pool, huge coffee shop.
$$$

Hotel Maya Yucatán
Calle 58, 483
Tel: 999 923 5395
Fax: 999 923 4642
www.hotelmayayucatan.com.mx
Pool, restaurant, lobby bar, travel
agency. **$$**

Hotel Misión Mérida
Calle 60, 491
Tel: 999 923 9500
Fax: 999 923 7665
www.hotelesmision.com
Stylish colonial architecture in
midtown. Pool, lobby bar,
restaurant. **$$$**

Hotel Reforma
Calle 59, 508
Tel: 999 924 7922
Two stories around central patio.
Pool, adjoining pizzeria. **$**

Hotel Santa Lucia
Calle 55, 608
Tel: 999 928 2672/2662
Fax: 999 924 6233/6375
www.hotelsantalucia.com.mx
Pleasant rooms around plant-filled
patio. Pool, cafeteria. **$**

Hotel Trinidad
Calle 62, 464
Tel: 999 923 2033
www.hotelestrinidad.com
Sunny garden patio, access to
nearby pool belonging to its sister
hotel, the Trinidad Galeria, book
exchange. **$**

PISTE

Hotel Chichén Itzá
Calle 15-A, 45
Tel: 985 851 0022
Airy lobby, big pool, restaurant. **$**
Pirámide Inn
Calle 15
Tel: 985 851 0115
Fax: 985 851 0114
www.piramideinn.com
Air-conditioned rooms, tropical
garden, pool, and a "photo tour" on
mezzanine floor where photos of
Maya sites as early as the 19th
century line the walls. Adjoins bus
station which has daily buses both
east and west. **$**

PROGRESO

The cheapest hotels are inland:
Hotel Progreso
Calle 29, 142
Tel: 969 935 0039
TV and fans or air-conditioning in
rooms. **$**

On the Malecón are:
Real de Mar
Calle 19, 144
Tel: 969 935 0798
Upstairs rooms with breezy balcony,
garden restaurant. **$**
Reef Yucatán
Telchac Puerto
Tel: 999 941 9494
www.reefyucatan.com
Awesome lobby, vast airy buffet
restaurant, and huge swimming
pool. Rates include room, meals
and all activities. **$$**
Tropical Suites
Malecón 143
Tel: 969 935 1263
Kitchenettes with refrigerator,
cooking facilities. **$**

PLAYA DEL CARMEN

Hotel Alhambra
Corner of Calle 8 and Av 5
Tel: 984 873 0735
Fax: 984 873 0699
Big white Moorish building. Rooms
with or without balcony, air-
conditioning. **$$**

Casa de Gopala
Corner of Calle 2 and Av 10
Tel/fax: 984 873 0054
Garden, pool, bar. **$$**
Hotel Jungla Caribe
Corner of Calle 8 and Av 5
Tel/fax: 984 873 0650
www.jungla-caribe.com
Small pool, bar in jungly garden.
Popular Jaguar restaurant overlooks
garden. **$$**
Hotel Mimi del Mar
Calle 4
Tel: 984 873 3187
www.mimidelmar.com
Beachfront rooms with balcony, air-
conditioning or fan, kitchenettes.
$$–$$$
Mom's Hotel
Corner of Calle 4 and Av 30
Tel/Fax: 984 873 0315
www.momshotel.com
Air-conditioned rooms, library,
restaurant, pool, internet access. **$**
Pelicano Inn
Corner of Calle 8 and Av 5
Tel: 984 873 0097
At the beach. Restaurant, bar,
breakfast included. **$$–$$$**
Hotel Prisma Caribe
Corner of Calle 28 and Av 10
www.prisma-caribe.com
Near beach. Air-conditioning,
hammocks, garden. **$–$$**
Hotel Rosa Mirador
Corner of Beachfront and Av 12
Tel: 984 873 0750
Fax: 984 873 0758
e-mail: rosamirador@hotmail.com
Rooms with fan. Garden, laundry. **$**
Hotel Suites Las Quintas
Corner of Avs Juarez and 30
Tel: 984 873 0120
Kitchen suites, pool. **$**
Treetops Hotel
Corner of Calle 8 and Av 10
Tel: 984 873 1495
Fax: 984 873 0351
www.treetopshotel.com
Attractive rooms with air
conditioning or fan. Pool and
swim-up bar, restaurant. **$$–$$$**
The Turquoise Reef Group
(US tel: 800 538 6802)
www.mexicoholiday.com
Operates several attractive
properties on the coast near to
Playa del Carmen. Rates range from
$47 to $290 for a double and they

include several properties – from
several in Playa del Carmen itself
($80 double upwards), **Posada del
Captain Lafitte** (on private beach
with pool), and **Shangri La Caribe**
(thatched-roof cabins on the beach
north of town with patio hammocks),
both north of Playa del Carmen;
Casa Jacques, luxurious residential
apartments in Playacar; **KaiLuum,** a
tent village resort on the beach 70
km (45 miles) south of Cancún;
Zamas in nearby Tulum; and the
delightfully remote **Costa de Cocos**
in Xcalak, at the southern tip of Sian
Ka'an peninsula. Here, fishing trips
as well as diving and snorkeling can
be arranged, and comfortable
rooms begin at $67 per person.

PUERTO MORELOS

Acamaya Reef
Off Cancún road, north of town
Tel/fax: 998 871 0132
www.acamayareef.com
RV park and campsite with
bungalows. **$$**
Hotel Ojo de Agua
By the beach
Tel: 998 871 0027
Fax: 998 871 0202
Rooms with kitchen or air-
conditioning. Restaurant, pool, bar.
$$
Posada Amor
Near town square and bus station.
Tel: 998 871 0033
Fax: 998 871 0178
Rooms with fans, restaurant, bar. **$**

RIO LAGARTOS

Genesis Retreat
Ek Balam
Tel: 985 852 7980
www.genesisretreat.com
An eco-hotel with cabañas, a
natural swimming pool, and locally
organized tours of the ruins and
nearby Maya village. **$**

Hotel Prices

The following categories are for two people sharing a double room. Hotel rates, especially in resort areas, rise about 10 or 15 percent in the peak season.

$$$ over US$100
$$ US$55–100
$ under US$55

TULUM

Hotel Acuario
Outside exit to site
Tel: 984 871 2195
Fax: 984 871 2194
Shabby but clean. Pool's overhead shower provides waterfall effect. Rooms with fan and TV. Adjoining restaurant. **$$**

Casa del Corazón, Casa Playa Maya and **Casa Solimán**
www.locogringo.com
Private houses to rent in the coastal Bahías de Punta Solimán between Xel-Há and Tulum.

Las Ranitas
Km. 9, Carr. Tulum-Boca Paila
Tel/Fax: 984 877 8554
www.lasranitas.com
Eco-friendly beachfront rooms with balcony, pool, and restaurant. **$$$**

Tita Tulum
Km. 8 Carr. Tulum-Boca Paila
Tel: 984 877 8513
Fax: 984 871 2033
www.titatulum.com
Beachfront *cabañas* and a restaurant. **$$**

UXMAL

Hacienda Uxmal
Near the ruins
Tel: 998 887 2450
www.mayaland.com
Where the early archeologists were based. Tiled verandas with rocking chairs, pool, restaurant. **$$$**

The Lodge at Uxmal
Tel: 998 887 2450
www.mayaland.com
Forty rooms at entrance to ruins, furnished by local craftsmen. Two pools, tennis, restaurants. **$$$**

Hotel Misión Uxmal
Tel: 997 976 2022/2000/2024
Fax: 997 976 2023
www.hotelesmision.com.mx
Two km (1 mile) north of turnoff to ruins, to which offers transport. Pool, restaurant. **$$$**

Villas Arqueologica Uxmal
Tel: 997 974 6020
Fax: 997 976 2040
www.clubmedvillas.com
Close to the ruins, run by Club Med. Pool, restaurant. **$$$**

VALLADOLID

Maria de la Luz
Calle 42, 193
Tel: 985 856 1181
Fax: 985 856 2071
On the main plaza. Has a pleasant terrace restaurant. Pool. **$$**

Mesón del Marqués
Calle 39, 203
Tel: 985 856 3042/2073
Fax: 985 856 2280
www.mesondelmarques.com
Garden with fountain, pool in tropical garden, restaurant. **$$–$$$**

Hotel Zaci
Calle 44, 192
Tel: 985 856 2167
Comfortable hotel with a leafy patio and a small pool. **$$**

Where to Eat

AKUMAL

La Buena Vida
Half Moon Bay
Restaurant and bar with pool. **$$**

La Cueva del Pescador
Akumal Bay
Tel: 984 875 9205
Serves seafood. **$$**

Turtle Bay Bakery
Near the main square
Popular breakfast spot. **$**

CAMPECHE

La Almena
In Hotel Baluartes, seafront
Tel: 981 816 3911
Elegant dining, international cuisine. **$$$**

Casa Vieja
Calle 10, 319
Tel: 981 811 8016/1311
Balcony overlooks Zócalo. Limited menu, minimal prices but great location. **$**

Cactus Steak House
Av Ruiz Cortinez at the Malecón
Tel: 981 811 1453
Seafood and chicken. **$$**

La Pigua
Av. Miguel Alemán, 179A
Tel: 981 811 3365
Seafood; specialties include coconut and mango shrimp. **$**

CANCUN

Blue Bayou
Hyatt Cancún Caribe, Km. 11
Tel: 998 848 7800
Piquant crawfish and other Cajun favorites. Live jazz. Dancing. **$$$**

Captain's Cove
Paseo Kukulcan Km. 16.5
Tel: 988 50016
Palapa-covered open huts over the water. Bargain breakfasts. **$$**

Casa Rolandi
Plaza Caracol, Km. 8.5
Tel: 998 883 2557
www.rolandi.com
Popular local Italian place. Pasta, seafood. **$$**

The Club Grill
Ritz Carlton Hotel
Tel: 998 881 0808
Cuban cigars, brandy, Baccarat crystal, seamless service. **$$$**

La Destilería
Blvd Kukulcan Km. 12.6
Tel: 998 885 1086/7
www.ladestileriacancun.com
International cuisine with Mexican accent. Tequila murals and store selling the best brands. **$$$**

La Habichuela
Margaritas 25 downtown
Tel: 998 884 3158
www.lahabichuela.com
Seafood, Mexican cuisine in attractive Maya setting. **$$–$$$**

Iguana Wana
Plaza Caracol
Tel: 998 883 0829
Distinctive decor. Great seafood, such as coconut shrimp in mango sauce. Good breakfast buffet. **$$**

Lorenzillo's
Paseo Kukulcan Km. 10.5
Tel: 998 883 1254/3073
Seafood, lobster, and prime beef
over the water and under the
largest *palapa* roof in the area. **$$$**

Mango Tango
Paseo Kukulcan Km. 14.2
Tel: 998 885 0303
Pasta, seafood, poultry, and beef
dishes in tropical surroundings. **$$$**

Matilda
Plaza las Americas
Tel: 998 884 9174
Downtown French bistro with fresh
bread, pastries, and roquefort
cheese and apple pizza. **$$**

Mikado
Marriott Hotel, Km.15
Tel: 998 881 2000
Japanese and Thai food in chic
surroundings. Patio dining. **$$$**

Modern Art Cafe
La Isla Village, Km. 12.5
Tel: 998 883 4511/2
Paintings, sculpture, ceramics and
good food. Evenings till 3am,
champagne brunch on weekends

OK Maguey Cantina
Kukulcan Plaza
Tel: 998 885 0503
Mexican cuisine. Breakfast, lunch.
Nightly mariachi show with dinner. **$$**

The Plantation House
Kukulcan 10.5
Tel: 998 883 1433
New Orleans-style mansion over the
water. Piano music. Seafood, duck,
lamb. **$$$**

Sanborns
Av Uxmal, near bus station downtown
Tel: 998 884 0002
The old reliable offers just about
everything and the *Sopa Especial* is
still the best recipe for upset
stomachs. **$$**

All the various malls along the Hotel
Strip contain food courts with the
familiar, internationally known fast
food counters.

CELESTUN

La Palapa
On the seafront
Tel: 998 916 2063
Local dishes. Good drink selection. **$**

CHETUMAL

Cafe Espresso
Central on seafront
Tel: 983 833 3013
Attractive decor. Open for breakfast,
dinner. Omelets, snacks, good
coffee. **$**

El Junco de Hong Kong
On seafront at Av 16 de Septiembre
Tel: 983 833 1700
Chinese. **$**

Sergio's
Corner of Obregon and 5 de Mayo
Tel: 983 832 0882
Lively, popular place, usually full.
Pizza, steaks, sturdy breakfasts. **$**

CHIAPAS

San Cristóbal de Las Casas
Mayambé
Guadalupe 66
Tel: 967 674 6278
Attractive restaurant in a covered
courtyard. Authentic Indian and
southeast Asian cuisine. **$**

Palenque Town
Restaurant Maya Cañada
Merle Green
Tel:916 345 00-42
Restaurant with tasty Mexican
seafood, fish and meat dishes. **$$**

COZUMEL

Casa Denis
1a Sur, 132
Tel: 987 872 0067
Cozumel's oldest restaurant and
still family-owned. **$$**

La Choza
Calle Adolfo Rosada Salas 198, at
Av 10
Tel: 987 872 0958
Yucatecan food in a *palapa*-roofed
restaurant. **$$**

Cocos Cozumel
Av 5, 180
Tel: 987 872 0241
Good place for every kind of
breakfast with eggs. **$**

Los Dorados de Villa
1a Sur, 72
Tel: 987 872 0196
For people-watching on the plaza. **$$**

Gurdos
Av Rafael E. Melgar, 23
Tel: 987 872 0946
Italian cuisine. **$$**

Mesa 17
Calles 17 and Av 25, Corpus Cristi
Tel: 987 878 4928
Mexican and International. **$$$**

IZAMAL

Kinich Kakmo
Calle 27, 299
Tel: 988 954 0489
Yucatecan specialties; next to the
entrance of the pyramid. **$–$$**

Restaurante El Toro
Calle 33, 303
Red tablecloths and a bullfighter
theme, but a limited menu. **$**

ISLA MUJERES

Although there's a good selection of
restaurants in town, the best are in
the big hotels: **Buho's** in Cabañas del
Mar (seafood); **Maria's Kan-Kin**
(French) in the hotel of the same
name; **Zazil-Ha** (Maya, Mexican,
Caribbean) in the Hotel Na-Balam.

MERIDA

Alberto's Continental
Calle 64, 482
Tel: 999 928 5367
Cuban tiled mosaic floor, rubber
tree lined indoor patio. Delicious
Yucatecan and Lebanese food; and
Kahlua coconut ice cream. **$$$**

Los Almendros
Calle 57, 468
Tel: 999 923 8135
Yucatecan food including Poc-Chuc
(pork loin stew). Friday evening
shows. **$$**

Restaurant Prices

The following categories are for
lunch or dinner per person, not
including drinks:

$$$	over US$25
$$	under US$25
$	under US$15

Restaurant Prices

The following categories are for lunch or dinner per person, not including drinks:

$$$ over US$25
$$ under US$25
$ under US$15

Amaro
Corner of Calles 59 and 60
Tel: 999 928 2451
Yucatecan dishes, pizzas, vegetarian. Patriotic poet Andres Quintana Roo was born in this building. **$**

La Bella Epoca
Calle 60, 497, Hotel del Parque
Tel: 999 928 1928
Chippendale chairs and menu encompassing Mexican, Arab, international and "naturalist" (health) food. **$$**

Cafeteria El Mesón
Calle 59, 500
Tel: 999 924 9022
Outdoor patio beside Hotel Caribe. **$**

La Casona
Calle 60, 434
Tel: 999 923 8348
Italian cuisine, Chihuahua beef. **$$**

Pancho's
Corner of Calles 59 and 60, 509
Tel: 999 942 0202
Lively patio bar with solid food and music. **$$**

Pasaje Picheta
Beyond the portals on the north side of the Grand Plaza, leads to an interior plaza with central tables offering self-service from a wide variety of food.

Pórtico del Peregrino
Calle 57, 501
Tel: 999 928 6163
International and Mexican cuisine served on romantic patio; delicious *pollo pibil* – chicken steamed in a banana leaf. **$–$$**

La Prosperidad
Calle 52, 491
Tel: 999 924 1407
Yucatecan cuisine. Live music at lunch and dinner. **$$**

La Sandwicheria
Corner of Calles 59 and 60
Fifteen different sandwich combinations in four sizes. Brightly lit, spotlessly clean. **$**

Yu-Liang's
Calle 60, 338
Tel: 999 920 0506
Chinese cuisine. **$**

PLAYA DEL CARMEN

Blue Lobster
Calle 12 and Av 5
Tel: 984 873 1360
Steak and lobster house. **$$$**

Buenos Aires
Corner of Calle 6 and Av 5
Tel: 984 873 2751
Quality Argentine steakhouse. **$$$**

El Chiringuito
Corner of Calle 10 and Av 5
Spanish cuisine, paella, tapas, live flamenco Thursdays. **$$**

The Coffee Press
Corner of Calle 2 and Av 5
Good breakfasts, lunches and home-made pies. Open until late. **$**

Cyberia
Corner of Calle 4 and Av 15
Daily 9am–9pm. Coffee, food, drinks, and internet access. **$**

Media Luna
Tel: 984 873 0526
Corner of Calle 10 and Av 5
Vegetarian and seafood. **$$**

La Parrilla
Corner of Calle 8 and Av 5
Tel: 984 873 0687
Mexican cuisine including "flamed dishes prepared at your table." Music every night. **$$**

Yaxche
Corner of Calle 8 and Av 5
Tel: 984 873 2502
Yucatecan food in a place named for the Maya sacred tree. **$–$$**

PROGRESO

Le Saint Bonnet
Calle 19, 150
Tel: 969 935 2299
Charming ambience on a raised terrace facing the beach; live music afternoons and weekend nights. **$**

TULUM

Il Giardino di Toni e Simone
Av Satelite
Tel: 984 804 1316
Tasty Italian cuisine, with steak and seafood on the menu. **$$**

VALLADOLID

Hostería del Marqués
In the Hotel Mesón del Marqués
Calle 39, 203
Tel: 985 856 2073
Hotel restaurant serving authentic Yucatecan cuisine. **$**

Nightlife

Mérida
In addition to a museum specifically dedicated to Yucatecan music in the **Casa de la Cultura** (Tuesday to Saturday, 9am–8pm) at the corner of Calles 63 and 64, there is music at 9pm six nights of the week:
Monday: folk dancing on main plaza.
Tuesday: big bands, Parque Santiago.
Wednesday: shows at the Olimpo.
Thursday: folklore and dance, corner of Calles 60 and 57.
Friday: Serenade, main university building.
Saturday: Fiesta Mexicana, corner of Paseo de Montejo and Calle 47.

Otherwise, discos and video bars are the substance of most Mérida nightlife. Several of the clubs, such as **Amarantus** (tel: 999 944 2817) and **Tequila Rock** (tel: 999 944 1828) can be found on the continuation of the Paseo de Montejo. The **Spasso** in the Hotel Hyatt (tel: 999 942 1234) is usually worth checking out. There are three movie theaters within a block or two of Calles 59 and 60.

Cancún
Nightlife is not hard to find in Cancún with virtually every hotel offering music and/or entertainment of one kind or another. There is usually some sort of low-grade folk dancing in the malls and there are a number of nightclubs, of which **La Boom** disco (Kukulcan

Km. 3.5; tel: 998 8497588;
Dady'O (Kukulcan Km. 9.5; tel: 998
883 3333), **Maax** (La Isla Mall, Km.
12.5) and the huge **Coco Bongo**
disco at the Bulldog Café (Hotel
Krystal, Km. 9; tel: 998 848 9800)
are among the liveliest. Boats leave
the Marina for a **Lobster Dinner
Cruise** and **Pirates Night** (tel: 998
883 3736).

Cozumel
Cozumel has the **Neptuno** (tel: 987
872 1537) and other discos and
bilingual karaoke bars. The central
plaza in San Miguel has a free
open-air concert Sunday nights.

Campeche
Campeche has very little nightlife to
speak of, although a few of the

larger restaurants and hotels have
late-opening bars and discos.

The city's **Sound & Light Show** is
presented at 8pm on Tuesday,
Fridays, and Sundays at the Puerto
de Tierra and the **Festival Folklorico**
in the Parque Santa Lucia on
Thursdays at 7.30pm and in the
Plaza de la República on Fridays at
7pm. In lively **Playa del Carmen**, the
sounds of nightlife flow from almost
every street. The **Blue Parrot Beach
Club** (tel: 984 873 0083) has a
variety of live music, DJs, and
dancers. **Alux** (Av Juárex and Calle
55; tel: 984 803 0713) is a
restaurant by day and a bar and
disco by night. It has been built into
a natural cave. The restaurant
Capitán Tutix (Calle 4 Nte) also has
live music.

Language

Pronunciation Tips

Although many Mexicans speak
some English, it is good to have
basic Spanish phrases at your
disposal; in remote areas, it is
essential. Most Guatemalans do
not speak English, except in tourist
regions. In general, locals are
delighted with foreigners who try to
speak the language, and they'll be
patient – if sometimes amused.
Pronunciation is not difficult. The
following is a simplified mini-lesson:

Vowels:
a as in *father*
e as in *bed*
i as in *police*
o as in *hole*
u as in *rude*

Consonants are approximately like
those in English, the main
exceptions being:
c is hard before **a**, **o**, or **u** (as in
English), and is soft before **e** or **i**,
when it sounds like **s**. Thus, *censo*
(census) sounds like *senso*.
g is hard before **a**, **o**, or **u** (as in
English), but before **e** or **i** Spanish **g**
sounds like a guttural **h**. **G** before
ua is often soft or silent, so that
agua sounds more like *awa*, and
Guadalajara like *Wadalajara*.
h is silent.
j sounds like the English h.
ll sounds like y.
ñ sounds like ny, as in *señor*.
q is followed by **u** as in English, but
the combination sounds like **k**
instead of like **kw**. ¿Qué quiere
Usted? is pronounced: Keh kee-er-
eh oosted?
r is often rolled.
x between vowels sounds like a
guttural **h**, e.g. in Mexico or Oaxaca.
y alone, as the word meaning

Shopping

Mérida
Three blocks south of Plaza Mayor
is the **Mercado Municipal** (corner
of Calles 56 and 67) which
specializes in Yucatán hammocks,
baskets, belts, *huipiles,*
(embroidered smocks) "Panama"
hats *(jipis)*, guayaberas (loose
shirts with large pockets). One
shop that specializes in
guayaberas is **Jack** (Calle 59,
507). **Maquech** (corner of Calles
59 and 60) specializes in
hammocks, Maya replicas, wool
carpets, and other handicrafts.
Gras Platería (Calle 60, 452)
displays Mexican opals,
terracotta, and silverwork. **Pasaje
Picheta** shopping center offers
arts and crafts, music cassettes,
embroidered clothing. On Calle 63
the **FONART** store has well-made
arts and crafts. Try the **Casa de las
Artesanías** (Calle 63) for regional
liquors and handicrafts of all
kinds. **Mérida English Library**
(Calle 53, 524; tel: 999 924 8401;
www.meridaenglishlibrary.com) has
a wide stock of books on Yucatán
and Mexico.

Cancún
There are several shopping malls
in Cancún. **La Isla Shopping**

Village (Blvd Kuklulcan Km. 12.5;
tel: 998 883 5025/883 4425) is
the most attractive and offers the
greatest variety. An antique
Mexico City streetcar departs from
here to tour downtown several
times a day. For luxury shopping
visit **Kukulcan Plaza** (Blvd
Kukulcan, km 13; tel: 998 885
2200). Choose tequila from
specialty shops such as **La
Destilería** (Blvd Kukulcan Km. 13;
tel: 998 885 1087;
www.ladestileriacancun.com).

Cozumel
Handcrafted items include Maya
pottery knock-offs, silver jewelry,
mother-of-pearl barrettes and pins,
onyx for table-top pyramids or
chess sets, gems, gold, and crystal.

Campeche
Craft items can be found at **Casa
de Artesanías Tukulná** (corner of
Calles 10 and 59; tel: 981 816
9088), **Arte Mexicano** (Calle 69,
9), and **Campechanisimas** (Calle
8, 189).
Markets are often good for
hammocks which should be of
pure cotton. **Becal** on Highway
180, southwest of Mérida, is
renowned for its Panama hats.

"and", is pronounced **ee**.
Note that **ch** and **ll** are separate letters of the Spanish alphabet; if looking in a phone book or dictionary for a word beginning with **ch**, you will find it after the final **c** entry. A name or word beginning with **ll** will be listed after the **l** entry (**ñ** and **rr** are also counted as separate letters.)

Useful Words/Phrases

please *por favor*
thank you *gracias*
you're welcome *de nada* (literally, for nothing)
I'm sorry *lo siento*
excuse me *con permiso* (if, for example, you would like to pass) *perdón* (if, for example, you have stepped on someone's foot)
yes *sí*
no *no*
can you speak English? *¿habla (usted) inglés?*
do you understand me? *¿me comprende? /¿me entiende?*
this is good *(esto) está bueno*
this is bad *(esto) está malo*
good morning *buenos días*
good night/evening *buenas noches*
goodbye *adiós*
where is...? *¿dónde está?*
exit *la salida*
entrance *la entrada*
money *dinero*
credit card *la tarjeta de crédito*
tax *impuesto*

At the Bar/Restaurant

In Spanish, *el menú* is not the main menu, but a fixed menu offered each day (usually for lunch) at a lower price. The main menu is *la carta*.
restaurant *un restaurante*
café, coffee shop *un café*
please bring me some coffee *un café, por favor*
please bring me... *tráigame por favor...*
beer *una cerveza*
cold water *agua fría*
hot water *agua caliente*
soft drink *un refresco*
daily special *el plato del día; el especial del día*

breakfast *desayuno*
lunch *almuerzo/comida*
dinner *cena*
first course *primer plato*
second course *plato principal*
may I have more beer? *¿Más cerveza, por favor?*
may I have the bill? *¿me da la cuenta, por favor?*
Waiter! (waitress!) *¡Señor! (¡Señorita! ¡Señora!)*

At the hotel

where is there an inexpensive hotel? *¿dónde hay un hotel económico?*
do you have an air-conditioned room? *¿tiene un cuarto con aire acondicionado?*
do you have a room with bath? *¿tiene un cuarto con baño?* **where is** *¿dónde está?*
the dining room? *¿el comedor?*
key *la llave*
manager – *el gerente*
owner (male) *el dueño*
owner (female) *la dueña*
can you cash a traveler's cheque? *¿puede cambiar un cheque de viajero?*

Communications

post office *el correo; la oficina de correos*
telegraph office *la oficina de telégrafos*
public telephone *el teléfono público*
letter *la carta*
postcard *la tarjeta postal*
envelope *el sobre*
stamp *un sello postal*

Places

police station *la estación de policía*
embassy *la embajada*
consulate *el consulado*
bank *el banco*
hotel *un hotel*
inn *una posada; una pension un apartamento*
apartment *un departamento*
cabaña *basic wooden beach chalet*
palapa *palm thatch-roofed beach shelter*

restroom *el sanitario/el baño de hombres/mujeres*
(private) bathroom *el baño privado*
public bathhouses *los baños públicos*
ticket office *la oficina de boletos, taquilla*
dry cleaners *la tintorería; la lavandería*

Shopping

department *el departamento*
market, market place – *el mercado*
souvenir shop *la tienda de recurditos*
what is the price? *¿cuánto cuesta?*
it's too expensive *es muy caro*
can you give me a discount? *¿me puede dar un descuento?*
do you have...? *¿tiene usted...?*
I will buy this *voy a comprar esto*
please show me another *muéstreme otro (otra) por favor*
just a moment, please *un momento, por favor*

Transport

airplane *avión*
airport *el aeropuerto*
ferry boat *el barco*
subway *el metro*
train station *la estación del ferrocarril*
train *el tren*
first class *primera clase*
second class *segunda clase*
deluxe *de lujo/ejecutivo*

Useful Phrases when Traveling
how much is a ticket to...? *¿cuánto cuesta un boleto a...?*
I want a ticket to... *quiero un boleto a...*
please stop here *pare aquí, por favor*
please go straight *recto, por favor*
how many kilometers is it from here to...? *¿cuántos kilómetros hay de aquí a...?*
how long does it take to go there...? *¿cuánto se tarda en llegar?*
left *a la izquierda*
right *a la derecha*
what is this place called? *¿cómo se llama este lugar?*
I'm going to... *Voy a...*

On the buses

bus *bus/camióneta*
express bus *el camióneta directo*
bus station *terminal de buses/camióneta*
bus stop *parada*
reserved seat *asiento reservado*
where does this bus go? *¿a dónde va esta camióneta?*
I am getting off here! (to call out to a bus driver when you want to get off) *¡Bajan!*

On the Road

car *el carro, el automóvil*
where is a petrol station? *¿dónde hay una gasolinera?*
a repair garage *un taller mecánico*
auto parts store *almacén de repuestos*
fill it up, please *lleno, por favor*
please check the oil *cheque el aceite, por favor*
radiator *el radiador*
battery *el acumulador*
I need... *necesito...*
spare wheel *la llanta de repuesto*
jack *un gato*
towtruck *una grúa*
mechanic *un mecánico*
tune-up *una afinación*
tire *una llanta*
a fuse *un fusible*
it's broken *está roto/a*
they're broken *están rotos/as*

Taxis

taxi *el taxi*
taxi stand *el sitio de taxis*
please call me a taxi *pídame un taxi, por favor*
what will you charge to take me to...? *¿cuánto me cobra para llevarme a...?*

Months of the Year

January	enero
February	febrero
March	marzo
April	abril
May	mayo
June	junio
July	julio
August	agosto
September	septiembre
October	octubre
November	noviembre
December	diciembre

Days of the Week

Monday	*lunes*
Tuesday	*martes*
Wednesday	*miércoles*
Thursday	*jueves*
Friday	*viernes*
Saturday	*sábado*
Sunday	*domingo*

Numbers

1 – *uno*
2 – *dos*
3 – *tres*
4 – *cuatro*
5 – *cinco*
6 – *seis*
7 – *siete*
8 – *ocho*
9 – *nueve*
10 – *diez*
11 – *once*
12 – *doce*
13 – *trece*
14 – *catorce*
15 – *quince*
16 – *dieciséis*
17 – *diecisiete*
18 – *dieciocho*
19 – *diecinueve*
20 – *veinte*
21 – *veintiuno*
25 – *veinticinco*
30 – *treinta*
40 – *cuarenta*
50 – *cincuenta*
60 – *sesenta*
70 – *setenta*
80 – *ochenta*
90 – *noventa*

100 – *cien*
101 – *ciento uno*
200 – *doscientos*
300 – *trescientos*
400 – *cuatrocientos*
500 – *quinientos*
600 – *seiscientos*
700 – *setecientos*
800 – *ochocientos*
900 – *novecientos*

1,000 – *mil*
2,000 – *dos mil*
10,000 – *diez mil*
100,000 – *cien mil*
1,000,000 – *un millón*
1,000,000,000 – *mil millones*

Understanding Creole

English is the official language of Belize, but the reality on the streets is somewhat different. There are dozens of Creole languages in the Caribbean; Belize Creole (spoken by about 180,000 people) is a hybrid of English and the diverse language groups of West Africa with a smattering of words derived from Spanish and Nicaraguan Miskito. Essentially vernacular (see examples below), Creole isn't taught, written or read: there are no definitive spellings. As is the case with many folk languages, Creole is particularly rich in proverbs. (See the book *Creole Proverbs of Belize* for further information.)

Fowl caca white an tink e lay egg
A chicken defecates white and thinks she's laid an egg. (Used in relation to a self-important person)
Dis-ya time no tan like befo time It was different in the old days.
Da weh da lee bwai mi di nyam?
What was the little boy eating?

Maya Glossary

Aguadas – seasonal water holes in lowland Maya region
Atol – drink made from maize dough or sometimes rice
Brujo – Maya priest
Cacique – political leader (originally "native chief" in Carib)
Ceiba – sacred kapok (silk-cotton) tree
Cenote – natural well in Yucatán
Chapín – colloquial term for a Guatamalan
Chicle – tree sap (from which chewing gum is derived)
Cofrade – cofradía member
Cofradía – religious group common among Maya in Guatamalan highlands
Corte – long skirt worn by Guatamalan Maya women
Creole – the people and language of Afro-Caribbean Belizeans
Criollo – native of Spanish descent
Finca – large farm estate (Guatemalan)
Guayabera – Loose shirt with large pockets

Huipil – Maya women's blouse
Indígena (or **Natural**) – polite term for native indian, used throughout Latin America.
Indio – pejorative term for native Indian
Ladino – Meaning 'Latin', it's used for any non-Indians, or for those Indians who have adopted Hispanic culture
Long Count – Maya calendar from Classic period (AD250-900) also known as Initial Series.
Marimba – Guatemalan musical instrument similar to xylophone
Mestizo – person of mixed Indian and Spanish heritage, who is generally part of Hispanic or Ladino society; common term in Mexico
Milpa – traditional maize field
Sacbe – "white road" between ancient cities or leading to a temple, especially in Yucatán
Típica – traditional handmade Guatemalan clothes and weavings produced for tourists
Traje – traditional Guatemalan clothing
Tzolkin – the counting of days according to ancient Maya calendar
Tzut – headscarf worn in highlands
Yaxche – Yucatec Maya for sacred Ceiba tree

Further Reading

There's a complete recommended book list to the region below, but useful supplementary guidebooks include Joyce Kelly's **An Archeological Guide to Northern Central America** and **An Archeological Guide to the Yucatán**. Michael Coe's **Tikal: A Handbook to the Ancient Ruins** is essential for in-depth exploration. In the Yucatán, Richard Perry's **Maya Missions** covers colonial Mexico superbly well. There are few bookshops in the Maya region that stock a good selection of the titles below. Antigua, in Guatemala, is the exception with a number of excellent stores.

Maya Civilization

The Ancient Maya by Robert Sharer (Stanford University, 1994). Authoritative, formidable study of the Maya.
The Art and Architecture of Ancient America by George Kubler (Penguin, 1984).
The Blood of Kings by Linda Schele and Mary Ellen Miller (Braziller [UK]; Thames & Hudson [US], 1992). The late Linda Schele was one of the greatest Mayanists of the late twentieth century who proved the Maya did not live a peaceful existence governed by priests and astronomers but were warlike and obsessed with bloodletting and sacrifice. Read with **A Forest of Kings**, written by Schele and David Freide (Quill/Morrow, 1990).
The Gods of Mexico by C.A. Burland (Eyre & Spottiswoode, 1967).
The Maya by Michael D. Coe (Thames & Hudson, 1993). This is the best place to start for a general introduction to the subject. Well illustrated with maps, drawings and photographs and written by one of the century's finest archeologists who also wrote the influential **Breaking the Maya Code** (Thames & Hudson, 1993) which confirmed that Mayan gylphs were a written language.
Maya Architecture by George Oakley Totten (Maya Press, 1926).
Maya Civilization by T. Patrick Culbert (Smithsonian, 1993). Concise, well-structured summary written by a leading archeologist.
Maya Civilization, editors Schmitt, de la Garza and Nalda (Thames & Hudson, 1998). Encyclopedic volume, outstandingly illustrated with lavish color plates. The subject is addressed as a series of essays, all written by notable Mayanists, covering everything from vegetation and ancient trade routes to ceramics and dynastic history. Important discussions on the power politics of the Classic Maya and the importance of Calakmul.
Maya: The Riddle and Rediscovery of a Lost Civilization by Charles Gallenkamp (Penguin, 1987). Serious but approachable analysis of Maya archeology, life and culture including the civilization's collapse.
Mayan Architecture by Henri Stierlin (Oldbourne, 1964).
Monuments of Civilization: Maya by Pierre Ivanoff (Cassell, 1975).
Mythology of the Americas by Cottie Burland, Irene Nicholson, and Harold Osborne (Hamlyn, 1970).
The Popol Vuh translated by Dennis Tedlock (Simon & Schuster, 1996). The K'iche "bible," the masterful book of creation that's both one of the most important pre-Columbian texts in the Americas and also a incredibly rich and imaginative read.
The Rise and Fall of the Maya Civilization by J. Eric S. Thompson (University of Oklahoma Press, 1966). Another excellent introduction to the Maya, and, though many of Thompson's more utopian theories have now been overturned, much of the text still reads well. Thompson's **Maya History and Religion** (Norman, 1970) is another useful study.
Silent Cities by Norman F. Carver (Shokokusha, 1966).
Tales and Legends of Ancient Yucatán by Ermilio Abreu Gomez (Dante, 1993).
Yucatán Before and After the Conquest by Diego de Landa, trans-

lated by William Gates (Dover Publications, 1978). On-the-spot reporting of Maya culture from a friar who witnessed the advance of the conquistadors.

Travel
Beyond the Mexique Bay by Aldous Huxley (Flamingo [UK], 1934). Vintage Huxley, full of purple prose, brilliant one-liners and quirky observations; the book covers Guatemala and Southern Mexico.
Incidents of Travel in Central America, Chiapas and Yucatán by John L. Stephens (Dover [UK], Prentice Hall [US], 1841). One the finest travel books ever written, the book sold in its thousands when originally published and remains in print today. Stephens and artist Catherwood traveled through the region during the Central American war but still managed to rediscover many ruins (including Copán) that were unknown in the west.
Sweet Waist of America by Anthony Daniels (Hutchinson, 1990). Mainly concerned with Guatemala, the book was written towards the end of the civil war. Daniels interviews a cross-section of Central American society including Guatemalan soldiers, priests, schoolchildren, and two military dictators.
Time Among the Maya by Ronald Wright (Henry Holt [UK], Abacus Travel [US], 1991). The finest contemporary travel account of the region, both erudite and entertaining. Wright completes the Ruta Maya "loop" between Yucatán, Belize, Guatemala, and Chiapas and meets an incredible assortment of characters. Combines dense study with incisive comment.
Yucatán Peninsula Handbook by Chicki Mallan and Joe Cummings (Moon, 1998).

History, Politics, and Society
Gift of the Devil by Jim Handy (South End Press, 1984) Excellent opinionated history of Guatemala. An essential text, but written before the end of the civil war so the Peace Accords are not covered.
In Focus Series (Latin American Bureau). Succinct guides to the

people politics and culture of the Maya countries. Individual editions on Guatemala, Belize, and Mexico.
Inside Guatemala; Inside Mexico; Inside Belize all by Tom Barry (Interhemispheric Education Resource Center, New Mexico, 1992). Concise and reliable summaries of the Maya countries, with sections on government and politics, religious issues, society, economics and the environment.
Unfinished Conquest by Víctor Perera (University of California Press, 1995). Perera is arguably Guatemala's best living writer; this title addresses the contradictions and imbalances of the state.
Rites: A Guatemalan Boyhood (Harcourt, Bruce Jovanovich, New York, 1986) is an autobiography of Perera's early years in Guatemala City's tiny Jewish community. **Last Lords of Palenque** (Little Brown/University of California Press, 1985) is a brilliant study of Mexico's Lacandón Maya.

Modern Maya Culture
Deciding to be Legal: a Maya Community in Houston by Jacqueline Maria Hagan (Temple University Press, 1994). Interesting account of the struggles and successes of Maya immigrants as they adjust to life in el norte.
I, Rigoberta Menchú – an Indian Woman in Guatemala by Rigoberta Menchú (Norton [US]/Verso [UK], 1984). Extremely harrowing autobiography of the K'iche' Maya Nobel Prize winner, who lost her mother, father, and brothers in the civil war. The second volume, **Crossing Borders** (Verso Books, 1997), is a much lighter, more optimistic read dealing with her life in exile and her return to Guatemala.
The Maya Atlas (North Atlantic Books, 1997). A insightful corroboration between academics and villagers, the Atlas documents the history and everyday experiences of the Toledo Maya of Belize.
The Maya of Guatemala by Philip Werne (Minority Rights Group, 1989). Concise study of the history and culture of the Guatemalan Maya and the difficulties they face.

Rigoberta Menchú and the Story of All Poor Guatemalans by David Stoll (Westview Press, 1999). Iconoclastic biography that erodes the credibility of significant chunks of I, Rigoberta Menchú. Stoll has also published an excellent account of the civil war in the Ixil, Guatemala, entitled **Between Two Armies** (Columbia University Press, 1993).
Son of Tecún Umán; Campesino (both University of Arizona Press, 1993); **Ignacio** (University of Pennsylvania Press, 1992) edited by James D. Sexton. Superb three-part autobiography of a Tz'utihil Maya from Lago de Atitlán told over a 20-year period during the civil war.

Literature
Belize 1798, The Road to Glory by Emory King (Tropical Books, 1991). Bombastic account of the Battle of St. George's Key written by one of Belize's larger-than-life American settlers, also the author of **Hey Dad, This is Belize**.
Long Night of the White Chickens by Francisco Goldman (Faber & Faber, 1993). Brilliant debut novel by a Guatemalan-American Goldman. It's an incredibly intricate tale of illegal baby adoptions, murder, and death squads that's set in Guatemala City and Boston.
Return of the Maya by Gaspar Pedro González (Yax Te', 1999). Fascinating tale of a Q'anjob' al Maya, and his crisis of identity in Ladino-dominated Guatemala, following his return from exile in Mexico. Claims to be the first novel to be written by a Maya writer.
On Heroes, Lizards and Passion by Zoila Ellis (Cubola Productions, 1994). Insightful tales of life in Belize, written by a local.
Zee Edgell Beka Lamb (Heinemann, 1987). Fascinating story of 1950s Belize.

Environment
Field Guide to the Birds of Mexico and Northern Central America by Steve N.G. Howell (Oxford University Press, 1994). The definitive reference book of the region's birds.
Pisces Diving Guides (Lonely Planet). Clear guides to the region's

reef life and dive sites. Editions include Cozumel and Belize.

Other Insight Guides

Insight Guide Belize. The definitive guide to Belize. Superb features, breathtaking photography and indispensable travel information.

Insight Guide Mexico. In-depth coverage of the entire country from Baja California to Chetumal with stunning photography and maps and revealing analysis.

Pocket Guides are concise yet reliable. They are designed for the visitor with limited time to spare and include a selection of carefully timed itineraries and personal recommendations. Companion titles in this series include: *Mexico City, the Baja Peninsula* and *Cancún & the Yucatán*.

Compact Guide: *Cancún & the Yucatán* is a mini-encyclopedia, with a wealth of travel information, competitively priced.

Insight Fleximap: *Mexico City* combines clear, detailed cartography with a durable laminated finish.

Feedback

We do our best to ensure the information in our books is as accurate and up-to-date as possible. The books are updated on a regular basis, using local contacts, who painstakingly add, amend and correct as required. However, some mistakes and omissions are inevitable and we are ultimately reliant on our readers to put us in the picture.

We would welcome your feedback on any details related to your experiences using the book "on the road". Maybe we recommended a hotel that you liked (or another that you didn't), as well as interesting new attractions, or facts and figures you have found out about the country itself. The more details you can give us (particularly with regard to addresses, e-mails and telephone numbers), the better.

We will acknowledge all contributions, and we'll offer an Insight Guide to the best letters received.

Please write to us at:
Insight Guides
PO Box 7910
London SE1 1WE
United Kingdom
Or send e-mail to:
insight@apaguide.co.uk

ART & PHOTO CREDITS

Picture Spreads

INSIGHT GUIDE
Guatemala Belize & Yucatán

Cartographic Editor **Zoë Goodwin**
Production **Stuart A Everitt**
Design Consultants
Carlotta Junger, Graham Mitchener
Picture Research
Hilary Genin, Monica Allende

Index

Numbers in italics refer to photographs

A
B
C
D
E
F

H
I
J

INSIGHT GUIDES

The classic series that puts you in the picture

INSIGHT GUIDES

The world's largest collection of visual travel guides & maps

TRULY ADVENTUROUS

TRULY ASIA

In the heart of Asia lies a land of many cultures, wonders and attractions. Especially for the adventure seeker to whom fear is not a factor. There are hundreds of thrills to experience. Mount Kinabalu. Mulu Caves. Taman Negara. These are just a few places where you'll always find that rewarding adrenaline rush. Where is this land, so challenging and exhilarating? It can only be Malaysia, Truly Asia.

Malaysia
Truly Asia